The Editor

DYMPNA CALLAGHAN is Dean's Professor in the Humanities at Syracuse University. She is the author of *Women and Gender in Renaissance Tragedy: A Study of* Othello, King Lear, The Duchess of Malfi, *and* The White Devil; *Shakespeare without Women*; *Shakespeare's Sonnets: An Introduction*; and co-author of *The Weyward Sisters: Shakespeare and Feminist Politics.* Her edited books include *Feminist Readings in Early Modern Culture: Emerging Subjects* (with Valerie Traub and Lindsay Kaplan), *John Webster's* Duchess of Malfi: *Contemporary Critical Essays,* Romeo and Juliet: *Texts and Contexts,* The Impact of Feminism in English Renaissance Studies, and *The Feminist Companion to Shakespeare.*

W. W. NORTON & COMPANY, INC.

Also Publishes

ENGLISH RENAISSANCE DRAMA: A NORTON ANTHOLOGY
edited by David Bevington et al.

THE NORTON ANTHOLOGY OF AFRICAN AMERICAN LITERATURE
edited by Henry Louis Gates Jr. and Nellie Y. McKay et al.

THE NORTON ANTHOLOGY OF AMERICAN LITERATURE
edited by Nina Baym et al.

THE NORTON ANTHOLOGY OF CHILDREN'S LITERATURE
edited by Jack Zipes et. al.

THE NORTON ANTHOLOGY OF CONTEMPORARY FICTION
edited by R. V. Cassill and Joyce Carol Oates

THE NORTON ANTHOLOGY OF ENGLISH LITERATURE
edited by M. H. Abrams and Stephen Greenblatt et al.

THE NORTON ANTHOLOGY OF LITERATURE BY WOMEN
edited by Sandra M. Gilbert and Susan Gubar

THE NORTON ANTHOLOGY OF MODERN AND CONTEMPORARY POETRY
edited by Jahan Ramazani, Richard Ellmann, and Robert O'Clair

THE NORTON ANTHOLOGY OF POETRY
edited by Margaret Ferguson, Mary Jo Salter, and Jon Stallworthy

THE NORTON ANTHOLOGY OF SHORT FICTION
edited by R. V. Cassill and Richard Bausch

THE NORTON ANTHOLOGY OF THEORY AND CRITICISM
edited by Vincent B. Leitch et al.

THE NORTON ANTHOLOGY OF WORLD LITERATURE
edited by Sarah Lawall et al.

THE NORTON FACSIMILE OF THE FIRST FOLIO OF SHAKESPEARE
prepared by Charlton Hinman

THE NORTON INTRODUCTION TO LITERATURE
edited by Alison Booth, J. Paul Hunter, and Kelly J. Mays

THE NORTON INTRODUCTION TO THE SHORT NOVEL
edited by Jerome Beaty

THE NORTON READER
edited by Linda H. Peterson and John C. Brereton

THE NORTON SAMPLER
edited by Thomas Cooley

THE NORTON SHAKESPEARE, BASED ON THE OXFORD EDITION
edited by Stephen Greenblatt et al.

For a complete list of Norton Critical Editions, visit
www.wwnorton.com/college/English/nce_home.htm

A NORTON CRITICAL EDITION

William Shakespeare

THE TAMING OF THE SHREW

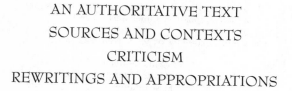

AN AUTHORITATIVE TEXT
SOURCES AND CONTEXTS
CRITICISM
REWRITINGS AND APPROPRIATIONS

Edited by

DYMPNA CALLAGHAN

SYRACUSE UNIVERSITY

W. W. NORTON & COMPANY
New York • London

W. W. Norton & Company has been independent since its founding in 1923, when William Warder and Mary D. Herter Norton first published lectures delivered at the People's Institute, the adult education division of New York City's Cooper Union. The firm soon expanded its program beyond the Institute, publishing books by celebrated academics from America and abroad. By mid-century, the two major pillars of Norton's publishing program—trade books and college texts—were firmly established. In the 1950s, the Norton family transferred control of the company to its employees, and today—with a staff of four hundred and a comparable number of trade, college, and professional titles published each year—W. W. Norton & Company stands as the largest and oldest publishing house owned wholly by its employees.

Composition by PennSet, Inc.
Manufacturing by the Maple-Vail Book Manfacturing Group.
Book design by Antonina Krass.
Production manager: Eric Pier-Hocking.

Library of Congress Cataloging-in-Publication Data

Shakespeare, William, 1564–1616.
   The taming of the shrew : an authoritative text, sources and contexts, criticism, rewritings, and appropriations / William Shakespeare ; edited by Dympna Callaghan. — 1st ed.
      p. cm. — (A Norton critical edition)
   Includes bibliographical references (p.   ).

   ISBN 978-0-393-92707-8 (pbk.)

   1. Man-woman relationships—Drama.   2. Married people—Drama.
3. Sex role—Drama.   4. Padua (Italy)—Drama.   5. Shakespeare, William, 1564–1616. Taming of the shrew.   I. Callaghan, Dympna.   II. Title

PR2832.A2C28 2009
822.3′3—dc22
                                                          2008053413

W. W. Norton & Company, Inc., 500 Fifth Avenue, New York, N.Y. 10110
www.wwnorton.com

W. W. Norton & Company Ltd., Castle House,
75/76 Wells Street, London W1T 3QT

3   4   5   6   7   8   9   0

Contents

Preface

I hate men.
I can't abide `em even now and then.
Than ever marry one of them, I'd rest a virgin rather,
For husbands are a boring lot and only give you bother.

So goes the song of Katherine in Cole Porter's frequently staged musical, *Kiss Me Kate* (1948), based on Shakespeare's *The Taming of the Shrew*. Although Shakespeare's Kate is a woman fueled by a comprehensive rage—she hates everyone, not just men—the lyrics of Porter's still widely performed musical offer a parody of modern feminist sentiments that demonstrate that distribution of power between the sexes remains as controversial as it was when Shakespeare was writing. The central pairing of the original play is the hostile alliance between Kate and the domineering and eccentric Petruchio. This marriage is contrasted with the union of Kate's sister, the mild and beautiful Bianca who elopes with Lucentio. Bianca's ostensible virtues seem to conform perfectly to the Renaissance ideal of "chaste, silent, and obedient" womanhood. Yet, by the end of the play, Bianca is a more difficult wife, or at least, a less compliant one, than her newly docile sister. It is not clear whether Kate's recently discovered quiescence signals that she has at last found happiness, or whether, overpowered by her husband's will, she has merely resigned herself to the abject submission she seems to champion in her final speech.

On the principle that "the course of true love never did run smooth" (*A Midsummer Night's Dream* 1.1.134), the plots of dramatic comedies typically involve a series of obstacles, errors, and confusions in the process of courtship that achieve their final resolution in marriages that are agreed upon or that actually take place in the final action. However, the principal couples in *Shrew* are well married before the end, and their weddings represent only the troubled beginnings of a transition toward established conjugality. Further, in the case of Kate and Petruchio, the passage from nuptials to sustained connubial intimacy is characterized by aggression and hostility. The play's status as a comedy is rendered further problematic by the fact that laughter is not the ready response to the domestic brutality entailed in Petruchio's design to "tame" his wife as he would a hawk. Most critics since the twentieth century have categorized the play as a "farce," a slapstick, knock-about romp whose violence is mediated by comedy. Farce may indeed serve as a distancing device that permits audiences to contemplate some of the most psychologically troubling and socially disruptive dimensions of marital intimacy. Foremost of these is the play's potentially disturbing conjunction of eroticism and violence.

Sources and Contexts

We can date with certainty neither the composition nor the first staging of *The Taming of the Shrew*. Written in the earlier part of Shakespeare's career, however, the play was probably first performed between 1591 and 1592, but only printed in 1623 in the First Folio some seven years after his death. The main plot of *Shrew*, unusually in the canon of Shakespeare's plays, has no clearly discernible literary source. One of the first rewritings of Shakespeare's text appears in a play of unknown authorship titled *A Pleasant Conceited History, Called The Taming of A Shrew* (1594; my emphasis), which shares many similarities with Shakespeare's play and was at one point thought to be a source for Shakespeare's *Shrew*. The current critical consensus is that *A Pleasant Conceited History* is a response to Shakespeare's *Shrew*, not its source. *Shrew*'s main plot finds its origins primarily in folk culture, which frequently treats post-nuptial relationships while in its literary counterpart the emphasis is on courtship as the romantic prelude to the wedding. The elaborate mating dance that precedes aristocratic unions is important in the plots of stage plays derived from courtly literature because the aim of such marriages was to forge economic and political ties that worked to consolidate power relations among elites. In the aristocratic world, marriage is a definitive conclusion and represents the achievement of dynastic alliance. Thus, conjugal alliance is inherently positive whether or not the particular pair of marital partners achieves personal felicity. Popular ballads and folktales, in contrast, focus on both "wooing *and* wedding." "Wedding," in this context is a verb that means "marrying," in contrast to the modern usage of "wedding" as a noun, meaning the religious or civil rite of matrimony followed by a wedding reception. In early modern popular culture, the nuptial celebration itself is significant primarily as the inauguration of the (potentially stormy) relationship that comes after it. While marriages in the folk tradition are as motivated by pecuniary considerations as more exalted unions are by wealth and power, cultural representations of these non-aristocratic marriages place much greater emphasis on whether the couple become either a harmonious or a disruptive part of the social fabric and on the maintenance of proper patriarchal authority within the household. This authority was comprised of what were deemed to be socially appropriate degrees of male domination and wifely submission in conjugal relationships, and mastery and submission in all other household relationships. It is important to remember that the early modern household often contained, like Petruchio's house, a sizable number of servants responsible for a wide range of activities from housework to farm labor, or to the management of property, or to the exercise of a trade. Thus, it was not only immediate blood relatives who were affected by the way power was brokered in a household, and especially within a marriage. Whether amicable or hostile, relations between marriage partners clearly impacted the wider social fabric of household and community.

Folk literature, then, addresses the entire gamut of experiences that are entailed in the "married state" and in the ongoing progress of an erotic relationship that has profound and far-reaching social effects, rather than on the notion of marriage as the culmination of courtship and, as essentially, the conclusion of a sexual relationship. Many of the motifs of the main plot are widely circulated in Indo-European folktales and are also to be found in the period's ballad literature. Representative of this folk tradition is the ballad *A Merry Jest of a Shrewd and Curst Wife Lapped in Morel's Skin*, reproduced in the Sources and Contexts section, from which Shakespeare may have derived some of the play's comic material about travel on horseback.

The problem of male authority and women's resistance to it, then, is hardly unique to Shakespeare. Patriarchy and the misogyny with which it is inherently imbued has a very long history indeed, and so not surprisingly, the theme of unruly women and male tyranny (the latter frequently presented with approbation rather than disapproval) has indirect literary precedents and was an already well-established theme in classical and medieval literature. For example, Chaucer's irrepressible Wife of Bath broaches the topic of dominance or "mastery" in marriage, and literary renditions of the widely circulated tale of long-suffering Griselda, a wife whose patience withstands the trials set by her husband, including the apparent murder of her children and his ostensible remarriage to a younger woman, are to be found in Boccaccio's *Decameron*, written in Italian and then Latinized by Petrarch, and in English in "The Clerk's Tale" in Chaucer's *The Canterbury Tales*.

As with the main plot, sources for the play's Induction (the two opening scenes) are also indirect. The motif of a commoner made to believe he is a lord probably has its earliest and non-European

origins in the *Arabian Nights*. The rural Warwickshire setting, however, belongs to the county of Shakespeare's birth and offers a
sharp contrast to the Italianate sophistication in which the main
action of the play takes place. Nonetheless, despite the familiarity
of an English setting, the Induction contains several references to
Ovid's *Metamorphoses*, a poem exemplary of the literature of the
Roman world at the time of the Emperor Augustus, and devoted
wholly to the concepts of change and transformation. Also featured
in Sources and Contexts are the stories of Daphne and Io from the
Metamorphoses in a modern translation by Charles Martin. Shakespeare, however, knew them both in Latin, and, even more importantly, in the English translation of 1567 by Arthur Golding. In
contrast to the Kate-Petruchio story, the play's subplot, the story of
Bianca and her wooers, possesses definable literary origins, princi-
pally George Gascoigne's comedy *Supposes*, a translation of Lu-
dovico Ariosto's *I Suppositi*, which was itself indebted to classical
Roman plays, Terence's *Eunuchus* and Plautus's *Captivi*. Apart
from the excerpt from *Supposes*, few of the materials in this
Sources and Contexts section can be construed as direct or indisputable sources for *Shrew* but cast light on the play by providing
some sense of the contemporary cultural discourses into which
Shakespeare intervenes.

Both marriage and metamorphoses are evoked in the play's title
and in its opening induction scene. Here, Christopher Sly, a
drunken beggar is ejected from an inn by the alewife. Coming upon
the dead-drunk Sly on their way from the hunt, a Lord and his
party decide to play a trick on him so that when he awakens he will
be told that he is himself a Lord who has suffered during a long illness from serious delusions about his true identity. When he awakens in a luxurious bed surrounded by fine objects, including
paintings depicting various episodes from Ovid's *Metamorphoses*, he
is convinced of his transformation. Ovid's poem provides an apt
parallel for Sly's transformation because in it unsuspecting mortals
often find themselves irreversibly turned into animals or plants,
usually without their consent and often specifically at the will of
the morally despicable but all-powerful god, Jove. Sly is also made
to believe that he is married to a lady, perfect in her wifely submission, who is represented by the transvestized boy page, Bartholemew. A further accoutrement of Sly's allegedly upgraded class is
provided by the play that is performed for his entertainment, clearly
in a more exalted genre, "more pleasing stuff" (Induction 2.134)
than the "commonty, a Christmas gambold or a tumbling-trick" (Induction 2.132–33) to which he is accustomed.

Sly proves a reluctant spectator, and at the end of Act 1 Scene 1,
the servingman and Bartholemew chide Sly for being inattentive

whereupon the party "sit and mark" (sit and watch, 1.1.246) the play in full view of the actual theater audience. This meta-theatrical effect serves to insist on the fictionality of the drama that then unfolds. Unlike *A Pleasant Conceited History*, written at about the same time as Shakespeare's *Shrew*, the Shakespeare play never returns to this episode, and we never learn how Sly reacted to what he saw. Nor do we see his return to his former condition of life. In fact, this is a thoroughly Ovidian strategy. In the *Metamorphoses*, transformation is frequently irreversible, and even when characters are restored to their former selves, such as the maiden Io who features in the Induction (Induction 2.52), it is with a sense of diminished agency. Io, for instance, recovering from life as a heifer, has trouble regaining human speech: "And though she gladly would have spoke: yet durst she not so do,/Without good heed, for fear she should have lowed like a cow."[1] Significantly, Ovidian themes imbue every aspect of Shakespeare's play even as they are transposed from the mythological register to the decidedly social one.

The play that Sly sees is, of course, *The Taming of the Shrew*. The form of metamorphosis encapsulated in the title is that of the unruly woman who somewhat miraculously becomes the (suspiciously) perfect wife. The performance opens with the arrival in the university city of Padua of the wealthy young Florentine, Lucentio, who is accompanied by his servant Tranio ostensibly to pursue his studies. Tranio urges that in the pursuit of scholastic Aristotelianism, that is, serious philosophy, they do not forget Ovid, who was not only the author of the *Metamorphoses* but also of the *Ars Amatoria* (*The Art of Love*), a lively verse advice manual on the business of courtship and seduction. Baptista and his two daughters arrive on the scene: the "intolerable" (5.2.98) Kate, known as a "hilding of a devilish spirit" (2.1.26) and the virtuous, mild, and much less dramatically interesting Bianca. Predictably, Lucentio falls in love with Bianca at first sight and thus overhears Baptista's resolution not to permit Bianca to marry until her elder sister, Kate, has secured a husband. Kate's temperament is thus the seemingly insurmountable obstacle that Bianca's suitors must overcome. Baptista also announces his intention to hire schoolmasters to teach music and poetry, and he requests that Hortensio and Gremio help him to engage them. This gives Lucentio the idea that he can pursue Bianca precisely by disguising himself as a tutor and having Tranio assume his own identity as Lucentio. This class transformation mirrors the Sly episode and suggests another form of transformation, namely, that whereby servants might become masters, a possibility that in real life was freighted with anxiety in a tightly

---

1. Arthur Golding, *Ovid's Metamorphoses* (1567). I have modernized the text.

structured social hierarchy such as that of early modern England. Thus the subplot weaves in carefully the main thread of the play—finding a suitor willing to take on the hellion, Kate, because anyone who hopes to marry Bianca has to find a mate for her impossible sister.

Act 2 Scene 1 sees Petruchio, "a mad-brain rudesby" (3.2.10) newly arrived in Padua vowing to marry a rich wife there. In making this assertion he refers to a veritable itinerary of unsuitable wives including the ancient and ugly Sibyl and the equally old and ugly Florentius, who is transformed into a young beauty when she solves a riddle her knight must answer. The last woman evoked by Petruchio is, since Kate is neither old nor ugly, more apt an analogy for what fate has in store for him, namely Xanthippe, the infamously "curst and shrewd" (1.2.68) wife of Socrates who was frequently depicted in Renaissance engravings dousing her philosopher husband with water. Petruchio resolves to woo Kate despite all admonitions about her temper, which manifests initially as sibling rivalry: "[S]he must have a husband. / I must dance barefoot on her wedding day" (2.1.32–33). This is the only point in the play when Kate voices any desire to be married, and indeed she never actually speaks her consent to marry Petruchio. When he first sees her, Kate has just broken a lute over the head of Bianca's disguised suitor, Hortensio, who is posing as a music master. This is also the second outburst of violence the audience has witnessed, and when the pair are first alone there is a fiery animosity between them that is arguably infused with a certain erotic energy, and this courting episode ends with Petruchio's resolve to tame Kate "And bring you from a wild Kate to a Kate / Conformable as other household Kates" (2.1.269–70). Petruchio plans to tame his shrew, a word that literally refers to a small rodent known to emit a sharp, high-pitched squeak. Tellingly too, much of the imagery used by Petruchio in his plan to "break" his wife's turbulent spirit derives from animal husbandry, specifically from hawk taming, and evokes the primordial domination of "man" over "nature." For the wedding of Kate in Act 3, the groom arrives late and in tatters. Further humiliating his now thoroughly enraged bride, he refuses her pleas to be allowed to stay for the wedding feast. Kate's transformation takes place in Act 4, that is, once the wedding is over and the marriage begins. In 4.1 Petruchio starves his wife and deprives her of sleep, and in 4.3 he holds out the promise of fine clothes, only to tear them to bits before her eyes. All of this, Petruchio does under cover of being the solicitous husband: "This is a way to kill a wife with kindness" (4.1.188) he tells us in a Machiavellian soliloquy at the end of 4.1, disclosing his strategy to the audience. By the last scene of Act 4, Kate is so thoroughly worn down that she will agree to almost anything Petruchio proposes: she swears the sun is the moon and an old man is a maid because "What you will have it named, even that it is, / And so shall it be so for Katherine" (4.5.22–23). Notably, however, she is not so worn down as to accede to Petruchio's abbreviated version of her name.

Early modern culture marked marriage as the most significant transition in the course of one's lifetime, and crucially a profound and irreversible transformation of one's identity was understood to accompany the shift from "maid" to wife and from bachelor to husband. The matter of free choice in marriage was hotly contested in Elizabethan England, and a woman's will in the matter was not necessarily understood as a consideration, especially in alliances that involved substantial wealth and property. Petruchio begins the process of overriding Kate's will when he asserts: "will you, nill you I will marry you" (2.1.263). The system of alliances among men is fully in operation in the matter of Bianca's match. When Baptista decides on Tranio posing as Lucentio as the best husband for his favorite daughter he makes the decision wholly on grounds of wealth. To seal the arrangement, Baptista requires verification of Lucentio's fortune from his father, Vincentio. Tranio sets about finding someone to pose as his (i.e., Lucentio's) wealthy father. He finds an old Mantuan gentleman in 4.2 and persuades him to take the role of Vincentio by inventing a story that all Mantuans found in the city are to be summarily executed due to a quarrel between the Dukes of Padua and Mantua.

However, of the two daughters, Kate marries with full parental consent while Bianca's marriage constitutes an act of filial disobedience. Bianca and Lucentio's marriage is also, in early modern terms, potentially illicit because they have eloped, and it is only—despite the disguise and deception the pair have practiced on Baptista—because the real Lucentio meets his criterion of vast wealth in the matter of selecting his daughter's husband that matters resolve themselves amicably at the end of the play. Indeed, Bianca's part in the deception of her father must be persuasive because Baptista in 4.4 is convinced that she loves the disguised Tranio, "Or both dissemble deeply their affections" (4.4.41).

At the wedding feast for Bianca and Lucentio in Act 5, the newlyweds gather together, including Hortensio, who having failed to secure Bianca's hand has settled for a rich widow. The husbands, and Baptista, lay a wager as to which of them has the most obedient wife. Having been trained like a hawk to come to her master's call, Kate comes as soon as she is bid, and to the astonishment of everyone, Kate wins the 500-crown wager for Petruchio and gives a homily on wifely obedience to the errant wives. While widows were notoriously willful, in part because they were often older and had

economic independence from second husbands and so the disobedience of Hortensio's wife is to be expected, Bianca's refusal to
obey Lucentio is remarkable. Their marriage, after all, had been a
love match. Has Bianca's personality also changed with marriage,
from pliant and obedient to willful? And has Kate's demeanor really
changed, or does she now dissemble? And are there aspects of personal identity that are intrinsic and unchanging—say, modesty or
gentleness—or does identity rather consist of a succession of social
roles: daughter, lover, spouse, servant, master? *Shrew*'s central
theme of "mastery" is thus brought to a head at the end of the play.
A word much used in early modern English, mastery refers to the
series of subjugations inherent in the social hierarchy, centrally, in
this play, those in which wives are subjected to husbands, but also
the pecking order whereby servants are dominated and controlled
by masters. We cannot know for certain whether Kate's transformation is genuine or permanent; nor do we ever come to know what
befalls Christopher Sly. The one identity shift that is reversed con-
sensually is the role switching between Lucentio and Tranio. Yet,
even this has sinister overtones as Lucentio's father avers when he
fears that the servant has usurped his master: "Oh, he hath murdered his master!" (5.1.73). Servants were more likely to be brutal-
ized and killed by their employers than the reverse, but probably
because they constituted crimes against authority and an inversion
of power, incidents in which servants murdered masters loomed
large in the cultural imagination.

   In typically Shakespearean fashion, the play does not resolve issues about the difference between domestic brutality and erotic intensity, or even about true love, but rather compels readers and
audiences to grapple with them for themselves. Why, for example,
is this a motherless household? John Fletcher's response in *A
Woman's Prize or The Tamer Tamed* (written 1609–1610) because it
rescinds Petruchio's putative victory over his wife, seems to indicate
that Fletcher, at least, felt that Shakespeare's Kate was indeed defeated and that her final speech is one of unequivocal submission,
even though her defeat has not been understood in the critical tradition as an established fact. Whether the play is misogynist,
whether it condones spousal abuse, or is on the contrary a happy
romp of a love story constitute the range of scholarly opinion on
the play reflected in the Criticism section. For Harold Bloom, the
play is a love story; for the Irish playwright George Bernard Shaw,
impersonating a woman's perspective and writing thirty years before women in Britain got the vote as the vigorous agitation for female suffrage was gathering momentum, the play is "barbarous" in
its diminishment of women. The Criticism section represents these
poles of opinion as well as a great deal in between. One of the most

important critical perspectives has been that of feminist criticism, though again, perhaps surprisingly, while it has rarely been wholly exonerated, the play has not been completely vilified by feminist critics who have tended to draw out its complex representation of gender relations. Indeed, the play has been at the very heart of recent feminist discussions of Shakespeare.

Shrew Rewritten for the Stage

Since this topic is of perennial interest, there is, as we might expect a long history of appropriation and rewriting of *The Taming of the Shrew*. The section Appropriations/Rewritings offers extracts from some of the earliest theatrical responses to the play by Shakespeare's contemporaries, including *A Pleasant Conceited History Called The Taming of A Shrew* (1594; my emphasis). In this play, the opening induction scenes that in Shakespeare take place in Warwickshire and are never returned to once the play shifts to its Italian setting in Padua, are brought up again in the last scene, so that *A Pleasant Conceited History* ends both thematically and geographically where it began, as *Shrew* does not. When *A Pleasant Conceited History* returns to the Sly episode at the end of the play, Sly asserts that he has learned from the play how to go home and tame his own wife.

Indicative of the popularity of the issues raised by Shakespeare's play, in 1611 John Fletcher, a playwright who is known to have collaborated with Shakespeare on other occasions, wrote a rebuttal to *Shrew* in which Petruchio, left a widower by his first wife, Katherine, is himself tamed by his new wife, Maria. This play was aptly titled *The Woman's Prize or the Tamer Tamed*, and, in contrast to Shakespeare's play, it delivers the victory in the battle of the sexes unequivocally to women. Reproduced here also are excerpts from a range of post-Shakespearean responses to the play including John Lacey's *Sauny the Scot: Or, The Taming of the Shrew: A Comedy* (c. 1667), a rewriting of Shakespeare's play published in 1698. James Worsdale's *A Cure for a Scold* (c. 1735) was a two-act version heavily dependent on Lacey and for this reason is not reproduced here. Two other versions put out by rival theaters in the early eighteenth century by Charles Johnson and Christopher Bullock, respectively, were both entitled *The Cobler of Preston*; Johnson's is excerpted. In the mid-eighteenth century, however, the popularity of these earlier versions was eclipsed by David Garrick's three-act play, *Catharine and Petruchio* (1754), which, as the title indicates, pared the Shakespearean text down to concentrate on the principal couple. David Garrick's heavily adapted version dominated the stage until the nineteenth century. Because of its singular importance in the annals of *Shrew's* theatrical history, *Catharine and Petruchio* is reproduced here in its entirety. Indeed the full text of *Shrew* was not performed again in England until 1844, and in America, until August Daly's 1847 production.

Thanks are due to the critics included in this volume, especially to Laurie Maguire and Marea Mitchell, who contributed new essays, to Emily Shortslef, who helped prepare the manuscript for the press, and, as ever, to my husband, Chris R. Kyle, for his insight and encouragement. My research assistant, the appropriately named Katie Vomero, has my heartfelt thanks not only for her labor but also because, as an exemplary undergraduate at Syracuse University, she reminded me that there is nothing more rewarding than making Shakespeare accessible to undergraduates.

The Text of
THE TAMING OF
THE SHREW

The Taming of the Shrew

Dramatis Personae

CHRISTOPHER SLY, *a beggar and tinker*
HOSTESS *of an alehouse*
A LORD
BARTHOLOMEW, *the Lord's page*
SERVANTS *and* HUNTSMEN *attending on the Lord*
PLAYERS

BAPTISTA MINOLA, *a gentleman of Padua*
KATE, *the shrew, Baptista's elder daughter; also referred to as Katharina and Katherine in speech prefixes, stage directions, and within the play*
BIANCA, *Baptista's younger daughter*
PETRUCHIO, *a gentleman of Verona, suitor to Kate*
GRUMIO, *Petruchio's personal servant*
CURTIS, *chief servant of Petruchio's house*
NATHANIEL, PHILIP, JOSEPH, NICHOLAS, PETER, *servants attending on Petruchio*
GREMIO, *of Padua, elderly suitor to Bianca*
HORTENSIO, *of Padua, suitor to Bianca, pretends to be Litio*
LUCENTIO, *of Pisa, son of Vincentio, suitor to Bianca, pretends to be Cambio*
TRANIO, *Lucentio's personal servant, pretends to be Lucentio*
BIONDELLO, *Lucentio's servant*
VINCENTIO, *Lucentio's father*
A PEDANT (MERCHANT), *of Mantua, pretends to be Vincentio*
A WIDOW, *in love with Hortensio*
A TAILOR
A HABERDASHER
AN OFFICER
SERVINGMEN, *attending on Baptista and Lucentio*

Induction, Scene I

Enter BEGGAR (CHRISTOPHER SLY) *and* HOSTESS.

SLY   I'll pheeze you, in faith.

HOSTESS   A pair of stocks, you rogue.

SLY   You're a baggage, the Slys are no rogues. Look in the
Chronicles. We came in with Richard Conqueror.
Therefore, *paucas pallabris*, let the world slide: Sessa!   5

HOSTESS   You will not pay for the glasses you have burst?

SLY   No, not a denier. Go, by Saint Jeronimy, go to thy cold
bed, and warm thee.

HOSTESS   I know my remedy; I must go fetch the thirdborough.

[*Exit* HOSTESS]

SLY   Third, or fourth, or fifth borough, I'll answer him   10
by law. I'll not budge an inch, boy. Let him come, and kindly.
[*Falls asleep.*]

Wind horns. Enter a LORD *from hunting, with his train.*

LORD   Huntsman, I charge thee, tender well my hounds.
Breathe Merriman, the poor cur is embossed,
And couple Clowder with the deep-mouthed brach.
Saw'st thou not, boy, how Silver made it good   15
At the hedge corner, in the coldest fault?
I would not lose the dog for twenty pound.

FIRST HUNTSMAN   Why, Belman is as good as he, my lord,
He cried upon it at the merest loss,
And twice today picked out the dullest scent,   20
Trust me, I take him for the better dog.

LORD   Thou art a fool. If Echo were as fleet,
I would esteem him worth a dozen such.
But sup them well, and look unto them all,
Tomorrow I intend to hunt again.   25

---

1. **pheeze you:** fix you.
2. **a pair of stocks:** a device consisting of a wooden beam with two leg holes into which offenders were locked by way of punishment.
3. **baggage:** contemptuous term for a woman; **Chronicles:** historical records.
4. **Richard the Conqueror:** Conflation of Richard Coeur de Lion (the lion-heart) and the Norman invader, William the Conqueror who successfully subjugated England in 1066.
5. *paucas pallabris:* shut up; Sly's misquote of the Spanish *pocas palabras*, "fewer words."
6. **denier:** small copper coin; **Jeronimy:** St. Jerome.
9. **thirdborough:** constable.
10. **answer him by law:** pursue a legal remedy.
11. **budge:** shift; **SD.** *Wind horns:* blow the horns.
12. **charge thee:** order you; **tender well:** take good care.
13. **Breathe:** rest; **embossed:** foaming at the mouth from exertion.
14. **deep-mouthed brach:** deep-voiced bitch.

FIRST HUNTSMAN   I will my Lord.

LORD   What's here? One dead, or drunk? See, doth he breathe?

SECOND HUNTSMAN   He breathes, my lord. Were he not warmed
with ale,
This were a bed but cold to sleep so soundly.

LORD   Oh monstrous beast, how like a swine he lies.   30
Grim death, how foul and loathsome is thine image.
Sirs, I will practice on this drunken man.
What think you, if he were conveyed to bed,
Wrapped in sweet clothes, rings put upon his fingers,
A most delicious banquet by his bed,   35
And brave attendants near him when he wakes,
Would not the beggar then forget himself?

FIRST HUNTSMAN   Believe me, lord, I think he cannot choose.

SECOND HUNTSMAN   It would seem strange unto him when he
waked.

LORD   Even as a flatt'ring dream, or worthless fancy.   40
Then take him up, and manage well the jest.
Carry him gently to my fairest chamber,
And hang it round with all my wanton pictures.
Balm his foul head in warm distillèd waters,
And burn sweet wood to make the lodging sweet.   45
Procure me music ready when he wakes,
To make a dulcet and a heavenly sound.
And if he chance to speak, be ready straight
And with a low submissive reverence
Say, "What is it your honor will command?"   50
Let one attend him with a silver basin
Full of rosewater, and bestrewed with flowers,
Another bear the ewer, the third a diaper,
And say, "Wilt please your lordship cool your hands?"
Someone be ready with a costly suit,   55
And ask him what apparel he will wear;
Another tell him of his hounds and horse,
And that his lady mourns at his disease.
Persuade him that he hath been lunatic,
And when he says he is, say that he dreams,   60
For he is nothing but a mighty lord.

38. **he cannot choose:** he cannot do otherwise.
40. **fancy:** imagination.
43. **hang it round with:** put up; **wanton pictures:** erotic art.
44. **distillèd:** perfumed.
45. **sweet wood:** fragrant wood.
47. **dulcet:** sweet.
52. **bestrewed:** covered with.
53. **ewer:** jug; **diaper:** towel.
55. **costly suit:** expensive clothes.
58. **his lady mourns at his disease:** his wife is upset by his illness.

This do, and do it kindly, gentle sirs.
It will be pastime passing excellent,
If it be husbanded with modesty.
FIRST HUNTSMAN   My lord, I warrant you we will play our part   65
As he shall think by our true diligence
He is no less than what we say he is.
LORD   Take him up gently, and to bed with him,
And each one to his office when he wakes.

Sound trumpets.

Sirrah, go see what trumpet 'tis that sounds.   70
Belike some noble gentleman that means,
Traveling some journey to repose him here.

Enter SERVINGMAN.

How now? Who is it?
SERVINGMAN   An't please your honor, players
That offer service to your lordship.

Enter PLAYERS.

LORD   Bid them come near. Now, fellows, you are welcome.   75
PLAYERS   We thank your honor.
LORD   Do you intend to stay with me tonight?
FIRST PLAYER   So please your lordship to accept our duty.
LORD   With all my heart. This fellow I remember
Since once he played a farmer's eldest son.   80
'Twas where you wooed the gentlewoman so well.
I have forgot your name, but sure that part
Was aptly fitted, and naturally performed.
SECOND PLAYER   I think 'twas Soto that your honor means.
LORD   'Tis very true. Thou didst it excellent.   85
Well, you are come to me in happy time,
The rather for I have some sport in hand
Wherein your cunning can assist me much.
There is a lord will hear you play tonight.
But I am doubtful of your modesties,   90
Lest overeyeing of his odd behavior—

63. **pastime passing excellent:** very good sport.
64. **husbanded with modesty:** managed sensibly.
69. **his office:** his appointed role.
70. **Sirrah:** term of address to a social inferior.
71. **Belike:** perhaps.
72. **repose him:** rest himself.
74. **An't please:** if it pleases; **players:** actors.
84. **Soto:** see p. 222.
87. **some sport in hand:** some trick afoot.
88. **cunning:** skill.
90. **modesties:** sense of decorum.
91. **overeyeing:** seeing.

For yet his honor never heard a play—
You break into some merry passion
And so offend him; for I tell you, sirs,
If you should smile, he grows impatient.   95
FIRST PLAYER   Fear not, my lord, we can contain ourselves,
Were he the veriest antic in the world.
LORD   Go, sirrah, take them to the buttery,
And give them friendly welcome every one.
Let them want nothing that my house affords.   100

                        Exit one with the PLAYERS.

Sirrah, go you to Barthol'mew my page,
And see him dressed in all suits like a lady.
That done, conduct him to the drunkard's chamber,
And call him "madam," do him obeisance.
Tell him from me, as he will win my love,   105
He bear himself with honorable action
Such as he hath observed in noble ladies
Unto their lords by them accomplishèd.
Such duty to the drunkard let him do
With soft low tongue, and lowly courtesy,   110
And say, "What is 't your honor will command,
Wherein your lady and your humble wife,
May show her duty, and make known her love?"
And then with kind embracements, tempting kisses,
And with declining head into his bosom,   115
Bid him shed tears, as being overjoyed
To see her noble lord restored to health,
Who for this seven years hath esteemèd him
No better than a poor and loathsome beggar.
And if the boy have not a woman's gift   120
To rain a shower of commanded tears,
An onion will do well for such a shift,
Which in a napkin being close conveyed
Shall in despite enforce a watery eye.
See this dispatched with all the haste thou canst.   125
Anon I'll give thee more instructions.

                        Exit a SERVINGMAN.

92. **heard a play:** went to a play.
93. **break into some merry passion:** start to laugh.
97. **veriest antic:** biggest lunatic.
98. **buttery:** larder.
100. **affords:** offers.
101. **Barthol'mew:** pronounced "Bartelmy."
102. **all suits:** entirely clothed.
104. **do him obeisance:** make the gestures of deference appropriate to a social superior.
123. **close conveyed:** hidden.
124. **in despite:** nevertheless.

I know the boy will well usurp the grace,
Voice, gait, and action of a gentlewoman.
I long to hear him call the drunkard husband,
And how my men will stay themselves from laughter,   130
When they do homage to this simple peasant,
I'll in to counsel them. Haply my presence
May well abate the overmerry spleen
Which otherwise would grow into extremes.

Induction, Scene 2

*Enter aloft the drunkard with attendants, some with
apparel, basin and ewer, and other appurtenances;
and* LORD.

SLY   For God's sake, a pot of small ale.

FIRST SERVINGMAN   Will 't please your lordship drink a cup of
sack?

SECOND SERVINGMAN   Will 't please your honor taste of these
conserves?

THIRD SERVINGMAN   What raiment will your honor wear today?

SLY   I am Christopher Sly. Call not me "honor" nor "lordship."   5
I ne'er drank sack in my life; and if you give me any conserves,
give me conserves of beef. Ne'er ask me what raiment I'll wear,
for I have no more doublets than backs, no more stockings
than legs, nor no more shoes than feet—nay sometime more
feet than shoes, or such shoes as my toes look through the   10
overleather.

LORD   Heaven cease this idle humor in your honor!
Oh that a mighty man of such descent,
Of such possessions and so high esteem,
Should be infusèd with so foul a spirit!   15

SLY   What, would you make me mad? Am not I Christopher
Sly, old Sly's son of Burton-heath, by birth a
pedlar, by education a cardmaker, by transmutation a

---

127. usurp the grace: imitate the demeanor.
132. Haply: perhaps.
133. abate: stop; **overmerry spleen:** too much laughter; the spleen was the organ believed
to be the seat of emotion.
1. small ale: weak, cheap beer.
2. sack: an expensive wine from Spain and the Canary Isles.
3. conserves: fruit preserved with sugar.
7. conserves of beef: beef preserved with salt.
8. doublets: jackets.
11. overleather: upper part of a shoe.
12. idle humor: foolish notion.
18. cardmaker: maker of the combs used in the wool-making process; **by transmutation:**
change.

bearherd, and now by present profession a tinker?
Ask Marian Hacket, the fat alewife of Wincot, if she know   20
me not. If she say I am not fourteen pence on the score for
sheer ale, score me up for the lying'st knave in Christendom.
What, I am not bestraught: here's—

THIRD SERVINGMAN   Oh, this it is that makes your lady mourn!

SECOND SERVINGMAN   Oh, this is it that makes your servants   25
droop.

LORD   Hence comes it that your kindred shuns your house
As beaten hence by your strange lunacy.
Oh noble lord, bethink thee of thy birth.
Call home thy ancient thoughts from banishment,
And banish hence these abject lowly dreams.   30
Look how thy servants do attend on thee,
Each in his office ready at thy beck.
Wilt thou have music? Hark, Apollo plays,   *Music.*
And twenty cagèd nightingales do sing.
Or wilt thou sleep? We'll have thee to a couch,   35
Softer and sweeter than the lustful bed
On purpose trimmed up for Semiramis.
Say thou wilt walk; we will bestrew the ground.
Or wilt thou ride? Thy horses shall be trapped,
Their harness studded all with gold and pearl.   40
Dost thou love hawking? Thou hast hawks will soar
Above the morning lark. Or wilt thou hunt?
Thy hounds shall make the welkin answer them
And fetch shrill echoes from the hollow earth.

FIRST SERVINGMAN   Say thou wilt course, thy greyhounds are as   45
swift
As breathèd stags, ay, fleeter than the roe.

SECOND SERVINGMAN   Dost thou love pictures? We will fetch
thee straight
Adonis painted by a running brook,

---

19. **bearheard:** keeper of a performing bear; **tinker:** itinerant pot mender.
20. **alewife of Wincot:** the female alehouse keeper at the village of Wincot, near Stratford.
21. **fourteen pence on the score:** the amount he has charged at the alehouse and of which the house keeps count.
22. **sheer:** pure.
23. **bestraught:** distraught.
29. **banishment:** when you were not here.
32. **beck:** summons.
37. **trimmed up:** decorated; **Semiramis:** notoriously sensual Queen of Assyria.
38. **bestrew:** scatter; carpet.
39. **trapped:** adorned.
43. **Welkin:** sky
45. **course:** hunt hares.
46. **breathèd stags:** stags that do not run out of breath easily.
48. **Adonis:** beloved of Venus and killed while hunting; the story is recounted in Shakespeare's narrative poem, *Venus and Adonis* and Ovid's *Metamorphoses* Book 10.

And Cytherea all in sedges hid,
Which seem to move and wanton with her breath,   50
Even as the waving sedges play with wind.
LORD   We'll show thee Io as she was a maid,
And how she was beguilèd and surprised,
As lively painted as the deed was done.
THIRD SERVINGMAN   Or Daphne roaming through a thorny wood,   55
Scratching her legs that one shall swear she bleeds,
And at that sight shall sad Apollo weep,
So workmanly the blood and tears are drawn.
LORD   Thou art a lord, and nothing but a lord.
Thou hast a lady far more beautiful   60
Than any woman in this waning age.
FIRST SERVINGMAN   And till the tears that she hath shed for thee
Like envious floods o'errun her lovely face,
She was the fairest creature in the world;
And yet she is inferior to none.   65
SLY   Am I a lord? And have I such a lady?
Or do I dream? Or have I dreamed till now?
I do not sleep: I see, I hear, I speak,
I smell sweet savors, and I feel soft things.
Upon my life, I am a lord indeed,   70
And not a tinker, nor Christopher Sly.
Well, bring our lady hither to our sight,
And once again a pot o' th' smallest ale.
SECOND SERVINGMAN   Will 't please your mightiness to wash
your hands?
Oh, how we joy to see your wit restored!   75
Oh, that once more you knew but what you are!
These fifteen years you have been in a dream,
Or when you waked, so waked as if you slept.
SLY   These fifteen years! By my fay, a goodly nap.
But did I never speak of all that time?   80
FIRST SERVINGMAN   Oh, yes, my lord, but very idle words,
For though you lay here in this goodly chamber,
Yet would you say ye were beaten out of door,
And rail upon the hostess of the house,
And say you would present her at the leet   85

---

49. **Cytherea:** another name for Venus, the goddess of love; **sedges:** marsh grass.
50. **wanton:** play seductively.
52. **Io:** transformed into a heifer by Jove who first seduced her; the story is recounted in Ovid's *Metamorphoses* Book 1.
55. **Daphne:** fleeing Jove's sexual pursuit, Daphne was transformed into a laurel tree; the story is recounted in Ovid's *Metamorphoses* Book 1.
61. **waning age:** declining from the perfection of Eden or the Golden Age.
63. **envious floods:** hateful.
69. **savors:** smells.
79. **fay:** faith
85. **leet:** local court (of the manor).

Because she brought stone jugs and no sealed quarts.
Sometimes you would call out for Cicely Hacket.

SLY   Ay, the woman's maid of the house.

THIRD SERVINGMAN   Why, sir, you know no house, nor no such
    maid,
    Nor no such men as you have reckoned up,   90
    As Stephen Sly, and old John Naps of Greece,
    And Peter Turph, and Henry Pimpernell,
    And twenty more such names and men as these,
    Which never were, nor no man ever saw.

SLY   Now Lord be thankèd for my good amends.   95

ALL   Amen.

Enter [PAGE *dressed as a*] LADY *with Attendants.*

SLY   I thank thee. Thou shalt not lose by it.

PAGE   How fares my noble lord?

SLY   Marry, I fare well, for here is cheer enough. Where is my wife?

PAGE   Here, noble lord. What is thy will with her?   100

SLY   Are you my wife, and will not call me husband?
    My men should call me "lord;" I am your goodman.

PAGE   My husband and my lord, my lord and husband,
    I am your wife in all obedience.

SLY   I know it well. What must I call her?

LORD   Madam.   105

SLY   Al'ce Madam, or Joan Madam?

LORD   Madam, and nothing else. So lords call ladies.

SLY   Madam wife, they say that I have dreamed
    And slept above some fifteen year or more.

PAGE   Ay, and the time seems thirty unto me,   110
    Being all this time abandoned from your bed.

SLY   'Tis much. Servants, leave me and her alone.
    Madam, undress you and come now to bed.

PAGE   Thrice noble lord, let me entreat of you
    To pardon me yet for a night or two,   115
    Or, if not so, until the sun be set.
    For your physicians have expressly charged,
    In peril to incur your former malady,
    That I should yet absent me from your bed.
    I hope this reason stands for my excuse.   120

---

86. **sealed quarts:** quart vessels which guaranteed the correct measure of ale or beer.
87. **Cicely Hacket:** a maid at the inn.
91. **Greece:** Greete, a small village near Stratford in the neighboring county of Gloucester-shire.
95. **amends:** recovery.
97. **Thou shalt not lose by it:** may you prosper for wishing me well.
99. **Marry:** indeed; literally, an oath meaning "by Mary," the Blessed Virgin.

SLY   Ay, it stands so that I may hardly tarry so long.
But I would be loath to fall into my dreams again.
I will therefore tarry in despite of the flesh and the blood.

Enter a [SERVINGMAN *as*] MESSENGER.

MESSENGER   Your honor's players, hearing your amendment,
Are come to play a pleasant comedy,   125
For so your doctors hold it very meet,
Seeing too much sadness hath congealed your blood,
And melancholy is the nurse of frenzy,
Therefore they thought it good you hear a play
And frame your mind to mirth and merriment,   130
Which bars a thousand harms and lengthens life.
SLY   Marry, I will let them play it. Is not a comonty
a Christmas gambold or a tumbling trick?
PAGE   No, my good lord, it is more pleasing stuff.
SLY   What, household stuff?
PAGE   It is a kind of history.   135
SLY   Well, we'll see 't. Come, madam wife, sit by my side
And let the world slip. We shall ne're be younger.

Act 1, Scene 1

Flourish. Enter LUCENTIO *and his man* TRIANO.

LUCENTIO   Tranio, since for the great desire I had
To see fair Padua, nursery of arts,
I am arrived for fruitful Lombardy,
The pleasant garden of great Italy,
And by my father's love and leave am armed   5
With his good will, and thy good company,
My trusty servant well approved in all,
Here let us breathe and haply institute
A course of learning and ingenious studies.

---

121. **it stands:** is the case; also a pun on erection.
124. **amendment:** recovery.
126. **meet:** suitable.
127. **sadness has congealed your blood:** reference to an early modern medical theory about the physiology of melancholy.
128. **melancholy is the nurse of frenzy:** depression leads to delirium.
132. **comonty:** comedy; **gambold:** frolic; **tumbling trick:** acrobatic entertainment.
134. **pleasing stuff:** entertaining.
135. **household stuff:** about domestic matters; but also all the things in a house; **history:** story.
137. **let the world slip:** let's sit and let the time go by.
1 SD. *Flourish:* trumpet fanfare.
2. **nursery of arts:** place where art is cultivated.
8. **let us breathe:** rest and stay.
9. **ingenious:** intellectual.

Pisa, renownèd for grave citizens,   10
Gave me my being, and my father first
A merchant of great traffic through the world,
Vincentio, come of the Bentivolii,
Vincentio's son, brought up in Florence,
It shall become to serve all hopes conceived   15
To deck his fortune with his virtuous deeds.
And therefore, Tranio, for the time I study,
Virtue and that part of philosophy
Will I apply that treats of happiness
By virtue specially to be achieved.   20
Tell me thy mind, for I have Pisa left
And am to Padua come, as he that leaves
A shallow plash, to plunge him in the deep,
And with satiety seeks to quench his thirst.
TRANIO   *Mi perdonato*, gentle master mine.   25
I am in all affected as yourself,
Glad that you thus continue your resolve
To suck the sweets of sweet philosophy.
Only, good master, while we do admire
This virtue and this moral discipline,   30
Let's be no stoics nor no stocks, I pray,
Or so devote to Aristotle's checks
As Ovid be an outcast quite abjured.
Balk logic with acquaintance that you have,
And practice rhetoric in your common talk;   35
Music and poesy use to quicken you;
The mathematics and the metaphysics,
Fall to them as you find your stomach serves you.
No profit grows where is no pleasure ta'en.
In brief, sir, study what you most affect.   40
LUCENTIO   Gramercies, Tranio, well dost thou advise.

---

10. **grave:** fine, upstanding.
12. **great traffic:** valuable trade.
13. **come of:** descended from.
15. **It . . . conceived:** Lucentio's career will meet the highest expectations.
16. **deck:** adorn.
19. **treats of:** deals with.
23. **plash:** pool.
24. **satiety:** having enough.
25. *Mi perdonato:* pardon me.
26. **affected as yourself:** of the same opinion as you.
28. **suck the sweets:** enjoy the pleasures.
31. **no stoics nor no stocks:** neither people who deliberately renounce pleasure nor people who are insensible to it.
32. **Aristotle's checks:** Aristotelian self-discipline.
33. **Ovid:** Roman love poet; **abjured:** renounced.
34. **Balk logic:** bandy words.
38. **as you find your stomach serves you:** whatever you find you have an appetite for.
40. **most affect:** like best.
41. **Gramercies:** many thanks.

If, Biondello, thou wert come ashore,
We could at once put us in readiness
And take a lodging fit to entertain
Such friends as time in Padua shall beget.   45
But stay awhile, what company is this?
TRANIO   Master, some show to welcome us to town.

Enter BAPTISTA *with his two daughters*, KATHERINA *and*
BIANCA; GREMIO *a pantaloon*; HORTENSIO, *suitor to* BIANCA.
LUCENTIO [*and*] TRANIO *stand by.*

BAPTISTA   Gentlemen, importune me no farther,
For how I firmly am resolved you know:
That is, not to bestow my youngest daughter   50
Before I have a husband for the elder.
If either of you both love Katherina,
Because I know you well and love you well,
Leave shall you have to court her at your pleasure.
GREMIO   To cart her rather. She's too rough for me.   55
There, there, Hortensio, will you any wife?
KATE   I pray you, sir, is it your will
To make a stale of me amongst these mates?
HORTENSIO   Mates, maid? How mean you that? No mates for you,
Unless you were of gentler, milder mold.   60
KATE   I'faith, sir, you shall never need to fear;
Iwis it is not halfway to her heart.
But if it were, doubt not her care should be
To comb your noddle with a three-legged stool
And paint your face, and use you like a fool.   65
HORTENSIO   From all such devils, good Lord deliver us!
GREMIO   And me too, good Lord!
TRANIO   Husht, master, here's some good pastime toward.
That wench is stark mad or wonderful froward.
LUCENTIO   But in the other's silence do I see   70
Maid's mild behavior and sobriety.
Peace, Tranio.
TRANIO   Well said, master. Mum, and gaze your fill.
BAPTISTA   Gentlemen, that I may soon make good
What I have said: Bianca, get you in.   75
And let it not displease thee, good Bianca,

42. **thou wert come ashore:** Biondello is a servant who has not yet arrived.
47. **SD. pantaloon:** old fool (a stock character of the Italian *commedio*).
55. **cart:** punish; exhibited in the streets in a cart was punishment for prostitution.
58. **a stale:** whore; laughingstock; **mates:** marriage partners.
62. **Iwis:** indeed; **her:** Kate is speaking about herself in the third person.
64. **noddle:** head.
68. **pastime toward:** show about to begin.
69. **froward:** stubborn; wilful.
73. **Mum:** be silent.

For I will love thee ne're the less, my girl.
KATE   A pretty peat! It is best put finger in the eye,
  and she knew why.
BIANCA   Sister, content you in my discontent.   80
  Sir, to your pleasure humbly I subscribe.
  My books and instruments shall be my company,
  On them to look, and practice by myself.
LUCENTIO   Hark, Tranio, thou mayst hear Minerva speak.
HORTENSIO   Signior Baptista, will you be so strange?   85
  Sorry am I that our good will effects
  Bianca's grief.
GREMIO   Why will you mew her up,
  Signior Baptista, for this fiend of hell,
  And make her bear the penance of her tongue?
BAPTISTA   Gentlemen, content ye. I am resolved.   90
  Go in, Bianca.

                                          [*Exit* BIANCA]

  And for I know she taketh most delight
  In music, instruments, and poetry,
  Schoolmasters will I keep within my house
  Fit to instruct her youth. If you, Hortensio,   95
  Or, Signior Gremio, you know any such,
  Prefer them hither; for to cunning men,
  I will be very kind and liberal
  To mine own children in good bringing up,
  And so farewell. Katherina, you may stay,   100
  For I have more to commune with Bianca.

                                                  Exit.

KATE   Why, and I trust I may go too, may I not?
  What, shall I be appointed hours, as though, belike,
  I knew not what to take, and what to leave? Ha.

                                                  Exit.

GREMIO   You may go to the devil's dam. Your gifts   105
  are so good, here's none will hold you. Their love is not

---

78. **pretty peat:** pampered pet; **put finger in the eye:** cry.
80. **content you:** no more discussion.
84. **Minerva:** goddess of wisdom.
87. **mew . . . up:** confine (literally meaning, "to coop up," a term derived from falconry).
88. **fiend of hell:** i.e., Kate.
97. **cunning:** learned.
101. **commune:** communicate, say.
103. **belike:** perhaps.
104. **what to take, and what to leave:** when to come and go.
105. **devil's dam:** devil's mother.
106. **hold:** restrain.

so great, Hortensio, but we may blow our nails together
and fast it fairly out. Our cake's dough on both sides.
Farewell. Yet for the love I bear, my sweet Bianca, if
I can by any means light on a fit man to teach her that   110
wherein she delights, I will wish him to her father.

HORTENSIO   So will I, Signior Gremio. But a word, I pray.
Though the nature of our quarrel yet never brooked parle,
know now, upon advice, it toucheth us both, that we may
yet again have access to our fair mistress and be happy   115
rivals in Bianca's love, to labor and effect one thing specially.

GREMIO   What's that, I pray?

HORTENSIO   Marry, sir, to get a husband for her sister.

GREMIO   A husband? A devil.

HORTENSIO   I say a husband.   120

GREMIO   I say a devil. Think'st thou, Hortensio, though
her father be very rich, any man is so very a fool to be
married to hell?

HORTENSIO   Tush, Gremio, though it pass your patience and
mine to endure her loud alarums, why, man, there be   125
good fellows in the world, and a man could light on
them, would take her with all faults, and money enough.

GREMIO   I cannot tell. But I had as lief take her dowry with this
condition; to be whipped at the high cross every morning.

HORTENSIO   Faith, as you say, there's small choice in rotten   130
apples. But come, since this bar in law makes us friends, it
shall be so far forth friendly maintained till by helping
Baptista's eldest daughter to a husband, we set his youngest
free for a husband, and then have to 't afresh. Sweet Bianca!
Happy man be his dole! He that runs fastest gets the ring. 135
How say you, Signior Gremio?

GREMIO   I am agreed, and would I had given him the best horse
in Padua to begin his wooing that would thoroughly woo her,
wed her, and bed her, and rid the house of her. Come on.

---

107. **blow our nails together:** be patient (rubbing one's nails is what one does while waiting).
108. **fast it fairly out:** wait it out; **Our cake's dough on both sides:** we are out of luck (proverbial expression).
110. **light on:** alight upon, i.e., come across.
113. **never brooked parle:** allowed negotiations.
114. **toucheth:** concerns.
116. **labor and effect:** endeavor and result.
124. **Tush:** a mild reproof.
125. **alarums:** noisy disturbances (literally, calls to arms).
128. **had as lief:** would just as soon.
129. **condition:** proviso; **high cross:** cross at the town center.
131. **bar in law:** legal impediment (imposed by Baptista).
134. **have to 't:** have at it, i.e., resume our former rivalry.
135. **Happy . . . dole:** joy to the winner; **gets the ring:** wins the prize.

Exeunt ambo. Manet TRANIO *and* LUCENTIO.

TRANIO   I pray, sir, tell me, is it possible   140
    That love should of a sudden take such hold?
LUCENTIO   Oh Tranio, till I found it to be true,
    I never thought it possible or likely.
    But see, while idly I stood looking on,
    I found the effect of love in idleness,   145
    And now in plainess do confess to thee,
    That art to me as secret and as dear
    As Anna to the Queen of Carthage was,
    Tranio, I burn, I pine, I perish, Tranio
    If I achieve not this young modest girl   150
    Counsel me, Tranio, for I know thou canst;
    Assist me, Tranio, for I know thou wilt.
TRANIO   Master, it is no time to chide you now,
    Affection is not rated from the heart.
    If love have touched you, naught remains but so,   155
    "Redime te captum quam queas minimo."
LUCENTIO   Gramercies, lad. Go forward. This contents.
    The rest will comfort, for thy counsel's sound.
TRANIO   Master, you looked so longly on the maid,
    Perhaps you marked not what's the pith of all.   160
LUCENTIO   Oh, yes, I saw sweet beauty in her face,
    Such as the daughter of Agenor had,
    That made great Jove to humble him to her hand,
    When with his knees he kissed the Cretan strand.
TRANIO   Saw you no more? Marked you not how her sister   165
    Began to scold, and raise up such a storm
    That mortal ears might hardly endure the din?
LUCENTIO   Tranio, I saw her coral lips to move,
    And with her breath she did perfume the air.
    Sacred and sweet was all I saw in her.   170
TRANIO   Nay, then 'tis time to stir him from his trance.
    I pray, awake, sir. If you love the maid,
    Bend thoughts and wits to achieve her. Thus it stands:
    Her elder sister is so curst and shrewd,

139. SD. ambo: both; *Manet:* they remain onstage.
145. love in idleness: pansy.
148. Anna: sister and confident of Dido, Queen of Carthage in Virgil's *Aeneid*.
153. chide: castigate.
154. rated: berated.
156. *Redime te captum quam queas minimo:* ransom yourself from capture as cheaply as you can.
160. pith: real issue.
162. daughter of Agenor: Europa, abducted by Jove.
163. Jove: king of the gods.
164. Cretan: of Crete.
173. Bend thoughts: turn your thoughts toward.
174. curst and shrewd: contrary and shrewish.

That till the father rid his hands of her,   175
Master, your love must live a maid at home,
And therefore has he closely mewed her up,
Because she will not be annoyed with suitors.
LUCENTIO   Ah, Tranio, what a cruel father's he!
But art thou not advised, he took some care   180
To get her cunning schoolmasters to instruct her?
TRANIO   Ay, marry, am I sir, and now 'tis plotted.
LUCENTIO   I have it, Tranio.
TRANIO   Master, for my hand,
Both our inventions meet and jump in one.
LUCENTIO   Tell me thine first.
TRANIO   You will be schoolmaster,   185
And undertake the teaching of the maid:
That's your device.
LUCENTIO   It is. May it be done?
TRANIO   Not possible, for who shall bear your part
And be in Padua here Vincentio's son,
Keep house, and ply his book, welcome his friends,   190
Visit his countrymen, and banquet them?
LUCENTIO   *Basta*, content thee, for I have it full.
We have not yet been seen in any house,
Nor can we be distinguished by our faces,
For man or master. Then it follows thus: 195
Thou shalt be master, Tranio, in my stead:
Keep house, and port, and servants, as I should,
I will some other be, some Florentine,
Some Neapolitan, or meaner man of Pisa.
'Tis hatched, and shall be so. Tranio, at once   200
Uncase thee. Take my colored hat and cloak.
When Biondello comes, he waits on thee,
But I will charm him first to keep his tongue.
TRANIO   So had you need.
In brief, sir, sith it your pleasure is,   205
And I am tied to be obedient,
For so your father charged me at our parting:
"Be serviceable to my son," quoth he,
Although I think 'twas in another sense,

---

184. **our inventions meet and jump in one:** we have the same realization at the same moment.
190. **ply his book:** study diligently.
191. **banquet:** used as a verb; host.
192. *Basta:* enough.
195. **man:** manservant.
197. **port:** state.
200. **'Tis hatched:** we have plan.
201. **uncase thee:** undress.
203. **charm him . . . to keep his tongue:** persuade him to stay quiet.

I am content to be Lucentio,   210
Because so well I love Lucentio.
LUCENTIO   Tranio, be so, because Lucentio loves,
And let me be a slave t' achieve that maid,
Whose sudden sight hath thralled my wounded eye.

      Enter BIONDELLO.

Here comes the rogue. Sirrah, where have you been?   215
BIONDELLO   Where have I been? Nay, how now, where
are you? Master, has my fellow Tranio stol'n your
clothes, or you stol'n his, or both? Pray, what's the news?
LUCENTIO   Sirrah, come hither. 'Tis no time to jest,
And therefore frame your manners to the time.   220
Your fellow Tranio here to save my life,
Puts my apparel and my count'nance on,
And I for my escape have put on his,
For in a quarrel since I came ashore,
I killed a man, and fear I was descried.   225
Wait you on him, I charge you, as becomes,
While I make way from hence to save my life.
You understand me?
BIONDELLO   I, sir,? Ne'er a whit.
LUCENTIO   And not a jot of Tranio in your mouth.
Tranio is changed into Lucentio.   230
BIONDELLO   The better for him. Would I were so too.
TRANIO   So could I, faith, boy, to have the next wish after,
That Lucentio indeed had Baptista's youngest daughter.
But, sirrah, not for my sake, but your master's, I advise
You use your manners discreetly in all kind of companies. 235
When I am alone, why, then I am Tranio,
But in all places else your master, Lucentio.
LUCENTIO   Tranio, let's go.
One thing more rests, that thyself execute
To make one among these wooers. If thou ask me why,   240
Sufficeth my reasons are both good and weighty.

                                          Exeunt.

      The presenters above speak.

FIRST SERVINGMAN   My lord, you nod. You do not mind the play.

---

214. thralled my wounded eye: enthralled my eyes that have been wounded by Cupid's
arrow.
220. frame your manners: adapt your behavior.
228. Ne'er a whit: not at all.
229. jot: the smallest mention.
239. rests: remains; **execute:** take action.
241. SD. *presenters:* actors.
242. nod: nod off.

SLY   Yes, by Saint Anne, do I. A good matter, surely.
  Comes there any more of it?
PAGE   My Lord, 'tis but begun.   245
SLY   'Tis a very excellent piece of work, madam lady. Would
  'twere done!   *They sit and mark.*

Act 1, Scene 2

Enter PETRUCHIO *and his man,* GRUMIO.

PETRUCHIO   Verona, for a while I take my leave,
  To see my friends in Padua, but of all
  My best belovèd and approvèd friend
  Hortensio, and I trow this is his house.
  Here, sirrah Grumio, knock, I say.   5
GRUMIO   Knock, sir? Whom should I knock? Is there
  any man has rebused your worship?
PETRUCHIO   Villain, I say, knock me here soundly.
GRUMIO   Knock you here, sir? Why, sir, what am I, sir,
  that I should knock you here, sir?   10
PETRUCHIO   Villain, I say, knock me at this gate
  And rap me well, or I'll knock your knave's pate.
GRUMIO   My master is grown quarrelsome.
  I should knock you first,
  And then I know after who comes by the worst.   15
PETRUCHIO   Will it not be?
  Faith, sirrah, and you'll not knock, I'll ring it.
  I'll try how you can *sol fa* and sing it.

     He wrings him by the ears.

GRUMIO   Help, masters, help! My master is mad.
PETRUCHIO   Now knock when I bid you, sirrah villain.   20

     Enter HORTENSIO.

HORTENSIO   How now, what's the matter? My old friend Grumio,
  and my good friend Petruchio? How do you all at Verona?
PETRUCHIO   Signior Hortensio, come you to part the fray?
  Con tutto il cuore bene trovato, may I say.

---

243. by Saint Anne: patron saint of married women.
246–47. Would, 'twere done!: I wish it was over!; **SD.** *mark: watch.*
6. knock: strike.
7. rebused: abused.
8. knock me: knock at the door for me.
17. ring it: a pun on "ring" and "wring."
18. sol fa: sing a scale; **sing it:** cry out in pain.
23. fray: brawl.
24. *Con tutto il cuore bene trovato*: With all my heart, well met (Italian).

HORTENSIO   *Alla nostra casa ben venuto molto honorata signior*   25
   mio Petruchio.
   Rise, Grumio, rise. We will compound this quarrel.
GRUMIO   Nay 'tis no matter, sir, what he 'leges in Latin.
   If this be not a lawful cause for me to leave his service.
   Look you, sir: he bid me knock him and rap him soundly,   30
   sir. Well, was it fit for a servant to use his master so,
   being perhaps, for aught I see, two-and-thirty, a peep out?
   Whom would to God I had well knocked at first,
   Then had not Grumio come by the worst.
PETRUCHIO   A senseless villain! Good Hortensio,   35
   I bade the rascal knock upon your gate,
   And could not get him for my heart to do it.
GRUMIO   Knock at the gate? O heavens! Spake you not
   these words plain, "Sirrah, knock me here, rap me
   here, knock me well, and knock me soundly"? And   40
   come you now with knocking at the gate?
PETRUCHIO   Sirrah, be gone or talk not, I advise you.
HORTENSIO   Petruchio, patience, I am Grumio's pledge.
   Why this a heavy chance twixt him and you,
   Your ancient trusty pleasant servant Grumio.   45
   And tell me now, sweet friend, what happy gale
   Blows you to Padua here from old Verona?
PETRUCHIO   Such wind as scatters young men through the
   world
   To seek their fortunes farther than at home,
   Where small experience grows but in a few.
   Signior Hortensio, thus it stands with me: 50
   Antonio my father is deceased,
   And I have thrust myself into this maze,
   Happily to wive and thrive as best I may.
   Crowns in my purse I have, and goods at home,   55
   And so am come abroad to see the world.
HORTENSIO   Petruchio, shall I then come roundly to thee
   And wish thee to a shrewd ill-favored wife?
   Thou'dst thank me but a little for my counsel.
   And yet I'll promise thee she shall be rich,   60

25–26. *Alla nostra casa ben venuto molto honorata signior mio Petruchio:* Welcome to
our house, very honorable Master Petruchio (Italian).
27. compound: settle.
28. 'leges: alleges; **Latin:** Grumio cannot tell the difference between Latin and Italian.
31. fit for a servant to use his master so: appropriate for a servant to behave thus toward
his master.
32. aught: anything; **a peep out:** inebriated; the expression derives from a card game, the
"pip" (peep) identifying the suit.
43. pledge: ally; guarantee.
44. heavy chance: sad occurrence.
53. this maze: conundrum.
54. wive: find a wife; marry.

And very rich. But thou'rt too much my friend,
And I'll not wish thee to her.

PETRUCHIO   Signior Hortensio, 'twixt such friends as we,
Few words suffice. And therefore, if thou know
One rich enough to be Petruchio's wife,   65
As wealth is burden of my wooing dance,
Be she as foul as was Florentius' love,
As old as Sibyl, and as curst and shrewd
As Socrates' Xanthippe, or a worse,
She moves me not, or not removes, at least,   70
Affection's edge in me, were she as rough
As are the swelling Adriatic seas.
I come to wive it wealthily in Padua;
If wealthily, then happily in Padua.

GRUMIO   Nay, look you, sir, he tells you flatly what his   75
mind is. Why, give him gold enough and marry him to
a puppet or an aglet-baby, or an old trot with ne're a tooth in
her head, though she have as many diseases as two-and-fifty
horses. Why, nothing comes amiss, so money comes withal.

HORTENSIO   Petruchio, since we are stepped thus far in,   80
I will continue that I broached in jest.
I can, Petruchio, help thee to a wife
With wealth enough, and young and beauteous,
Brought up as best becomes a gentlewoman.
Her only fault, and that is faults enough,   85
Is that she is intolerable curst,
And shrewd, and froward, so beyond all measure,
That were my state far worser than it is,
I would not wed her for a mine of gold.

PETRUCHIO   Hortensio, peace. Thou know'st not gold's effect. 90
Tell me her father's name, and 'tis enough,
For I will board her, though she chide as loud
As thunder, when the clouds in autumn crack.

HORTENSIO   Her father is Baptista Minola,
An affable and courteous gentleman.   95
Her name is Katherina Minola,

---

66. **burden:** as in the sense of the burden or repeated refrain of a song.
67. **Florentius' love:** alludes to the story of an ugly old woman who becomes young and beautiful after marriage in John Gower's *Confessio Amantis* [Confessions of Love].
68. **Sibyl:** female oracle of antiquity.
69. **Socrates' Xanthippe:** Socrates' wife, a famous shrew.
70. **moves:** disturbs; does not remove.
77. **aglet baby:** doll worn as an ornament; **trot:** derogative term for an elderly woman.
86. **intolerable curst:** intolerably contrary.
87. **froward:** Stubborn; willful.
92. **I will board her:** woo her.
93. **clouds in autumn crack:** an allusion to the violently stormy autumnal weather.

Renowned in Padua for her scolding tongue.
PETRUCHIO   I know her father, though I know not her,
And he knew my deceasèd father well.
I will not sleep, Hortensio, till I see her,   100
And therefore let me be thus bold with you,
To give you over at this first encounter,
Unless you will accompany me thither.
GRUMIO   I pray you, sir, let him go while the humor lasts. A'
my word, and she knew him as well as I do, she would think   105
scolding would do little good upon him. She may perhaps call
him half a score knaves or so. Why, that's nothing; an he begin
once, he'll rail in his rope tricks. I'll tell you what, sir, and she
stand him but a little, he will throw a figure in her face and
so disfigure her with it that she shall have no more eyes to   110
see withal than a cat. You know him not, sir.
HORTENSIO   Tarry, Petruchio, I must go with thee,
For in Baptista's keep my treasure is.
He hath the jewel of my life in hold,
His youngest daughter, beautiful Bianca,   115
And her withholds from me. Other more
Suitors to her and rivals in my love,
Supposing it a thing impossible,
For those defects I have before rehearsed,
That ever Katherina will be wooed.   120
Therefore this order hath Baptista ta'en,
That none shall have access unto Bianca
Till Katherine the Curst have got a husband.
GRUMIO   Katherine the Curst,
A title for a maid of all titles the worst.   125
HORTENSIO   Now shall my friend Petruchio do me grace,
And offer me disguised in sober robes,
To old Baptista as a schoolmaster
Well seen in music, to instruct Bianca,
That so I may by this device at least   130

---

97. **scolding:** nagging.
106–7. **call him half a score knaves:** call him a rogue ten times.
108. **rail in his rope tricks:** curb his violent rhetoric.
108–9. **and she stand him but a little:** if she tolerates him even a little.
109–10. **throw a figure in her face and so disfigure her:** use abusive language; a "figure"
literally means a figure of speech.
110–11. **no more eyes to see withal than a cat:** obscure expression of uncertain
meaning.
113. **my treasure:** Bianca; also the dowry that would be his if he married her.
114. **the jewel of my life:** Bianca; referring again to his love for her and her father's
wealth.
119. **defects:** obstacles (to marrying Bianca); **before rehearsed:** spoken of previously.
124–25. **Curst . . . worst:** a rhymed couplet.
126. **do me grace:** do a favor.
127. **sober robes:** proper clothes.

Have leave and leisure to make love to her,
And unsuspected court her by herself.

Enter GREMIO *and* LUCENTIO *disguised.*

GRUMIO   Here's no knavery. See, to beguile the old-
folks, how the young folks lay their heads together.
Master, master, look about you. Who goes there, ha?   135
HORTENSIO   Peace, Grumio, it is the rival of my love.
Petruchio, stand by a while.
GRUMIO   A proper stripling, and an amorous.

[*They stand aside*]

GREMIO   O, very well, I have perused the note.
Hark you, sir, I'll have them very fairly bound,   140
All books of love, see that at any hand,
And see you read no other lectures to her.
You understand me. Over and beside
Signior Baptista's liberality,
I'll mend it with a largess. Take your paper too,   145
And let me have them very well perfumed,
For she is sweeter than perfume itself
To whom they go to. What will you read to her?
LUCENTIO   Whate'er I read to her, I'll plead for you,
As for my patron, stand you so assured,   150
As firmly as yourself were still in place,
Yea, and perhaps with more successful words
Than you, unless you were a scholar, sir.
GREMIO   Oh this learning, what a thing it is.
GRUMIO   [*Aside*] Oh this woodcock, what an ass it is.   155
PETRUCHIO   Peace, sirrah.
HORTENSIO   Grumio, mum. [*Advancing*] God save you, Signior
Gremio.
GREMIO   And you are well met, Signior Hortensio.
Trow you whither I am going?
To Baptista Minola.   160
I promised to enquire carefully
About a schoolmaster for the fair Bianca,
And by good fortune I have lighted well
On this young man, for learning and behavior

131. **to make love to:** to woo.
133–34. **to beguile the old-folks . . . the young folks lay their heads together:** the young
conspire together against the old.
138. **proper stripling:** handsome lad.
143. **Over and beside:** over and above.
145. **a largess:** gift of money.
155. **woodcock:** easily snared bird
157. **Grumio, mum:** be quiet Grumio.
159. **trow:** know.

Fit for her turn, well read in poetry   165
And other books, good ones, I warrant ye.
HORTENSIO   'Tis well. And I have met a gentleman
  Hath promised me to help me to another,
  A fine musician to instruct our mistress.
  So shall I no whit be behind in duty   170
  To fair Bianca, so beloved of me.
GREMIO   Beloved of me, and that my deeds shall prove.
GRUMIO   [*Aside*] And that his bags shall prove.
HORTENSIO   Gremio, 'tis now no time to vent our love.
  Listen to me, and if you speak me fair,   175
  I'll tell you news indifferent good for either.
  Here is a gentleman whom by chance I met,
  Upon agreement from us to his liking,
  Will undertake to woo curst Katherine,
  Yea, and to marry her, if her dowry please.   180
GREMIO   So said, so done, is well.
  Hortensio, have you told him all her faults?
PETRUCHIO   I know she is an irksome brawling scold.
  If that be all, masters, I hear no harm.
GREMIO   No, sayst me so, friend? What countryman?   185
PETRUCHIO   Born in Verona, old Antonio's son:
  My father dead, my fortune lives for me,
  And I do hope good days and long to see.
GREMIO   Oh sir, such a life with such a wife were strange.
  But if you have a stomach, to 't a God's name,   190
  You shall have me assisting you in all.
  But will you woo this wildcat?
PETRUCHIO   Will I live?
GRUMIO   Will he woo her? Ay, or I'll hang her.
PETRUCHIO   Why came I hither but to that intent?
  Think you a little din can daunt mine ears?   195
  Have I not in my time heard lions roar?
  Have I not heard the sea, puffed up with winds,
  Rage like an angry boar chafèd with sweat?
  Have I not heard great ordnance in the field?
  And heaven's artillery thunder in the skies?   200
  Have I not in a pitchèd battle heard

173. **bags:** money bags with a pun on testicles.
174. **vent:** express.
176. **indifferent:** equally.
178. **Upon agreement from us to his liking:** if we agree to his terms.
185. **What countryman?:** Where are you from?
190. **a stomach to 't:** the appetite for it; **a God's name:** in God's name.
192. **wildcat:** pun on "cat" and Katherine or Kate.
194. **but to that intent:** for that purpose.
195. **daunt mine ears:** deafened me.
198. **chafèd:** irritated.
199. **ordnance:** military ordinance.

Loud 'larums, neighing steeds, and trumpets clang?
And do you tell me of a woman's tongue,
That gives not half so great a blow to hear,
As will a chestnut in a farmer's fire?   205
Tush, tush, fear boys with bugs.

GRUMIO   For he fears none.

GREMIO   Hortensio, hark.
This gentleman is happily arrived,
My mind presumes for his own good, and yours.   210

HORTENSIO   I promised we would be contributors,
And bear his charge of wooing, whatsoe're.

GREMIO   And so we will, provided that he win her.

GRUMIO   I would I were as sure of a good dinner.

Enter TRANIO *brave, and* BIONDELLO.

TRANIO   Gentlemen, God save you. If I may be bold,   215
Tell me, I beseech you, which is the readiest way
To the house of Signior Baptista Minola?

BIONDELLO   He that has the two fair daughters, is't he you mean?

TRANIO   Even he, Biondello.

GREMIO   Hark you, sir, you mean not her to—   220

TRANIO   Perhaps him and her, sir. What have you to do?

PETRUCHIO   Not her that chides, sir, at any hand, I pray.

TRANIO   I love no chiders, sir. Biondello, let's away.

LUCENTIO   [*aside*] Well begun, Tranio.

HORTENSIO   Sir, a word ere you go.
Are you a suitor to the maid you talk of, yea or no?   225

TRANIO   And if I be sir, is it any offence?

GREMIO   No, if without more words you will get you hence.

TRANIO   Why sir, I pray, are not the streets as free
For me, as for you?

GREMIO   But so is not she.

TRANIO   For what reason, I beseech you?   230

GREMIO   For this reason, if you'll know,
That she's the choice love of Signior Gremio.

HORTENSIO   That she's the chosen of Signior Hortensio.

TRANIO   Softly, my masters. If you be gentlemen
Do me this right: hear me with patience.   235
Baptista is a noble gentleman,

---

202. 'larums: alarms.
205. a chestnut in a farmer's fire: the sound of a chestnut popping. Again, Petruchio dismisses the problem of a shrewish wife as a mere domestic issue as opposed to momentous matters of war and the world of men beyond the household.
206. fear boys with bugs: frighten boys with bugbears or bugaboos.
212. bear his charge of wooing: cover the expenses incurred in courtship.
214. I would: I wish; as sure: as certain.
215. SD. brave: dressed in fine clothes.

To whom my father is not all unknown,
And were his daughter fairer than she is,
She may more suitors have, and me for one.
Fair Leda's daughter had a thousand wooers,   240
Then well one more may fair Bianca have.
And so she shall. Lucentio shall make one,
Though Paris came in hope to speed alone.

GREMIO   What, this gentleman will out-talk us all.

LUCENTIO   Sir, give him head. I know he'll prove a jade.   245

PETRUCHIO   Hortensio, to what end are all these words?

HORTENSIO   Sir, let me be so bold as ask you,
Did you yet ever see Baptista's daughter?

TRANIO   No, sir, but hear I do that he hath two,
The one, as famous for a scolding tongue,   250
As is the other, for beauteous modesty.

PETRUCHIO   Sir, sir, the first's for me. Let her go by.

GREMIO   Yea, leave that labor to great Hercules,
And let it be more than Alcides' twelve.

PETRUCHIO   Sir, understand you this of me, in sooth,   255
The youngest daughter whom you hearken for,
Her father keeps from all access of suitors,
And will not promise her to any man
Until the elder sister first be wed.
The younger then is free, and not before.   260

TRANIO   If it be so, sir, that you are the man
Must stead us all, and me amongst the rest,
And if you break the ice, and do this feat,
Achieve the elder, set the younger free
For our access, whose hap shall be to have her   265
Will not so graceless be to be ingrate.

HORTENSIO   Sir you say well, and well you do conceive,
And since you do profess to be a suitor,
You must as we do, gratify this gentleman,
To whom we all rest generally beholding.   270

TRANIO   Sir, I shall not be slack. In sign whereof,
Please ye we may contrive this afternoon,

---

240. **Leda's daughter:** Helen of Troy.
243. **Paris:** Trojan prince who abducted Helen; **speed:** prevail.
245. **give him head:** let him have his way; **a jade:** old horse.
252. **Let her go by:** leave her out of the matter.
253. **Hercules:** i.e., someone of superhuman strength.
254. **Alcides' twelve:** Hercules, also known as Alcides, was assigned twelve ostensibly impossible tasks.
255. **in sooth:** in truth.
262. **stead us:** help us.
265–66. **whose hap shall be to have her . . . to be ingrate:** the successful suitor to Bianca will show his gratitude to Petruchio.
267. **conceive:** understand.
270. **we all rest generally beholding:** we are all beholden or indebted to him.

And quaff carouses to our mistress' health,
And do as adversaries do in law,
Strive mightily, but eat and drink as friends.   275
GRUMIO, BIONDELLO   Oh excellent motion! Fellows, let's be gone.
HORTENSIO   The motion's good indeed, and be it so.
Petruchio, I shall be your *ben venuto*.

Exeunt.

Act 2, Scene 1

Enter KATHERINA *and* BIANCA.

BIANCA   Good sister, wrong me not, nor wrong yourself,
To make a bondmaid and a slave of me.
That I disdain. But for these other goods,
Unbind my hands, I'll pull them off myself,
Yea, all my raiment, to my petticoat,   5
Or what you will command me will I do,
So well I know my duty to my elders.
KATE   Of all thy suitors here, I charge tell
Whom thou lov'st best. See thou dissemble not.
BIANCA   Believe me, sister, of all the men alive,   10
I never yet beheld that special face,
Which I could fancy more than any other.
KATE   Minion, thou liest. Is't not Hortensio?
BIANCA   If you affect him, sister, here I swear
I'll plead for you myself, but you shall have him.   15
KATE   Oh, then belike you fancy riches more.
You will have Gremio to keep you fair.
BIANCA   Is it for him you do envy me so?
Nay, then you jest, and now I well perceive
You have but jested with me all this while.   20
I prithee, sister Kate, untie my hands.
KATE   If that be jest, then all the rest was so.   *Strikes her.*

Enter BAPTISTA.

BAPTISTA   Why, how now, dame, whence grows this insolence?

---

273. **quaff carouses:** toast.
276. **motion:** proposal.
278. ***ben venuto; benvenuto:*** welcome (Italian).
2. **bondmaid:** an indentured female servant.
3. **goods:** things.
5. **raiment:** garment.
13. **Minion:** contemptuous term.
14. **affect:** like.
16. **belike:** perhaps.

Bianca, stand aside. Poor girl, she weeps.
Go ply thy needle, meddle not with her.   25
For shame, thou hilding of a devilish spirit,
Why dost thou wrong her that did ne're wrong thee?
When did she cross thee with a bitter word?
KATE   Her silence flouts me, and I'll be revenged.

                              Flies after BIANCA.

BAPTISTA   What, in my sight? Bianca, get thee in.   *Exit* [BIANCA].   30
KATE   What, will you not suffer me? Nay, now I see
She is your treasure, she must have a husband.
I must dance barefoot on her wedding day,
And for your love to her lead apes in hell.
Talk not to me, I will go sit and weep,   35
Till I can find occasion of revenge.
BAPTISTA   Was ever gentleman thus grieved as I?
But who comes here?

        Enter GREMIO, LUCENTIO, *in the habit of a mean man,*
        PETRUCHIO *with* TRANIO *with his boy bearing a lute and*
        books.

GREMIO   Good morrow, neighbor Baptista.
BAPTISTA   Good morrow, neighbor Gremio. God save   40
you, gentlemen.
PETRUCHIO   And you good sir. Pray, have you not a daughter
Called Katherina, fair and virtuous?
BAPTISTA   I have a daughter, sir, called Katherina.
GREMIO   You are too blunt. Go to it orderly.   45
PETRUCHIO   You wrong me, Signior Gremio. Give me leave.
I am a gentleman of Verona, sir,
That hearing of her beauty and her wit,
Her affability and bashful modesty,
Her wondrous qualities and mild behavior,   50
Am bold to show myself a forward guest
Within your house to make mine eye the witness
Of that report which I so oft have heard,
And for an entrance to my entertainment,
I do present you with a man of mine   55
Cunning in music and the mathematics,
To instruct her fully in those sciences,
Whereof I know she is not ignorant.
Accept of him, or else you do me wrong.

26. **hilding:** vicious.
29. **flouts:** mocks.
34. **lead apes in hell:** proverbially the occupation of spinsters.
38. **SD.** *mean:* poor; *his boy:* Biondello.
56. **Cunning:** learned.

His name is Litio, born in Mantua.   60
BAPTISTA   You're welcome, sir, and he, for your good sake.
  But for my daughter, Katherine, this I know,
  She is not for your turn, the more my grief.
PETRUCHIO   I see you do not mean to part with her,
  Or else you like not of my company.   65
BAPTISTA   Mistake me not, I speak but as I find.
  Whence are you sir? What may I call your name?
PETRUCHIO   Petruchio is my name, Antonio's son,
  A man well known throughout all Italy.
BAPTISTA   I know him well. You are welcome for his sake.   70
GREMIO   Saving your tale, Petruchio, I pray, let us that are
  poor petitioners speak too. *Bacare*, you are marvelous forward.
PETRUCHIO   Oh, pardon me, Signior Gremio, I would fain be
  doing.
GREMIO   I doubt it not, sir. But you will curse your wooing.   75
  Neighbors, this is a gift very grateful, I am sure of it. To
  express the like kindness, myself, that have been more kindly
  beholding to you than any, freely give unto you this young
  scholar, that hath been long studying at Rheims, as cunning
  in Greek, Latin, and other languages, as the other in music and   80
  mathematics. His name is Cambio. Pray, accept his service.
BAPTISTA   A thousand thanks, Signior Gremio.
  Welcome, good Cambio. But, gentle sir,
  Methinks you walk like a stranger.
  May I be so bold to know the cause of your coming?   85
TRANIO   Pardon me, sir, the boldness is mine own,
  That, being a stranger in this city here,
  Do make myself a suitor to your daughter,
  Unto Bianca, fair and virtuous.
  Nor is your firm resolve unknown to me   90
  In the preferment of the eldest sister.
  This liberty is all that I request,
  That upon knowledge of my parentage,
  I may have welcome 'mongst the rest that woo,
  And free access and favor as the rest.   95
  And toward the education of your daughters
  I here bestow a simple instrument,
  And this small packet of Greek and Latin books,
  If you accept them, then their worth is great.

60. **Litio:** old Italian word for garlic.
63. **She is not for your turn:** she would not suit you.
72. ***Bacare:*** stand back.
84. **walk like a stranger:** stand apart.
91. **In the preferment of:** in the precedence you give to.
97. **a simple instrument:** the lute.

BAPTISTA	Lucentio is your name? Of whence, I pray?	100
TRANIO	Of Pisa, sir, son to Vincentio.	
BAPTISTA	A mighty man of Pisa. By report	

    I know him well. You are very welcome, sir.
    [*To* HORTENSIO] Take you the lute, [*To* LUCENTIO] and you the
      set of books;
    You shall go see your pupils presently. Holla, within!   105

      Enter a SERVANT.

    Sirrah, lead these gentlemen
    To my daughters, and tell them both
    These are their tutors. Bid them use them well.

      [*Exit* SERVANT, *with* LUCENTIO *and* HORTENSIO]

    We will go walk a little in the orchard,
    And then to dinner. You are passing welcome,   110
    And so I pray you all to think yourselves.

PETRUCHIO   Signior Baptista, my business asketh haste,
    And every day I cannot come to woo.
    You knew my father well, and in him me,
    Left solely heir to all his lands and goods,   115
    Which I have bettered rather than decreased.
    Then tell me, if I get your daughter's love,
    What dowry shall I have with her to wife?

BAPTISTA   After my death the one half of my lands,
    And in possession twenty thousand crowns.   120

PETRUCHIO   And for that dowry, I'll assure her of
    Her widowhood, be it that she survive me,
    In all my lands and leases whatsoever.
    Let specialties be therefore drawn between us,
    That covenants may be kept on either hand.   125

BAPTISTA   Ay, when the special thing is well obtained,
    That is, her love; for that is all in all.

PETRUCHIO   Why, that is nothing, for I tell you, father,
    I am as peremptory as she proud-minded.
    And where two raging fires meet together   130
    They do consume the thing that feeds their fury.
    Though little fire grows great with little wind,
    Yet extreme gusts will blow out fire and all.
    So I to her, and so she yields to me,
    For I am rough and woo not like a babe.   135

BAPTISTA   Well mayst thou woo, and happy be thy speed.

---

108. **use them well:** treat them.
110. **passing:** more than.
124. **specialties:** contract terms.
125. **covenants:** legal agreements.
135. **woo not like a babe:** I don't woo gently; I'm not naive.

But be thou armed for some unhappy words.
PETRUCHIO　Ay, to the proof, as mountains are for winds,
　That shakes not, though they blow perpetually.

　Enter HORTENSIO *with his head broke.*

BAPTISTA　How now, my friend, why dost thou look so pale?　140
HORTENSIO　For fear, I promise you, if I look pale.
BAPTISTA　What, will my daughter prove a good musician?
HORTENSIO　I think she'll sooner prove a soldier.
　Iron may hold with her, but never lutes.
BAPTISTA　Why, then thou canst not break her to the lute?　145
HORTENSIO　Why, no, for she hath broke the lute to me.
　I did but tell her she mistook her frets,
　And bowed her hand to teach her fingering,
　When, with a most impatient devilish spirit,
　"Frets call you these?" quoth she, "I'll fume with them."　150
　And with that word she struck me on the head,
　And through the instrument my pate made way.
　And there I stood amazèd for a while
　As on a pillory, looking through the lute,
　While she did call me rascal, fiddler,　155
　And twangling Jack, with twenty such vile terms,
　As had she studied to misuse me so.
PETRUCHIO　Now, by the world, it is a lusty wench!
　I love her ten times more than e'er I did.
　Oh how I long to have some chat with her!　160
BAPTISTA　Well, go with me, and be not so discomfited.
　Proceed in practice with my younger daughter;
　She's apt to learn and thankful for good turns.
　Signior Petruchio, will you go with us
　Or shall I send my daughter Kate to you?　165

　　　　　　　　　　　　　Exit. Manet PETRUCHIO.

PETRUCHIO　I pray you do. I'll attend her here,
　And woo her with some spirit when she comes.
　Say that she rail, why then I'll tell her plain,
　She sings as sweetly as a nightingale.
　Say that she frown, I'll say she looks as clear　170
　As morning roses newly washed with dew.
　Say she be mute and will not speak a word,

138. **to the proof:** impermeable, weatherproof.
139. SD. **broke:** injured.
144. **Iron may hold with her:** only force will have any effect.
147. **mistook her frets:** made mistakes in the fingering.
160. **some chat with her:** a pun on the name "Kate."
163. **apt to learn and thankful for good turns:** willing to learn and grateful for help.
165. SD. *Manet:* Only.
166. **attend her:** wait for her.

Then I'll commend her volubility
And say she uttereth piercing eloquence.
If she do bid me pack, I'll give her thanks,   175
As though she bid me stay by her a week.
If she deny to wed, I'll crave the day
When I shall ask the banns and when be marrièd.
But here she comes, and now, Petruchio speak.

    Enter KATHERINA.

Good morrow, Kate, for that's your name, I hear.   180
KATE   Well have you heard, but something hard of hearing.
They call me Katherine, that do talk of me.
PETRUCHIO   You lie, in faith, for you are called plain Kate,
And bonny Kate, and sometimes Kate the curst.
But Kate, the prettiest Kate in Christendom,   185
Kate of Kate Hall, my super-dainty Kate,
For dainties are all Kates, and therefore, Kate
Take this of me, Kate of my consolation.
Hearing thy mildness praised in every town,
Thy virtues spoke of, and thy beauty sounded,   190
Yet not so deeply as to thee belongs,
Myself am moved to woo thee for my wife.
KATE   Moved? In good time. Let him that moved you hither
Remove you hence. I knew you at the first
You were a movable.
PETRUCHIO   Why, what's a movable?   195
KATE   A joint stool.
PETRUCHIO   Thou hast hit it. Come, sit on me.
KATE   Asses are made to bear, and so are you.
PETRUCHIO   Women are made to bear, and so are you.
KATE   No such jade as you, if me you mean.
PETRUCHIO   Alas, good Kate, I will not burden thee,   200
For knowing thee to be but young and light.
KATE   Too light for such a swain as you to catch,
And yet as heavy as my weight should be.
PETRUCHIO   Should be? Should buzz.
KATE   Well ta'en, and like a buzzard.
PETRUCHIO   Oh slow-winged turtle, shall a buzzard take thee?   205
KATE   Ay, for a turtle, as he takes a buzzard.
PETRUCHIO   Come, come you wasp, i'faith you are too angry.

187. **dainties are all Kates**: a pun on "cates," delicacies, confections.
194. **A movable**: piece of furniture; a capricious person; a "flip-flopper."
196. **A joint stool**: a stool made by an expert joiner or carpenter.
198. **Women are made to bear**: to bear children; to have men on top of them during intercourse.
199. **jade**: broken-down horse.
204. **Should buzz**: punning on Kate's last word, "be"/"bee."
207. **wasp**: shrew; pun on the insect.

KATE   If I be waspish, best beware my sting.

PETRUCHIO   My remedy is then to pluck it out.

KATE   Ay, if the fool could find it where it lies.   210

PETRUCHIO   Who knows not where a wasp does wear his sting?
In his tail.

KATE   In his tongue?

PETRUCHIO   Whose tongue?

KATE   Yours, if you talk of tales, and so farewell.

PETRUCHIO   What, with my tongue in your tail? Nay, come again,
Good Kate, I am a gentleman.

KATE   That I'll try.   *She strikes him*   215

PETRUCHIO   I swear I'll cuff you if you strike again.

KATE   So may you lose your arms.
If you strike me, you are no gentleman,
And if no gentleman, why then no arms.

PETRUCHIO   A herald, Kate? Oh put me in thy books.   220

KATE   What is your crest, a coxcomb?

PETRUCHIO   A combless cock, so Kate will be my hen.

KATE   No cock of mine. You crow too like a craven.

PETRUCHIO   Nay, come Kate, come. You must not look so sour.

KATE   It is my fashion when I see a crab.   225

PETRUCHIO   Why, here's no crab, and therefore look not sour.

KATE   There is, there is.

PETRUCHIO   Then show it me.

KATE   Had I a glass, I would.

PETRUCHIO   What, you mean my face?

KATE   Well aimed of such a young one.   230

PETRUCHIO   Now, by Saint George, I am too young for you.

KATE   Yet you are withered.

PETRUCHIO   'Tis with cares.

KATE   I care not.

PETRUCHIO   Nay, hear you Kate. In sooth, you scape not so.

KATE   I chafe you if I tarry. Let me go.

PETRUCHIO   No, not a whit. I find you passing gentle.   235
'Twas told me you were rough, and coy, and sullen,

214. my tongue in your tail: bawdily implies cunnilingus.
216. cuff: hit.
217. arms: this begins a pun on arms, that is limbs used to strike, and the coat of arms
depicted on an heraldic shield.
220. put me in thy books: books of heraldry, (continuing the pun), also favor.
221. crest: armorial insignia; coxcomb: fool's hat.
222. combless cock: without aggression.
223. craven: cock who has lost the fight.
225. crab: crabby person.
232. with cares: with worry.
233. In sooth: indeed.
234. chafe: get irritated.
235. a whit: at all.

And now I find report a very liar,
For thou art pleasant, gamesome, passing courteous,
But slow in speech, yet sweet as springtime flowers.
Thou canst not frown, thou canst not look askance,   240
Nor bite the lip, as angry wenches will,
Nor hast thou pleasure to be cross in talk,
But thou with mildness entertain'st thy wooers,
With gentle conference, soft and affable.
Why does the world report that Kate doth limp?   245
Oh sland'rous world! Kate like the hazle twig
Is straight and slender and as brown in hue
As hazelnuts, and sweeter than the kernels.
Oh, let me see thee walk. Thou dost not halt.
KATE   Go, fool, and whom thou keep'st command.   250
PETRUCHIO   Did ever Dian so become a grove
As Kate this chamber with her princely gait?
O, be thou Dian, and let her be Kate.
And then let Kate be chaste and Dian sportful.
KATE   Where did you study all this goodly speech?   255
PETRUCHIO   It is extempore, from my mother wit.
KATE   A witty mother, witless else her son.
PETRUCHIO   Am I not wise?
KATE   Yes, keep you warm.
PETRUCHIO   Marry, so I mean, sweet Katherine, in thy bed.
And therefore setting all this chat aside,   260
Thus in plain terms: your father hath consented
That you shall be my wife; your dowry 'greed on,
And will you, nill you, I will marry you.
Now, Kate, I am a husband for your turn,
For by this light, whereby I see thy beauty,   265
Thy beauty that doth make me like thee well,
Thou must be married to no man but me.

          Enter BAPTISTA, GREMIO, TRANIO.

For I am he am born to tame you, Kate,
And bring you from a wild Kate to a Kate
Conformable as other household Kates.   270

---

240. **askance:** suspiciously.
245. **doth limp:** is lame (Petruchio is examining her as if he is buying a horse).
247. **brown in hue:** dark complexion.
251. **Dian:** the goddess Diana, the chaste huntress.
256. **extempore, from my mother wit:** unrehearsed; extempory and natural.
258. **keep you warm:** as in the proverb, "He is wise enough that can keep himself warm."
260. **chat:** pun on Kate, following upon Petruchio's use of Kate's full name, Katherine, in the previous line.
263. **will you, nill you:** whether you want to or not.
264. **for your turn:** to suit you.
270. **household Kates:** domestic items.

Here comes your father. Never make denial,
I must, and will have Katherine to my wife.
BAPTISTA   Now, Signior Petruchio, how speed you with my daughter?
PETRUCHIO   How but well, sir? How but well?
It were impossible I should speed amiss.   275
BAPTISTA   Why, how now, daughter Katherine, in your dumps?
KATE   Call you me daughter? Now I promise you
You have showed a tender fatherly regard,
To wish me wed to one half lunatic,
A madcap ruffian and a swearing Jack,   280
That thinks with oaths to face the matter out.
PETRUCHIO   Father, 'tis thus: yourself and all the world
That talked of her have talked amiss of her.
If she be curst, it is for policy,
For she's not froward, but modest as the dove,   285
She is not hot, but temperate as the morn,
For patience she will prove a second Grissel,
And Roman Lucrece for her chastity.
And to conclude, we have 'greed so well together
That upon Sunday is the wedding day.   290
KATE   I'll see thee hanged on Sunday first.
GREMIO   Hark, Petruchio, she says she'll see thee hanged first.
TRANIO   Is this your speeding? Nay then goodnight our part.
PETRUCHIO   Be patient gentlemen, I choose her for myself.
If she and I be pleased, what's that to you?   295
'Tis bargained twixt us twain being alone,
That she shall still be curst in company.
I tell you, 'tis incredible to believe
How much she loves me. Oh, the kindest Kate,
She hung about my neck, and kiss on kiss   300
She vied so fast, protesting oath on oath,
That in a twink she won me to her love.
Oh, you are novices. 'Tis a world to see
How tame, when men and women are alone,
A meacock wretch can make the curstest shrew.   305
Give me thy hand, Kate, I will unto Venice

---

275. speed amiss: not succeed.
276. in your dumps: sullen, in a bad mood.
280. a swearing Jack: ill-mannered man.
281. face the matter out: brazen it out.
285. froward: stubborn, willful.
287. Grissel: Patient Griselda who endured the cruelly abusive behavior of her husband, which he administered as a test of her wifely obedience. Among others, this story is told by Chaucer in *The Clerk's Tale*.
288. Lucrece: chaste matron who committed suicide after she was raped and was thus held to be a model of virtuous womanhood.
302. in a twink: instant.
305. meacock: mewling wretch; **curstest:** most curst.

To buy apparel 'gainst the wedding day.
Provide the feast, father, and bid the guests,
I will be sure my Katherine shall be fine.
BAPTISTA   I know not what to say, but give me your hands,   310
God send you joy, Petruchio. 'Tis a match.
GREMIO, TRANIO   Amen, say we. We will be witnesses.
PETRUCHIO   Father, and wife, and gentlemen, adieu.
I will to Venice. Sunday comes apace,
We will have rings, and things, and fine array,   315
And kiss me Kate, we will be married a Sunday.

Exit PETRUCHIO *and* KATHERINE.

GREMIO   Was ever match clapped up so suddenly?
BAPTISTA   Faith, gentlemen, now I play a merchant's part,
And venture madly on a desperate mart.
TRANIO   'Twas a commodity lay fretting by you,   320
'Twill bring you gain, or perish on the seas.
BAPTISTA   The gain I seek is quiet in the match.
GREMIO   No doubt but he hath got a quiet catch.
But now, Baptista, to your younger daughter,
Now is the day we long have lookèd for.   325
I am your neighbor, and was suitor first.
TRANIO   And I am one that love Bianca more
Than words can witness, or your thoughts can guess.
GREMIO   Youngling, thou canst not love so dear as I.
TRANIO   Graybeard, thy love doth freeze.
GREMIO   But thine doth fry.   330
Skipper, stand back, 'tis age that nourisheth.
TRANIO   But youth in ladies' eyes that florisheth.
BAPTISTA   Content you gentlemen, I will compound this strife.
'Tis deeds must win the prize, and he of both
That can assure my daughter greatest dower,   335
Shall have my Bianca's love.
Say, Signior Gremio, what can you assure her?
GREMIO   First, as you know, my house within the city

307. **'gainst:** for.
310. **but give me your hands:** this is a crucial moment in the text in which Kate apparently gives her assent via the practice known as "handfasting," even if it is not her verbal assent. She certainly doesn't repeat her earlier objections.
313. **wife:** future wife.
314. **apace:** quickly.
317. **clapped up:** hastily agreed.
319. **desperate mart:** volatile market.
320. **a commodity lay fretting:** risky business.
329. **Youngling:** youngster.
330. **thy love doth freeze:** is too cold and lacking passion; **thine doth fry:** is too hot and passionate.
331. **Skipper:** one who skips youthfully, a term of contempt.
333. **compound:** resolve. Baptista's suggested resolution to the competition between the suitors is an entirely financial one.

Is richly furnishèd with plate and gold,
Basins and ewers to lave her dainty hands;   340
My hangings all of Tyrian tapestry;
In ivory coffers I have stuffed my crowns;
In cypress chests my arras counterpoints,
Costly apparel, tents, and canopies,
Fine linen, Turkey cushions bossed with pearl,   345
Valance of Venice gold in needlework,
Pewter and brass, and all things that belongs
To house or housekeeping. Then at my farm
I have a hundred milch kine to the pail,
Six score fat oxen standing in my stalls,   350
And all things answerable to this portion.
Myself am struck in years, I must confess,
And if I die tomorrow, this is hers,
If whilst I live she will be only mine.
TRANIO   That "only" came well in. Sir, list to me.   355
I am my father's heir and only son,
If I may have your daughter to my wife,
I'll leave her houses three or four as good
Within rich Pisa walls, as any one
Old Signior Gremio has in Padua,   360
Besides two thousand ducats by the year
Of fruitful land, all which shall be her jointure.
What, have I pinched you, Signior Gremio?
GREMIO   Two thousand ducats by the year of land,
My land amounts not to so much in all.   365
That she shall have, besides an argosy
That now is lying in Marcellus' road.
What, have I choked you with an argosy?
TRANIO   Gremio, 'tis known my father hath no less
Than three great argosies, besides two galliasses   370

340. **lave:** wash.
341. **Tyrian:** purple, from Tyre.
343. **cypress chests:** storage chests made of cypress wood; **arras counterpoints:** tapestry coverlets.
345. **Turkey cushions bossed with pearl:** embossed cushions from Turkey.
346. **Valance of Venice gold in needlework:** fringes of drapery stitched with gold from Venice. Like the Turkish cushions, the Venetian valances are a sign of Gremio's wealth.
349. **milch kine to the pail:** cows for milking.
351. **things answerable to this portion:** appropriate to the dowry.
352. **struck in years:** old.
363. **have I pinched you:** made you uncomfortable.
364. **Two thousand ducats by the year of land:** Tranio outbids his master's rival with the solidity of land, and does not even trouble to compete with Gremio's detailed itemization of household goods.
366. **an argosy:** largest kind of trading vessel.
367. **Marcellus' road:** where the ship is anchored, outside the port of Marseilles.
368. **choked you:** silenced.
370. **galliasses:** capacious cargo ships.

And twelve tight galleys. These I will assure her,
And twice as much whate'er thou offrest next.
GREMIO   Nay, I have offered all. I have no more,
And she can have no more than all I have.
If you like me, she shall have me and mine.   375
TRANIO   Why, then the maid is mine from all the world
By your firm promise, Gremio is outvied.
BAPTISTA   I must confess your offer is the best,
And let your father make her the assurance,
She is your own, else you must pardon me.   380
If you should die before him, where's her dower?
TRANIO   That's but a cavil. He is old, I young.
GREMIO   And may not young men die as well as old?
BAPTISTA   Well gentlemen, I am thus resolved,
On Sunday next, you know   385
My daughter Katherine is to be married.
Now on the Sunday following, shall Bianca
Be bride to you, if you make this assurance;
If not, to Signior Gremio.
And so I take my leave, and thank you both.   *Exit.* 390
GREMIO   Adieu, good neighbor. Now I fear thee not.
Sirrah, young gamester, your father were a fool
To give thee all, and in his waning age
Set foot under thy table. Tut, a toy.
An old Italian fox is not so kind, my boy.   *Exit.* 395
TRANIO   A vengeance on your crafty withered hide!
Yet I have faced it with a card of ten.
'Tis in my head to do my master good.
I see no reason but supposed Lucentio
Must get a father, called supposed Vincentio,   400
And that's a wonder. Fathers commonly
Do get their children, but in this case of wooing,
A child shall get a sire, if I fail not of my cunning.   *Exit.*

---

371. **tight:** watertight.
381. **where's her dower?:** How would Bianca fare financially in the event that the son does not live to inherit his father's wealth?
392. **gamester:** gambler.
393. **in his waning age:** declining years.
394. **Set foot under thy table:** to become a dependent. Gremio doubts that Tranio's (Lucentio's) father will be foolish enough to give all his wealth away while still alive. **Tut, a toy:** nonsense.
395. **An old Italian fox is not so kind:** a cunning old man is not so easy to trick.
397. **faced:** trumped; a continuation of the bidding theme but now in reference to a card game.
399. **supposed:** an allusion to the source of the subplot, Gascoigne's *Supposes*.
400. **get:** beget; generate.
403. **child . . . sire:** in finding a spouse, the child, not his father needs to be in charge.

Act 3, Scene 1

Enter LUCENTIO, HORTENSIO, *and* BIANCA.

LUCENTIO   Fiddler, forbear, you grow too forward, sir,
Have you so soon forgot the entertainment
Her sister Katherine welcomed you withal?

HORTENSIO   But, wrangling pedant, this is
The patroness of heavenly harmony.   5
Then give me leave to have prerogative,
And when in music we have spent an hour,
Your lecture shall have leisure for as much.

LUCENTIO   Preposterous ass, that never read so far,
To know the cause why music was ordained.   10
Was it not to refresh the mind of man
After his studies or his usual pain?
Then give me leave to read philosophy,
And while I pause, serve in your harmony.

HORTENSIO   Sirrah, I will not bear these braves of thine.   15

BIANCA   Why, gentlemen, you do me double wrong,
To strive for that which resteth in my choice.
I am no breeching scholar in the schools,
I'll not be tied to hours nor 'pointed times,
But learn my lessons as I please myself,   20
And to cut off all strife, here sit we down.
Take you your instrument, play you the whiles,
His lecture will be done ere you have tuned.

HORTENSIO   You'll leave his lecture when I am in tune?

LUCENTIO   That will be never. Tune your instrument.   25

BIANCA   Where left we last?

LUCENTIO   Here, madam:
Hic ibat Simois, hic est Sigeia tellus,
Hic steterat Priami regia celsa senis.

BIANCA   Conster them.   30

LUCENTIO   *Hic ibat*, as I told you before, *Simois*, I am Lucentio,
hic est; son unto Vincentio of Pisa, *Sigeia tellus*,
disguised thus to get your love, *Hic steterat*, and that
Lucentio that comes a wooing, *Priami*, is my man Tranio,

---

1. **forbear:** desist.
9. **Preposterous:** inversion of the natural order.
15. **braves:** challenges.
18. **breeching scholar:** schoolboy capable of being whipped.
20. **as I please myself:** this is a rather Kate-like assertion of self-will on Bianca's part.
21. **to cut off all strife:** to end the quarrel between the two tutors.
28–29. ***Hic ibat Simois, hic est Sigeia tellus,/Hic steterat Priami regia celsa senis:***
"Here flowed the Simois; here is the Sigeian plain/Here stood old Priam's lofty palace,"
Ovid, *Heroides* 1: 33–4, from Penelope's letter to her husband, Ulysses.
30. **Conster:** construe; explain; translate.

regia, bearing my port, *celsa senis* that we might beguile   35
   the old pantaloon.
HORTENSIO   Madam, my instrument's in tune.
BIANCA   Let's hear. Oh fie, the treble jars.
LUCENTIO   Spit in the hole, man, and tune again.
BIANCA   Now let me see if I can conster it. *Hic ibat Simois*,   40
   I know you not, *hic est Sigeia tellus*, I trust you not,
   Hic steterat Priami, take heed he hear us not, *regia*,
   presume not, *celsa senis*, despair not.
HORTENSIO   Madam, 'tis now in tune.
LUCENTIO   All but the bass.
HORTENSIO   The bass is right, 'tis the base knave that jars.   45
LUCENTIO   How fiery and forward our pedant is,
   Now, for my life, the knave doth court my love,
   Pedascule, I'll watch you better yet.
BIANCA   [*To* LUCENTIO] In time I may believe, yet I mistrust.
LUCENTIO   Mistrust it not, for sure Aeacides   50
   Was Ajax called so from his grandfather.
BIANCA   I must believe my master, else, I promise you,
   I should be arguing still upon that doubt,
   But let it rest. Now, Litio, to you:
   Good master, take it not unkindly, pray,   55
   That I have been thus pleasant with you both.
HORTENSIO   You may go walk, and give me leave a while.
   My lessons make no music in three parts.
LUCENTIO   Are you so formal, sir? Well, I must wait
   And watch withal, for but I be deceived,   60
   Our fine musician groweth amorous.
HORTENSIO   Madam, before you touch the instrument,
   To learn the order of my fingering,
   I must begin with rudiments of art,
   To teach you gamut in a briefer sort,   65
   More pleasant, pithy, and effectual,
   Than hath been taught by any of my trade,
   And there it is in writing fairly drawn.
BIANCA   Why, I am past my gamut long ago.
HORTENSIO   Yet read the gamut of Hortensio.   70
BIANCA   [*Reads*] *Gamut* I am, the ground of all accord,
   A re, to plead Hortensio's passion:

---

35. port: identity.
36. pantaloon: old fool (male).
38. the treble jars: is not in tune.
45. the base knave that jars: it is Lucentio that annoys Hortensio.
47. the knave doth court my love: Hortensio is pursuing Bianca.
48. *Pedascule*: mini-pedant (not a real word).
50–51. Aeacides/Was Ajax called so from his grandfather: Aeacides was a descendant of Aeacus, the grandfather of Ajax. Lucentio is continuing Bianca's lesson from the *Heroides*.

B mi, Bianca, take him for thy lord
C fa ut, that loves with all affection:
D sol re, one clef, two notes have I,   75
E la mi, show pity or I die.
Call you this gamut? Tut, I like it not.
Old fashions please me best; I am not so nice
To charge true rules for old inventions.

    Enter a MESSENGER.

MESSENGER   Mistress, your father prays you leave your books   80
    And help to dress your sister's chamber up.
    You know tomorrow is the wedding day.
BIANCA   Farewell, sweet masters both, I must be gone.
    [*Exeunt* BIANCA *and* MESSENGER]
LUCENTIO   Faith, mistress, then I have no cause to stay.   [*Exit.*]
HORTENSIO   But I have cause to pry into this pedant.   [*Exit.*]   85
    Methinks he looks as though he were in love.
    Yet if thy thoughts, Bianca, be so humble
    To cast thy wand'ring eyes on every stale,
    Seize thee that list, if once I find thee ranging,
    Hortensio will be quit with thee by changing.   *Exit.*   90

Act 3, Scene 2

    Enter BAPTISTA, GREMIO, TRANIO, KATHERINE, BIANCA, *and*
    others, attendants.

BAPTISTA   Signior Lucentio, this is the 'pointed day
    That Katherine and Petruchio should be married,
    And yet we hear not of our son-in-law.
    What will be said, what mockery will it be
    To want the bridegroom when the priest attends   5
    To speak the ceremonial rites of marriage?
    What says Lucentio to this shame of ours?
KATE   No shame but mine, I must forsooth be forced
    To give my hand opposed against my heart

---

83. I must be gone: though there is no stage direction in the *Folio*, Bianca leaves the stage, immediately followed by Lucentio, and thus leaving Hortensio on stage alone for his final pronouncement.
88. stale: bait.
89. Seize thee that list: whoever wants you can have you; **ranging:** inconstant.
90. changing: Hortensio will change the object of his affections.
1. 'pointed: appointed.
5. To want the bridegroom when the priest attends: for the bridegroom to keep the priest waiting.
8. forsooth: in truth.
9. my hand opposed against my heart: marrying against my will; giving one's hand in marriage meant giving one's heart.

Unto a mad-brain rudesby, full of spleen,   10
Who wooed in haste and means to wed at leisure.
I told you, I, he was a frantic fool,
Hiding his bitter jests in blunt behavior.
And to be noted for a merry man,
He'll woo a thousand, 'point the day of marriage,   15
Make friends, invite, and proclaim the banns,
Yet never means to wed where he hath wooed.
Now must the world point at poor Katherine,
And say, "Lo, there is mad Petruchio's wife,
If it would please him come and marry her."   20

TRANIO   Patience, good Katherine, and Baptista too.
Upon my life, Petruchio means but well,
Whatever fortune stays him from his word,
Though he be blunt, I know him passing wise;
Though he be merry, yet withal he's honest.   25

KATE   Would Katherine had never seen him though.

                               Exit weeping.

BAPTISTA   Go, girl, I cannot blame thee now to weep,
For such an injury would vex a very saint,
Much more a shrew of impatient humor.

    Enter BIONDELLO.

BIONDELLO   Master, master, news, and such old news as you   30
never heard of.

BAPTISTA   Is it new and old too? How may that be?

BIONDELLO   Why, is it not news to hear of Petruchio's coming?

BAPTISTA   Is he come?

BIONDELLO   Why, no sir.   35

BAPTISTA   What then?

BIONDELLO   He is coming.

BAPTISTA   When will he be here?

BIONDELLO   When he stands where I am and sees you there.

TRANIO   But say, what to thine old news?   40

BIONDELLO   Why, Petruchio is coming, in a new hat and an old
jerkin, a pair of old breeches thrice turned; a pair of boots
that have been candle-cases, one buckled, another laced: an
old rusty sword ta'en out of the town armory, with a broken
hilt, and chapeless; with two broken points; his horse hipped,   45
with an old mothy saddle, and stirrups of no kindred, besides,

10. **a mad-brain rudesby:** a mad, rude fellow; **spleen:** temper.
12. **a frantic fool:** mad idiot.
16. **Make friends:** secure relationships with the bride's family.
30–31. **such old news as you/never heard of:** rare, unusual.
42. **thrice turned:** three times repaired.
43. **candle-cases:** old boots only fit to hold candle ends.
45. **chapeless:** missing part of the scabbard; **hipped:** lame.
46. **stirrups of no kindred:** unmatched.

possessed with the glanders and like to mose in the chine,
troubled with the lampass, infected with the fashions, full of
windgalls, sped with spavins, rayed with the yellows, past
cure of the fives, stark spoiled with the staggers, begnawn with   50
the bots, swayed in the back, and shoulder-shotten, near-
legged before, and with a half-cheeked bit, and a headstall
of sheep's leather, which, being restrained to keep him from
stumbling, hath been often burst and now repaired with knots;
one girth six times pieced, and a woman's crupper of velure,   55
which hath two letters for her name, fairly set down in studs,
and here and there pieced with packthread.

BAPTISTA   Who comes with him?

BIONDELLO   Oh sir, his lackey, for all the world caparisoned
like the horse: with a linen stock on one leg and   60
a kersey boot-hose on the other, gartered with a red and
blue list; an old hat, and the humor of forty fancies pricked
in't for a feather—a monster, a very monster in apparel,
and not like a Christian footboy or a gentleman's lacky.

TRANIO   'Tis some odd humor pricks him to this fashion,   65
Yet oftentimes he goes but mean appareled.

BAPTISTA   I am glad he's come, howsoe're he comes.

BIONDELLO   Why, sir, he comes not.

BAPTISTA   Didst thou not say he comes?

BIONDELLO   Who, that Petruchio came?   70

BAPTISTA   Ay, that Petruchio came.

BIONDELLO   No, sir, I say his horse comes with him on his back.

BAPTISTA   Why, that's all one.

BIONDELLO   Nay by S. Jamy,

---

47. glanders: an equine disease that causes swelling and discharge; **mose in the chine:** symptoms of the above disease.
48. lampass: a growth in the mouth that prevents eating.
49. windgalls: tumors; **spavins:** inflamed cartilage; **rayed:** colored; **the yellows:** jaundice.
49–50. past cure of the fives: avives, an equine glandular disease.
50. stark spoiled with the staggers: totally ruined with a disease that impairs balance; **begnawn:** eaten up with.
51. bots: parasitic worms; **shoulder-shotten:** dislocated shoulder.
51–52. near-legged before: knock-kneed forelegs.
52. a half-cheeked: only on halfway; **headstall:** the piece of the bridle that goes overhead.
55. one girth six times pieced: girth strap with six holes; **crupper of velure:** velvet loop under the horse's tail to secure the saddle.
56. letters for her . . . studs: studded monogram.
57. packthread: parcel twine.
59. lackey: footman; **caparisoned:** attired.
61. kersey boot-hose: coarse woolen stocking.
62. list: cloth border.
62–63. the humor of forty fancies pricked in't for a feather: decorated in innumerable, different styles.
63. a monster: monstrous.
73. all one: makes no difference.
74. S. Jamy: St. James of Compostella; probably from a lost ballad.

I hold you a penny,   75
A horse and a man
Is more than one,
And yet not many.

Enter PETRUCHIO *and* GRUMIO.

PETRUCHIO   Come, where be these gallants? Who's at home?
BAPTISTA   You are welcome, sir.   80
PETRUCHIO   And yet I come not well.
BAPTISTA   And yet you halt not.
TRANIO   Not so well appareled as I wish you were.
PETRUCHIO   Were it better, I should rush in thus.
But where is Kate? Where is my lovely bride?   85
How does my father? Gentles, methinks you frown.
And wherefore gaze this goodly company,
As if they saw some wondrous monument,
Some comet, or unusual prodigy?
BAPTISTA   Why, sir, you know this is your wedding day.   90
First were we sad, fearing you would not come,
Now sadder that you come so unprovided.
Fie, doff this habit, shame to your estate,
An eyesore to our solemn festival.
TRANIO   And tell us what occasion of import   95
Hath all so long detained you from your wife,
And sent you hither so unlike yourself?
PETRUCHIO   Tedious it were to tell and harsh to hear,
Sufficeth, I am come to keep my word,
Though in some part enforced to digress,   100
Which at more leisure I will so excuse
As you shall well be satisfied withal.
But where is Kate? I stay too long from her.
The morning wears, 'tis time we were at church.
TRANIO   See not your bride in these unreverent robes.   105
Go to my chamber, put on clothes of mine.
PETRUCHIO   Not I, believe me. Thus I'll visit her.
BAPTISTA   But thus, I trust, you will not marry her.
PETRUCHIO   Good sooth, even thus. Therefore, ha' done with
words.

---

75. **hold:** wager.
79. **gallants:** stylish gentlemen.
86. **Gentles:** ladies and gentlemen.
88. **some wondrous monument:** an omen or portent.
89. **prodigy:** phenomenon.
92. **unprovided:** unprepared.
93. **doff:** remove; **estate:** social rank.
95. **occasion of import:** compelling circumstances.
105. **unreverent:** inappropriate and demeaning.
109. **sooth:** truth.

To me she's married, not unto my clothes.   110
Could I repair what she will wear in me,
As I can change these poor accoutrements,
'Twere well for Kate and better for myself.
But what a fool am I to chat with you,
When I should bid good morrow to my bride   115
And seal the title with a lovely kiss.   *Exit [with* GREMIO].
TRANIO   He hath some meaning in his mad attire.
We will persuade him, be it possible,
To put on better ere he go to church.
BAPTISTA   I'll after him and see the event of this.   120
        Exit [with BIANCA, GREMIO, *and* ATTENDANTS].
TRANIO   But sir, love concerneth us to add
Her father's liking, which to bring to pass,
As before imparted to your worship,
I am to get a man—whate'er he be,
It skills not much, we'll fit him to our turn,   125
And he shall be Vincentio of Pisa,
And make assurance here in Padua
Of greater sums than I have promisèd,
So shall you quietly enjoy your hope,
And marry sweet Bianca with consent.   130
LUCENTIO   Were it not that my fellow schoolmaster
Doth watch Bianca's steps so narrowly,
'Twere good, methinks, to steal our marriage,
Which once performed, let all the world say no,
I'll keep mine own, despite of all the world.   135
TRANIO   That by degrees we mean to look into,
And watch our vantage in this business.
We'll overreach the greybeard Gremio,
The narrow-prying father Minola,
The quaint musician, amorous Litio,   140
All for my master's sake, Lucentio.

    Enter GREMIO.

Signior Gremio, came you from the church?
GREMIO   As willingly as e'er I came from school.
TRANIO   And is the bride and bridegroom coming home?
GREMIO   A bridegroom say you? 'Tis a groom indeed,   145

111. **Could I repair what she will wear in me:** if I could change those aspects of my character that will be trying to her; if I could only compensate for the way she will wear me
down.
132. **narrowly:** closely.
133. **to steal our marriage:** to elope.
136. **by degrees:** by and by.
137. **vantage:** advantage, keep our best interests in mind.
138. **overreach:** do better than.
143. **As willingly as e'er I came from school:** eagerly.

A grumbling groom, and that the girl shall find.
TRANIO   Curster than she? Why, 'tis impossible.
GREMIO   Why, he's a devil, a devil, a very fiend.
TRANIO   Why she's a devil, a devil, the devil's dam.
GREMIO   Tut, she's a lamb, a dove, a fool to him.   150
    I'll tell you, Sir Lucentio. When the priest
    Should ask if Katherine should be his wife,
    "Ay, by Gog's wouns," quoth he, and swore so loud
    That all amazed the priest let fall the book,
    And as he stooped again to take it up,   155
    This mad-brained bridegroom took him such a cuff,
    That down fell priest and book, and book and priest,
    "Now take them up," quoth he, "if any list."
TRANIO   What said the wench when he rose again?
GREMIO   Trembled and shook, forwhy, he stamped and swore,   160
    As if the vicar meant to cozen him.
    But after many ceremonies done
    He calls for wine. "A health," quoth he, as if
    He had been aboard carousing to his mates
    After a storm, quaffed off the muscatel   165
    And threw the sops all in the sexton's face
    Having no other reason
    But that his beard grew thin and hungerly,
    And seemed to ask him sops as he was drinking.
    This done, he took the bride about the neck,   170
    And kissed her lips with such a clamorous smack,
    That at the parting all the church did echo,
    And I seeing this, came thence for very shame,
    And after me, I know, the rout is coming.
    Such a mad marriage never was before.   175
    Hark, hark, I hear the minstrels play.   *Music plays.*

    Enter PETRUCHIO, KATE, BIANCA, HORTENSIO, BAPTISTA.

PETRUCHIO   Gentlemen and friends, I thank you for your pains.
    I know you think to dine with me today,

147. **Curster:** more shrewish.
149. **the devil's dam:** the mother of the devil.
153. **by Gog's wouns:** by God's wounds (a blasphemous oath).
156. **took him such a cuff:** gave him such a blow.
158. **quoth:** said; **if any list:** if anyone wishes.
160. **forwhy:** because.
161. **cozen:** dupe.
164. **aboard carousing to his mates:** on board ship drinking with his male companions.
165. **muscatel:** a sweet wine.
166. **sops:** pieces of cake soaked in wine; **sexton:** church warden.
168. **hungerly:** hungrily.
174. **rout:** crowd.
177. **pains:** trouble.

And have prepared great store of wedding cheer,
But so it is, my haste doth call me hence,   180
And therefore here I mean to take my leave.
BAPTISTA   Is't possible you will away tonight?
PETRUCHIO   I must away today before night come.
Make it no wonder. If you knew my business,
You would entreat me rather go than stay.   185
And, honest company, I thank you all,
That have beheld me give away myself
To this most patient, sweet, and virtuous wife.
Dine with my father, drink a health to me,
For I must hence, and farewell to you all.   190
TRANIO   Let us entreat you stay till after dinner.
PETRUCHIO   It may not be.
GREMIO   Let me entreat you.
PETRUCHIO   It cannot be.
KATE   Let me entreat you.
PETRUCHIO   I am content.
KATE   Are you content to stay?
PETRUCHIO   I am content you shall entreat me stay,
But yet not stay, entreat me how you can.   195
KATE   Now if you love me, stay.
PETRUCHIO   Grumio, my horse.
GRUMIO   Ay, sir, they be ready, the oats have eaten the horses.
KATE   Nay, then,
Do what thou canst, I will not go today,
No, nor tomorrow, not till I please myself.   200
The door is open, sir, there lies your way.
You may be jogging whiles your boots are green.
For me, I'll not be gone till I please myself.
'Tis like you'll prove a jolly, surly groom,
That take it on you at the first so roundly.   205
PETRUCHIO   O Kate, content thee. Prithee, be not angry.
KATE   I will be angry. What hast thou to do?
Father, be quiet. He shall stay my leisure.
GREMIO   Ay, marry sir, now it begins to work.
KATE   Gentlemen, forward to the bridal dinner.   210
I see a woman may be made a fool
If she had not a spirit to resist.
PETRUCHIO   They shall go forward, Kate, at thy command,
Obey the bride, you that attend on her.

179. **cheer:** celebration.
180. **doth call me hence:** must go from hence [here].
193. **content:** agreed; satisfied.
202. **jogging whiles your boots are green:** leave early (proverb).
205. **take it on you at the first so roundly:** you take on the role (of husband-ruler) so carelessly.

Go to the feast, revel and domineer,   215
Carouse full measure to her maidenhead,
Be mad and merry, or go hang yourselves.
But for my bonny Kate, she must with me.
Nay, look not big, nor stamp, nor stare, nor fret,
I will be master of what is mine own.   220
She is my goods, my chattels. She is my house,
My household-stuff, my field, my barn,
My horse, my ox, my ass, my anything,
And here she stands, touch her whoever dare.
I'll bring mine action on the proudest he   225
That stops my way in Padua. Grumio,
Draw forth thy weapon, we are beset with thieves.
Rescue thy mistress if thou be a man.
Fear not, sweet wench. They shall not touch thee, Kate,
I'll buckler thee against a million.   *Exeunt.* PETRUCHIO,   230
KATE [*and* GRUMIO].
BAPTISTA   Nay, let them go, a couple of quiet ones.
GREMIO   Went they not quickly, I should die with laughing.
TRANIO   Of all mad matches never was the like.
LUCENTIO   Mistress, what's your opinion of your sister?
BIANCA   That being mad herself, she's madly mated.   235
GREMIO   I warrant him, Petruchio is Kated.
BAPTISTA   Neighbors and friends, though bride and bridegroom
   wants
For to supply the places at the table,
You know there wants no junkets at the feast.
Lucentio, you shall supply the bridegroom's place,   240
And let Bianca take her sister's room.
TRANIO   Shall sweet Bianca practice how to bride it?
BAPTISTA   She shall, Lucentio. Come, gentlemen, let's go.

                                   Exeunt.

---

215. **domineer:** celebrate riotously.
216. **Carouse:** toast.
219. **look not big, nor stamp, nor stare, nor fret:** This is an implicit stage direction.
221. **chattels:** moveable goods.
222. **household-stuff:** domestic goods.
227. **bring mine action on the proudest he:** attack, take legal action against the most formidable adversary.
228. **stops:** bars.
229. **thieves:** the guests who want to keep Kate at the wedding banquet.
230. **buckler:** shield.
237–38. **wants/For to supply:** are absent.
239. **junkets:** delicacies.
241. **room:** place.
242. **bride it:** behave like a bride.

Act 4, Scene 1

Enter GRUMIO.

GRUMIO   Fie, fie on all tired jades, on all mad masters, and all
foul ways. Was ever man so beaten? Was ever man so rayde?
Was ever man so weary? I am sent before to make a fire, and
they are coming after to warm them. Now were not I a little
pot and soon hot, my very lips might freeze to my teeth, my   5
tongue to the roof of my mouth, my heart in my belly, ere I
should come by a fire to thaw me. But I with blowing the fire
shall warm myself, for considering the weather, a taller man
than I will take cold. Holla, hoa, Curtis!

Enter CURTIS.

CURTIS   Who is that calls so coldly?   10
GRUMIO   A piece of ice. If thou doubt it, thou mayst
slide from my shoulder to my heel with no
greater a run but my head and my neck. A fire, good Curtis.
CURTIS   Is my master and his wife coming, Grumio?
GRUMIO   Oh ay, Curtis, ay, and therefore fire, fire! Cast on no   15
water.
CURTIS   Is she so hot a shrew as she's reported?
GRUMIO   She was, good Curtis, before this frost. But thou
know'st, winter tames man, woman, and beast; for it
hath tamed my old master, and my new mistress, and myself,   20
fellow Curtis.
CURTIS   Away, you three inch fool! I am no beast.
GRUMIO   Am I but three inches? Why, thy horn is a foot,
and so long am I, at the least. But wilt thou make a fire,
or shall I complain on thee to our mistress, whose hand—   25
she being now at hand—thou shalt soon feel, to thy
cold comfort, for being slow in thy hot office.
CURTIS   I prithee, good Grumio, tell me, how goes the world?
GRUMIO   A cold world, Curtis, in every office but thine, and
therefore fire. Do thy duty, and have thy duty, for my   30
master and mistress are almost frozen to death.
CURTIS   There's fire ready, and therefore, good Grumio,
the news.
GRUMIO   Why "Jack boy, ho boy," and as much news as wilt thou.

---

1. **jades:** decrepit horses.
2. **rayde:** filthied.
4–5. **little pot:** small fellow.
15–16. **Cast on no water:** from a well-known ballad, "Scotland Is Burning."
22. **three inch fool:** reference to Grumio's size.
23. **thy horn is a foot:** your horn is a foot long; bawdy jest on penis length or cuckold's
horn, the conventional sign of a man whose wife was unfaithful.
34. **Jack boy, ho boy:** from a song.

CURTIS   Come, you are so full of cony-catching.   35
GRUMIO   Why, therefore fire, for I have caught extreme
  cold. Where's the cook? Is supper ready, the house
  trimmed, rushes strewed, cobwebs swept, the servingmen
  in their new fustian, the white stockings, and every officer
  his wedding garment on? Be the Jacks fair within,   40
  the Jills fair without, the carpets laid, and everything in order?
CURTIS   All ready; and therefore, I pray thee, news.
GRUMIO   First, know my horse is tired, my master and mistress
  fallen out.
CURTIS   How?   45
GRUMIO   Out of their saddles into the dirt, and thereby
  hangs a tale.
CURTIS   Let's ha't, good Grumio.
GRUMIO   Lend thine ear.
CURTIS   Here.   50
GRUMIO   [Strikes him] There.
CURTIS   This 'tis to feel a tale, not to hear a tale.
GRUMIO   And therefore 'tis called a sensible tale, and this
  cuff was but to knock at your ear, and beseech listening.
  Now I begin. Inprimis, we came down a foul   55
  hill, my master riding behind my mistress.
CURTIS   Both of one horse?
GRUMIO   What's that to thee?
CURTIS   Why, a horse.
GRUMIO   Tell thou the tale. But hadst thou not crossed me, thou 60
  shouldst have heard how her horse fell and she under her
  horse; thou shouldst have heard in how miry a place, how she
  was bemoiled, how he left her with the horse upon her, how
  he beat me because her horse stumbled, how he waded
  through the dirt to pluck him off me, how he swore, how she   65
  prayed that never prayed before, how I cried, how the horses
  ran away, how her bridle was burst, how I lost my crupper, with
  many things of worthy memory, which now shall die in
  oblivion, and thou return unexperienced to thy grave.
CURTIS   By this reckoning he is more shrew than she.   70

35. cony-catching: target of petty thieves and confidence men.
38. trimmed: prepared; decorated; rushes strewed: reeds used as a floor covering.
39. fustian: coarse cotton cloth; officer: every person with an office or position in the
household.
40. Jacks: male servants; leather drinking vessel.
41. Jills: female servants; small, metal drinking vessel; carpets: tablecloths.
46–47. thereby hangs a tale: that's quite a story.
52. to feel a tale, not to hear a tale: a response to being struck—he feels the blow.
54. cuff: strike.
55. Inprimis: in the first place.
57. of one horse: on one horse.
62. miry: muddy.
63. bemoiled: muddied with.
69. unexperienced: still not knowing.

GRUMIO   Ay, and that thou and the proudest of you all shall
find when he comes home. But what talk I of this?
Call forth Nathaniel, Joseph, Nicholas, Phillip, Walter,
Sugarsop and the rest. Let their heads be slickly combed,
their blue coats brushed, and their garters of an indifferent   75
knit. Let them curtsy with their left legs, and not
presume to touch a hair of my master's horsetail till
they kiss their hands. Are they all ready?
CURTIS   They are.
GRUMIO   Call them forth.   80
CURTIS   Do you hear, ho? You must meet my master
to countenance my mistress.
GRUMIO   Why, she hath a face of her own.
CURTIS   Who knows not that?
GRUMIO   Thou, it seems, that calls for company to   85
countenance her.
CURTIS   I call them forth to credit her.

Enter four or five servingmen.

GRUMIO   Why, she comes to borrow nothing of them.
NATHANIEL   Welcome home, Grumio.
PHILLIP   How now, Grumio?   90
JOSEPH   What, Grumio.
NICHOLAS   Fellow Grumio.
NATHANIEL   How now, old lad?
GRUMIO   Welcome, you, how now, you, what you, fellow you,
and thus much for greeting. Now my spruce   95
companions, is all ready, and all things neat?
NATHANIEL   All things is ready. How near is our master?
GREMIO   E'ne at hand, alighted by this; and therefore be
not—Cock's passion, silence! I hear my master.

Enter PETRUCHIO *and* KATE.

PETRUCHIO   Where be these knaves? What, no man at door   100
To hold my stirrup, nor to take my horse?
Where is Nathaniel, Gregory, Phillip?
ALL SERVANTS   Here, here sir, here sir.
PETRUCHIO   Here sir, here sir, here sir, here sir!
You logger-headed and unpolished grooms.   105

---

75. **indifferent:** matched; plain.
77. **master's horsetail:** tail of my master's horse.
82. **to countenance her:** to face her.
87. **to credit her:** to greet her, a pun on 'credit' as loaning money follows.
95. **spruce:** spruced-up.
98. **E'ne:** even; already; **by this:** by this time.
99. **Cock's passion:** God's (Christ's) passion on the cross.
100. **Where be:** where are.
105. **logger-headed:** blockheaded.

What? No attendance? No regard? No duty?
Where is the foolish knave I sent before?
GRUMIO   Here sir, as foolish as I was before.
PETRUCHIO   You peasant swain, you whoreson, malt-horse drudge!
 Did I not bid thee meet me in the park   110
 And bring along these rascal knaves with thee?
GRUMIO   Nathaniel's coat, sir, was not fully made,
 And Gabriel's pumps were all unpinked i'th' heel.
There was no link to color Peter's hat,
 And Walter's dagger was not come from sheathing.   115
There were none fine but Adam, Ralph, and Gregory,
The rest were ragged, old, and beggarly,
Yet, as they are, here are they come to meet you.
PETRUCHIO   Go, rascals, go, and fetch my supper in.

Exeunt SERVANTS.

 [*Sings*]

"Where is the life that late I led?   120
Where are those—" Sit down, Kate,
And welcome. Soud, soud, soud, soud.

 Enter SERVANTS *with supper.*

Why, when, I say? Nay, good sweet Kate, be merry.
Off with my boots, you rogues, you villains, when?

 [*Sings*]

"It was the Friar of Orders gray,   125
As he forth walked on his way."
Out, you rogue, you pluck my foot awry.
Take that, and mend the plucking of the other.
Be merry, Kate. Some water, here. What, hoa!

 Enter one with water.

Where's my Spaniel Troilus? Sirrah, get you hence,   130
And bid my cousin Ferdinand come hither.

---

109. **swain:** youth; **whoreson:** son of a whore; **malt-horse drudge:** mindless servant;
literally, workhorse used to grind malt in a brewery.
110. **the park:** the grounds of a grand house.
113. **unpinked i'th':** without a pattern formed by perforation.
114. **link:** burnt torch, used to blacken articles of clothing.
115. **come from sheathing:** being fitted with a sheath.
120. **"Where is the life that late I led?":** catch from a ballad.
122. **Soud:** a nonsensical word.
125. **the Friar of Orders gray:** member of a monastic order who wore grey.
127. **pluck my foot awry:** in pulling off his boot, the servant wrenches Petruchio's leg.
128. **Take that:** an implicit stage direction that Petruchio strikes his servant.
130. **Spaniel Troilus:** breed and name of his dog, named after the Trojan prince, brother
of Hector.

One, Kate, that you must kiss and be acquainted with.
Where are my slippers? Shall I have some water?
Come, Kate, and wash, and welcome heartily.
You whoreson villain, will you let it fall?   135
KATE   Patience, I pray you, 'twas a fault unwilling.
PETRUCHIO   A whoreson, beetle-headed, flap-eared knave.
Come, Kate, sit down, I know you have a stomach.
Will you give thanks, sweet Kate, or else shall I?
What's this? Mutton?
FIRST SERVINGMAN   Ay.
PETRUCHIO   Who brought it?
PETER   I.   140
PETRUCHIO   'Tis burnt, and so is all the meat.
What dogs are these? Where is the rascal cook?
How durst you villains bring it from the dresser
And serve it thus to me that love it not?
There, take it to you, trenchers, cups, and all: 145
You heedless jolt-heads, and unmannered slaves.
What, do you grumble? I'll be with you straight.
KATE   I pray you, husband, be not so disquiet,
The meat was well, if you were so contented.
PETRUCHIO   I tell thee, Kate, 'twas burnt and dried away,   150
And I expressly am forbid to touch it;
For it engenders choler, planteth anger,
And better 'twere that both of us did fast,
Since of ourselves, ourselves are choleric,
Than feed it with such overroasted flesh: 155
Be patient, tomorrow 't shall be mended,
And for this night we'll fast for company.
Come, I will bring thee to thy bridal chamber.   *Exeunt.*

        Enter SERVANTS *severally.*

NATHANIEL   Peter, didst ever see the like?
PETER   He kills her in her own humor.   160
GRUMIO   Where is he?

        Enter CURTIS, *a servant.*

---

135. **will you let it fall:** you are dropping it.
137. **beetle-headed:** thick-headed.
138. **you have a stomach:** you are hungry.
139. **give thanks:** say grace.
142. **What dogs:** i.e., servants.
143. **dresser:** sideboard, from whence the meat is served.
145. **take it to you:** take it away; **trenchers:** plates.
146. **jolt-heads:** blockhead.
152. **choler:** hot-tempered; refers to the now obsolete theory of the humors or bodily temperaments into which people's dispositions were categorized; **planteth:** implants.
154. **choleric:** hot tempered (a reference to the theory of the humors that were believed to govern physiology and personality).

CURTIS   In her chamber,
  Making a sermon of continency to her,
  And rails, and swears, and rates, that she, poor soul,
  Knows not which way to stand, to look, to speak   165
  And sits as one new risen from a dream.
  Away, away, for he is coming hither.   *[Exeunt]*

    Enter PETRUCHIO.

PETRUCHIO   Thus have I politicly begun my reign,
  And 'tis my hope to end successfully.
  My falcon now is sharp, and passing empty,   170
  And till she stoop, she must not be full gorged,
  For then she never looks upon her lure.
  Another way I have to man my haggard,
  To make her come, and know her keeper's call.
  That is, to watch her, as we watch these kites,   175
  That bate and beat and will not be obedient.
  She ate no meat today, nor none shall eat.
  Last night she slept not, nor tonight she shall not.
  As with the meat, some undeserved fault
  I'll find about the making of the bed,   180
  And here I'll fling the pillow, there the bolster,
  This way the coverlet, another way the sheets.
  Ay, and amid this hurly I intend,
  That all is done in reverent care of her,
  And in conclusion, she shall watch all night,   185
  And if she chance to nod, I'll rail and brawl,
  And with the clamor keep her still awake.
  This is a way to kill a wife with kindness,
  And thus I'll curb her mad and headstrong humor.
  He that knows better how to tame a shrew,   190
  Now let him speak. 'Tis charity to show.

                                        Exit.

163. **of continency:** about sexual continence.
166. **new risen:** just woken.
170. **passing empty:** quite hungry.
171. **stoop:** submits; **full gorged:** sated.
172. **lure:** bait.
173. **haggard:** falcon.
175. **watch her:** keep her awake; **kites:** birds of prey; pun on Kate.
183. **hurly:** commotion.
185. **watch:** stay awake.
188. **kill a wife with kindness:** proverb.

Act 4, Scene 2

Enter TRANIO *and* HORTENSIO.

TRANIO   Is't possible, friend Litio, that Mistress Bianca
　　Doth fancy any other but Lucentio?
　　I tell you, sir, she bears me fair in hand.
HORTENSIO   Sir, to satisfy you in what I have said,
　　Stand by, and mark the manner of his teaching.   15

Enter BIANCA [*and* LUCENTIO *as* CAMBIO]

LUCENTIO   Now, mistress, profit you in what you read?
BIANCA   What, master, read you? First, resolve me that.
LUCENTIO   I read that I profess, *The Art to Love*.
BIANCA   And may you prove, sir, master of your art.
LUCENTIO   While you, sweet dear, prove mistress of my heart.   10
HORTENSIO   Quick proceeders, marry! Now tell me, I pray,
　　You that durst swear that your mistress Bianca
　　Loved none in the world so well as Lucentio.
TRANIO   Oh, despiteful love, unconstant womankind,
　　I tell thee, Litio, this is wonderful.   15
HORTENSIO   Mistake no more, I am not Litio,
　　Nor a musician as I seem to be,
　　But one that scorn to live in this disguise
　　For such a one as leaves a gentleman
　　And makes a god of such a cullion.   20
　　Know, sir, that I am called Hortensio.
TRANIO   Signior Hortensio, I have often heard
　　Of your entire affection to Bianca,
　　And since mine eyes are witness of her lightness,
　　I will with you, if you be so contented,   25
　　Forswear Bianca and her love forever.
HORTENSIO   See how they kiss and court. Signior Lucentio,
　　Here is my hand, and here I firmly vow
　　Never to woo her more, but do forswear her
　　As one unworthy all the former favors   30
　　That I have fondly flattered her withal.
TRANIO   And here I take the like unfeignèd oath,
　　Never to marry with her, though she would entreat,
　　Fie on her, see how beastly she doth court him.
HORTENSIO   Would all the world but he had quite forsworn.   35

3. **she bears me fair in hand:** makes me think I have a chance of obtaining her love.
8. ***The Art to Love:*** Ovid's *Ars Amatoria*.
11. **proceeders:** degree candidates; **marry:** indeed.
20. **cullion:** base person.
24. **lightness:** wanton.
25. **contented:** pleased.
34. **beastly:** basely; like a beast.

For me, that I may surely keep mine oath.
I will be married to a wealthy widow,
Ere three days pass, which hath as long loved me
As I have loved this proud disdainful haggard.
And so farewell, Signior Lucentio.   40
Kindness in women, not their beauteous looks
Shall win my love, and so I take my leave,
In resolution as I swore before.   [*Exit*]
TRANIO   Mistress Bianca, bless you with such grace,
As 'longeth to a lovers blessèd case.   45
Nay, I have ta'en you napping, gentle love,
And have forsworn you with Hortensio.
BIANCA   Tranio, you jest. But have you both forsworn me?
TRANIO   Mistress, we have.
LUCENTIO   Then we are rid of Litio.
TRANIO   I' faith he'll have a lusty widow now,   50
That shall be wooed and wedded in a day.
BIANCA   God give him joy.
TRANIO   Ay, and he'll tame her.
BIANCA   He says so, Tranio?
TRANIO   Faith, he is gone unto the taming school.   55
BIANCA   The taming school—what, is there such a place?
TRANIO   Ay, mistress, and Petruchio is the master,
That teacheth tricks eleven and twenty long
To tame a shrew and charm her chattering tongue.

        Enter BIONDELLO.

BIONDELLO   Oh master, master, I have watched so long   60
That I am dog-weary, but at last I spied
An ancient angel coming down the hill
Will serve the turn.
TRANIO   What is he, Biondello?
BIONDELLO   Master, a marcantant, or a pedant,
I know not what, but formal in apparel,   65
In gait and countenance surely like a father.
LUCENTIO   And what of him, Tranio?
TRANIO   If he be credulous and trust my tale,
I'll make him glad to seem Vincentio,
And give assurance to Baptista Minola   70
As if he were the right Vincentio.
Take in your love, and then let me alone.

---

39. haggard: wild hawk.
45. 'longeth: contraction of "belongeth"; belongs.
59. charm: persuade to silence.
62. ancient angel: reliable old man; literally, an "angel" is a gold coin.
64. marcantant: merchant; **pedant:** scholar.

Enter a PEDANT.

PEDANT   God save you, sir.
TRANIO   And you, sir, you are welcome.
    Travel you far on, or are you at the farthest?
PEDANT   Sir, at the farthest for a week or two,   75
    But then up farther, and as far as Rome,
    And so to Tripoli, if God lend me life.
TRANIO   What countryman, I pray?
PEDANT   Of Mantua.
TRANIO   Of Mantua, sir? Marry, God forbid.
    And come to Padua careless of your life?   80
PEDANT   My life, sir? How I pray? For that goes hard.
TRANIO   'Tis death for anyone in Mantua
    To come to Padua. Know you not the cause?
    Your ships are stayed at Venice, and the Duke,
    For private quarrel 'twixt your Duke and him,   85
    Hath published and proclaimed it openly.
    'Tis marvel, but that you are but newly come,
    You might have heard it else proclaimed about.
PEDANT   Alas, sir, it is worse for me than so,
    For I have bills for money by exchange   90
    From Florence, and must here deliver them.
TRANIO   Well, sir, to do you courtesy,
    This will I do, and this I will advise you.
    First tell me, have you ever been at Pisa?
PEDANT   Ay, sir, in Pisa have I often been,   95
    Pisa renownèd for grave citizens.
TRANIO   Among them know you one Vincentio?
PEDANT   I know him not, but I have heard of him,
    A merchant of incomparable wealth.
TRANIO   He is my father, sir, and sooth to say,   100
    In count'nance somewhat doth resemble you.
BIONDELLO   [*Aside*] As much as an apple doth an oyster,
    and all one.
TRANIO   To save your life in this extremity,
    This favor will I do you for his sake;   105
    And think it not the worst of all your fortunes
    That you are like to Sir Vincentio.
    His name and credit shall you undertake,
    And in my house you shall be friendly lodged.
    Look that you take upon you as you should.   110
    You understand me, sir. So shall you stay
    Till you have done your business in the city.
    If this be courtesy, sir, accept of it.

---

81. **goes hard:** is tough.

PEDANT   Oh sir, I do, and will repute you ever
   The patron of my life and liberty.   115
TRANIO   Then go with me to make the matter good,
   This, by the way, I let you understand,
   My father is here looked for every day
   To pass assurance of a dower in marriage
   'Twixt me and one Baptista's daughter here.   120
   In all these circumstances I'll instruct you.
   Go with me to clothe you as becomes you.   *Exeunt.*

Act 4, Scene 3

Enter KATHERINA *and* GRUMIO.

GRUMIO   No, no forsooth, I dare not for my life.
KATE   The more my wrong, the more his spite appears.
   What, did he marry me to famish me?
   Beggars that come unto my father's door
   Upon entreaty have a present alms,   5
   If not, elsewhere they meet with charity.
   But I, who never knew how to entreat,
   Nor never needed that I should entreat,
   Am starved for meat, giddy for lack of sleep,
   With oaths kept waking, and with brawling fed.   10
   And that which spites me more than all these wants,
   He does it under name of perfect love,
   As who should say, if I should sleep or eat
   'Twere deadly sickness or else present death.
   I prithee, go and get me some repast,   15
   I care not what, so it be wholesome food.
GRUMIO   What say you to a neat's foot?
KATE   'Tis passing good. I prithee, let me have it.
GRUMIO   I fear it is too choleric a meat.
   How say you to a fat tripe finely broiled?   20
KATE   I like it well. Good Grumio, fetch it me.
GRUMIO   I cannot tell, I fear 'tis choleric.
   What say you to a piece of beef and mustard?
KATE   A dish that I do love to feed upon.
GRUMIO   Ay, but the mustard is too hot a little.   25
KATE   Why then, the beef, and let the mustard rest.
GRUMIO   Nay then, I will not. You shall have the mustard

---

116. **make the matter good:** do what we have said we will do, put the plan into action.
119. **dower:** dowry.
5. **have a present alms:** are given charity.
15. **repast:** meal.
17. **neat's:** ox's.
19. **too choleric a meat:** a meat that induces choler or bad-temperedness.

Or else you get no beef of Grumio.
KATE   Then both, or one, or anything thou wilt.
GRUMIO   Why then, the mustard without the beef.   30
KATE   Go, get thee gone, thou false deluding slave,   *Beats him.*
That feed'st me with the very name of meat.
Sorrow on thee and all the pack of you
That triumph thus upon my misery.
Go get thee gone, I say.   35

     Enter PETRUCHIO *and* HORTENSIO *with meat.*

PETRUCHIO   How fares my Kate? What, sweeting, all amort?
HORTENSIO   Mistress, what cheer?
KATE   Faith, as cold as can be.
PETRUCHIO   Pluck up thy spirits, look cheerfully upon me.
Here, love, thou seest how diligent I am
To dress thy meat myself and bring it thee.   40
I am sure, sweet Kate, this kindness merits thanks.
What, not a word? Nay then, thou lov'st it not,
And all my pains is sorted to no proof.
Here, take away this dish.
KATE   I pray you, let it stand.
PETRUCHIO   The poorest service is repaid with thanks,   45
And so shall mine before you touch the meat.
KATE   I thank you, sir.
HORTENSIO   Signior Petruchio, fie, you are to blame.
Come, Mistress Kate, I'll bear you company.
PETRUCHIO   Eat it up all, Hortensio, if thou lovest me.   50
Much good do it unto thy gentle heart.
Kate, eat apace. And now, my honey love,
Will we return unto thy father's house
And revel it as bravely as the best,
With silken coats and caps and golden rings,   55
With ruffs and cuffs, and farthingales, and things,
With scarves, and fans, and double change of bravery,
With amber bracelets, beads, and all this knavery.
What, hast thou dined? The tailor stays thy leisure,
To deck thy body with his ruffling treasure.   60

     Enter TAILOR.

Come, tailor, let us see these ornaments.
Lay forth the gown.

---

36. amort: dejected.
40. dress: prepare.
57. double change of bravery: two changes of fine clothes.
60. ruffling: with ruffles.
61. ornaments: i.e., clothes that ornament the person.

Enter HABERDASHER.

                            What news with you, sir?
HABERDASHER   Here is the cap your worship did bespeak.
PETRUCHIO   Why, this was molded on a porringer,
  A velvet dish. Fie, fie, 'tis lewd and filthy.   65
  Why, 'tis a cockle or a walnut-shell,
  A knack, a toy, a trick, a baby's cap.
  Away with it! Come, let me have a bigger.
KATE   I'll have no bigger. This doth fit the time,
  And gentlewomen wear such caps as these.   70
PETRUCHIO   When you are gentle, you shall have one too,
  And not till then.
HORTENSIO   That will not be in haste.
KATE   Why, sir, I trust I may have leave to speak,
  And speak I will. I am no child, no babe.
  Your betters have endured me say my mind,   75
  And if you cannot, best you stop your ears.
  My tongue will tell the anger of my heart,
  Or else my heart, concealing it, will break,
  And rather than it shall, I will be free
  Even to the uttermost as I please in words.   80
PETRUCHIO   Why, thou sayst true. It is paltry cap,
  A custard coffin, a bauble, a silken pie.
  I love thee well in that thou lik'st it not.
KATE   Love me, or love me not, I like the cap,
  And it I will have, or I will have none. [*Exit* HABERDASHER]   85
PETRUCHIO   Thy gown? Why, ay. Come, tailor, let us see't.
  Oh, mercy, God, what masking stuff is here?
  What's this? A sleeve? 'Tis like demi-cannon.
  What, up and down carved like an apple tart?
  Here's snip, and nip, and cut, and slish and slash,   90
  Like to a censer in a barber's shop.
  Why, what i' devil's name, tailor, call'st thou this?
HORTENSIO   I see she's like to have neither cap nor gown.
TAILOR   You bid me make it orderly and well,
  According to the fashion, and the time.   95
PETRUCHIO   Marry, and did. But if you be remembered,
  I did not bid you mar it to the time.
  Go hop me over every kennel home,

63. **bespeak:** order.
64. **porringer:** porridge bowl.
75. **betters:** people better than you.
82. **custard coffin:** a custard pastry; **bauble:** trinket.
87. **masking stuff:** outfit appropriate for a masque or costume party, i.e., unsuitable.
88. **demi-cannon:** big cannon.
89. **carved:** cut.
91. **censer:** incense burner.
98. **hop me over every kennel home:** hop over every gutter.

For you shall hop without my custom, sir.
I'll none of it. Hence, make your best of it.   100
KATE   I never saw a better fashioned gown,
More quaint, more pleasing, nor more commendable.
Belike you mean to make a puppet of me.
PETRUCHIO   Why, true, he means to make a puppet of thee.
TAILOR   She says your worship means to make a puppet of her.   105
PETRUCHIO   Oh monstrous arrogance! Thou liest, thou thread,
   thou thimble,
Thou yard, three-quarters, half-yard, quarter, nail,
Thou flea, thou nit, thou winter cricket, thou.
Braved in mine own house with a skein of thread!
Away, thou rag, thou quantity, thou remnant,   110
Or I shall so bemete thee with thy yard
As thou shalt think on prating whilst thou liv'st.
I tell thee, I, that thou hast marred her gown.
TAILOR   Your worship is deceived. The gown is made
Just as my master had direction.   115
Grumio gave order how it should be done.
GRUMIO   I gave him no order. I gave him the stuff.
TAILOR   But how did you desire it should be made?
GRUMIO   Marry, sir, with needle and thread.
TAILOR   But did you not request to have it cut?   120
GRUMIO   Thou hast faced many things.
TAILOR   I have.
GRUMIO   Face not me. Thou hast braved many men.
Brave not me; I will neither be faced nor braved. I say
   unto thee, I bid thy master cut out the gown, but I did   125
   not bid him cut it to pieces.
Ergo thou liest.
TAILOR   Why here is the note of the fashion to testify.
PETRUCHIO   Read it.
GRUMIO   The note lies in 's throat if he say I said so.   130
TAILOR   "Inprimis, a loose-bodied gown."
GRUMIO   Master, if ever I said "loose-bodied gown," sew
   me in the skirts of it and beat me to death with a bottom
   of brown thread. I said a gown.
PETRUCHIO   Proceed.   135
TAILOR   "With a small compassed cape."

109. **Braved:** confronted.
111. **bemete:** fitting; **yard:** yardstick.
112. **prating:** prattling, talking excessively.
117. **stuff:** cloth.
121. **faced:** the facing of the garment.
123. **Face:** as in "face off."
127. **Ergo:** therefore.
131. **Inprimis:** in the first place; **loose-bodied:** not close-fitting.
133–34. **a bottom of . . . thread:** a ball or skein.
136. **small compassed:** a little flared.

GRUMIO   I confess the cape.

TAILOR   "With a trunk sleeve."

GRUMIO   I confess two sleeves.

TAILOR   "The sleeves curiously cut."   140

PETRUCHIO   Ay, there's the villainy.

GRUMIO   Error i' th' bill, sir, error i' th' bill. I commanded the
sleeves should be cut out and sewed up again, and that I'll
prove upon thee, though thy little finger be armed in a thimble.

TAILOR   This is true that I say, and I had thee in place   145
where, thou shouldst know it.

GRUMIO   I am for thee straight. Take thou the bill, give
me thy mete-yard, and spare not me.

HORTENSIO   God-a-mercy, Grumio, then he shall have no odds.

PETRUCHIO   Well, sir, in brief, the gown is not for me.   150

GRUMIO   You are i' th' right, sir, 'tis for my mistress.

PETRUCHIO   Go, take it up unto thy master's use.

GRUMIO   Villain, not for thy life! Take up my mistress'
gown for thy master's use.

PETRUCHIO   Why sir, what's your conceit in that?   155

GRUMIO   Oh, sir, the conceit is deeper than you think for:
Take up my mistress' gown to his master's use. Oh fie, fie, fie!

PETRUCHIO   [Aside] Hortensio, say thou wilt see the tailor paid.
[To TAILOR] Go, take it hence. Be gone, and say no more.

HORTENSIO   [Aside] Tailor, I'll pay thee for thy gown tomorrow.   160
Take no unkindness of his hasty words.
Away, I say. Commend me to thy master.

                                                    Exit TAILOR.

PETRUCHIO   Well, come my Kate. We will unto your father's
Even in these honest mean habiliments.
Our purses shall be proud, our garments poor,   165
For 'tis the mind that makes the body rich.
And as the sun breaks through the darkest clouds,
So honor peereth in the meanest habit.
What, is the jay more precious than the lark
Because his feathers are more beautiful?   170
Or is the adder better than the eel

---

138. trunk sleeve: full sleeve.
140. curiously: ornately.
148. mete-yard: measuring stick.
149. no odds: no change.
153–54. Take up my mistress' gown for thy master's use: the joke is on (1) cross-
dressing, and (2) lifting Kate's skirts so that Petruchio can have intercourse with her.
155. conceit: design or invention.
162. Commend me: remember me to (a social politeness).
164. habiliments: clothes.
165. proud: full.
168. peereth: is visible; **meanest:** most lowly.

Because his painted skin contents the eye?
Oh no, good Kate, neither art thou the worse
For this poor furniture and mean array.
If thou account'st it shame, lay it on me,   175
And therefore frolic; we will hence forthwith,
To feast and sport us at thy father's house.
[*To* GRUMIO] Go call my men, and let us straight to him,
And bring our horses unto Long Lane end.
There will we mount, and thither walk on foot.   180
Let's see, I think 'tis now some seven o'clock,
And well we may come there by dinnertime.

KATE   I dare assure you, sir, 'tis almost two,
And 'twill be suppertime ere you come there.

PETRUCHIO   It shall be seven ere I go to horse.   185
Look what I speak, or do, or think to do,
You are still crossing it. Sirs let 't alone.
I will not go today, and ere I do,
It shall be what o'clock I say it is.

HORTENSIO   Why, so this gallant will command the sun.   190

Act 4, Scene 4

Enter TRANIO [*disguised as* LUCENTIO], *and the* PEDANT
dressed like VINCENTIO.

TRANIO   Sir, this is the house. Please it you that I call?

PEDANT   Ay, what else. And but I be deceived,
Signior Baptista may remember me
Near twenty years ago in Genoa,
When we were lodgers at the Pegasus.   5

TRANIO   'Tis well, and hold your own in any case
With such austerity as 'longeth to a father.

Enter BIONDELLO.

PEDANT   I warrant you. But, sir, here comes your boy.
'Twere good he were schooled.

TRANIO   Fear you not him. Sirrah Biondello,   10
Now do your duty thoroughly, I advise you.
Imagine 'twere the right Vincentio.

BIONDELLO   Tut, fear not me.

---

172. **painted:** patterned.
174. **furniture:** apparel; **mean array:** inferior dress.
187. **crossing:** contradicting.
190. **gallant:** fine gentleman.
5. **we were lodgers at the Pegasus:** stayed at the Pegasus Inn.
9. **he were schooled:** if he had received instructions.

TRANIO   But hast thou done thy errand to Baptista?

BIONDELLO   I told him that your father was at Venice   15
And that you looked for him this day in Padua.

TRANIO   Th'art a tall fellow. Hold thee that to drink. [*Gives money.*]
Here comes Baptista. Set your countenance, sir.

Enter BAPTISTA *and* LUCENTIO. PEDANT *booted and barehaded.*

TRANIO   Signior Baptista, you are happily met.
Sir, this is the gentleman I told you of.   20
I pray you, stand good father to me now,
Give me Bianca for my patrimony.

PEDANT   Soft, son. Sir, by your leave, having come to Padua
To gather in some debts, my son Lucentio
Made me acquainted with a weighty cause   25
Of love between your daughter and himself.
And for the good report I hear of you,
And for the love he beareth to your daughter,
And she to him, to stay him not too long,
I am content in a good father's care   30
To have him matched, and if you please to like
No worse than I, upon some agreement
Me shall you find ready and willing
With one consent to have her so bestowed,
For curious I cannot be with you,   35
Signior Baptista, of whom I hear so well.

BAPTISTA   Sir, pardon me in what I have to say,
Your plainness and your shortness please me well.
Right true it is your son Lucentio here
Doth love my daughter, and she loveth him,   40
Or both dissemble deeply their affections.
And therefore, if you say no more than this,
That like a father you will deal with him
And pass my daughter a sufficient dower,
The match is made, and all is done.   45
Your son shall have my daughter with consent.

TRANIO   I thank you, sir. Where then do you know best

---

17. **a tall fellow**: an admirable chap; **Hold thee that to drink**: buy yourself a drink; Tranio is giving Biondello a tip.
18. **Set your countenance**: assume a straight face; **SD.** *Pedant booted and barehaded*: to look as if he has been traveling. Since the Pedant is already on stage, the indication is that he comes forward and makes some adjustment to his clothing.
22. **patrimony**: inheritance from one's father.
29. **stay**: delay.
31. **matched**: engaged.
35. **curious**: unstraightforward.
44. **dower**: dowry.

We be affied and such assurance ta'en
As shall with either parts agreement stand.

BAPTISTA   Not in my house, Lucentio, for you know   50
Pitchers have ears, and I have many servants.
Besides, old Gremio is harkening still,
And happily we might be interrupted.

TRANIO   Then at my lodging, and it like you.
There doth my father lie, and there this night   55
We'll pass the business privately and well.
Send for your daughter by your servant here.
My boy shall fetch the scrivener presently.
The worst is this, that at so slender warning,
You are like to have a thin and slender pittance.   60

BAPTISTA   It likes me well. Cambio, hie you home,
And bid Bianca make her ready straight.
And if you will, tell what hath happened:
Lucentio's father is arrived in Padua,
And how she's like to be Lucentio's wife.   65

                              [*Exit* LUCENTIO]

BIONDELLO   I pray the gods she may with all my heart.
TRANIO   Dally not with the gods, but get thee gone.

                                        Exit.

Signior Baptista, shall I lead the way?
Welcome. One mess is like to be your cheer.
Come, sir, we will better it in Pisa.   70
BAPTISTA   I follow you.   *Exeunt.*

        Enter LUCENTIO *and* BIONDELLO.

BIONDELLO   Cambio.
LUCENTIO   What sayst thou, Biondello?
BIONDELLO   You saw my master wink and laugh upon you?
LUCENTIO   Biondello, what of that?   75
BIONDELLO   Faith, nothing, but he's left me here behind
to expound the meaning or moral of his signs and tokens.
LUCENTIO   I pray thee, moralize them.

---

48. **We be affied and such assurance ta'en:** where should be betrothed and make the legal arrangements?
48. **affied:** affianced.
51. **Pitchers have ears:** people will eavesdrop.
52. **harkening:** listening.
56. **pass:** give; bequeath.
58. **scrivener:** the scribe who would write up the details of the agreement.
59. **so slender warning:** such short notice.
60. **a thin and slender pittance:** small hospitality.
61. **It likes me well:** I like it.
69. **One mess is like to be your cheer:** one dish is likely to be your meal.
78. **moralize them:** explain them.

BIONDELLO   Then thus. Baptista is safe talking with the
   deceiving father of a deceitful son.   80
LUCENTIO   And what of him?
BIONDELLO   His daughter is to be brought by you to the supper.
LUCENTIO   And then?
BIONDELLO   The old priest at Saint Luke's church is at your
   command at all hours.   85
LUCENTIO   And what of all this?
BIONDELLO   I cannot tell, except they are busied about a
   counterfeit assurance. Take you assurance of her *cum
   privilegio ad imprimendum solum*, to th' church take the
   priest, clerk, and some sufficient honest witnesses.   90
   If this be not that you look for, I have no more to say,
   But did Bianca farewell forever and a day.
LUCENTIO   Hear'st thou, Biondello?
BIONDELLO   I cannot tarry. I knew a wench married in an
   afternoon as she went to the garden for parsely to stuff a   95
   rabbit, and so may you, sir. And so, adieu, sir. My master
   hath appointed me to go to Saint Luke's to bid the priest be
   ready to come against you come with your appendix.   *Exit.*
LUCENTIO   I may, and will, if she be so contented.
   She will be pleased, then wherefore should I doubt?   100
   Hap what hap may, I'll roundly go about her.
   It shall go hard if Cambio go without her.   *Exit.*

Act 4, Scene 5

Enter PETRUCHIO, KATE, HORTENSIO.

PETRUCHIO   Come on, i' God's name, once more toward our
   father's.
   Good Lord, how bright and goodly shines the moon!
KATE   The moon? The sun. It is not moonlight now.
PETRUCHIO   I say it is the moon that shines so bright.
KATE   I know it is the sun that shines so bright.   5
PETRUCHIO   Now, by my mother's son, and that's myself,
   It shall be moon, or star, or what I list

---

88. **assurance:** marriage contract.
88–89. ***cum privilegio ad imprimendum solum:*** an assurance that the marriage is completely legitimate; literally, "with the exclusive right to print."
95–96. **to the garden for parsley to stuff a rabbit:** she pretended to have gone out to pick
parsley, but in fact she went secretly to get married.
98. **against you come:** in the event that you come; **appendix:** wife; appendage.
99. **be so contented:** agrees.
101. **Hap what hap may:** whatever happens; **roundly:** completely.
102. **It shall go hard:** it will be hard luck.
7. **list:** wish.

Or ere I journey to your father's house.
Go on, and fetch our horses back again.
Evermore crossed and crossed, nothing but crossed.   10
HORTENSIO   Say as he says, or we shall never go.
KATE   Forward, I pray, since we have come so far,
  And be it moon, or sun, or what you please,
  And if you please to call it a rush candle,
  Henceforth I vow it shall be so for me.   15
PETRUCHIO   I say it is the moon.
KATE   I know it is the moon.
PETRUCHIO   Nay, then you lie. It is the blessèd sun.
KATE   Then, God be blessed, it is the blessèd sun,
  But sun it is not, when you say it is not,   20
  And the moon changes even as your mind.
  What you will have it named, even that it is,
  And so it shall be so for Katherine.
HORTENSIO   Petruchio, go thy ways. The field is won.
PETRUCHIO   Well, forward, forward. Thus the bowl should run,   25
  And not unluckily against the bias.
  But soft, company is coming here.

     Enter VINCENTIO.

Good morrow, gentle mistress, where away?
Tell me, sweet Kate, and tell me truly too,
Hast thou beheld a fresher gentlewoman?   30
Such war of white and red within her cheeks!
What stars do spangle heaven with such beauty
As those two eyes become that heavenly face?
Fair lovely maid, once more good day to thee.
Sweet Kate, embrace her for her beauty's sake.   35
HORTENSIO   A will make the man mad to make the woman
  of him.
KATE   Young budding virgin, fair, and fresh, and sweet,
  Whither away, or where is thy abode?
  Happy the parents of so fair a child;   40
  Happier the man whom favourable stars
  Allots thee for his lovely bedfellow.
PETRUCHIO   Why, how now, Kate? I hope thou art not mad.
  This is a man, old, wrinkled, faded, withered,
  And not a maiden, as thou sayst he is.   45

---

10. crossed: contradicted (by Kate).
25. the bowl should run: an allusion to the game of bowls; the arc the bowl should take unluckily against the bias.
27. soft: hush, stop talking.
31. war of white and red: an allusion to the poetic tradition of female beauty derived from Petrarch, in which the ideal woman had white skin and cheeks like roses.
36. A will: you will.

KATE   Pardon, old father, my mistaking eyes,
  That have been so bedazzled with the sun
  That everything I look on seemeth green.
  Now I perceive thou art a reverend father.
  Pardon, I pray thee, for my mad mistaking.   50
PETRUCHIO   Do, good old grandsire, and withal make known
  Which way thou travelest. If along with us,
  We shall be joyful of thy company.
VINCENTIO   Fair sir, and you, my merry mistress,
  That with your strange encounter much amazed me,   55
  My name is called Vincentio, my dwelling Pisa,
  And bound I am to Padua, there to visit
  A son of mine, which long I have not seen.
PETRUCHIO   What is his name?
VINCENTIO   Lucentio, gentle sir.
PETRUCHIO   Happily met, the happier for thy son.   60
  And now by law as well as reverend age,
  I may entitle thee my loving father.
  The sister to my wife, this gentlewoman,
  Thy son by this hath married. Wonder not,
  Nor be not grieved. She is of good esteem,   65
  Her dowry wealthy, and of worthy birth;
  Beside, so qualified as may beseem
  The spouse of any noble gentleman.
  Let me embrace with old Vincentio,
  And wander we to see thy honest son,   70
  Who will of thy arrival be full joyous.
VINCENTIO   But is this true, or is it else your pleasure,
  Like pleasant travelers, to break a jest
  Upon the company you overtake?
HORTENSIO   I do assure thee, father, so it is.   75
PETRUCHIO   Come, go along, and see the truth hereof,
  For our first merriment hath made thee jealous.
                              Exeunt [all but HORTENSIO]
HORTENSIO   Well, Petruchio, this has put me in heart.
  Have to my widow, and if she be froward,
  Then hast thou taught Hortensio to be untoward.   *Exit.*   80

51. **withal:** in addition.
62. **my loving father:** father-in-law, i.e., his wife's sister's father.
72. **else:** also.
77. **jealous:** suspicious.
78. **put me in heart:** lifted my spirits.
79. **froword:** stubborn, willful.
80. **untoward:** intractable.

Act 5, Scene 1

Enter BIONDELLO, LUCENTIO *and* BIANCA. GREMIO *is out before.*

BIONDELLO   Softly and swiftly, sir, for the priest is ready.
LUCENTIO   I fly, Biondello; but they may chance to need
thee at home, therefore leave us.

Exit [with BIANCA].

BIONDELLO   Nay, faith, I'll see the church a' your back,
and then come back to my master's as soon as I can.   5
GREMIO   I marvel Cambio comes not all this while.

Enter PETRUCHIO, KATE, VINCENTIO, GRUMIO, *with attendants.*

PETRUCHIO   Sir, here's the door. This is Lucentio's house.
My father's bears more toward the market-place.
Thither must I, and here I leave you, sir.
VINCENTIO   You shall not choose but drink before you go.   10
I think I shall command your welcome here,
And by all likelihood some cheer is toward.

Knock.

GREMIO   They're busy within. You were best knock louder.

PEDANT *looks out of the window.*

PEDANT   What's he that knocks as he would beat down the gate?
VINCENTIO   Is Signior Lucentio within, sir?   15
PEDANT   He's within, sir, but not to be spoken withal.
VINCENTIO   What if a man bring him a hundred pound or
two to make merry withal?
PEDANT   Keep your hundred pounds to yourself. He
shall need none so long as I live.   20
PETRUCHIO   Nay, I told you your son was well beloved in
Padua. Do you hear, sir, to leave frivolous circumstances,
I pray you tell Signior Lucentio that his father is
come from Pisa and is here at the door to speak with
him.   25
PEDANT   Thou liest. His father is come from Padua and
here looking out at the window.
VINCENTIO   Art thou his father?

SD. *out before:* stands in front.
4. **a':** at.
8. **My father's:** Baptista's.
22. **circumstances:** details.

PEDANT   Ay, sir, so his mother says, if I may believe her.
PETRUCHIO   [*To Vincentio*] Why, how now, gentleman? Why,   30
this is flat knavery to take upon you another man's name.
PEDANT   Lay hands on the villain. I believe a means
to cozen somebody in this city under my countenance.

Enter BIONDELLO.

BIONDELLO   [*Aside*] I have seen them in the church together,
God send 'em good shipping. But who is here? Mine old   35
Master Vincentio. Now we are undone and brought to nothing.
VINCENTIO   Come hither, crackhemp.
BIONDELLO   I hope I may choose, sir.
VINCENTIO   Come hither, you rogue. What, have you forgot me?
BIONDELLO   Forgot you? No, sir. I could not forget you, for   40
I never saw you before in all my life.
VINCENTIO   What, you notorious villain, didst thou never
see thy master's father, Vincentio?
BIONDELLO   What, my old worshipful old master? Yes
marry, sir, see where he looks out of the window.   45
VINCENTIO   Is 't so, indeed?

He beats Biondello.

BIONDELLO   Help, help, help! Here's a madman will murder
me.
PEDANT   Help, son! Help Signior Baptista!
PETRUCHIO   Prithee, Kate, let's stand aside and see the end of   50
this controversy.

Enter PEDANT *with servants,* BAPTISTA, TRANIO.

TRANIO   Sir, what are you that offer to beat my
servant?
VINCENTIO   What am I, sir? Nay, what are you, sir? Oh immortal
gods! Oh fine villain! A silken doublet, a velvet   55
hose, a scarlet cloak, and a copintank hat. Oh, I am undone,
I am undone! While I play the good husband at home,
my son and my servant spend all at the university.
TRANIO   How now, what's the matter?
BAPTISTA   What, is the man lunatic?   60
TRANIO   Sir, you seem a sober ancient gentleman by
your habit, but your words show you a madman. Why

---

33. cozen: dupe by a confidence trick; **under my countenance:** by assuming my identity.
35. good shipping: good luck.
36. undone: caught; **brought to nothing:** ruined.
37. crackhemp: villan; literally one who will break the hemp rope of the hangman.
38. choose: decide my own course.
56. copintank hat: high-crowned.
57. good husband: frugal householder.

sir, what 'cerns it you if I wear pearl and gold? I thank
my good father, I am able to maintain it.

VINCENTIO   Thy father! Oh villain, he is a sailmaker in Bergamo.   65

BAPTISTA   You mistake, sir, you mistake, sir. Pray, what do
you think is his name?

VINCENTIO   His name? As if I knew not his name. I have
brought him up ever since he was three years old, and
his name is Tranio.   70

PEDANT   Away, away, mad ass! His name is Lucentio, and he
is mine only son and heir to the lands of me, Signior Vincentio.

VINCENTIO   Lucentio! Oh, he hath murdered his master! Lay
hold on him, I charge you, in the Duke's name. Oh, my
son, my son! Tell me, thou villain, where is my son Lucentio?   75

TRANIO   Call forth an officer. Carry this mad knave to
the jail. Father Baptista, I charge you see that he be
forthcoming.

VINCENTIO   Carry me to the jail?

GREMIO   Stay, officer, he shall not go to prison.   80

BAPTISTA   Talk not, Signior Gremio. I say he shall go to prison.

GREMIO   Take heed, Signior Baptista, lest you be cony-
catched in this business. I dare swear this is the right Vincentio.

PEDANT   Swear, if thou dar'st.

GREMIO   Nay, I dare not swear it.   85

TRANIO   Then thou wert best say that I am not Lucentio.

GREMIO   Yes, I know thee to be Signior Lucentio.

BAPTISTA   Away with the dotard. To the jail with him.

Enter BIONDELLO, LUCENTIO *and* BIANCA.

VINCENTIO   Thus strangers may be haled and abused. Oh
monstrous villain!   90

BIONDELLO   Oh, we are spoiled, and yonder he is. Deny him,
forswear him, or else we are all undone.

Exit BIONDELLO, TRANIO *and* PEDANT, *as fast as may be.*

LUCENTIO   Pardon, sweet father.   *Kneels.*

VINCENTIO   Lives my sweet son?

BIANCA   Pardon, dear father.   95

BAPTISTA   How hast thou offended? Where is Lucentio?

LUCENTIO   Here's Lucentio, right son to the right Vincentio,
That have by marriage made thy daughter mine,
While counterfeit supposes bleared thine eyne.

---

63. **'cerns**: concerns.
88. **dotard**: doddering old fool.
89. **strangers . . . abused**: people from out of town (referring to himself), may be mistreated; **haled**: molested.
91. **spoiled**: ruined.
99. **bleared**: clouded.

GREMIO   Here's packing, with a witness, to deceive us all.   100
VINCENTIO   Where is that damnèd villain Tranio,
  That faced and braved me in this matter so?
BAPTISTA   Why, tell me, is not this my Cambio?
BIANCA   Cambio is changed into Lucentio.
LUCENTIO   Love wrought these miracles. Bianca's love   105
  Made me exchange my state with Tranio,
  While he did bear my countenance in the town,
  And happily I have arrivèd at the last
  Unto the wishèd haven of my bliss.
  What Tranio did, myself enforced him to;   110
  Then pardon him, sweet Father, for my sake.
VINCENTIO   I'll slit the villain's nose that would have sent
  me to the jail.
BAPTISTA   But do you hear, sir, have you married my
  daughter without asking my good will?   115
VINCENTIO   Fear not, Baptista, we will content you. Go to.
  But I will in to be revenged for this villany.   *Exit.*
BAPTISTA   And I to sound the depth of this knavery.   *Exit.*
LUCENTIO   Look not pale, Bianca. Thy father will not frown.

                                              Exeunt.

GREMIO   My cake is dough, but I'll in among the rest,   120
  Out of hope of all, but my share of the feast.
KATE   Husband, let's follow, to see the end of this ado.
PETRUCHIO   First kiss me, Kate, and we will.
KATE   What, in the midst of the street?
PETRUCHIO   What, art thou ashamed of me?   125
KATE   No, sir, God forbid, but ashamed to kiss.
PETRUCHIO   Why, then let's home again. Come, sirrah, let's away.
KATE   Nay, I will give thee a kiss. Now pray thee, love, stay.
PETRUCHIO   Is not this well? Come, my sweet Kate.
  Better once than never, for never too late.   *Exeunt.*   130

Act 5, Scene 2

Enter BAPTISTA, VINCENTIO, GREMIO, *the* PEDANT, LUCEN-
TIO, *and* BIANCA; TRANIO, BIONDELLO, GRUMIO, *and* WIDOW;
The servingmen with TRANIO *bringing in a banquet.*

LUCENTIO   At last, though long, our jarring notes agree,
  And time it is, when raging war is done,

100. **packing:** conspiring.
112. **slit the villain's nose:** nose-slitting was an Elizabethan punishment.
118. **to sound the depth:** investigate.
120. **My cake is dough:** I have the short end of the stick.

To smile at scapes and perils overblown.
My fair Bianca, bid my father welcome,
While I with selfesame kindness welcome thine.   5
Brother Petruchio, sister Katherina,
And thou, Hortensio with thy loving widow,
Feast with the best, and welcome to my house.
My banquet is to close our stomachs up
After our great good cheer. Pray you, sit down,   10
For now we sit to chat as well as eat.

PETRUCHIO   Nothing but sit and sit, and eat and eat.

BAPTISTA   Padua affords this kindness, son Petruchio.

PETRUCHIO   Padua affords nothing but what is kind.

HORTENSIO   For both our sakes I would that word were true.   15

PETRUCHIO   Now, for my life, Hortensio fears his widow.

WIDOW   Then never trust me if I be afeard.

PETRUCHIO   You are very sensible, and yet you miss my sense.
I mean Hortensio is afeard of you.

WIDOW   He that is giddy thinks the world turns round.   20

PETRUCHIO   Roundly replied.

KATE   Mistress, how mean you that?

WIDOW   Thus I conceive by him.

PETRUCHIO   Conceives by me! How likes Hortensio that?

HORTENSIO   My widow says, thus she conceives her tale.   25

PETRUCHIO   Very well mended. Kiss him for that, good widow.

KATE   "He that is giddy thinks the world turns round,"
I pray you tell me what you meant by that.

WIDOW   Your husband, being troubled with a shrew,
Measures my husband's sorrow by his woe.   30
And now you know my meaning.

KATE   A very mean meaning.

WIDOW   Right, I mean you.

KATE   And I am mean indeed, respecting you.

PETRUCHIO   To her, Kate!

HORTENSIO   To her, Widow!   35

PETRUCHIO   A hundred marks my Kate does put her down.

HORTENSIO   That's my office.

PETRUCHIO   Spoke like an officer. Ha' to thee, lad.

          Drinks to HORTENSIO.

BAPTISTA   How likes Gremio these quick-witted folks?

---

9. **close our stomachs up:** fill us.
15. **I would:** I wish.
17. **afeard:** afraid.
21. **Roundly:** wittily.
24. **Conceives:** engenders a child; has an understanding.
36. **hundred marks:** about £67.
37. **office:** duty.

GREMIO   Believe me, sir, they butt together well.   40
BIANCA   Head, and butt. An hasty-witted body
  Would say your head and butt were head and horn.
VINCENTIO   Ay, mistress bride, hath that awakened you?
BIANCA   Ay, but not frighted me, therefore I'll sleep again.
PETRUCHIO   Nay, that you shall not. Since you have begun,   45
  Have at you for a bitter jest or two.
BIANCA   Am I your bird? I mean to shift my bush,
  And then pursue me as you draw your bow.
  You are welcome all.   *Exit* BIANCA.
PETRUCHIO   She hath prevented me. Here, Signior *Tranio*,   50
  This bird you aimed at, though you hit her not.
  Therefore a health to all that shot and missed.
TRANIO   Oh, sir, Lucentio slipped me like his greyhound,
  Which runs himself and catches for his master.
PETRUCHIO   A good swift simile, but something currish.   55
TRANIO   'Tis well, sir, that you hunted for yourself.
  'Tis thought your deer does hold you at a bay.
BAPTISTA   Oh, oh, Petruchio, Tranio hits you now.
LUCENTIO   I thank thee for that gird, good Tranio.
HORTENSIO   Confess, confess, hath he not hit you here?   60
PETRUCHIO   A has a little galled me, I confess,
  And as the jest did glance away from me,
  'Tis ten to one it maimed you two outright.
BAPTISTA   Now in good sadness, son Petruchio,
  I think thou hast the veriest shrew of all.   65
PETRUCHIO   Well, I say no. And therefore for assurance,
  Let's each one send unto his wife,
  And he whose wife is most obedient,
  To come at first when he doth send for her
  Shall win the wager which we will propose.   70
HORTENSIO   Content. What's the wager?
LUCENTIO   Twenty crowns.
PETRUCHIO   Twenty crowns!
  I'll venture so much of my hawk or hound,
  But twenty times so much upon my wife.   75
LUCENTIO   A hundred then.

---

41. Head, and butt: butt heads; **hasty-witted:** quick-witted, clever.
42. head and horn: cuckold's horns, i.e., the horns that were thought to be worn by a man whose wife was unfaithful to him.
47. bird: target; **bush:** place.
51. This bird you aimed at: this woman you hoped to win.
53. slipped me: got away from me.
55. currish: dog-like.
57. your deer does hold you at a bay: keep you at a distance (punning on "deer" and "dear").
59. gird: biting sarcasm.
65. veriest: truest.
71. Content: agreed.

HORTENSIO   Content.
PETRUCHIO   A match, 'tis done.
HORTENSIO   Who shall begin?
LUCENTIO   That will I.   80
 Go, Biondello, bid your mistress come to me.
BIONDELLO   I go.   *Exit.*
BAPTISTA   Son, I'll be your half, Bianca comes.
LUCENTIO   I'll have no halves. I'll bear it all myself.

  Enter BIONDELLO.

 How now, what news?
BIONDELLO   Sir, my mistress sends you word   85
 That she is busy and she cannot come.
PETRUCHIO   How? She's busy and she cannot come?
 Is that an answer?
GREMIO   Ay, and a kind one too.
 Pray God, sir, your wife send you not a worse.
PETRUCHIO   I hope better.
HORTENSIO   Sirrah Biondello   90
 Go and entreat my wife to come to me forthwith.
         Exit BIONDELLO.
PETRUCHIO   Oh ho, entreat her. Nay, then she must needs come.
HORTENSIO   I am afraid, sir, do what you can.

  Enter BIONDELLO.

 Yours will not be entreated. Now, where's my wife?
BIONDELLO   She says you have some goodly jest in hand.   95
 She will not come. She bids you come to her.
PETRUCHIO   Worse and worse. She will not come.
 Oh vile, intolerable, not to be endured.
 Sirrah Grumio, go to your mistress,
 Say I command her come to me.   *Exit.* 100
HORTENSIO   I know her answer.
PETRUCHIO   What?
HORTENSIO   She will not.
PETRUCHIO   The fouler fortune mine, and there an end.

  Enter KATHERINA.

BAPTISTA   Now, by my halidom, here comes Katherina.
KATE   What is your will, sir, that you send for me?
PETRUCHIO   Where is your sister and Hortensio's wife?   105
KATE   They sit conferring by the parlor fire.
PETRUCHIO   Go fetch them hither. If they deny to come,

_____

93. **I am afraid:** I expect.
103. **halidom:** holy dame; the Blessed Mother.

Swinge me them soundly forth unto their husbands.
Away, I say, and bring them hither straight.
LUCENTIO   Here is a wonder, if you talk of a wonder.   110
HORTENSIO   And so it is. I wonder what it bodes.
PETRUCHIO   Marry, peace it bodes, and love, and quiet life,
   An awful rule, and right supremacy,
   And, to be short, what not that's sweet and happy.
BAPTISTA   Now fair befall thee, good Petruchio,   115
   The wager thou hast won, and I will add
   Unto their losses twenty thousand crowns,
   Another dowry to another daughter,
   For she is changed as she had never been.
PETRUCHIO   Nay, I will win my wager better yet,   120
   And show more sign of her obedience,
   Her new built virtue and obedience.

   Enter KATE, BIANCA, *and* WIDOW.

See where she comes, and brings your froward wives
As prisoners to her womanly persuasion.
Katherine, that cap of yours becomes you not.   125
Off with that bauble, throw it underfoot.
WIDOW   Lord, let me never have a cause to sigh
   Till I be brought to such a silly pass.
BIANCA   Fie, what a foolish duty call you this?
LUCENTIO   I would your duty were as foolish, too.   130
   The wisdom of your duty, fair Bianca,
   Hath cost me five hundred crowns since suppertime.
BIANCA   The more fool you for laying on my duty.
PETRUCHIO   Katherine, I charge thee tell these headstrong women
   What duty they do owe their lords and husbands.   135
WIDOW   Come, come, you're mocking. We will have no telling.
PETRUCHIO   Come on, I say, and first begin with her.
WIDOW   She shall not.
PETRUCHIO   I say she shall, and first begin with her.
KATE   Fie, fie, unknit that threat'ning, unkind brow,   140
   And dart not scornful glances from those eyes
   To wound thy lord, thy king, thy governor.
   It blots thy beauty as frosts do bite the meads,
   Confounds thy fame as whirlwinds shake fair buds,
   And in no sense is meet or amiable.   145
   A woman moved is like a fountain troubled,
   Muddy, ill-seeming, thick, bereft of beauty,
   And while it is so, none so dry or thirsty

108. **Swinge me them:** beat them.
113. **awful rule:** command.
114. **what not that's sweet:** everything that is sweet and happy.
123. **froward:** disobedient, wayward.

Will deign to sip or touch one drop of it.
Thy husband is thy lord, thy life, thy keeper,   150
Thy head, thy sovereign—one that cares for thee,
And for thy maintenance commits his body
To painful labor both by sea and land,
To watch the night in storms, the day in cold,
Whilst thou liest warm at home, secure and safe,   155
And craves no other tribute at thy hands
But love, fair looks, and true obedience;
Too little payment for so great a debt.
Such duty as the subject owes the prince,
Even such a woman oweth to her husband,   160
And when she is froward, peevish, sullen, sour,
And not obedient to his honest will,
What is she but a foul contending rebel,
And graceless traitor to her loving lord?
I am ashamed that women are so simple   165
To offer war where they should kneel for peace,
Or seek for rule, supremacy, and sway,
When they are bound to serve, love, and obey.
Why are our bodies soft, and weak, and smooth,
Unapt to toil and trouble in the world,   170
But that our soft conditions and our hearts
Should well agree with our external parts?
Come, come, you froward and unable worms,
My mind hath been as big as one of yours,
My heart as great, my reason haply more,   175
To bandy word for word and frown for frown;
But now I see our lances are but straws,
Our strength as weak, our weakness past compare,
That seeming to be most which we indeed least are.
Then vail your stomachs, for it is no boot,   180
And place your hands below your husband's foot,
In token of which duty, if he please,
My hand is ready, may it do him ease.
PETRUCHIO   Why, there's a wench! Come on, and kiss me, Kate.
LUCENTIO   Well, go thy ways old lad for thou shalt ha't.   185
VINCENTIO   'Tis a good hearing when children are toward.
LUCENTIO   But a harsh hearing when women are froward.
PETRUCHIO   Come, Kate, we'll to bed
We three are married, but you two are sped.

161. **froward:** willful, disobedient.
163. **contending:** warring.
165. **simple:** foolish.
173. **unable worms:** weak, incapable creatures.
175. **haply:** perhaps.
180. **vail your stomachs:** don't be so proud; **boot:** use, profit.

'Twas I won the wager, though you hit the white,   190
And being a winner, God give you good night.

Exit PETRUCHIO

HORTENSIO   Now go thy ways, thou hast tamed a curst shrew.
LUCENTIO   'Tis a wonder, by your leave, she will be tamed so.

---

190. I won the wager, though you hit the white: "I won the bet even though you hit your target." The allusion here is to archery where the "white" is the center of the target; also a pun on Bianca's name, which means "white" in Italian.
193. by your leave: if you don't mind my saying so.

A Note on the Text

In the minds of many readers, textual scholarship is more or less synonymous with the art of obfuscation. However, textual matters entail the important, detailed, and notoriously complex work of deciding how to represent the writings of the past with an eye to readers of the present. Even where only one version of a play survives, we have access to the print shop's transcription of the author's words, and only rarely to the author's words written in his own hand. In the case of Shakespeare, only a few lines in a co-authored play, *Sir Thomas More*, survive in his own hand, and not a single line of a play or poem. This is neither surprising nor mysterious given the rate of survival of early modern documents. What is important, however, is to remind ourselves that we are always reading a mediated version of what Shakespeare wrote, and that even if we had access to the manuscript copies of his plays, his "foul papers" as they are called, we might find out that he had written a number of versions without sharing our modern idea that there is but one complete and final version of a text. While these are indeed compelling and complex matters, their investigation is not the goal of this edition because while textual scholarship requires the investigation of every possible circumstance and anomaly in the production of a given text, the goal of textual editing is clarity. For this reason, I have tried to leave the text as unencumbered with textual apparatus as possible.

In the absence of Quarto editions that predate the Folio's version of the play, the only authoritative text of *The Taming of the Shrew* in existence is the First Folio, published in 1623. The anonymous 1594 play, *A Pleasant Conceited History, Called The Taming of A Shrew*, whose main characters have different names, arguably constitutes not so much a competing version as an entirely different, and most likely, non-Shakespearean play. Certainly, *A Pleasant Conceited History* is not ascribed to Shakespeare, even on the occasions of its reprinting in 1596 and 1607. For these reasons, the text of this edition is based on the First Folio. The text follows the First Folio as closely as possible. I have silently modernized the text, and all other deviations from the Folio are in the interests of clarification and within long-standing traditions of editorial practice. For example, act and scene divisions have been inserted in conformity with modern editorial conventions, and some speech prefixes have been amended in the interests of clarity.

In the Criticism section of this volume, all line numbers for Shakespeare's *The Taming of the Shrew* refer to the Norton Critical Edition.

SOURCES AND
CONTEXTS

OVID

From Metamorphoses†

Apollo and Daphne

Daphne, the daughter of the river god
Peneus, was the first love of Apollo;
this happened not by chance, but by the cruel
outrage of Cupid; Phoebus, in the triumph
of his great victory against the Python,   5
observed him bending back his bow and said,
    "What are *you* doing with such manly arms,
lascivious boy? That bow befits *our* brawn,
wherewith we deal out wounds to savage beasts
and other mortal foes, unerringly: 10
just now with our innumerable arrows
we managed to lay low the mighty Python,
whose pestilential belly covered acres!
Content yourself with kindling love affairs
with your wee torch—and don't claim *our* glory!"   15
    The son of Venus answered him with this:
"Your arrow, Phoebus, may strike everything;
mine will strike you: as animals to gods,
your glory is so much the less than mine!"
    He spoke, and soaring upward through the air   20
on wings that thundered, in no time at all
had landed on Parnassus' shaded height;
and from his quiver drew two arrows out
which operated at cross-purposes,
for one engendered flight, the other, love;   25
the latter has a polished tip of gold,
the former has a tip of dull, blunt lead;
with this one, Cupid struck Peneus' daughter,
while the other pierced Apollo to his marrow.
    One is in love now, and the other one   30
won't hear of it, for Daphne calls it joy
to roam within the forest's deep seclusion,
where she, in emulation of the chaste
goddess Phoebe, devotes herself to hunting;

† From *Ovid's Metamorphoses*, trans. Charles Martin (New York: Norton, 2007), pp. 33–46.
Copyright © 2004 by Charles Martin. Used by permission of W. W. Norton & Company,
Inc.

one ribbon only bound her straying tresses.   35
   Many men sought her, but she spurned her suitors,
loath to have anything to do with men,
and rambled through the wild and trackless groves
untroubled by a thought for love or marriage.
   Often her father said, "You owe it to me,   40
child, to provide me with a son-in-law
and grandchildren!"
                      "Let me remain a virgin,
father most dear," she said, "as once before
Diana's father, Jove, gave her that gift."
   Although Peneus yielded to you, Daphne,   45
your beauty kept your wish from coming true,
your comeliness conflicting with your vow:
at first sight, Phoebus loves her and desires
to sleep with her; desire turns to hope,
and his own prophecy deceives the god.   50
   Now just as in a field the harvest stubble
is all burned off, or as hedges are set ablaze
when, if by chance, some careless traveler
should brush one with his torch or toss away
the still-smoldering brand at break of day—   55
just so the smitten god went up in flames
until his heart was utterly afire,
and hope sustained his unrequited passion.
   He gazes on her hair without adornment:
"What if it were done up a bit?" he asks,   60
and gazes on her eyes, as bright as stars,
and on that darling little mouth of hers,
though sight is not enough to satisfy;
he praises everything that he can see—
her fingers, hands, and arms, bare to her shoulders—   65
and what is hidden prizes even more.
   She flees more swiftly than the lightest breeze,
nor will she halt when he calls out to her:
"Daughter of Peneus, I pray, hold still,
hold still! I'm not a foe in grim pursuit!   70
Thus lamb flees wolf, thus dove from eagle flies
on trembling wings, thus deer from lioness,
thus any creature flees its enemy,
but I am stalking you because of love!
   "Wretch that I am: I'm fearful that you'll fall,   75
brambles will tear your flesh because of me!
The ground you're racing over's very rocky,
slow down, I beg you, restrain yourself in flight,
and I will follow at a lesser speed.
   "Just ask yourself who finds you so attractive!   80

I'm not a caveman, not some shepherd boy,
no shaggy guardian of flocks and herds—
you've no idea, rash girl, you've no idea
whom you are fleeing, that is why you flee!
    "Delphi, Claros, Tenedos are all mine,   85
I'm worshipped in the city of Patara!
Jove is my father, I alone reveal
what was, what is, and what will come to be!
The plucked strings answer my demand with song!
    "Although my aim is sure, another's arrow   90
proved even more so, and my careless heart
was badly wounded—the art of medicine
is my invention, by the way, the source
of my worldwide fame as a practitioner
of healing through the natural strength of herbs. 95
    "Alas, there is no herbal remedy
for the love that I must suffer, and the arts
that heal all others cannot heal their lord—"
    He had much more to say to her, but Daphne
pursued her fearful course and left him speechless, 100
though no less lovely fleeing him; indeed,
disheveled by the wind that bared her limbs
and pressed the blown robes to her straining body
even as it whipped up her hair behind her,
the maiden was more beautiful in flight!   105
    But the young god had no further interest
in wasting his fine words on her; admonished
by his own passion, he accelerates,
and runs as swiftly as a Gallic hound
chasing a rabbit through an open field;   110
the one seeks shelter and the other, prey—
he clings to her, is just about to spring,
with his long muzzle straining at her heels,
while she, not knowing whether she's been caught,
in one swift burst, eludes those snapping jaws,   115
no longer the anticipated feast;
so he in hope and she in terror race.
    But her pursuer, driven by his passion,
outspeeds the girl, giving her no pause,
one step behind her, breathing down her neck;   120
her strength is gone; she blanches at the thought
of the effort of her swift flight overcome,
but at the sight of Peneus, she cries,
"Help me, dear father! If your waters hold
divinity, transform me and destroy   125
that beauty by which I have too well pleased!"
    Her prayer was scarcely finished when she feels

a torpor take possession of her limbs—
her supple trunk is girdled with a thin
layer of fine bark over her smooth skin;   130
her hair turns into foliage, her arms
grow into branches, sluggish roots adhere
to feet that were so recently so swift,
her head becomes the summit of a tree;
all that remains of her is a warm glow.   135

    Loving her still, the god puts his right hand
against the trunk, and even now can feel
her heart as it beats under the new bark;
he hugs her limbs as if they were still human,
and then he puts his lips against the wood,   140
which, even now, is adverse to his kiss.

    "Although you cannot be my bride," he says,
"you will assuredly be my own tree,
O Laurel, and will always find yourself
girding my locks, my lyre, and my quiver too—   145
you will adorn great Roman generals
when every voice cries out in joyful triumph
along the route up to the Capitol;
you will protect the portals of Augustus,
guarding, on either side, his crown of oak;   150
and as I am—perpetually youthful,
my flowing locks unknown to the barber's shears—
so you will be an evergreen forever
bearing your brilliant foliage with glory!"

    Phoebus concluded. Laurel shook her branches   155
and seemed to nod her summit in assent.

Jove and Io (1)

There is a grove in Thessaly, enclosed
on every side by high and wooded hills:
they call it Tempe. The river Peneus,
which rises deep within the Pindus range,
pours its turbulent waters through this gorge   5
and over a cataract that deafens all
its neighbors far and near, creating clouds
that drive a fine, cool mist along, until
it drips down through the summits of the trees.

    Here is the house, the seat, the inner chambers   10
of the great river; here Peneus holds court
in his rocky cavern and lays down the law
to water nymphs and tributary streams.

    First to assemble were the native rivers,
uncertain whether to congratulate,   15

or to commiserate with Daphne's father:
the Sperchios, whose banks are lined with poplars,
the ancient Apidanus and the mild
Aeas and Amprysus; others came later—
rivers who, by whatever course they take,   20
eventually bring their flowing streams,
weary of their meandering, to sea.

    Inachus was the only river absent,
concealed in the recesses of his cave:
he added to his volume with the tears   25
he grimly wept for his lost daughter Io,
not knowing whether she still lived or not;
but since he couldn't find her anywhere,
assumed that she was nowhere to be found—
and in his heart, he feared a fate far worse.   30

    For Jupiter had seen the girl returning
from her father's banks and had accosted her:
"O maiden worthy of almighty Jove
and destined to delight some lucky fellow
(I know not whom) upon your wedding night,   35
come find some shade," he said, "in these deep woods—"
(showing her where the woods were *very* shady)
"while the sun blazes high above the earth!

    "But if you're worried about entering
the haunts of savage beasts all by yourself,   40
why, under the protection of a god
you will be safe within the deepest woods—
and no plebeian god, for I am he
who bears the celestial scepter in his hand,
I am he who hurls the roaming thunderbolt—   45
don't run from me!"

                  But run she did, through Lerna
and Lyrcea, until the god concealed
the land entirely beneath a dense
dark mist and seized her and dishonored her.

    Juno, however, happened to look down   50
on Argos, where she noticed something odd:
swift-flying clouds had turned day into night
long before nighttime. She realized
that neither falling mist nor rising fog
could be the cause of this phenomenon,   55
and looked about at once to find her husband,
as one too well aware of the connivings
of a mate so often taken in the act.

    When he could not be found above, she said,
"Either I'm mad—or I am being had."   60
She glided down to earth from heaven's summit

immediately and dispersed the clouds.
    Having intuited his wife's approach,
Jove had already metamorphosed Io
into a gleaming heifer—a beauty still,   65
even as a cow. Despite herself,
Juno gave this illusion her approval,
and feigning ignorance, asked him whose herd
this heifer had come out of, and where from;
Jove, lying to forestall all inquiries   70
as to her origin and pedigree,
replied that she was born out of the earth.
Then Juno asked him for her as a gift.
    What could he do? Here is his beloved:
to hand her over is unnatural,   75
but not to do so would arouse suspicion;
shame urged him onward while love held him back.
Love surely would have triumphed over shame,
except that to deny so slight a gift
to one who was his wife and sister both   80
would make it seem that this was no mere cow!
    Her rival given up to her at last,
Juno feared Jove had more such tricks in mind,
and couldn't feel entirely secure
until she'd placed this heifer in the care   85
of Argus, the watchman with a hundred eyes:
in strict rotation, his eyes slept in pairs,
while those that were not sleeping stayed on guard.
No matter where he stood, he looked at Io,
even when he had turned his back on her.   90
    He let her graze in daylight; when the sun
set far beneath the earth, he penned her in
and placed a collar on her indignant neck.
She fed on leaves from trees and bitter grasses,
and had no bed to sleep on, the poor thing,   95
but lay upon the ground, not always grassy,
and drank the muddy waters from the streams.
    Having no arms, she could not stretch them out
in supplication to her warden, Argus;
and when she tried to utter a complaint   100
she only mooed—a sound which terrified her,
fearful as she now was of her own voice.
    Io at last came to the riverbank
where she had often played; when she beheld
her own slack jaws and newly sprouted horns   105
in the clear water, she fled, terrified!
    Neither her naiad sisters nor her father
knew who this heifer was who followed them

and let herself be petted and admired.
Inachus fed her grasses from his hand;   110
she licked it and pressed kisses on his palm,
unable to restrain her flowing tears.
    If words would just have come, she would have spoken,
telling them who she was, how this had happened,
and begging their assistance in her case;   115
but with her hoof, she drew lines in the dust,
and letters of the words she could not speak
told the sad story of her transformation.
    "Oh, wretched me," cried Io's father, clinging
to the lowing calf's horns and snowy neck.   120
"Oh, wretched me!" he groaned. "Are you the child
for whom I searched the earth in every part?
Lost, you were less a grief than you are, found!
    "You make no answer, unable to respond
to our speech in language of your own,   125
but from your breast come resonant deep sighs
and—all that you can manage now—you *moo!*
    "But I—all unaware of this—was busy
arranging marriage for you, in the hopes
of having a son-in-law and grandchildren.   130
Now I must pick your husband from my herd,
and now must find your offspring there as well!
    "Nor can I end this suffering by death;
it is a hurtful thing to be a god,
for the gates of death are firmly closed against me,   135
and our sorrows must go on forever."
    And while the father mourned his daughter's loss,
Argus of the hundred eyes removed her
to pastures farther off and placed himself
high on a mountain peak, a vantage point   140
from which he could keep watch in all directions.
    The ruler of the heavens cannot bear
the sufferings of Io any longer,
and calls his son, born of the Pleiades,
and orders him to do away with Argus.   145
    Without delay, he takes his winged sandals,
his magic, sleep-inducing wand, and cap;
and so equipped, the son of father Jove
glides down from heaven's summit to the earth,
where he removes and leaves behind his cap   150
and winged sandals, but retains the wand;
and sets out as a shepherd, wandering
far from the beaten path, driving before him
a flock of goats he rounds up as he goes,
while playing tunes upon his pipe of reeds.   155

The guardian of Juno is quite taken
by this new sound: "Whoever you might be,
why not come sit with me upon this rock,"
said Argus, "for that flock of yours will find
the grass is nowhere greener, and you see   160
that there is shade here suitable for shepherds."
    The grandson of great Atlas takes his seat
and whiles away the hours, chattering
of this and that—and playing on his pipes,
he tries to overcome the watchfulness   165
of Argus, struggling to stay awake;
even though Slumber closes down some eyes,
others stay vigilant. Argus inquired
how the reed pipes, so recently invented,
had come to be, and Mercury responded: 170

Pan and Syrinx

"On the idyllic mountains of Arcadia,
among the hamadryads of Nonacris,
one was renowned, and Syrinx was her name.
Often she fled—successfully—from Satyrs,
and deities of every kind as well,   5
those of the shady wood and fruited plain.
    "In her pursuits and in virginity
Diana was her model, and she wore
her robe hitched up and girt above the knees
just as her goddess did; and if her bow   10
had been made out of gold, instead of horn,
anyone seeing her might well have thought
she *was* the goddess—as, indeed, some did.
    "Wearing his crown of sharp pine needles, Pan
saw her returning once from Mount Lycaeus,   15
and began to say. . . ."
                            There remained to tell
of how the maiden, having spurned his pleas,
fled through the trackless wilds until she came
to where the gently flowing Ladon stopped
her in her flight; how she begged the water nymphs   20
to change her shape, and how the god, assuming
that he had captured Syrinx, grasped instead
a handful of marsh reeds! And while he sighed,
the reeds in his hands, stirred by his own breath,
gave forth a similar, low-pitched complaint!   25
    The god, much taken by the sweet new voice
of an unprecedented instrument,
said this to her: "At least we may converse

with one another—I can have that much."

    That pipe of reeds, unequal in their lengths,   30
and joined together one-on-one with wax,
took the girl's name, and bears it to this day.

    Now Mercury was ready to continue
until he saw that Argus had succumbed,
for all his eyes had been closed down by sleep.   35
He silences himself and waves his wand
above those languid orbs to fix the spell.

    Without delay he grasps the nodding head
and where it joins the neck, he severs it
with his curved blade and flings it bleeding down   40
the steep rock face, staining it with gore.
O Argus, you are fallen, and the light
in all your lamps is utterly put out:
one hundred eyes, one darkness all the same!

Jove and Io (2)

But Saturn's daughter rescued them and set
those eyes upon the feathers of her bird,
filling his tail with constellated gems.

    Her rage demanded satisfaction, *now*:
the goddess set a horrifying Fury   5
before the eyes and the imagination
of her Grecian rival; and in her heart
she fixed a prod that goaded Io on,
driving her in terror through the world
until at last, O Nile, you let her rest   10
from endless labor; having reached your banks,
she went down awkwardly upon her knees,
and with her neck bent backward, raised her face
as only she could do it, to the stars;
and with her groans and tears and mournful mooing,   15
entreated Jove, it seemed, to put an end
to her great suffering.

                  Jove threw his arms
around the neck of Juno in embrace,
imploring her to end this punishment:
"In future," he said, "put your fears aside: 20
never again will you have cause to worry—
about *this* one." And swore upon the Styx.

    The goddess was now pacified, and Io
at once began regaining her lost looks,
till she became what she had been before;   25
her body lost all of its bristling hair,
her horns shrank down, her eyes grew narrower,

her jaws contracted, arms and hands returned,
and hooves divided themselves into nails;
nothing remained of her bovine nature,   30
unless it was the whiteness of her body.
She had some trouble getting her legs back,
and for a time feared speaking, lest she moo,
and so quite timidly regained her speech.
    She is a celebrated goddess now,   35
and worshipped by the linen-clad Egyptians.
Her son, Epaphus, is believed to be
sprung from the potent seed of mighty Jove,
and temples may be found in every city
wherein the boy is honored with his parent.   40

GEORGE GASCOIGNE

Supposes[†]

The names of the Actors.

BALIA, *the Nurse.*
POLYNESTA, *the young woman.*
CLEANDER, *the Doctor, suter to Polynesta.*
PASYPHILO, *the Parasite.*
CARION, *the Doctor's man.*
DULYPO, *fayned servant and lover of Polynesta.*
EROSTRATO, *fayned master and suter to Polynesta.*
DALIO & CRAPYNO } *servants to fayned Erostrato.*
SCENÆSE, *a gentleman stranger.*
PAQUETTO & PETRUCIO } *his servants.*
DAMON, *father to Polinesta.*
NEUOLA, *and two other his servants.*
PSYTERIA, *an old hag in his house.*
PHYLOGANO, *a* Scycilian *gentleman, father to Erostrato.*
LYTIO, *his servant.*
FERRARESE, *an Innkeeper of* Ferrara.
       The Comedy presented as it were in Ferrara.

---

† From *Early Plays from the Italian*, ed. R. Warwick Bond (Oxford: Clarendon Press, 1911). Word glosses are those of D. C. Callaghan. Apart from the title, the spelling of this text has not been modernized and appears exactly in the form presented to its Elizabethan readers. If you have difficulty with any of the words, try sounding them out loud in order to grasp their meaning phonetically.

Actus primus. Scena I.

BALIA, *the Nurse.*   POLYNESTA, *the young woman.*

Here is nobody, come foorth *Polynesta*, let vs looke about to be
sure least any man heare our talke: for I thinke within the house
the tables, the plankes, the beds, the portals, yea and the cupboards them selues haue eares.

POL   You might as well haue sayde, the windowes and the   5
doores: do you not see howe they harken?

BA   Well you jest faire, but I would aduise you take heede, I
have bidden you a thousande times beware: you will be spied
one day talking with *Dulippo*.

PO   And why should I not talke with *Dulippo*, as well as with   10
any other, I pray you?

BA   I haue giuen you a wherfore for this why many times: but
go too, followe your owne aduise till you ouerwhelme vs all
with soden mishappe.

PO   A great mishappe I promise you: marie Gods blessing on   15
their heart that sette suche a brouche on my cappe.

BA   Well, looke well about you: a man would thinke it were inough for you secretly to reioyce, that by my helpe you haue
passed so many pleasant nightes togither: and yet by my
trouth I do it more than halfe agaynst my will, for I would   20
rather you had setled your fansie in some noble familie, yea
and it is no small griefe vnto me, that (reiecting the suites of
so many nobles and gentlemen) you have chosen for your darling a poore seruaunt of your fathers, by whome shame and
infamie is the best dower you can looke for to attayne.   25

PO   And I pray you whome may I thanke but gentle nourse?
that continually praysing him, what for his personage, his curtesie, and aboue all, the extreme passions of his minde, in fine
you would neuer cease till I accepted him, delighted in him,
and at length desired him with no lesse affection, than he   30
earst desired me.

BA   I can not denie, but at the beginning I did recommende
him vnto you (as in deede I may say that for my selfe I haue a
pitiful heart) seeing the depth of his vnbridled affection, and
that continually he neuer ceassed to fill mine eares with lam-   35
entable complaynts.

PO   Nay rather that he filled your pursse with bribes and rewards, Nourse.

BA   Well you may iudge of Nourse as you liste. In deede I haue
thought it always a deede of charitie to helpe the miserable   40
yong men, whose tender youth consumeth with the furious
flames of loue. But be you sure if I had thought you would
haue passed to the termes you nowe stand in, pitie nor pen-

cion, peny nor pater noster shoulde euer haue made Nurse
once to open hir mouth in the cause.   45

PO   No of honestie, I pray you, who first brought him into my
chamber? who first taught him the way to my bed but you? fie
Nourse fie, neuer speake of it for shame, you will make me
tell a wise tale anone.

BA   And haue I these thanks for my good wil? why then I see   50
wel I shall be counted the cause of all mishappe.

PO   Nay rather the author of my good happe (gentle Nourse)
for I would thou knewest I loue not *Dulipo*, nor any of so
meane estate, but haue bestowed my loue more worthily than
thou deemest: but I will say no more at this time.   55

BA   Then I am glad you haue changed your minde yet.

PO   Nay I neither haue changed, nor will change it.

BA   Then I vnderstande you not, how sayde you?

PO   Mary I say that I loue not *Dulipo*, nor any suche as he, and
yet I neither haue changed nor wil change my minde.   60

BA   I can not tell, you loue to lye with *Dulipo* very well: this
geare is Greeke to me: either it hangs not well togither, or I
am very dull of vnderstanding: speake plaine I pray you.

PO   I can speake no plainer, I haue sworne to ye contrary.

BA   Howe? make you so deintie to tell it Nourse, least she   65
shoulde reueale it? you haue trusted me as farre as may be, (I
may shewe to you) in things that touche your honor if they
were knowne: and make you strange to tell me this? I am sure
it is but a trifle in comparison of those things wherof heretofore you haue made me priuie.   70

PO   Well, it is of greater importance than you thinke Nourse:
yet would I tell it you vnder condition and promise that you
shall not tell it agayne, nor giue any signe or token to be sus-
pected that you know it.

BA   I promise you of my honestie, say on.   75

PO   Well heare you me then: this yong man whome you haue
always taken for *Dulipo*, is a noble borne *Sicilian*, his right
name *Erostrato*, sonne to *Philogano*, one of the worthiest men
in that countrey.

BA   How *Erostrato*? is it not our neighbour, whiche ___?   80

PO   Holde thy talking nourse, and harken to me, that I may ex-
plane the whole case vnto thee. The man whome to this day
you haue supposed to be *Dulipo*, is (as I say) *Erostrato*, a gentleman that came from *Sicilia* to studie in this Citie, & euen
at his first arriuall met me in the street, fel enamored of me, 85
& of suche vehement force were the passions he suffred, that
immediatly he cast aside both long gowne and bookes, & determined on me only to apply his study. And to the end he

The
first s
pose
grow
of all
the s
poses

64: ye: the

might the more cõmodiously bothe see me and talke with me,
he exchanged both name, habite, clothes and credite with his 90
seruãt *Dulipo* (whom only he brought with him out of *Sicilia*)
and so with the turning of a hand, of *Erostrato* a gentleman,
he became *Dulipo* a seruing man, and soone after sought
seruice of my father, and obteyned it.

BA   Are you sure of this? 95

PO   Yea out of doubt: on the other side *Dulippo* tooke vppon
him the name of *Erostrato* his maister, the habite, the credite,
bookes, and all things needefull to a studente, and in shorte
space profited very muche, and is nowe esteemed as you see.

BA   Are there no other *Sicylians* heere: nor none that passe this 100
way, which may discouer them?

PO   Very fewe that passe this way, and fewe or none that tarrie
heere any time.

BA   This hath been a straunge aduenture: but I pray you howe
hang these thinges togither? that the studente whom you say 105
to be the servant, and not the maister, is become an earnest
suter to you, and requireth you of your father in mariage?

PO   That is a pollicie deuised betweene them, to put Doctor
Dotipole out of conceite: the olde dotarde, he that so instantly
dothe lye vpon my father for me. But looke where he comes, 110
as God helpe me it is he, out vpon him, what a luskie yonker
is this? yet I had rather be a Noonne a thousande times, than
be combred with suche a Coystrell.

BA   Daughter you haue reason, but let vs go in before he come
any neerer. 115

> POLYNESTA *goeth in, and* BALYA *stayeth a little whyle
> after, speaking a worde or two to the doctor, and then
> departeth.*

Scena 2.

CLEANDER, *Doctor.*   PASIPHILO, *Parasite.*

BALYA, *Nourse.*

Were these dames heere, or did mine eyes dazil?

PA   Nay fyr heere were *Polynesta* and hir nourse.

CLE   Was my *Polynesta* heere? alas I knewe hir not.

BA   <aside> He muste haue better eyesight that shoulde marry
your *Polynesta*, or else he may chaunce to ouersee the best 5
poynt in his tables sometimes.

---

111. **luskie yonker:** lusty youngster (Polynesta is being ironic)
112. **Noonne:** nun
113. **combred with such a Coystrell:** harassed with such a varlet i.e., lumbered with such
a despicable person

PA Syr it is no maruell, the ayre is very mistie too day: I my
selfe knew hir better by hir apparell than by hir face.

CLE In good fayth and I thanke God I haue mine eye sighte
goode and perfit, little worse than when I was but twentie   10
yeres olde.

PA How can it be otherwise? you are but yong.

CLE I am fiftie yeres olde.

PA <aside> He telles ten lesse than he is.

CLE What sayst thou of ten lesse?   15

PA I say I woulde haue thoughte you tenne lesse, you looke
like one of six and thirtie, or seuen and thirtie at the moste.

CLE I am no lesse than I tell.

PA You are like inough too liue fiftie more: shewe me your
hande.   20

CLE Why is *Pasiphilo* a Chiromancer?

PA What is not *Pasiphilo*? I pray you shewe mee it a little.

CLE Here it is.

PA O how straight and infracte is this line of life? you will liue
to the yeeres of *Melchisedech*.   25

CLE Thou wouldest say, *Methusalem*.

PA Why is it not all one?

CLE I perceiue you are no very good Bibler *Pasiphilo*.

PA Yes sir an excellent good Bibbeler, specially in a bottle: Oh
what a mounte of Venus here is? but this lighte serueth not   30
very well, I will beholde it an other day, when the ayre is
clearer, and tell you somewhat, peraduenture to your con-
tentation.

CLE You shal do me great pleasure: but tell me, I pray thee
Pasiphilo, whome doste thou thinke *Polynesta* liketh better,   35
Erostrato or me?

PA Why? you out of doubt: She is a gentlewoman of a noble
minde, and maketh greater accompte of the reputation she
shall haue in marrying your worship, than that poore scholer,
whose birthe and parentage God knoweth, and very fewe else.   40

CLE Yet he taketh it vpon him brauely in this countrey.

PA Yea, where no man knoweth the contrarie: but let him
braue it, bost his birth, and do what he can, the vertue and
knowledge that is within this body of yours, is worth more
than all the countrey he came from.   45

CLE It becommeth not a man to praise him selfe: but in deede
I may say, (and say truely,) that my knowledge hath stoode me
in better steade at a pinche, than coulde all the goodes in the
worlde. I came out of *Otranto* when the Turkes wonne it, and
first I came to *Padua*, after hither, where by reading, counsail-   50

43. **bost:** boast

ing, and pleading, within twentie yeares I haue gathered and
gayned as good as ten thousande Ducats.

PA   Yea mary, this is the righte knowledge: Philosophie, Poetrie,
Logike, and all the rest, are but pickling sciences in comparison to this.   55

CLE   But pyckling in deede, whereof we haue a verse:

   The trade of Lawe doth fill the boystrous bagges,
   They swimme in silke, when others royst in ragges.

PA   O excellent verse, who made it? *Virgil*?

CLE   *Virgil*? tushe it is written in one of our gloses.   60

PA   Sure who soeuer wrote it, the morall is excellent, and worthy to be written in letters of golde. But too the purpose: I
thinke you shall neuer recouer the wealth that you loste at
Otranto.

CLE   I thinke I haue dubled it, or rather made it foure times as   65
muche: but in deed, I lost mine only sonne there, a childe of
fiue yeres old.

PA   O great pitie.

CLE   Yea, I had rather haue lost al the goods in ye world.

PA   Alas, alas: by God and grafts of suche a stocke are very   70
gayson in these dayes.

CLE   I know not whether he were slayne, or the Turks toke him
and kept him as a bond slaue.

PA   Alas, I could weepe for compassion, but there is no remedy
but patience, you shall get many by this yong damsell with the   75
grace of God.

CLE   Yea, if I get hir.

PA   Get hir? why doubt you of that?

CLE   Why? hir father holds me off with delayes, so that I must
needes doubt.   80

PA   Content your selfe sir, he is a wise man, and desirous to
place his Daughter well: he will not be too rashe in hys determination, he will thinke well of the matter: and lette him
thinke, for the longer he thinketh, the more good of you shall
he thinke: whose welth? whose vertue? whose skill? or whose   85
estimation can he compare to yours in this Citie?

CLE   And hast thou not tolde him that I would make his
Daughter a dower of two thousand Ducates?

PA   Why, euen now, I came but from thence since.

CLE   What said he?   90

PA   Nothing, but that *Erostrato* had profered the like.

---

60. **gloses:** glosses, i.e., in the commentaries on our texts with a joke on specious
remarks.
71. gayson: rare

CLE   *Erostrato?* how can he make any dower, and his father yet
aliue?

PA   Thinke you I did not tell him so? yes I warrãt you, I forgot
nothing that may furder your cause: and doubte you not, *Eros-*   95
trato shal neuer haue hir vnlesse it be in a dreame.

CLE   Well gentle *Pasiphilo*, go thy wayes and tell *Damon* I require nothing but his daughter: I wil none of his goods: I shal
enrich hir of mine owne: & if this dower of two thousand
Ducates seem not sufficiẽt, I wil make it fiue hundreth more,   100
yea a thousand, or what so euer he will demaũd rather thẽ
faile: go to *Pasiphilo*, shew thy selfe frẽdly in working this
feate for me: spare for no cost, since I haue gone thus farre, I
wilbe loth to be out bidden. Go.

PA   Where shall I come to you againe?   110

CLE   At my house.

PA   When?

CLE   When thou wilte.

PA   Shall I come at dinner time?

CLE   I would byd thee to dinner, but it is a Saincts euen which   115
I haue euer fasted.

PA   <aside> Faste till thou famishe.

CLE   Harke.

PA   <aside> He speaketh of a dead mans faste.

CLE   Thou hearest me not.   120

PA   <aside> Nor thou vnderstandest me not.

CLE   I dare say thou art angrie I byd the not to dinner: but
come if thou wilte, thou shalt take such as thou findest.

PA   What? think you I know not where to dine?

CLE   Yes *Pasiphilo* thou art not to seeke.   125

PA   No be you sure, there are enowe will pray me.

CLE   That I knowe well enough *Pasiphilo*, but thou canst not be
better welcome in any place than to me, I will tarrie for thee.

PA   Well, since you will needes, I will come.

CLE   Dispatche then, and bring no newes but good.   130

PA   <aside> Better than my rewarde by the rood.

CLEANDER *exit*, PASIPHILO *restat*.

Scena iij.

*   *   *

DULIPO   Hard hap had I when I first began this vnfortunate enterprise: for I supposed the readiest medicine to my miserable
affects had bene to change name, clothes, & credite with my
servant, & to place my selfe in *Damons* seruice: thinking that
as sheuering colde by glowing fire, thurst by drinke, hunger by   5

131. **rood**: cross

pleasant repasts, and a thousande suche like passions finde
remedie by their contraries, so my restlesse desire might haue
founde quiet by continuall contemplation. But alas, I find that
only loue is vnsaciable: for as the flie playeth with the flame
till at last she is cause of hir owne decay, so the louer that   10
thinketh with kissing and colling to content his vnbrideled
apetite, is cōmonly seene the only cause of his owne consumption. Two yeeres are nowe past since (vnder the colour
of *Damons* seruice) I haue bene a sworne servant to *Cupid*: of
whom I haue receiued as much fauour & grace as euer man   15
founde in his seruice. I haue free libertie at al times to behold
my desired, to talke with hir, to embrace hir, yea (be it spoken
in secrete) to lie with hir. I reape the fruites of my desire: yet
as my ioyes abounde, euen so my paines encrease. I fare like
the couetous man, that hauing all the world at will, is neuer   20
yet content: the more I haue, the more I desire. Alas, what
wretched estate haue I brought my selfe vnto, if in the ende of
all my farre fetches, she be giuen by hir father to this olde
doting doctor, this buzard, this bribing villaine, that by so
many meanes seeketh to obtain hir at hir fathers hāds? I know 25
she loueth me best of all others, but what may that preuaile
when perforce she shalbe cōstrained to marie another? Alas,
the pleasant tast of my sugred ioyes doth yet remaine so perfect in my remēbrance, that the least soppe of sorow seemeth
more soure thā gal in my mouth. If I had neuer knowen de-   30
light, with better contentatiō might I haue passed these
dreadful dolours. And if this olde *Mumpsimus* (whom the
pockes consume) should win hir, then may I say, farewell the
pleasant talke, the kind embracings, yea farewel the sight of
my *Polynesta*: for he like a ielouse wretch will pen hir vp, that 35
I thinke the birdes of the aire shall not winne the sighte of hir.
I hoped to haue caste a blocke in his waie, by the meanes that
my servant (who is supposed to be *Erostrato*, and with my
habite and credite is wel esteemed) should proffer himself a
suter, at the least to counteruaile the doctors proffers. But my 40
maister knowing the wealth of the one, and doubting the state
of the other, is determined to be fed no longer with faire
wordes, but to accept the doctor, (whom he right well
knoweth) for his sonne in law. Wel, my seruant promised me
yesterday to deuise yet againe some newe conspiracie to driue 45
maister doctor out of conceite, and to laye a snare that the
foxe himselfe might be caught in: what it is, I knowe not, nor
I saw him not since he went about it: I will goe see if he be
within, that at least if he helpe me not, he maye yet prolong
my life for this once.   50

*   *   *

Actus .ij. Scena .j.

DULIPO.   EROSTRATO.

I thinke if I had as many eyes as *Argus*, I coulde not haue sought
a man more narrowly in euery streete and euery by lane, there
are not many Gentlemen, scholers, nor Marchauntes in the
Citie of *Ferara*, but I haue mette with them, excepte him:
peraduenture hee is come home an other way: but looke where   5
he commeth at the last.

ERO   In good time haue I spied my good maister.

DU   For the loue of God call me *Dulipo* (not master,) main-
tayne the credite that thou haste hitherto kepte, and let me
alone.   10

ERO   Yet sir let me sometimes do my duetie vnto you, especially
where no body heareth.

DU   Yea, but so long the Parat vseth to crie knappe in sporte,
that at the last she calleth hir maister knaue in earnest: so
long you will vse to call me master, that at the last we shall be   15
heard. What newes?

ERO   Good.

DU   In deede?

ERO   Yea excellent, we haue as good as won the wager.

DU   Oh, how happie were I if this were true?   20

ERO   Heare you me, yesternight in the euening I walked out,
and founde *Pasiphilo*, and with small entreating I had him
home to supper, where by suche meanes as I vsed, he became
my great friend, and tolde me the whole order of our aduer-
saries determination: yea and what *Damon* doth intende to do   25
also, and hath promised me that frõ time to time, what he can
espie he will bring me word of it.

DU   I can not tel whether you know him or no, he is not to trust
vnto, a very flattering and a lying knaue.

ERO   I know him very well, he can not deceiue me: and this   30
that he hath told me I know must needes be true.

DU   And what was it in effect?

ERO   That *Damon* had purposed to giue his daughter in
mariage to this doctor, vpõ the dower that he hath profered.

DU   Are these your good newes? your excellent newes?   35

ERO   Stay a whyle, you will vnderstande me before you heare
me.

DU   Well, say on.

---

2. **narrowly**: carefully
13. **Parat**: Parrot; **knappe**: snap!
34. **dower**: dowry

ERO   I answered to that, I was ready to make hir the lyke dower.

DU   Well sayde.

ERO   Abide, you heare not the worst yet.

DU   O God, is there any worsse behinde?

ERO   Worsse? why what assurance coulde you suppose that I might make without some special consent from *Philogano* my father?

DU   Nay you can tell, you are better scholer than I.

ERO   In deede you haue lost your time: for the books that you tosse now a dayes, treate of smal science.

DU   Leaue thy iesting, and proceede.

ERO   I sayd further, that I receyued letters lately from my father, whereby I vnderstoode that he woulde be heere very shortly to performe all that I had profered: therefore I required him to request *Damon* on my behalf, that he would stay his promise to the doctor for a fourtnight or more.

DU   This is somewhat yet, for by this meanes I shal be sure to linger and liue in hope one fourtnight longer: but, at the fourthnights ende when *Philogano* commeth not, how shall I then do? yea and though he came, howe may I any way hope of his consent, when he shall see, that to follow this amorous enterprise, I haue set aside all studie, all remembraunce of my duetie, and all dread of shame. Alas, alas, I may go hang my selfe.

ERO   Comforte your selfe man, and trust in me: there is a salue for euery sore, and doubt you not, to this mischeefe we shall finde a remedie.

DU   O friend reuiue me, that hitherto since I first attempted this matter haue bene continually dying.

ERO   Well harken a while then: this morning I tooke my horse and rode into the fieldes to solace my self, and as I passed the foorde beyonde *S. Anthonies* gate, I met at the foote of the hill a gentleman riding with two or three men: and as me thought by his habite and his lookes, he should be none of the wisest. He saluted me, and I him: I asked him from whence he came, and whither he would? he answered that he had come from *Venice*, then from *Padua*, nowe was going to *Ferrara*, and so to his countrey, which is *Scienna*: As soone as I knewe him to be a *Scenese*, sodenly lifting vp mine eyes, (as it were with an admiration) I sayd vnto him, are you a *Scenese*, and come to *Ferrara*? why not, sayde he: quoth I (halfe and more with a trembling voyce) know you the daunger that should ensue if you be knowne in *Ferrara* to be a *Scenese*? he more than halfe amased, desired me earnestly to tell him what I ment.

DU   I vnderstande not wherto this tendeth.

---

49. iesting: jesting

ERO   I beleeue you: but harken to me.

DU   Go too then.   85

ERO   I answered him in this sorte: Gentleman, bycause I haue
heretofore founde very curteous entertaynement in your
countrey, (beeing a studēt there,) I accompt my self as it were
bounde to a *Scenese*: and therefore if I knewe of any
mishappe towards any of that countrey, God forbid but I   90
should disclose it: and I maruell that you knewe not of the in-
iurie that your countreymen offered this other day to the Em-
bassadours of Counte *Hercules*.

DU   What tales he telleth me: what appertayne these to me?

ERO   If you will harken a whyle, you shall finde them no tales,   95
but that they appertayne to you more than you thinke for.

DU   Foorth.

ERO   I tolde him further, these Ambassadoures of Counte *Her-*
cules had dyuers Mules, Waggens, and Charettes, ladē with
diuers costly iewels, gorgeous furniture, & other things which 100
they caried as presents, (passing that way) to the king of
Naples: the which were not only stayd in *Sciene* by the officers
whom you cal Customers, but serched, ransacked, tossed &
turned, & in the end exacted for tribute, as if they had bene
the goods of a meane marchaunt.   105

DU   Whither the diuell wil he? is it possible that this geare ap-
pertaine any thing to my cause? I finde neither head nor foote
in it.

ERO   O how impaciēt you are: I pray you stay a while.

DU   Go to yet a while then.   110

ERO   I proceeded, that vpon these causes the Duke sent his
Chauncelor to declare the case vnto the Senate there, of
whome he had the moste vncurteous answere that euer was
heard: whervpon he was so enraged with all of that countrey,
that for reuenge he had sworne to spoyle as many of them as 115
euer should come to *Ferara*, and to sende them home in their
dublet and their hose.

DU   And I pray thee how couldest thou vpon the sudden deuise
or imagine suche a lye? and to what purpose?

ERO   You shall heare by and by a thing as fitte for our purpose,   120
as any could haue happened.

DU   I would fayne heare you conclude.

ERO   You would fayne leape ouer the stile, before you come at
the hedge: I woulde you had heard me, and seene the gestures
that I enforced to make him beleeue this.   125

DU   I beleeue you, for I knowe you can counterfet wel.

ERO   Further I sayde, the duke had charged vpon great penal-
ties, that the Inholders and vitlers shoulde bring worde dayly of

---

99. **dyuers**: diverse, various
128. **vitlers**: victualers, i.e., food suppliers

as many *Sceneses* as came to their houses. The gentleman beeing (as I gessed at the first) a mã of smal *sapientia*, when he 130
heard these newes, would haue turned his horse an other way.

DU By likelyhoode he was not very wise when hee would
beleeue that of his countrey, which if it had bene true euery
man must needes haue knowen it.

ERO Why not? when he had not beene in his countrey for a 135
moneth paste, and I tolde him this had hapned within these
seuen dayes.

DU Belike he was of small experience.

ERO I thinke, of as litle as may be: but beste of all for our purpose, and good aduenture it was, that I mette with such an 140
one. Now harken I pray you.

DU Make an ende I pray thee.

ERO He, as I say, when he hard these words, would haue
turned the bridle: and I fayning a countenance as though I
were somewhat pensiue and carefull for him, paused a while, 145
& after with a great sighe saide to him: Gentleman, for the
curtesie that (as I said) I haue found in your countrey, & bicause your affaires shall be the better dispatched, I will finde
the meanes to lodge you in my house, and you shal say to euery mã, that you are a *Sicilian* of *Cathanea*, your name 150
Philogano, father to me that am in deede of that countrey and
citie, called here *Erostrato*. And I (to pleasure you) will (during your abode here) do you reuerence as you were my father.

DU Out vpon me, what a grosse hedded foole am I? now I perceiue whereto this tale tendeth. 155

ERO Well, and how like you of it?

DU Indifferently, but one thing I doubt.

ERO What is that?

DU Marie, that when he hath been here twoo or three dayes,
he shal heare of euery man that there is no such thing be- 160
twene the Duke and the Towne of *Sciene*.

ERO As for that let me alone, I doe entertaine and will entertaine him so well, that within these two or three daies I will
disclose vnto him all the whole matter, and doubte not but to
bring him in for performance of as muche as I haue promised 165
to *Damon*: for what hurte can it be to him, when he shall
binde a strange name and not his owne?

DU What, thinke you he will be entreated to stande bounde for
a dower of two thousand Ducates by the yeere?

ERO Yea why not, (if it were ten thousande) as long as he is not 170
in deede the man that is bound?

DU Well, if it be so, what shall we be the neerer to our purpose?

---

130. **mã**: man; **sapienta**: wisdom
150. **mã**: man

ERO   Why? when we haue done as muche as we can, how can
we doe any more?   175

DU   And where haue you left him?

ERO   At the Inne, bicause of his horses: he and his men shall
lie in my house.

DU   Why brought you him not with you?

ERO   I thought better to vse your aduise first.   180

DU   Well, goe take him home, make him all the cheere you can,
spare for no cost, I will alowe it.

ERO   Content, looke where he commeth.

DU   Is this he? goe meete him, by my trouthe he lookes euen
lyke a good soule, he that fisheth for him, mighte bee sure to   185
catche a cods heade: I will rest here a while to discipher him.

> EROSTRATO *espieth the Scenese and goeth towards him:*
> DULIPO *standeth aside.*

*   *   *

ANONYMOUS

From A Merry Jest of a Shrewd and Curst Wife Lapped in Morel's Skin, for Her Good Behavior c. 1550†

Listen friends, and hold you still,
Abide a while and dwell:
A merry jest tell you I will,
And how that it befell.
As I went walking upon a day,   5
Among my friends to sport:
To an hour I took the way,
To rest me for my comfort.

A great feast was kept there than,
And many one, was thereat: 10
With wives and maidens and many a good man,
That made good game and chat.
It befell then at that tide,
An honest man was there:
A cursed Dame sat by his side,   15
That often did him dere.

---

187. **cods heade**: an old codger
† Transcription based on 1580 edition reproduced on Early English Books Online.
16. **dere**: vex.

His wife she was I tell you plain,
This dame ye may me trow:
To play the master she would not lain,
And make her husband bow   20
At every word that she did speak,
To be peace he was full fain:
Or else she would take him on the cheek,
Or put him to other pain.

When she did wink, he dared not stir,   25
Nor play wherever he went:
With friend or neighbor to make good cheer,
When she her brows bent.
These folk had two maidens faire and free,
Which were their daughters dear: 30
This is true, believe you me,
Of conditions, was none their peer.

The youngest was meek and gentle iwis,
Her fathers condition she had:
The eldest her mothers withouten miss,   35
Sometime frantic and sometimes mad.
The father had his pleasure in the one always,
And glad he was her to behold:
The mother in the other, this is no nay,
For in all her cursedness she made her bold.   40

And at the last she was, in faith,
As curst as her mother in word and deed:
Her mischievous pageants sometime to play,
Which caused her father's heart to bleed.
For he was woe and nothing glad,   45
And of her would fain be rid:
He wished to God that some man her had,
But yet to marriage he dared her not bid.

Full many there came the youngest to have,
But her father was loath her to forgo: 50
None there came the eldest to crave,
For fear it should turn them to woe.

18. **trow:** believe.
19. **lain:** pretend.
22. **fain:** willing.
33. **iwis:** indeed.
35. **withouten miss:** without doubt.
39. **this is no nay:** cannot be contradicted.
46. **fain:** willingly, gladly.

The father was loathe any man to beguile,
For he was true and just withal:
Yet there came one within a while,   55
That her demanded in the hall.

Another there came right soon also,
The youngest to have he would be fain:
Which made the father's heart full woe,
That he and the youngest should part in twain.   60
But the mother was fell, and might her not see,
Wherefore of her she would have been rid:
The young man full soon she granted pardie,
Great gold and silver with her she bid.

Saying full soon, he would her have,   65
And wedded they were short tale to make:
The Father said, "So God me save,
For heaviness and sorrow, I tremble and quake."
Also his heart was in great care,
How he should bestow the eldest iwis: 70
Which should make his purse full bare,
Of her he would be rid by heaven's bliss.

As hap was that this young man should,
Desire the eldest without fail:
To marriage he said full fain he would,   75
That he might her have for his avail.
The Father said with words anon,
"Gold and silver I would thee give:
If thou her marry, by sweet Saint John,
But thou shouldst repent it all thy life.   80

She is conditioned I tell thee plain,
Most like a fiend, this is no nay:
Her Mother doth teach her, withouten lain,
To be master of her husband another day.

---

58. **fain:** willing.
61. **fell:** ruthless.
63. **pardie:** by God, assuredly.
64. **she bid:** i.e. her mother put up as a dowry.
70. **iwis:** indeed.
71. **full:** completely.
73. **As hap was:** it happened.
75. **full fain:** very willingly.
76. **avail:** at my disposal.
81. **plain:** complain.
82. **no nay:** beyond contradiction.
83. **lain:** pretence.

If thou shouldst her marry, and with her not agree,   85
Her mother thou shouldst, have always in thy top:
By night and day, that shouldst vex thee,
Which sore would stick, then in thy crop.

And I could not amend it by God of might,
For I dare not speak my self for my life: 90
Sometime among, be it wrong or right,
I let her have all for fear of strife.
If I ought say, she doth me treat,
Except I let her have her will:
As a child that should be beat,   95
She will me charm; the devil her kill.

Another thing thou must understand,
Her mother's good will thou must have also:
If she be thy friend, by sea or by land,
Amiss with thee, then can it not go.   100
For she doth love with all her mind,
And would not see her fare amiss:
If thou to her darling could be kind,
Thou couldst not want by heaven's bliss.

If thou to the mother, now wilt seek,   105
Behave thy self then like a man:
And show thy self both humble and meek,
But when thou hast her doe what thou can.
Thou wotest what I said to thee before,
I counsel thee mark my words well: 110
It were great pity, thou wert forlore.
With such a devilish fiend of hell."

"I care not for that," the young man said,
"If I can get her mother's good will:
I would be glad to have that maid,   115
Me thinketh she is withouten evil."
"Alas good man I am sorry for thee,
That thou wilt cast thy self away,
Thou art so gentle and so free.
Thou shalt never tame her I dare well say.   120

But I have done I will say no more,
Therefore farewell and go thy way:

85. **in thy top:** coming down on you.
88. **crop craw:** i.e. stuck in your throat.
109. **Thou wotest:** thou knowest; you know.
111. **thou wert:** you were; **forlore:** destroyed.

Remember what I said to thee before,
And beware of repentance another day."

[After the marriage of the young man to the shrewish daughter]

"I was never so vexed this time beforne,
As I am now of this wife alone:
A vengeance on her that ever she was borne,   775
For she maketh me often full woebegone.
And I cannot tell, where me to turn
For me to wend, by God in fay
Which cause me often for to mourn
Or yet to know what for to say.   780

"I am worse, then mad or wood,
And yet I am loathe with her to begin,
I fear me I shall never make her good
Except I do wrap her in black Morel's skin,
That can no more draw at plough nor cart,   785
It shall be to late to call for her kin,
When she begineth once for to smart,
For little ease thereby she shall win.

"Morel is old, he can labor no more,
Nor doe no good but always eat,   790
I trow I have kept him thus long in store,
To work a charm that shall be feat.
The whoreson is blind and lame also
Behind and before, he cannot steer,
When he from the stable to the street should go,   795
He falleth down, right then in the mire.

"Yet I am loathe him for to kill
For he hath done me good service by now,
But if my wife fulfill not my will
I must him flea by God I trow   800
But at this point now will I be,
I will be master as it is reason,
And make her subject unto me
For she must learn a new lesson.

773. **beforne:** before.
778. **fay:** faith.
784. **Morel's skin:** the hide of his old horse.
791. **trow:** believe.
800. **trow:** believe.

"Her father did warn me of this before,   805
How I should it find in every degree:
But I did take it for half a scorn,
And would not believe him then pardie.
But now I perceive it very well,
He did it for good will iwis: 810
Wherefore I think that Morels fell,
Must mend all thing that is amiss.

"Thus he that will not believe his friend,
As her dear father was unto me:
He is worthy for to find,   815
Always great pain and misery.
But I may not choose him to believe,
For the deed doth prove himself in fay:
Ever she is ready me for to grieve,
And thinks to continue so always.   820

"But now I will home to prove her mind,
And see what welcome I shall have:
She may be to me, so unkind,
That she shall repent it, so God me save.
For if I should of her complain,   825
Folk would me mock, and give me scorn:
And say I were worthy of this pain,
Because it was she wed me so well beforne."

*How the good man was welcomed, when he returned home
again.*

The good man came riding to the gate,
And knocked as he had been wood: 830
His servant right soon did meet him thereat,
And bid him welcome with right mild mood.
The master said, "What doth my dame now?
Is she as frantic yet as she was:
Than will I tame her I make God avow,   835
And make her sing full loud alas.

"Where art thou wife? Shall I have any meat,
Or am I not so welcome unto thee
That at my commandment I shall ought get?
I pray thee heartily soon tell thou me.   840

808. pardie: assuredly.
810. iwis: certainly.
818. fay: faith.
828. beforne: before.

If thou doe not serve me and that anon,
I shall thee show mine anger iwis:
I swear by God and by Saint John,
Thy bones will I swaddle so have I bliss."

Forth she came, as brim a boar   845
And like a dog she berated him then:
Saying thus: "I set no store,
By thee thou wretch thou art no man,
Get thee hence out of my sight,
For meat nor drink thou getest none here: 850
I swear to thee by Mary bright,
Of me thou getest here no good cheer."

"Well, wife," he said thou dost me compel,
To do that thing, that I were loathe:
If I bereave Morel of his old fell: 855
Thou shalt repent it by the faith now goeth.
For I see well that it will no better be,
But in it thou must, after the new guise:
It had been better so mote I thee,
That thou hadst not begun this enterprise."   860

How the good man caused Morel to be slain and the hide salted,
to lay his wife therein to sleep.

"Now will I begin, my wife to tame,
That all the world shall it know,
I would be loathe her for to shame,
Though she do not care, ye may me trow.
Yet will I her honestly regard,   865
And it preserve wherever ye may,
But Morel that is in yonder yard,
His hide therefore he must lose in fay."

And so he commanded anon,
To slay old Morel his great horse: 870
And flay him then, the skin from the bone,
To wrap it about his wife's white corpse.
Also he commanded of a birchen tree,
Rods to be made of a good great heap:

---

842. **iwis:** certainly.
845. **brim:** fierce.
855. **fell:** hide.
859. **mote:** must.
868. **fay:** faith.
873. **birchen:** birch.

And swear by dear God in Trinity,   875
His wife in his cellar should skip and leap.

"The hide must be salted then," he said eke,
"Because I would not have it stink:
I hope herewith she will be meek,
For this I trow will make her shrink.   880
And bow at my pleasure, when I her bed,
And obey my commandments both loud and still,
Or else I will make her body bleed,
And with sharp rods beat her my fill."

Anon with that to her he began to call,   885
She bid abide in the devil's name:
"I will not come what so befall,
Sit still with sorrow and mickle shame.
Thou shalt not rule me as pleaseth thee,
I will well thou know by God's dear Mother,   890
But thou shalt be ruled always by me,
And I will be master and none other."

"Wilt thou be master, dear wife in fay?
Then must we wrestle for the best game:
If thou win then may I say,   895
That I have done myself great shame.
But first I will make thee sweat, good Joan,
Red blood even to the heels adown,
And lap thee in Morel's skin alone,
That the blood shall be seen even from the crown."   900

"Sayest thou me that, thou wretched knave!
It were better thou hadst me never seen:
I swear to thee so God me save,
With my nails I will scratch out both thine eyen,
And therefore think not to touch me once,   905
For by the mass if thou begin that,
Thou shalt be handled for the nonce,
That all thy brains on the ground shall squat."

"Why then there is no remedy I see,
But needs I must doe even as I thought: 910

877. **eke:** also.
880. **trow:** believe.
888. **mickle:** much.
893. **fay:** faith.
899. **lap:** wrap.
904. **eyen:** eyes

Seeing it will none other wise be,
I will thee not spare by God that me bought.
For now I am set thee for to charm,
And make thee meek by God's might,
Or else with rods while thou art warm,   915
I shall thee scourge with reason and right."

"Now good Morel's skin,
Receive my curst wife in.

How the curst wife in Morel's skin lay,
Because she would not her husband obey.

"Now will I my sweet wife trim,
According as she deserveth to me: 920
I swear by God and by Saint Sim,
With birchen rods well beat shall she be.
And after that in Morel's salt skin,
I will her lay and full fast bind,
That all her friends, and eke her kin,   925
Shall her long seek or they her find."

Then he her met, and to her began to say,
"How sayst thou wife wilt thou be master yet?"
She swear by God's body, and by that day,
And suddenly with her fist she did him hit.   930
And defied him devil at every word,
Saying, "Precious whoreson what doest thou think?
I set not by thee a stinking turd
Thou shalt not get of me neither meat nor drink!"

"Sayest thou me that wife," quoth he. Then   935
With that in his arms he began her catch
Straight to the cellar with her he ran
And fastened the door with lock and latch
And threw the key down him beside,
Asking her than if she would obey   940
Then she said, "Nay, for all thy pride,"
But she was master and would abide always.

"Then," quoth he, "We must make a fray
And with that her clothes he began to tear
"Out upon thee whoreson!" then she did say,   945

919. **trim:** get into shape.
921. **Saint Sim:** St. Simon.
922. **birchen:** birch.

"Wilt thou rob me of all my gear
It cost thee naught thou arrant thief!"
And quickly she gat him by the head
With that she said God give thee a mischief
And them that fed thee first with bread.   950

They wrestled together thus they two
So long that the clothes asunder went
And to the ground he threw her tho
That clean from the back her smock he rent.
In every hand a rod he got,   955
And laid upon her a right good pace:
Asking of her, "What game was that?"
And she cried out, "Whoreson! Alas, alas!"

"What wilt thou do? Wilt thou kill me?
I have made thee a man of naught: 960
Thou shalt repent it, by God's pity,
That ever this deed thou hast ywrought."
"I care not for that, dame," he did say,
"Thou shalt give over or we depart
The mastership all, or all this day   965
I will not cease to make thee smart."

Ever he laid on, and ever she did cry,
"Alas, alas, that ever I was born!
Out upon thee murderer! I thee defy!
Thou hast my white skin, and my body all to torn   970
Leave off betime I counsel thee."
"Nay, by God, dame, I say not so yet,
I swear to thee, by Mary so free
We begin but now, this is the first fit."

"Once again, we must dance about   975
And then thou shalt rest in Morel's skin."
He gave her than so many a great clout
That on the ground the blood was seen.
Within a while, he cried new rods new
With that she cried full loud alas,   980
"Dance yet about dame, thou came not where it grew!"
And suddenly with that in a swoon she was.

He spied that and up he her hent,
And wrung her hard then by the nose:

953. **tho:** then.
962. **ywrought:** done.
983. **hent:** seized.

With her to Morel's skin, straight he went,   985
And therein full fast he did her close.
Within a while, she did revive,
Through the gross salt that did her smart:
She thought she should never have gone on live,
Out of Morel's skin so sore is her heart.   990

When she did spy that therein she lay,
Out of her wit she was full nie:
And to her husband then did she say,
"How canst thou do this villainy?"
"Nay how sayest thou, thou cursed wife?   995
In this foul skin I will thee keep,
During the time of all thy life,
Therein for ever to wail and weep."

With that her mood began to sink,
And said, "Dear husband, for grace I call: 1000
For I shall never sleep nor wink,
Till I get your love whatso'er befall.
And I will never to you offend,
In no manner of wise, of all my life:
Nor to do nothing that may pretend,   1005
To displease you with my wits five."

"For Father nor Mother whatsoever they say
I will not anger you by God in throne:
But glad will your commandments obey,
In presence of people and eke alone."   1010
"Well, on that condition thou shalt have,
Grace and fain bed to rest thy body in:
But if thou rage more so God me save,
I will wrap thee again in Morel's skin."

Then he took her out in his arms twain,   1015
And beheld her so piteously with blood arrayed,
"How thinkst thou wife, shall we arraign
Have such business more?" to her he said,
She answered, "Nay, my husband dear,
While I you know, and you know me,   1020
Your commandments I will both far and near,
Fulfill always in every degree."

992. nie: near.
1010. eke: also.
1012. fain: gladly.

"Well then, I promise thee by God even now,
Between thee and me shall never be strife,
If thou to my commandments quickly bow   1025
I will the cherish all the days of my life."
In bed she was laid and healed full soon,
As fair and clear as she was before,
What he her bid was quickly done,
To be diligent iwis she took no scorn.   1030

Then was he glad, and thought in his mind
"Now have I done, myself great good,
And her also, we shall it find,
Though I have shed part of her blood.
For as me think, she will be meek: 1035
Therefore I will her Father and Mother,
Bid to guest, now the next week,
And of our neighbors, many other."

How the good man did bid her Father and Mother to guest, and
many of his neighbors, that they might see his wife's patience.

Great pain he made his wife to take,
Against the day that they should come: 1040
Of them was none that there did lack,
I dare well say unto my doom.
The Father and Mother and neighbors all.
Did thither come to make good cheer,
Soon they were set in general,   1045
The wife was diligent as did appear.

Father and Mother was welcome then,
And so were they all in good fay:
The husband sate there like a man,
The wife did serve them all that day.   1050
The good man commanded what he would have,
The wife was quick at hand,
"What now?" thought the Mother, "This arrant knave,
Is master as I understand."

"What may this mean?" Then she began think,   1055
"That my daughter so diligent is:
Now can I neither eat nor drink,
Till I it know by heaven's bliss."

1030. **iwis:** indeed.
1048. **fay:** faith.
1049. **sate:** sat.

When her daughter came again,
To serve at the board as her husband bade,   1060
The Mother stared with her eyen twain,
Even as one that had been mad.

All the folk, that at the board sate,
Did her behold then everyone:
The Mother [up] from the board her got,   1065
Following her daughter and that anon,
And in the kitchen she her found,
Saying unto her in this wise:
"Daughter thou shalt well understand,
I did not teach thee after this guise."   1070

"Ah, good Mother, ye say full well,
All things with me is not as ye ween:
If ye had been in Morel's fell,
As well as I it should be seen."
"In Morel's fell. What devil is that?"   1075
"Marry, Mother I will it you show:
But beware that you come not thereat,
Lest you your self then do beshrew.

"Come down now in this cellar so deep,
And Morel's skin there you shall see: 1080
With many a rod that hath made me to weep,
When the blood ran down fast by my knee."
The Mother this beheld and cried out, "Alas!"
And ran out of the cellar as she had been wood,
She came to the table where the company was,   1085
And said, "Out whoreson; I will see thy heart blood."

"Peace, good Mother, or so have I bliss,
Ye must dance else as did my wife:
And in Morel's skin lie, that well salted is,
Which you should repent all the days of your life."   1090
All they that were there, held with the young man,
And said he did well in every manner degree,

1060. **board**: table.
1070. **guise**: fashion.
1072. **ye ween**: you think.
1073. **fell**: hide.
1075. **fell**: hide.
1076. **Marry**: by Mary (an oath).
1078. **beshrew**: become perverted.
1084. **as she had been wood**: in a state of shocked insensibility.

When dinner was done, they departed all then,
The mother no longer durst there be.

The Father abode last and was full glad,   1095
And gave his children his blessing iwis,
Saying the young man full well done had,
And merrily departed without amiss,
This young man was glad ye may be sure,
That he had brought his wife to this,   1100
God give us grace in rest to endure,
And hereafter to come unto his bliss.

Thus was Morel slain out of his skin.
To charm a shrew so have I bliss:
Forgive the young man if he did sin,   1105
But I think he did nothing amiss.
He did all thing even for the best.
As it well proved then,
God save our wives from Morel's nest,
I pray you say all, "Amen."   1110

Thus endeth the jest of Morel's skin,
Where the curst wife was lapped in,
Because she was of a shrewd leer.
Thus was she served in this manner.

FINIS

1096. iwis: indeed.
1114. served: treated.

CRITICISM

LAURIE MAGUIRE

The Naming of the Shrew[†]

Of the many topics which provide a thematic arc for Shakespeare's writing, linking plays from every period and genre, the topic of names is one of the most consistent. Sometimes it is emphatically central, as in Juliet's soliloquy, "What's in a name?" This metaphysical interrogative is the heart of a play which shows the lovers' tragic attempts to escape the adversarial expectations and associations of their surnames: to be a Capulet means to "hate . . . all Montagues" (1.1.70) and vice versa. Sometimes the topic of names is subliminal, as in the tendency of characters to exemplify their names: the martial Caius Martius (whose second name instantiates the Roman god of war) or the loquacious Volumnia (whose name "indicates her passion for words"; McDonald 44) in *Coriolanus*; the appropriately named heroines of the late romances: the lost Perdita (*Winter's Tale* 3.3.33), the sea-born Marina (*Pericles* 3.3.13), the "admired Miranda" (*Tempest* 3.1.37–8) or faithful Fidele ("Thy name well fits thy faith; thy faith thy name" (*Cymbeline* 4.2.381); the jester Feste and his anti-festive opponent, Malvolio, in *Twelfth Night* (contrast the pacifist *Ben*-volio in *Romeo and Juliet*). Sometimes the interest in names is fleetingly foregrounded in a pun. In *2 Henry IV* Falstaff dismisses the (anachronistically) disruptive Pistol: "Discharge yourself of our company Pistol" (*2H4* 2.4.106). *1 Henry IV* bears the paronomastic marker of Falstaff's earlier identity as Oldcastle when Hal addresses him as "My old lad of the castle" (1.2.41–2). Sometimes names resonate ironically. In *Two Gentlemen of Verona*, as William Carroll points out, the introduction of a character "named (and with the characteristics of) Proteus into a friendship plot automatically destabilizes the genre, since true friendship depends absolutely on fidelity and constancy, the inverse of the protean" (31).

Naming is character creation *in parvo*. i.e., much in little. As Harry Levin says, "the *persona* begins with the name" (55). For Wellek and Warren "each appellation is a kind of vivifying, animiz-

---

† This essay was written especially for this Norton Critical Edition. Printed by permission of the author.

ing, individuating" (219). Throughout the canon, from early Shakespeare to late, names cue the topic of identity, the relation between a character's name and the creation of his or her subjectivity. Onomastics is thus a subdivision of the Elizabethan interest in language: the relation between signifier and signified, word and meaning, label and personality. Indeed Elizabethan dictionaries regularly included appendixes of proper names (places names, people names, mythological names). Names were words, and like words, they had "meaning." In 1609 John Wynborne in *The New Age of Old Names* asked rhetorically "What bee termes, but names?" (sig. B3v), and in 1655 Edward Lyford compared those who did not know the meaning of their names to those who spoke nonsense, not knowing the meaning of words (sig. A2v).

Names in literature are never neutral. David Lodge explains that "we don't expect our neighbour Mr Shepherd to look after sheep, or mentally associate him with that occupation. If he is a character in a novel, however, pastoral and perhaps biblical associations will inevitably come into play" (36). It is this onomastic predetermination—what we today would call cultural programming—which Shakespeare investigates (and his characters reject). Shakespeare's concern, like Derrida's, is "to problematize the proper name and proper (literal) meaning, the proper in general" (*Of Grammatology* lxxxiv).

Discussion of names permeates the dialogue in *The Taming of the Shrew*: characters remember, mistake, duplicate, and comment on names. The play begins with the inebriated tinker Christopher Sly mistaking a historical name. Insulted by the hostess's denigration of him as a rogue, he asserts his identity from noble lineage: "The Slys are no rogues . . . we came in with Richard Conqueror" Ind. 1.3–4). In the same scene the Lord greets his traveling players with a theatrical reminiscence about Soto, "a farmer's elder son," in which the Lord tells the actor "I have forgot your name; but sure that part / Was aptly fitted and naturally perform'd" (Ind.1.80; 82–3). One scene later Sly's new identity is heralded and reinforced by a new name:

> FIRST SERVINGMAN   Will't please *your lordship* drink a cup of sack?
>
> SECOND SERVINGMAN   Will't please *your honor* taste of these conserves?
>
> THIRD SERVINGMAN   What raiment will *your honor* wear today? (Induction 2.2–4; emphasis added)

Although Sly initially clings to his old name—"I am Christopher Sly, call not me honor nor lordship" (Induction 2.5–6)—he gradually accepts his new identity, in which he displays an interest in the way to address a wife:

SLY   What must I call her?
LORD   Madam.
SLY   Al'ce madam, or Joan madam?
LORD   Madam, and nothing else. So lords call ladies. (Induction 2.104–7)[1]

The play ends with a pun on the name of one of its central characters, Bianca, when Petruchio tells Bianca's husband: "'Twas I won the wager though you hit the white" (5.2.190). In between, the relation between name and identity is constantly asserted or tested:

Call you me daughter? (2.1.277)[2]
[Thou] feed'st me with the very name of meat. (4.3.32)
[T]his is flat knavery, to take upon you another man's name. (5.1.31)

In a crucial exchange in Act 5, Vincentio confronts Tranio (in Lucentio's attire), while Baptista tries to smooth over the fracas:

BAPTISTA   You mistake, sir, you mistake, sir. Pray what do you think is his name?
VINCENTIO   His name! as if I knew not his name! I have brought him up ever since he was three years old, and his name is Tranio. (5.1.68–70)

Vincentio clings to the belief that identity and onomastics are fixed: to be called Tranio must mean to be Tranio.

At the center of the play's investigation of name and identity is a heroine with two names: Katherine and Kate.[3] The former is the heroine's customary name but, on first meeting her, Petruchio instantly renames her ("Good morrow, Kate") and defiantly underlines his renaming: "for that's your name, I hear" (2.1.180). It is this blatantly untrue explanation which prompts Katherine's onomastic corrective: "They call me Katherine that do talk of me" (2.1.182). One may see in Petruchio's renaming an assertion of Adamic dominion over independent creatures: the control (diminution) of Katherine's name anticipates the control (reduction) of her personality. Or, if one is a twentieth-century New Critic, one may read the diminutive positively: Petruchio offers Katherine the opportunity to embrace a new identity through adopting a new name. It is not the change from Katherine to Kate which interests me

---

1. Despite this guidance, Sly immediately addresses his lady with a form of his own: "Madam wife" (Induction 2.12).
2. This question carries the same implications that a similar question ("Are you our daughter?") has in *King Lear* (1.4.218). Just as personal name is linked to identity so positional name in a relationship brings with it certain behavioral expectations appropriate to hierarchy (Weidhorn 307).
3. I exclude Katherina as a third name as it is, technically, a variant of Katherine.

here so much as the existence of dual names.[4] For though Katherine is bombarded by her abbreviation (Petruchio uses it eleven times in his first seven lines) she later slyly reasserts the full form in the controversial sun/moon scene in which she sanctions Petruchio's right to rename everything: "What you will have it named, even that it is / And so it shall be so for Katherine" (4.5.22–3). In the final scene the two forms coexist. Petruchio can encourage "Kate" to a flyting match with the widow—"To her, Kate! . . . A hundred marks, my Kate does put her down" (5.2.34; 36)—yet ninety lines later apostrophise his wife as "Katherine":

> Katherine, that cap of yours becomes you not,
> Off with that bable, throw it underfoot. (5.2.125–6)

> Katherine, I charge thee tell these headstrong women
> What duty they do owe their lords and husbands. (5.2.134–5)

No other Shakespearean heroine is binominal in this way. If name is related to identity, Katherine's two names do not make her more knowable, more identifiable, but less so.

Critics have tried to align each of Katherine's names with a set of behaviors (public/private; dutiful/independent), with Petruchio's two forms in Act 5 indicating that wives can be both independent and submissive, depending on the husband's assessment of the situation. But bifurcation in this way is not straightforward as Katherine/Kate is not the only dyad. "Kate" itself is open to dual interpretation or definition. In 3.2, for instance, Gremio uses "Kate" as a verb: "I warrant him, Petruchio is Kated" (237). His coinage summarizes Katherine's resistance to Petruchio, encapsulating Katherine's combative actions and attitudes. "Kate" thus becomes a term for set behavioral patterns, like "Herod" in *Hamlet* ("it out-Herods Herod"; *Hamlet* 3.2.13–14) or "(Au)fidius" in *Coriolanus*: "I would not have been so fidius'd for all the chests in Corioles" (2.1.130–1). But if Gremio here turns "Kate" into a generic verb with negative associations, Petruchio uses "Kate" as a generic noun with a different set of associations. In their first meeting he puns on the noun "cate": "For dainties are all Kates" (2.1.187). The term works, like Gremio's, as generic generalization and summary, this time of the "bonny Kate," the "prettiest," the "super-dainty Kate" of the previous three lines, and an anticipation of his concluding threat (or offer) of generalized domestication: "a Kate / Conformable as other household Kates" (2.1.270). The point is not that one correlation is right and the other wrong—"Kate" equals bad behaviour (Gremio's correlation) or gentle manners (Petru-

---

4. Of interest also is the way critics and editors regularly deny Katherine her most basic request—her full name—but that is another topic.

chio's correlation)—but that the name is associated by both with Katherine's behavior rather than with her identity. We are supposed to infer identity from behavior, of course: a character who acts shrewishly must *be* a shrew (just as one who speaks dutifully must be dutiful). But performance rather than identity is under investigation throughout the play. Nowhere is this more visible than in the last scene, in Katherine's famous lengthy speech of (apparent) submission to her new husband.

Critical debate (like actorly interpretation) tends to polarize into opposed interrogatives: is this speech sincere or not? The answer to this binary question depends on another binary, to do with the outcome of the play's taming plot: is Katherine tamed (and thus means what she says, her earlier character extinguished) or is she resistant (and the speech is ironic)? Answers in favor of either of these questions find ample support: 40-plus lines of irony are too much to sustain, therefore the speech is genuine; Petruchio cannot want a tamed wife, therefore it is ironic; Katherine is simply saying she loves this man so much she would do anything for him, therefore it is genuine (and inoffensively so); the male behavior Katherine describes does not correspond to the actions of any of the play's male characters, therefore the speech is ironic; and so on.

These questions, and the answers to them, depend on a precise correlation of behavior with identity, of speech with conviction. The speech is or is not (genuine/playful); it cannot be both. But if the focus is not on meaning but on performance, the ground shifts slightly as theater productions often make clear, with actresses increasingly exposing the gap between (temporary) ad hoc performance and (permanent) identity. A production at the Royal Shakespeare Theatre in Stratford in 1995–96, directed by Gale Edwards, foregrounded the performative aspects of Katherine's speech metatheatrically, the culmination of a production which self-consciously stressed performativity throughout. Tranio was given every understudy's dream—unexpected promotion to the leading romantic male (and was slightly piqued at the end not to be able to retain this role). His first appearance as one of Bianca's suitors, in the bidding scene of 2.1, was a source of considerable thespian stress (after which he had to resort to his asthma inhaler). Petruchio's confident boasting about his ability to handle Katherine—the blustering autobiographical "have I not in my time heard lions roar?" of 1.2.195—was clearly an audition piece, one with which his man Grumio was so wearily familiar that he could accompany all Petruchio's gestures mechanically. With this background, Katherine's last speech, then, was staged in terms of theater rather than gender: not a case of female submission but of theatrical triumph. Katherine got the moment she, as an actress, had been waiting for: the opportunity to upstage Petruchio.

The curtain dropped almost immediately—with such an interpretation one could not play the last lines. A production by the Oxford Stage Company (OSC) in 2006 rooted itself in the theatrical even more obviously and thematically, exploring life as a series of roles. As the director Chris Pickles wrote in the programme: "Isn't life about pretending? Not necessarily literally pretending to be another person, but don't we all get through life by partially hiding who we really are and what we really feel?" I want to turn now to this production and what it can teach us about interpreting Katherine's dual names.

In this production the onstage theater company was "a man down" (at moments of personnel pressure, *sotto voce* ad libs and scripted extra-textual explanations occurred). Consequently Sly was pressed into service in situations of increasing theatrical desperation (for the onstage company) and theatrical challenge (for the real actor): he played Baptista, Grumio, the tailor, the pedant, Vincentio, the jailer, and the widow. This doubling [*sic*] led to a scene in which Sly had to play four roles simultaneously (5.1): the Pedant-impersonating-Vincentio confronted by the real Vincentio, interrupted by Baptista and threatened with incarceration by the jailer. The scene's increasing theatrical challenges led to a climax of thespian exasperation when Sly-as-Baptista instructs Sly-as-jailer to arrest Sly-as-pedant and carry himself off to prison; Sly-as-Sly momentarily balked at the impossibility of the request. The OSC had primed us well for this scene: in watching Sly perform throughout, in focusing on his performance(s), we were watching role-play rather than identity, action rather than ontology.

Although Sly warmed to the unfamiliar and initially alarming experience of acting, he slipped in and out of his role as Sly. Sly-as-Baptista was visibly taken aback by the virago Katherine when she barked her first lines in his face, "I pray you, sir, is it your will / To make a stale of me amongst these mates?" (1.1.57–8). Her imperative "Father, be quiet" at 3.2.209 when Baptista has said nothing had Sly checking his script in bewilderment lest he have missed a line, an action he repeated in different circumstances as Sly/Vincentio in 4.5: here, when Petruchio greeted Vincentio as "gentle mistress," Sly scanned his text to correct what he believed to be his misunderstanding of the plot. Instinctive real-life honesty overtook Sly's theatrical effort in 4.2 when Tranio asked him (Sly-as-Pedant) "[K]now you one Vincentio?" "I know him not," Sly replied, to the company's onstage alarm before quickly correcting his blunder: "BUT—I *have* heard of him" (4.2.97–8).[5] The stress on the con-

---

5. Even the professionals could be tricked in this way. Petruchio's series of boasts beginning "Have I not in my time heard lions roar . . .?" (1.2.195 ff.) was so convincing that an awe-struck Hortensio asked *"Have you?"*

trasting conjunction and the auxiliary verb turned Shakespeare's text into an improvised rescue line (a rescue of which Sly-as-actor was visibly proud). As the tailor in 4.3, Sly had three attempts at his opening line—"Here is the cap your worship did bespeak" (4.3.63)—before finding an interpretation and accent which met the company's approval.

The importance of onomastics to identity was underlined throughout this production in stage business with names. Sly initially hesitated over the unfamiliar names in his script: "If you [*pause*], Hortensio / Or, Signior [*See-nee-or*] Gremio" (1.1.95–6). Two lines into his first speech as Baptista, Sly tells the suitors of his resolve not to marry his "youngest daughter" before the "elder." Accompanied by two actresses he had no means of knowing which was which; the actresses tried to assist (a small squeak at "youngest," a cough at "elder") but the information did not prevent Sly initially moving toward Bianca on his following line, "If either of you both love Katherina" (1.1.52). Lucentio-as-Cambio persistently responded to his own name when it was addressed to Tranio-as-Lucentio or voiced by others, even to the point of bounding in from offstage for an apparently missed cue:

> PETRUCHIO   What is his name?
> VINCENTIO   Lucentio, gentle sir. (4.5.59)
> LUCENTIO   [*entering in haste*]: Yes?

(Lucentio's onomastic instincts applied logically in reverse: he failed to respond to Cambio.)

The play is, of course, structured to call attention to the theatrical throughout for it is not just one play-within-a-play but a series. When Baptista and his daughters enter, Lucentio expresses surprise: "What company is this?" Tranio suggests, improbably, that it is "some show to welcome us to town" (1.1.46, 47) and the two stand aside to watch the performance of the Minolas. In 1.2 Hortensio, Grumio, and Petruchio "stand by awhile" (136) to watch Gremio and Cambio. Hijacking the pedant in Act 4, Tranio tells him "In all these circumstances I'll instruct you; / Go with me to clothe you as becomes you" (4.2.121–2), a line one imagines being spoken regularly offstage in the South Bank theaters; in 4.4 the pedant practices his role as Vincentio (3–5). In 5.1 when the two Vincentios come to blows Petruchio and Katherine "stand aside and see the end of this controversy" (5.1.50–51).[6] One of the play's sources, Gascoigne's drama *Supposes*, is similarly attentive to over-

---

6. This plurality of inset dramas means that the editorial indication "Aside" is unusually problematic. Aside to whom? To which audience? In her forthcoming Arden 3 edition Barbara Hodgdon eschews all asides.

hearings and over-observings, as well as to characters' performance. Boasting of his success in beguiling the traveling Sicilian, Dulippo stresses his theatrical gestures, facial expressions, pauses, and sighs: "I would you had heard mee, and seene the gestures that I enforced to make him beleeve this" (sig. C6v); "I feigning a countenance as thogh I were somewhat pensive and carefull for him, paused a while, and after with a great sigh said . . ." (sig. C7r).

Juliet Dusinberre observes another kind of inset performance in the play: one character's observation of him or her *self*. Analyzing Bianca's ability to turn on tears as required (a skill of which Kate accuses her at 1.1.78–9) and the boy player's use of an onion in a handkerchief when playing a stereotyped woman's part, Dusinberre comments:

> The boy feigns the woman's sorrow, and the woman's sorrow is feigned. . . . Disguise makes explicit in women what one writer describes as "an ambiguity which corresponded to an ambiguity in the self, divided between surveyor and surveyed." . . . The woman observes her disguised self. But when the woman is played by a boy, she watches two people, herself disguised and the boy who plays her. (248)

This observation about doubleness, detachment, and disguise is made in the context of an argument about gender; but it could equally be part of an argument about theater. (And one cannot separate the two: gender is a performance, as the success of recent all-male productions of Shakespeare show.) And it accords perfectly with Chris Pickles's observation (cited above) that we negotiate life through performance, through hiding or acting a part; the natural consequence of this is Dusinberre's conclusion that we observe ourselves performing, are aware of our role playing.

Nowhere was the OSC Sly more aware of his situation as improvising actor than in 5.1, his key scene of multiple identities. The action found its climax in Vincentio's response to Tranio's summoning of an officer. The officer is instructed "Carry this mad knave to the jail. Father Baptista, I charge you see that he be forthcoming" to which Vincentio objects "Carry me to the jail?" (5.1.79). He objects because he is the innocent party. Sly-as-Vincentio, however, protested not about his character's innocence but about the impossibility of the stage business for him as Sly. It was not judicial outrage but theatrical incredulity which lay behind his wail, "Carry *me* to the jail?" But he rose to the challenge, twisting his own arm up behind his back and hitting himself on the head with his truncheon as he frogmarched himself away.

Sly's understanding of, and theatrical grasp of, the complexities of this scene as he realized that he had consecutive speeches as different characters (speeches, moreover which required a change of location from up a stepladder, peering as "*out of the window*" [TLN 2397] back down to ground level and therefore always involved a pause in dialogue while we watched the actor maneuvering role and space) meant that the company bravely eschewed this scene's potential for classic knockabout farce. Farce is dependent on speed, on quick-fire contradictions, on moving the action so quickly that the audience and onstage characters have no time to think. But here we had ample time to think. The scene was helplessly funny, as it invariably is in performance, but for unusually different reasons. In this scene of plural names for one character—Baptista, two Vincentios, the Jailer—we watched not the characters Sly was acting but Sly acting the characters. In Paul de Man's terms, we watched the dancer not the dance. Multiply nameable but completely unknowable, Sly's thespian dilemma foregrounded the world of impersonation, the world of role-play, the world of anonymity.

I use anonymity here not in its etymological sense but in the philosophical sense pioneered by Maurice Natanson when he declared: "Anonymity, in general parlance, means the state of being unknown, without identity, a kind of hiddenness" (22). Natanson's discussion of anonymity links the unknowable to role-play. All individuals have names but most of our daily business is conducted with people as roles rather than as individuals: the bus conductor, the bank teller, the postal clerk. Anonymity occurs not just because or when these named characters function anonymously in our world but because or when they function as functions. Anonymity for Natanson means seeing people not as agents but as typified roles (37). The *dramatis personae* of Gascoigne's *Supposes* makes this point clearly, linking the characters to their functions through the definite article: "*Balia*, the nurse. / *Polynesta*, the yong woman. / *Cleander*, the doctor" (sig. B2r).

The OSC staging of 5.1 exposed Sly's life as a series of roles: from beggar/tinker to Lord to father-of-daughters, servant, pedant, tailor, father-of-son, jailor. (Incidentally, this scene contains more references to name and identity than does any other scene in the play.) Casting Sly quadruply in this scene raised the theatrical and ontological stakes. Almost every time a character addressed Sly (as Vincentio, the Pedant-as-Vicentio, Baptista, or the jailor) or emphasized an assertion with a gesture toward one of these characters ("this is the right Vincentio"), he gestured toward blank space. We bent our eye on vacancy. Not only was this unproblematic, it was the point: in theater "this" is what you say it is, even when "this" is nothing.

To focus on Sly's roles and his negotiation of a situation's changing demands was to focus on characters as functions. Act 5, scene

1 is the center of three sequential scenes (4.5, 5.1, 5.2) about theater and role play. Katherine's "performance" in 4.5 paved the way
for Sly's tour de force in 5.1 which paved the way for Katherine's
lengthy submission speech in 5.2. The sun/moon debate of 4.5 exploited all the usual performance markers of cognition, recognition, and exaggeration. In capitulating, Katherine even smiled
for the first time; she was playing with Petruchio and was deliberately overlapping theater, identity, and language. The presence of
Sly in 4.5 as Vincentio removed any possibility of this being a scene
of literal taming, coercion, or submission. It was clearly a scene of
theater, of fiction, of make-believe. Sly-Vincentio's role as an audience or plaything for Petruchio and Katherine reminded us of the
play's *raison d'être* (and by extension that of the sun/moon debate)
as a performance for Sly. And his temporary disorientation when
addressed as a woman further prevented us from reading the scene
and the play literally (as his namesake does in *A Shrew*).[7] Sly was
no more a woman than he was Vincentio (or, for that matter, Sly).
Plays, like identity, are about roles; roles begin with language ("I
say it is the sun"); and language works by agreement ("But sun it is
not when you say it is not"). If language plays a role defined by convention (agreement) or context so too does theater: in Plautus's
Menaechmi the prologue says "All this is Epidamnus—as long as
this play lasts, anyway. In another play it will be another place"
(104). Gascoigne's *Supposes* is also aware of this: below the *dramatis personae* we read "The comedie presented *as it were* in Ferrara"
(sig. B2r, my emphasis).

This sequence of scenes highlighting characters' ad hoc functions led us to Katherine's long speech in 5.2. To ask if or when she
was performing as Katherine and when as Kate was a redundant
question. The point was: she was performing. No more than Sly
can she be two people at once, in two places at once. She cannot
be the actor and the acted upon, the triumpher and the tamed, the
person who imprisons herself. The Oxford Shakespeare Company
production played the speech neutrally—not devoted obedience,
not irony, nor anything on the signifying scale in between. Consequently we watched the gap; we watched Katherine's unknowabil-
ity. The name was irrelevant; she had slipped between the two, into
the gap which is the space of anonymity. She was an actor (as are
we all) saying her lines.

Katherine's speech was pre-echoed in the country-house scene of

---

7. At the end of his experience in *A Shrew* Sly shows his critical limitations by taking the
   play's title literally: "I know now how to tame a shrew" (sig. G2v). The productions of
   The Shrew which most underline the play's capacity for misogyny tend to be those which
   omit the Sly framework (Jonathan Miller's BBC film of 1980, and his RSC production of
   1987) and therefore remove the taming plot's status as performance.

4.3 when Petruchio instructs her to say thank you: "The poorest service is repaid with thanks, / And so shall mine before you touch the meat" (4.3.45–6). Manners, reduced to their most basic function, are a performance for a reward. (Some psychologists argue that to teach toddlers "please" and "thank you" is to teach them hypocrisy: they perform these codes without sincerity simply as a means to an end). Katherine's line "I thank you sir" became a lengthy comic turn as she proved unable to say the words ("I th- . . . I th- . . . I th- . . ."). When she finally succeeded, she repeated the line to herself six times with a variety of emphases and intonations ("I *thank* you sir; I thank *you*, sir" etc). Practice, repetition, rehearsal: the line may well have been sincere but what we watched was the performance of sincerity—a performance we saw again in 5.2.

For Natanson, as we saw above, anonymity is the gap between named personhood and the performance of a role. His comments apply equally to multiple names. Anonymity in *The Taming of the Shrew* resides at the junction of Kate and Katherine; the heroine is multiply named but completely unknowable. She has entered the realm of anonymity. William Flesch echoes Natanson: "there is something fictional about all people, something susceptible to anonymity, in the vanishing space beyond generality . . . where pure interiority . . . and pure exteriority . . . coincide" (475). Anonymity for Flesch, as for Natanson, is about role-play: fictionality is to enact a part, to play someone (or someone else). Wilde's Lady Bracknell remarked that "Three addresses always inspire confidence, even in tradesmen." Her comment cannot be transferred to multiple names in heroines. Katherine's two names do not inspire confidence that we can "know" her as a mimetically real character.

I want to return to the appropriation of names as generic verbs with which I began. Shakespeare converts proper nouns into verbs four times in the canon: Kate in *Taming of the Shrew*, Phebe in *As You Like It* ("she Phebes me"; 4.3.39), Herod in *Hamlet*, and Aufidius in *Coriolanus*. How do critics and audiences work out the meaning of such neologisms—or how does Shakespeare teach us to read them? In *Shrew, As You Like It, Hamlet, Coriolanus*, the texts seem to provide internal glosses for their onomastic coinages. The line in *Shrew* is the most complicated so let me first consider the other three.

In *As You Like It*, the surrounding context provides several glosses. Rosalind asks the shepherd Silvius if he wishes to hear the letter Phebe has sent to Rosalind. Silvius is keen to hear it "for I never heard it yet; / Yet heard too much of Phebe's cruelty." This cues Rosalind's response: "She Phebes me. Mark how the tyrant writes" (*As You Like It* 4.3.36–9). Phebe's cruelty and her tyranny are stressed. Thus, "she Phebes me" clearly means "she acts like Phebe toward me, i.e., cruelly."

The *Hamlet* reference ("it out-Herods Herod"; *Hamlet* 3.2.9) is also clear and unambiguous: to "Herod" is obviously to be extreme in cruelty or language. The phrase is unlikely to be misinterpreted because Herod was a familiar figure from medieval mystery plays and his name was equated with performance style. In the Coventry mystery cycle we have the famous stage direction "Herod rages in the pageant and in the street also" (line 783). To be Herod is to rage. Nonetheless, Shakespeare provides a gloss: the player is first warned against "o'erdoing Termagant" (another mystery play authority, usually presented as a "violent, overbearing personage"; OED termagant, n. (a.) 1); this warning is followed by the synonymous summary "it out-Herods Herod" (3.2.13–14). It is an example of Shakespeare condensing terms as he teaches his audience language: the prefix "o'er" which carries the meaning of excess is first attached to a familiar verb ("o'erdoing"); then it—or rather, its synonym, "out"—is attached to a verb-conversion, "out-Herods Herod," as Shakespeare concentrates his meaning and form.

In the example from *Coriolanus* ("I would not have been so fidius'd for all the chests in Corioles"; 2.1.130–1) to "fidius" someone is to thrash them. Here, as in my previous examples, Shakespeare's dialogue provides the definition, with Menenius asking if Coriolanus has "disciplined Aufidius soundly" (2.1.125). This is a more elegant variant of my colloquial "thrash," as befits Menenius's consistently temperate style.

In *The Shrew* we have a similar pattern, with the coinage appearing to gloss the previous line, but there are at least three possible interpretations. Bianca observes that "Being mad herself, she's madly mated" and Gremio responds "Petruchio is Kated." Gremio's line may express agreement with Bianca: that is, he may be restating her point, summarizing it in a synonymous form. In this case to "Kate" someone is to give someone a taste of their own medicine. Petruchio has been hoist by his own petard. Or his line may be a contradiction of Bianca's. She has suggested that the couple are well matched but Gremio counters that Kate has turned the tables on her husband. In this case to "Kate" someone is to checkmate them or to gain the upper hand. Or, if we allow that rhyme can link not just sound but sense there is an equation of Kateing with mating: that is, for Petruchio to mate is to be married to Kate. Marriage means not something general but something unique to two individuals, in this instance a Kate and a Petruchio. (I am grateful to my colleague Elisabeth Dutton for this suggestion.)

Jonathan Bate's RSC Shakespeare comes close to suggesting this when it offers "mated with Kate" as its gloss on this line, but oddly it also offers "infected with the Kate," a gloss it adopts from Brian Morris's Arden 2 edition where Morris writes to catch "the 'Kate' (as if it were the name of an illness)." This is the one thing the phrase surely does not mean. Morris cites as an analogy, Beatrice's line in *Much Ado* (1.1.73–5) where she worries that Claudio has "caught the Benedick"; if so, "it will cost him a thousand pound ere 'a be cured." I dismiss Morris's analogy because it is far from analogous—using a proper name as a generic noun ("the Benedick") is not the same thing as turning a proper noun into a generic verb ("Kated"), especially when there are other obviously parallel examples of this verbal tic: she Phebes me, out-Herods Herod, fidius'd.

Whatever is meant by "Petruchio is Kated" (and I shall return to this question), in all four instances of noun conversions, behavior is encapsulated in a generic verb. We might now ask: whose behavior? I have yoked the four examples together as if they were equal, but *Coriolanus* seems the odd one out. In the other examples the name equals the behavior the verb inscribes: whatever "Kate" may mean, it is clear that her actions, like those of Herod and Phebe, determine the meaning of the derivative verb. Not so the case of "fidius'd" where it is Coriolanus whose actions dictate the meaning. To "fidius" someone means not to act like Aufidius but to act like Coriolanus. It means not to be active but to be passive; not to give blows but to receive them. Verbs, we are taught in childhood grammar lessons, are "doing words"; but Aufidius no longer does the action of his own verb. He has lost agency; he has also, incidentally, lost the full form of his name. The two, as Katherine realizes when she overturns Petruchio's use of her diminutive form Kate, are related.

There is, however, a further complication. The phrase "medius fidius" is used by the Schoolmaster in *Two Noble Kinsmen* 3.5.11. In her Arden 3 edition Lois Potter identifies this as one of the exclamatory interjections listed in Lily's *Latin Grammar*. It is an abbreviation, meaning "may the divine Fidius [Jupiter] help me." Thus "Kated" and "Aufidius" derive at least some of their force from punning associations with other words. That leaves "to Phebe" and "out-Herod" as the outsiders. (I am grateful to Richard Proudfoot for the points in this paragraph.)

The question of association leads me to a final point, which is identity by association. It is remarkable how all these examples connect people (as Elisabeth Dutton observes; personal communication). Aufidius has to stay by Coriolanus to be "fidius'd"; it is specifically Petruchio for whom mating is Kating. In fact, the example from *Shrew* is more interlinked in this respect than the others, first by the rhyme, and second by the change of subject: Bianca is talking about Kate ("*she's* madly mated"), Gremio about Petruchio ("*Petruchio* is Kated"). Third, both these subjects are in passive constructions: Kate is mated, Petruchio is Kated. There is a complex linguistic matching going on here, an interdependence, an assertion of individuality even as that individuality is temporarily lost in the identity of the other. This seems entirely appropriate for a play about marriage. New Critics often argues that Petruchio and Katherine "deserve each other"—whether positively (they are kindred fiery spirits) or negatively (he gives her a taste of her own medicine and so extinguishes her personality). The language here tempts me to argue in support of the benign interpretation.

* * *

What Shakespeare shows us in *The Taming of the Shrew* is how doubling—the Elizabethan thespian ability to act two (or more) people in close succession, on different occasions, but not at the same time—becomes anonymity. The verbal doubling of Katherine with Kate proves to be a highly significant theatrical trope in a play which examines the tools of the dramatist's art: language, imagination, disguise, illusion, willing suspension of disbelief, behavioral psychology. Katherine has two names, is two people, just as the boy playing her is two people, male and female, just as the play is two plays—one for Sly and one for us. That this theatrical exploration of doubleness extends to personal names is made patently clear throughout, from the Italian significance of Lucentio's assumed name, Cambio ("change"), through Petruchio's pun on "Bianca" to the disappearance of the literal Sly in favor of a Katherine who, performing as Kate, becomes figuratively "sly" (see Burns).[8] The way in which the investigation of dramatic change, role-playing, and anonymity permeates all levels of *The Taming of the Shrew* makes this a remarkably accomplished comedy for such an early date—not a crude farce about the *taming* of the shrew, but a sophisticated exploration of the multiple *naming* of the shrew.

WORKS CITED

Anon. *The Coventry Corpus Christi Plays.* Eds. Pamela M. King and Clifford Davidson. Kalamazoo: Medieval Institute Publications, Western Michigan UP, 2000.
Burns, Margie. "The Ending of the Shrew." *Shakespeare Studies* 18 (1986): 41–64.
Carroll, William C. See Shakespeare.
De Man, Paul. *Allegories of Reading.* New Haven, Conn: Yale UP, 1979.
Derrida, Jacques. *Of Grammatology.* Trans. Gayatri Chakravorty Spivak. Baltimore: Johns Hopkins UP, 1976.
Dusinberre, Juliet. *Shakespeare and the Nature of Women.* London: Macmillan, 3rd ed. 2003.
Flesch, William. "Anonymity and Unhappiness in Proust and Wittgenstein." *Criticism* 29/4 (1987): 459–76.
Foakes, R. A., and Rickert, C. T., eds. *Henslowe's Diary.* Cambridge: CUP, 1961.
Gascoigne, George. *Supposes.* London, 1566.

8. In a final irony unanticipated by Shakespeare, the most problematic debate in textual circles originates in a variant name, Henslowe's significant/ insignificant 1594 entry for *The Taming of a Shrew* at Newington Butts (see Foakes and Rickert 22).

Levin, Harry. *Shakespeare and the Revolution of the Times*. New York: OUP, 1965, reprinted 1976.

Lodge, David. *The Art of Fiction*. Harmondsworth: Penguin, 1992.

Lyford, Edward. *The True Interpretation and Etymology of Christian Names*. London, 1655.

McDonald, Russ. "The Language of Tragedy." In *The Cambridge Companion to Shakespearean Tragedy*. Ed. Claire McEachern. Cambridge: CUP, 2002. Pp. 23–49.

Natanson, Maurice. *Anonymity: A Study in the Philosophy of Alfred Schutz*. Bloomington: Indiana UP, 1986.

Pickles, Chris. Program note for *Taming of the Shrew*, Oxford Stage Company, 2006.

Plautus. *The Brothers Menaechmus*. Trans. E. F. Watling. In *The Pot of Gold and Other Plays*. Harmondsworth: Penguin, 1965.

Shaaber, M. A. "The First Rape of Fair Hellen by John Trussell." *Shakespeare Quarterly* 8 (1957): 407–48.

Shakespeare, William. *The Complete Works*. Eds. Jonathan Bate and Eric Rasmussen. Basingstoke: Macmillan, 2007.

———. *Mr William Shakespeare His Comedies, Histories, Tragedies*. London: 1623.

———. *The Riverside Shakespeare*. Gen. ed. G. B. Evans. Boston: Houghton Mifflin, 1974

———. *The Taming of the Shrew*. Ed. Brian Morris. Arden 2. London: Methuen, 1982.

———. *The Two Gentlemen of Verona*. Ed. William C. Carroll. Arden 3. Walton on Thames: Thomson Learning, 2004.

Warner, William. *Albion's England*. London, 1586.

Weidhorn, Manfred. "The Relation of Title and Name to Identity in Shakespearean Tragedy." *SEL* 9 (1969): 303–19.

Wellek, René, and Austin Warren. *Theory of Literature*. Harmondsworth: Penguin, 1942, reprinted 1976.

Wilde, Oscar. *The Importance of Being Earnest*. Ed. Russell Jackson. London: Ernest Benn, 1980.

Wynborne, John. *The New Age of Old Names*. London, 1609.

SIR ARTHUR QUILLER-COUCH

The Taming of the Shrew[†]

* * *

To call *The Shrew* a masterpiece is not only to bend criticism into sycophancy and a fawning upon Shakespeare's name. It does worse. Accepted, it sinks our standard of judgment, levels it, and by levelling forbids our understanding of how a great genius operates; how consummate it can be at its best, how flagrantly bad at its worst.

We hold that no-one walking on any such safe respectable level between heaven and hell can ever grasp the range of a Shakespeare to whom, in the writing of Comedy, *The Shrew* came in the day's work with (let us say) *Twelfth Night* or *The Tempest*. To pretend that *The Shrew*, with its 'prentice grasp on poetry, can compare for a moment with *A Midsummer-Night's Dream* or with *Twelfth Night* is an affectation, as foolish as most other human folly; as to assert

---

[†] From Introduction to *The Taming of the Shrew* (Cambridge: Cambridge University Press, 1962). Reprinted by permission of Cambridge University Press.

The Shrew's underplot (the whole Ariosto intrigue) as master-work. Any careful, candid examination will expose it as patchwork, and patched none too cleverly.

But the trouble about *The Shrew* is that, although it reads rather ill in the library, it goes very well on the stage, in spite of the choice of managers and adapters to present it without the Induction—the one block of it which indelibly stamps it as Shakespeare's. Samuel Pepys on April 7, 1667, went to the King's house and

> there saw *The Taming of a Shrew* which hath some very good pieces in it, but generally is but a mean play; and the best part, 'Sawny' done by Tracy; and hath not half its life, by reason of the words, I suppose, not being understood at least by me.

Being a play which invites rant and in places even demands it, *The Shrew* as naturally tempts the impersonator of Petruchio to unintelligible shouting and mouthing. Yet there is a delicacy in the man underlying his boisterousness throughout, which should be made to appear, and, allowed to appear, is certain to please. He has to tame this termagant bride of his, and he does it in action with a very harsh severity. But while he storms and raves among servants and tailors, showing off for her benefit, to her his speech remains courteous and restrained—well restrained and, with its ironical excess, elaborately courteous. It is observable that, through all the trials he imposes on her, he never says the sort of misprising word that hurts a high-mettled woman more than any rough deed and is seldom if ever by any true woman forgotten or quite forgiven. This underlying delicacy observed by the actor presenting Petruchio, the play can never fail to 'act well,' or—as Pope and Johnson put it—to divert.

As for Katharina, only a very dull reader can miss recognising her, under her froward mask, as one of Shakespeare's women, marriageable and willing to mate; a Beatrice opposing a more repellent barrier, yet behind it willing, even seeking, to surrender. Her true quarrel with her sister Bianca (who has something in her of the pampered cat, with claws) slips out in the words which *A Shrew* gives to her—

> But yet I will consent and marry him;
> For I, methinks, have been too long a maid,
> And match him to [too], or else his manhood's good;[1]

and in her outburst upon her father in *The Shrew*—

> *She* is your treasure, *she* must have a husband.[2]

---

1. Sc. 5.70–72. [Note, this is not Shakespeare's play but the anonymous related text discussed in the Introduction to this volume—*Editor*.]
2. Act 2, Sc. I.
3. Act 5, Sc. I.

And there are truly few prettier conclusions in Shakespeare than
her final submission—

> Nay, I will give thee a kiss, now pray thee, love, stay.[3]

IX

There have been shrews since Xantippe's time and since
Solomon found that a scolding woman was a scourge shaken to and
fro: and it is not discreet perhaps for an editor to discuss, save historically, the effective ways of dealing with them. Petruchio's was
undoubtedly drastic and has gone out of fashion. But avoiding the
present times and recalling Dickens, most fertile of inventors since
Shakespeare, with Dickens's long gallery of middle-aged wives who
make household life intolerable by various and odious methods,
one cannot help thinking a little wistfully that the Petruchian discipline had something to say for itself. It may be that these curses on
the hearth are an inheritance of our middle-class, exacerbating
wives by deserting them, most of the day, for desks and professional
routine; that the high feudal lord would have none of it, and as little would the rough serf or labourer with an unrestrained hand. Let
it suffice to say that *The Taming of the Shrew* belongs to a period,
and is not ungallant, even so. The works of our author do not enforce set lessons in morals. If we require moral instruction of them
we must take them in the large and let the instruction almost imperceptibly sink in and permeate. He teaches no express doctrine
anywhere, unless it be the value of charity as interpreting law. He is
nowhere an expositor of creed or dogma, but simply always an ex-
horter, by quiet, catholic influence, to valiancy and noble conduct
of life. Indeed it were no paradox to use even of this rough play the
saying of St Jerome concerning the Son of Sirach, that we read
Shakespeare not for establishment of doctrine but for improvement
of manners.

GEORGE BERNARD SHAW

The Taming of the Shrew[†]

Assuming the guise of a protesting lady, Shaw wrote The Pall Mall
Gazette *a letter which appeared on June 8, 1888.* (It is reprinted in
Archibald Henderson's George Bernard Shaw: Man of the Century.)

---

† From *Shaw on Shakespeare*, ed. Edwin Wilson (Freeport, N.Y.: Books for Libraries Press,
1971). Reprinted by permission of the Society of Authors.

Sir

They say that the American woman is the most advanced woman to be found at present on this planet. I am an Englishwoman, just come up, frivolously enough, from Devon to enjoy a few weeks of the season in London, and at the very first theatre I visit I find an American woman playing Katharine in The Taming of the Shrew—a piece which is one vile insult to womanhood and manhood from the first word to the last. I think no woman should enter a theatre where that play is performed; and I should not have stayed to witness it myself, but that, having been told that the Daly Company has restored Shakespear's version to the stage, I desired to see with my own eyes whether any civilized audience would stand its brutality.

Of course, it was not Shakespear: it was only Garrick adulterated by Shakespear. Instead of Shakespear's coarse, thick-skinned money hunter, who sets to work to tame his wife exactly as brutal people tame animals or children—that is, by breaking their spirit by domineering cruelty—we had Garrick's fop who tries to "shut up" his wife by behaving worse than she—a plan which is often tried by foolish and ill-mannered young husbands in real life, and one which invariably fails ignominiously, as it deserves to. The gentleman who plays Petruchio at Daly's—I neither know nor desire to know his name—does what he can to persuade the audience that he is not in earnest, and that the whole play is a farce, just as Garrick before him found it necessary to do; but in spite of his fine clothes, even at the wedding, and his winks and smirks when Katharine is not looking, he cannot make the spectacle of a man cracking a heavy whip at a starving woman other than disgusting and unmanly. In an age when woman was a mere chattel, Katharine's degrading speech about

> "Thy husband is thy lord, thy life, thy keeper,
> Thy head, thy sovereign: one that cares for thee [with a whip]
> And for thy maintenance; commits his body
> To painful labour, both by sea and land," etc.

might have passed with an audience of bullies. But imagine a parcel of gentlemen in the stalls at the Gaiety Theatre, half of them perhaps living idly on their wives' incomes, grinning complacently through it as if it were true or even honourably romantic. I am sorry that I did not come to town earlier that I might have made a more timely protest. In the future I hope all men and women who respect one another will boycott The Taming of the Shrew until it is driven off the boards.

Yours truly,
Horatio Ribbonson
St. James's Hotel, and Fairheugh Rectory, North Devon, June 7th.

GEORGE R. HIBBARD

The Taming of the Shrew: A Social Comedy†

The trouble about *The Shrew* is that, although it reads rather ill in the library, it goes very well on the stage." This curious piece of dramatic criticism * * * with its tone of hurt surprise, is an index to the kind of critical reaction *The Shrew* has generally evoked. * * * It does not fit in with the view that Shakespearean comedy is essentially romantic; it offers, or seems to offer, little encouragement to those who see character and its development as the central interest in his writing; it can hardly be described as "lyrical"; it even casts some doubt on the validity of the epithet "gentle" as applied to its author. * * * But *The Shrew*, living up to its name, obstinately refuses to be put down. It will not rest in the decent obscurity of the back-premises of criticism to which scholars have consigned it. It goes on giving pleasure to theatre audiences, as it has done for more than three and a half centuries. * * *

The discrepancy between the judgment of the academic critic, on the one hand, and of the common playgoer, on the other, is such as to make one ask whether the latter may not be in the right after all.

* * *

The Shrew * * * is, in my opinion, despite the large element of farce and sheer knockabout that it contains, a true comedy, a significant critical comment on the life and society of the England in which it was written.

What then is it about? The title, though well calculated to draw an audience, is misleading on this point. At best it covers only half of the action, the part of it that deals with Petruchio and Katharina. It is irrelevant so far as the story of Bianca and her wooers is concerned. The main theme is, however, announced directly and unequivocally the moment that Baptista appears with his two daughters, accompanied by Gremio and Hortensio in I.i. His first words are:

> Gentlemen, importune me no farther,
> For how I firmly am resolved you know;
> That is, not to bestow my youngest daughter
> Before I have a husband for the elder[1] [1.1.48–51]

---

† From *Shakespearean Essays*, ed. Alwin Thaler and Norman Sanders (Knoxville: University of Tennessee Press, 1964). Reprinted by permission of The University of Tennessee Press.

1. All quotations from the play are taken from the New Cambridge edition (Cambridge, 1928). Line numbers to the play have been added in brackets and refer to this Norton Critical Edition.

The Shrew is a play about marriage, and about marriage in Elizabethan England. The point needs to be stressed, because its obvious affiliations with Latin comedy and with Italian comedy can
easily obscure its concern with what were, when it was first produced, topical and urgent issues in this country, coming home to
men's business and women's bosoms in the literal sense of both
words. It is perfectly true that it does owe much to Latin comedy.
Grumio's comment in I.ii, when he says: "See, to beguile the old
folks, how the young folks lay their heads together," is a succinct
reminder of the debt. And not only is the subplot taken from Ariosto's *I Suppositi*, but also much of the characterization in it has
been influenced by the *Commedia dell' arte*. Gremio is described as
"a pantaloon" in the Folio stage direction that precedes his entrance in I.i, and as "the old Pantaloon" by Lucentio when he is
wooing Bianca in III.i. The Pedant of Mantua derives from the
same tradition, and, to add to the Italianate atmosphere, there are
even bits of Italian in the dialogue. Nevertheless, an Elizabethan
audience would have found nothing strange or outlandish in Baptista's problem and nothing perverse or improbable about the measures he proposes to take in an effort to solve it. Among the
propertied classes at any rate (there is practically no information
about the rest) marriages were arranged by parents, and it was a
matter of prestige as well as of prudence to see that daughters were
provided with husbands of a suitable status and income. In an essay as delightful as it is informative Wallace Notestein writes:

> The romantic hopes of young women, at least in the moneyed
> classes, were seldom realized and those who desired in their
> husbands good looks and seemly attire, or the solid virtues,
> had sometimes to compromise with their ideals. The women
> who had worldly aspirations had more chance of gaining the
> helpmates they craved. The marriages arranged for them by
> their parents were based largely on property considerations,
> with rank and old family not overlooked. The reader of Eliza-
> bethan and early Stuart letters hardly recovers from his aston-
> ishment at the mercenary ways in which parents planned the
> marriages of their children. They were the more inclined to
> take pains in such matters because many of them were subject
> to old feudal tenures that were an anachronism but still on the
> statute books. . . . Moreover they were bound by community
> opinion to busy themselves about the marriages of their sons
> and daughters. *Those who failed to make good matches for their
> progeny, or who left a daughter unbestowed, were censured by
> the neighbours and indeed by the children themselves.* There
> was another good reason why parents came to the fore in all
> the marital plans for their children. It was they who had to

make settlements upon their sons and provide dowries for their daughters. Young people in the propertied world were not supposed to marry without an income. (My italics)[2]

Such being the general situation, the young man who was prepared to take advantage of it was also common enough. Joel Hurstfield, who reaches much the same conclusion as Notestein in the chapter he devotes to marriage in *The Queen's Wards*, actually cites an instance from real life of a young man who behaved as Petruchio does when he first reaches Padua, though the sequel was rather different:

> "Body of our Lord!"; cried the young Henry Kingston when he heard that a wealthy middle-aged widow had appeared on the marriage market. "I will go marry this old widow and pay my debts. Then when I have buried her will I marry a young wench and get children!" Marry her he did; but she held him in thrall for thirty-eight years and it was his, not her, death which parted them.[3]

And, just as there was nothing particularly unusual in a young man marrying a widow much older than himself for her money, so also matches between old men and young women, for the begetting of an heir, were also commonplace. To quote Notestein once more:

> Arranged marriages, whether necessary or not, worked special hardship in cases where older men were joined to very young women. The rate of mortality among young wives meant that many a man married three or four times. In the third or fourth venture he might be intent upon finding a mate young enough to assure him of a male heir. Hence it was not uncommon for a man of forty-five to marry a girl of eighteen. It was not hard for him to command such a bride and from his own class. Parents were in many cases only too glad to bestow their daughters upon a man of settled habits and of an assured income.[4]

There is, in fact, nothing inherently farcical in the initial situation out of which *The Shrew* develops; it reflects life as it was lived. Indeed, Baptista, in his concern for his daughters' education, shows himself more liberal-minded and enlightened than many Elizabethan fathers were.

But, while the arranged marriage was the normal thing, there was also opposition to it. It came from two main sources. On the

2. Wallace Notestein, "The English Woman, 1580–1650," in *Studies in Social History*, ed. J. H. Plumb (London, 1955), pp. 86–7.
3. Joel Hurstfield, *The Queen's Wards: Wardship and Marriages under Elizabeth I*, (London: Longmans, Green) (1958), p. 150.
4. Notestein, pp. 89–90.

one hand, there were divines and moralists who saw the *mariage de convenance* as a consequence of parental covetousness and as having a degrading effect on those who suffered under it. On the other, there were the writers of romances and the poets who, by elevating true love to the status of an absolute, must have done much to affect the attitude and the outlook of the young. The author of the pamphlet *Tell-Trothes New-Yeares Gift*, which appeared in 1593 and is, therefore, almost exactly contemporary with *The Shrew*, states that jealousy supplies hell with more souls than any other human passion. He then continues:

> The first cause [of jealousy] is a constrained loue, when as parentes do by compulsion coople two bodies, neither respectinge the ioyning of their hartes, nor hauing any care of the continuance of their wellfare, but more regardinge the linkinge of wealth and money together, then of loue with honesty: will force affection without liking, and cause loue with Ielosie. For either they marry their children in their infancy, when they are not able to know what loue is, or else they match them with inequallity, ioyning burning sommer with kea-cold winter, their daughters of twenty yeares olde or vnder, to rich cormorants of three score or vpwards. Whereby, either the dislike that likely growes with yeares of discretion engendereth disloyalty in the one, or the knowledge of the others disability leades him to Ielosie.[5]

Shortly before this pamphlet was published, the unfortunate case of "Mr. Page's wife of Plymouth" seems to have excited considerable interest. Driven into marriage with an older man whom she did not love, Mrs. Page conspired with her lover, George Strangwidge, to murder her husband. The crime was discovered, and Mrs. Page and Strangwidge were executed in 1590. But there was much sympathy for her, and it was effectively voiced by Thomas Deloney in his broadside ballad on the subject, published in 1591. In it Mrs. Page says:

> In blooming yeares my Fathers greedy minde,
> Against my will, a match for me did finde:
> Great wealth there was, yea, gold and siluer store,
> But yet my heart had chosen one before.
>
> Mine eies dislikt my fathers liking quite,
> My hart did loth my parents fond delight:
> My childish minde and fancie told to mee,
> That with his age my youth could not agree.

---

5. *Tell-Trothes New-Yeares Gift* and *The Passionate Morrice*, ed. F. J. Furnivall (London, 1876), p. 5.

> On knees I prayde they would not me constraine;
> With teares I cryde their purpose to refraine;
> With sighes and sobbes I did them often moue,
> I might not wed whereas I could not loue.[6]

As a result of these two currents of ideas, some concessions were gradually being made to the wishes and inclinations of those most intimately concerned. The children were beginning to acquire the right to have at least a negative voice in the matter. And this too is represented in the play. Baptista, after reaching a business agreement with Petruchio in II.i, has the grace to add that it will only be carried out,

> when the special thing is well obtained,
> This is, her love; for that is all in all. [2.1.126–7]

That he really attaches very little importance to love in the case of either daughter, is made very evident in the course of the play, but the gesture towards it is probably representative of the actual situation in England at the time.

A case, of sorts, can be made out for the view that *The Shrew* is designed to bring out and contrast the two opposed attitudes to marriage that existed at the time when it was written: the idea of marriage as a purely business matter, which may be called realistic since it corresponds to the facts, and the idea of it as a union of hearts and minds, which may be called romantic. That some kind of contrast is intended is evident from the conduct of the two plots, which alternate with each other in a regular and contrapuntal fashion until the final scene, where they come together and are rounded off. In this reading of the play the realistic attitude is embodied in Petruchio who makes no secret of his mercenary intentions. To Hortensio, who asks him why he has come to Padua, he replies:

> Antonio, my father, is deceased,
> And I have thrust myself into this maze,
> Haply to wive and thrive as best I may. (I.ii.) [1.2.51–3]

A few lines later he clinches the matter when, having said that the age and appearance of the lady are of no importance so long as she is rich, he adds:

> I come to wive it wealthily in Padua;
> If wealthily, then happily in Padua. [1.2.72–3]

He plainly belongs to the old conservative school of thought, and his views on wives and their place are in keeping. In III.ii, having

---

6. *Works of Thomas Deloney*, ed. F. O. Mann (Oxford, 1912), p. 483.

married Katharina, he pretends to defend her against her friends and kinsmen, ostensibly telling them but in fact telling her:

> Nay, look not big, nor stamp, nor stare, nor fret,
> I will be master of what is my own.
> She is my goods, my chattels, she is my house,
> My household stuff, my field, my barn,
> My horse, my ox, my ass, my any thing. [3.2.220–24]

The words are substantially a version of the tenth commandment and they serve as a forcible reminder of the weight of authority and tradition behind the attitude to woman which they express. In accordance with this same body of ideas, Petruchio feels that his wife should be in complete subjection to him; uses the appropriate means to subdue her to his will; and having achieved this purpose, explains its significance to Hortensio in V.ii by saying:

> Marry, peace it bodes, and love, and quiet life,
> An awful rule and right supremacy;
> And, to be short, what not, that's sweet and happy.
> [5.2. 112–14]

In contrast to this story, in which the woman is treated as a chattel, enjoys none of the pleasures of courtship and is humiliated and subdued, there runs alongside it the tale of Bianca. She enjoys the pleasures of being wooed by no fewer than four men, of making her own choice from among them, of deceiving her father, of stealing a runaway marriage, of having it approved of by both the fathers concerned, and, most important of all, of continuing to get her own way with her husband after marriage as well as before it.

Put in these terms, *The Shrew* looks like an argument for the romantic attitude. But this conclusion only has to be stated for it to be found unacceptable. The scenes involving Petruchio and Katharina have much more vitality than those involving Bianca. We are left at the end with the conviction that the arranged match is a far more durable and solid thing than the romantic one. The most eloquent speech in the whole play is Katharina's, extolling the principle of male dominance and female subjection as a law of nature, and it follows on Petruchio's triumph over Lucentio in the matter of the wager. The main interest of the play is in Petruchio and Katharina, not in the rest.

Does this mean, then, that Shakespeare has come down on the side of the arranged marriage and the old order? In general terms it would seem unlikely, for in his subsequent comedies love is the central value. More to the point, however, such an inference will not square with the evidence of the second half of II.i, which is a pointed and effective piece of comic satire on the marriage market.

In the first half of the scene Petruchio has wooed Katharina and the match between them has been fixed. Petruchio makes his exit saying:

> Father, and wife, and gentlemen, adieu,
> I will to Venice—Sunday comes apace—
> We will have rings, and things, and fine array,
> And kiss me, Kate, we will be married o' Sunday. [2.1.313–16]

The way is now open for Baptista to dispose of his younger daughter and he wastes no time in setting about it. The scene that follows, between him and Gremio and Tranio, is conducted on a blatantly commercial level. Baptista's opening words, referring to the match that has just been concluded between Katharina and Petruchio, set the tone:

> Faith, gentlemen, now I play a merchant's part,
> And venture madly on a desperate mart. [2.1.318–19]

Tranio catches the allusion at once, and endorses it by saying:

> 'Twas a commodity lay fretting by you,
> 'Twill bring you gain, or perish on the seas. [2.1.320–21]

Both of them regard Katharina as a questionable piece of goods that Baptista has done well to get off his hands. At this point Gremio puts in his claim for the hand of Bianca and Tranio promptly asserts his counterclaim. Both begin by saying that they love her, but the statement really amounts to nothing—in any case Tranio is only standing in for Lucentio—and Baptista immediately brings the whole thing down to the only terms that matter when he stops the incipient quarrel with the words:

> Content you, gentlemen, I will compound this strife.
> 'Tis deeds must win the prize, and he, of both,
> That can assure my daughter greatest dower,
> Shall have Bianca's love. [2.1.333–36]

The dower involved here is the money the husband assured to his wife on marriage, in order to provide for her widowhood if he should die before her. It was an essential part of the marriage contract in Shakespeare's England. *Deeds* in this context mean, not the service with which the lover of romance won his lady, but property and cash. There is surely a pun on the sense of *title-deeds*. Bianca's fate is to be settled by an auction, not by a knightly combat. Gremio makes his bid; Tranio puts in a better; Gremio increases his offer; Tranio outbids him once more, and actually uses the word "out-vied" to describe his success. The satire is unmistakable. It is clinched by Baptista's weighing of the two offers and settling, with a careful proviso, for the higher. Turning to Tranio, he says:

> I must confess your offer is the best,
> And, let your father make her the assurance,
> She is your own—else, you must pardon me,
> If you should die before him, where's her dower?
> [2.1.378–81]

But, being a good business man, he keeps the second customer in reserve. If Tranio's father fails to back up his son's offer, Bianca will be married to Gremio after all.

The scene leaves one in no doubt about the play's attitude to the marriage market.

* * *

Katharina's shrewishness is not bad temper, but the expression of her self-respect. Indeed, it even looks like a deliberately adopted form of self-defence, a means of testing the quality of the men she meets, in order to ensure that she has some say in the matter of marriage and is not sold off to a wealthy milksop. She is certainly not opposed to the prospect of marriage. The opening of II.i makes this plain enough, for in it she ill-treats Bianca for being so successful with men, and, when her father seeks to restrain her, she cries out in a jealous fury:

> What, will you not suffer me? Nay, now I see
> She is your treasure, she must have a husband,
> I must dance bare-foot on her wedding-day
> And for your love to her lead apes in hell. [2.1.31–4]

She detests the idea of being an old maid and of her younger sister preceding her in marriage. She is attached to traditional notions of order and fitness. Provided that she can find a man who will stand up to her and earn her respect, she is ready and even eager to marry. Her subsequent behaviour, including her final speech, is all of a piece with her character and attitude as revealed in these two appearances and in the analogy drawn by Petruchio at the end of IV.i between the process by which he tames her and the methods used to tame a haggard, for the Elizabethans believed that falcons and the like were really of an affectionate nature and could be brought to love the man who trained them. Gervase Markham, for example, after listing the various kinds of hawks, adds these words: "all these Hawkes are hardy, meeke, and louing to the man." Moreover, in his subsequent directions for training them, he lays great stress on kindness, writing as follows:

> All Hawkes generally are manned after one manner, that is to say, by watching and keeping them from sleep, by a contin-

uall carrying of them vpon your fist, and by a most familiar
stroaking and playing with them, with the Wing of a dead
Foule or such like, and by often gazing and looking of them in
the face, with a louing and gentle Countenance, and so making them acquainted with the man.[7]

"Hardy (i.e. bold), meeke, and louing to the man" is a very accurate
description of Katharina's real character.

* * *

That *The Shrew* is a gay, high-spirited, rollicking play, full of broad
farcical scenes and richly comic narrative passages is self-evident.
What I have tried to show is that it also has a serious side to it. Underneath the comic exaggeration it is basically realistic. It portrays
the marriage situation, not as it appeared in the romances of the
day, but as it was in Shakespeare's England. And the criticism it
brings to bear on it is constructive as well as destructive. Baptista,
the foolish father who knows nothing about his daughters yet seeks
to order their lives, is defeated all along the line. So is Gremio, the
old pantaloon, who thinks he can buy a wife. The play's disapproval
of the arranged match, in which no account is taken of the feelings
of the principals, could not be plainer. Within the framework of
marriage as it existed at the time, it comes out in favour of the
match based on real knowledge and experience, over against the
more fanciful kind of wooing that ignores facts in favour of book-
ishly conventional attitudes and expressions of feeling. Paradoxically
enough it is Katharina and Petruchio, for each of whom it is the
other, as the other really is, that matters, who embody the new revo-
lutionary attitude to marriage, rather than Lucentio and Bianca. In
many ways *The Shrew*, in its rougher fashion, anticipates *Much Ado*,
where the same two ways to the altar are contrasted with each other,
though in a much subtler and more brilliant manner.

NATASHA KORDA

Household Kates: Domesticating Commodities in *The Taming of the Shrew*[†]

Commentary on Shakespeare's *The Taming of the Shrew* has frequently noted that the play's novel taming strategy marks a departure from traditional shrew-taming tales. Unlike his predecessors,
Petruchio does not use force to tame Kate; he does not simply beat

---

7. Gervase Markham, *Country Contentments*, 4th edition (London, 1631), pp. 36–7.
† *Shakespeare Quarterly* 47.2 (Summer 1996): 109–31. © The Johns Hopkins University
   Press. Reprinted with permission of The Johns Hopkins University Press.

his wife into submission.[1] Little attention has been paid, however, to the historical implications of the play's unorthodox methodology, which is conceived in specifically economic terms: "I am he am born to tame you, Kate," Petruchio summarily declares, "And bring you from a wild Kate to a Kate / Conformable as other household Kates" (2.1.269–71).[2] Petruchio likens Kate's planned domestication to a domestication of the emergent commodity form itself, whose name parallels the naming of the shrew. The *Oxford English Dictionary* defines *cates* as "provisions or victuals bought (as distinguished from, and usually more delicate or dainty than, those of home production)." The term is an aphetic form of *acate*, which derives from the Old French *achat*, meaning "purchase."[3] Cates are thus by definition exchange-values—commodities, properly speaking—as opposed to use-values, or objects of home production.[4] In order to grasp the historical implications of *Shrew*'s unorthodox methodology and of the economic terms Shakespeare employs to shape its taming strategy, I would like first to situate precisely the form of its departure from previous shrew-taming tales. What differentiates *The Taming of the Shrew* from its precursors is not so much a concern with domestic economy—which has always been a central preoccupation of shrew-taming literature—but rather a shift in *modes of production* and thus in the very terms through which domestic economy is conceived. The coordinates of this shift are contained within the term *cates* itself, which, in distinguishing goods that are purchased from those that are produced within and for the home, may be said to map the historical shift from domestic use-value production to production for the market.

Prior to Shakespeare's play, shrews were typically portrayed as reluctant producers within the household economy, high-born wives who refused to engage in the forms of domestic labor expected of them by their humble tradesman husbands. In the ballad "The Wife Wrapped in a Wether's Skin," for example, the shrew refuses to

---

1. See *The Taming of the Shrew*, ed. Brian Morris (London and New York: Methuen, 1981), 1–149, esp. 70; Richard Hosley, "Sources and Analogues of *The Taming of the Shrew*," *Huntington Library Quarterly* 27 (1963–64): 289–308; and John C. Bean, "Comic Structure and the Humanizing of Kate in *The Taming of the Shrew*" in *The Woman's Part: Feminist Criticism of Shakespeare*, Carolyn Ruth Swift Lenz, Gayle Greene, and Carol Thomas Neely, eds. (Urbana, Chicago, and London: U of Illinois P, 1980), 65–78.
2. Quotations from *The Taming of the Shrew* follow the Arden Shakespeare text, edited by Brian Morris. Line numbers in brackets refer to this Norton Critical Edition.
3. *The Oxford English Dictionary*, 2d ed., prepared by J. A. Simpson and E.S.C. Weiner, 20 vols. (Oxford: Clarendon Press, 1987), 2:978 and 1:66; hereafter cited simply as *OED*.
4. "He who satisfies his own need with the product of his own labour admittedly creates use-values, but not commodities. . . . In order to become a commodity, the product must be transferred to the other person . . . through the medium of exchange" (Karl Marx, *Capital: A Critique of Political Economy, Volume One*, trans. Ben Fowkes [New York: Vintage Books, 1977], 131).

brew, bake, wash, card, or spin on account of her "gentle kin" and delicate complexion:

> There was a wee cooper who lived in Fife,
> Nickety, nackity, noo, noo, noo
> And he has gotten a gentle wife. . . .
> Alane, quo Rushety, roue, roue, roue
>
> She wadna bake, nor she wadna brew,
> For the spoiling o her comely hue.
>
> She wadna card, nor she wadna spin,
> For the shaming o her gentle kin.
>
> She wadna wash, nor she wadna wring,
> For the spoiling o her gouden ring.[5]

The object of the tale was simply to put the shrew to work, to restore her (frequently through some gruesome form of punishment[6]) to her proper productive place within the household economy. When the cooper from Fife, who cannot beat his ungentle wife due to her gentle kin, cleverly wraps her in a wether's skin and tames her by beating the hide instead, the shrew promises: "Oh, I will bake, and I will brew, / And never mair think on my comely hue. / Oh, I will card, and I will, spin, / And never mair think on my gentle kin," etc. Within the tradition of shrew-taming literature prior to Shakespeare's play, the housewife's domestic responsibilities were broadly defined by a feudal economy based on household production, on the production of use-values for domestic consumption.

With the decline of the family as an economic unit of production, however, the role of the housewife in late-sixteenth-century England was beginning to shift from that of skilled producer to savvy consumer. In this period household production was gradually being replaced by nascent capitalist industry, making it more economical for the housewife to purchase what she had once produced. Brewing and baking, for example, once a routine part of the housewife's activity, had begun to move from the home to the market, becoming the province of skilled (male) professionals.[7]

---

5. Muriel Bradbrook cites this ballad as a possible source for *Shrew* in "Dramatic Role as Social Image: a Study of *The Taming of the Shrew*," *Muriel Bradbrook on Shakespeare* (Sussex, UK: Harvester Press; Totowa, NJ: Barnes and Noble Books, 1984), 57–71, esp. 60. Brian Morris discusses the ballad in his introduction to the Arden edition and in Appendix III, where he reprints several versions of it (75 and 310–16).

6. The prescribed method of shrew-taming prior to Shakespeare's play was typically violent.

7. See Susan Cahn, *Industry of Devotion: The Transformation of Women's Work in England, 1500–1660* (New York: Columbia UP, 1987), esp. 42–46. Cf. Alice Clark, *Working Life of Women in the Seventeenth Century* (New York: E. P. Dutton, 1919); and Roberta Hamilton, *The Liberation of Women: A Study of Patriarchy and Capitalism* (London and Boston: George Allen and Unwin, 1978).

Washing and spinning, while still considered "women's work," were becoming unsuitable activities for middle-class housewives and were increasingly delegated to servants, paid laundresses, or spinsters.[8] The housewife's duties were thus gradually moving away from the production of use-values within and for the home and toward the consumption of market goods, or cates, commodities produced outside the home. The available range of commodities was also greatly increased in the period, so that goods once considered luxuries, available only to the wealthiest elites, were now being found in households at every level of society.[9] Even "inferior artificers and many farmers," as William Harrison notes in his *Description of England*, had "learned . . . to garnish their cupboards with plate, their joint beds with tapestry and silk hangings, and their tables with carpets and fine napery."[1] *The Taming of the Shrew* may be said both to reflect and to participate in this cultural redefinition by portraying Kate not as a reluctant producer but rather as an avid and sophisticated consumer of market goods. When she is shown shopping in 4.3 (a scene I will discuss at greater length below), she displays both her knowledge of and preference for the latest fashions in apparel. Petruchio's taming strategy is accordingly aimed not at his wife's productive capacity—he never asks Kate to brew, bake, wash, card, or spin—but at her consumption. He seeks to educate Kate in her new role as a consumer of household cates.

Before examining in precisely what way Petruchio seeks to tame Kate's consumption of cates, I would like to introduce a further complication into this rather schematic account of the shift from household production to consumption, being careful not to conflate material change with ideological change. The ideological redefinition of the home as a sphere of consumption rather than production in sixteenth-century England did not, of course, correspond to the lived reality of every early modern English housewife. Many women continued to work productively, both within and outside the home.[2] Yet the acceptance of this ideology, as Susan Cahn

8. See Cahn, 53–56.
9. On conspicuous consumption in early modern England, see F. J. Fisher, *London and the English Economy, 1500–1700* (London and Ronceverte: The Hambledon Press, 1990), 105–18; Joan Thirsk, *Economic Policy and Projects: The Development of a Consumer Society in Early Modern England* (Oxford: Clarendon Press, 1978); Chandra Mukerji, *From Graven Images: Patterns of Modern Materialism* (New York: Columbia UP, 1983); and *Consumption and the World of Goods*, John Brewer and Roy Porter, eds. (London and New York: Routledge, 1993).
1. William Harrison, *The Description of England: The Classic Contemporary Account of Tudor Social Life*, ed. Georges Edelen (New York: The Folger Shakespeare Library and Dover Publications, 1994), 200.
2. See Martha C. Howell's rich and complex account of the types of female labor that took place, both within and outside the home, in late-medieval and early modern northern European cities. Howell's book resists the nostalgic overvaluation of female production in precapitalist society which has informed much of the earlier work on this subject and, in particular, that of the housework theorists.

points out, became the "price of upward social mobility" in the period and, as such, exerted a powerful influence on all social classes.[3] The early modern period marked a crucial change in the *cultural valuation* of housework, a change that is historically linked—as the body of feminist-materialist scholarship which Christine Delphy has termed "housework theory"[4] reminds us—to the rise of capitalism and development of the commodity form.[5]

According to housework theory, domestic work under capitalism is not considered "real" work because "women's productive labor is confined to use-values while men produce for exchange."[6] It is not that housework disappears with the rise of capitalism; rather, it becomes economically devalued. Because the housewife's labor has no exchange-value, it remains unremunerated and thus economically "invisible."[7] Read within this paradigm, *Shrew* seems to participate in the ideological erasure of housework by not representing it on the stage, by rendering it, quite literally, invisible. The weakness of this analysis of the play, however, is that it explains only what Kate does not do onstage and provides no explanation for what she actually does.

In continuing to define the housewife's domestic activity solely within a matrix of use-value production, housework theory—despite its claim to offer an historicized account of women's subjection under capitalism—treats housework as if it were itself, materially speaking, an unchanging, transhistorical entity, which is not, as we have seen, the historical case. For though the market commodity's infiltration of the home did not suddenly and magically absolve the housewife of the duty of housework, it did profoundly alter *both* the material form and the cultural function of such work insofar as it became an activity increasingly centered around the proper order, maintenance, and display of household cates—objects having, by definition, little or no use-value.

3. See Cahn, 7 and 156.
4. In an article first published in 1978, Christine Delphy maintained: "We owe to the new feminists . . . the posing, for the first time in history, of the question of housework as a *theoretical* problem." She asserted that no coherent "theory of housework" had thus far been produced and offered her own preliminary attempt at such a systematic theorization ("Housework or domestic work" in *Close to Home: A materialist analysis of women's oppression*, ed. and trans. Diana Leonard [Amherst: U of Massachusetts P, 1984], 78–92, esp. 78).
5. As Annette Kuhn observes, feminist materialists of the 1970s "seized upon [housework] as the key to an historically concrete understanding of women's oppression, . . . as the central point at which women's specific subordination in capitalism is articulated" (*Feminism and Materialism: Women and Modes of Production*, Annette Kuhn and AnnMarie Wolpe, eds. [London and Boston: Routledge and Kegan Paul, 1978], 198).
6. See Karen Sachs, "Engels Revisited" in *Women, Culture, and Society*, Michelle Zimbalist Rosaldo and Louise Lamphere, eds. (Stanford: Stanford UP, 1974), 221–22; and Kuhn, "Structures of Patriarchy and Capital in the Family" in Kuhn and Wolpe, eds., 42–67, esp. 54.
7. On the economic invisibility of housework, see Delphy, 84.

Privileging delicacy of form over domestic function, cates threaten to sever completely the bond linking exchange-value to any utilitarian end; they are commodities that unabashedly assert their own superfluousness. It is not simply that cates, as objects of exchange, are to be "distinguished from" objects of home production, however, as the *OED* asserts. Rather, their very purpose is to signify this distinction, to signify their own distance from utility and economic necessity. What replaces the utilitarian value of cates is a symbolic or cultural value: cates are, above all, signifiers of social distinction or differentiation.[8] Housework theory cannot explain *Shrew*'s recasting of the traditional shrew-taming narrative because it can find no place in its strictly economic analysis for the housewife's role within a *symbolic* economy based on the circulation, accumulation, and display of status objects, or what Pierre Bourdieu terms "symbolic" (as distinct from "economic") capital.[9] How did the presence of status objects, or cates, within the nonaristocratic household transform, both materially and ideologically, the "domesticall duties" of the housewife? To what degree was her new role as a consumer and caretaker of household cates perceived as threatening? What new mechanisms of ideological defense were invented to assuage such perceived threats? I shall argue that it is precisely the cultural anxiety surrounding the housewife's new managerial role with respect to household cates which prompted Shakespeare to write a new kind of shrew-taming narrative.

* * *

If Petruchio's punning appellation of Kate as a "super-dainty" cate seems an obvious misnomer in one sense—she can hardly be called "delicate"—in another it is quite apt, as his gloss makes clear. The substantive *dainty*, deriving from the Latin *dignitatem* (worthiness, worth, value), designates something that is "estimable, sumptuous, or rare."[1] In describing her as a "dainty," Petruchio appears to be referring to her value as a commodity, or cate, on the marriage market (he has just discovered that her dowry is worth "twenty thousand crowns") [2.1.120].

Yet Petruchio's reference to Kate as "super-dainty" refers to her not as a commodity or object of exchange between men but rather as a *consumer* of commodities. According to the *OED*, in its adjectival form the term *dainty* refers to someone who is "nice, fastidious, particular; sometimes, over-nice" as to "the quality of food,

8. On commodities as signs of distinction, see Pierre Bourdieu, *Distinction: A Social Critique of the Judgement of Taste* (Cambridge, MA: Harvard UP, 1984); and Jean Baudrillard, *For a Critique of the Political Economy of the Sign*, trans. Charles Levin (St. Louis, MO: Telos Press, 1981).
9. Bourdieu, "Symbolic capital" in *Outline of a Theory of Practice*, trans. Richard Nice (Cambridge: Cambridge UP, 1977), 171–83.
1. *OED*, 4:218.

comforts, etc." In describing Kate as "super-dainty," Petruchio implies that she belongs to the latter category; she is "over-nice," not so much discriminating as blindly obedient to the dictates of fashion. Sliding almost imperceptibly from Kate as a consumer of cates to her status as a cate, Petruchio's gloss ("For dainties are all Kates") elides the potential threat posed by the former by subsuming it under the aegis of the latter. His pun on *Kates/cates* dismisses the significance of Kate's role as a consumer (as does Newman's reading) by effectively reducing her to an object of exchange between men.

The pun on *Kates/cates* is repeated at the conclusion of Petruchio's "chat" with Kate (in the pronouncement quoted at the beginning of this essay) and effects a similar reduction: "And therefore, setting all this chat aside, / Thus in plain terms," Petruchio proclaims, summing up his unorthodox marriage proposal, "I am he am born to tame you, Kate, / And bring you from a wild Kate to a Kate / Conformable as other household Kates" [2.1.268–70]. And yet, in spite of his desire to speak "in plain terms," Petruchio cannot easily restrict or "tame" the signifying potential of his own pun. For once it is articulated, the final pun on *Kates/cates* refuses to remain tied to its modifier, "household," and insists instead upon voicing itself, shrewishly, where it shouldn't (i.e., each time Kate is named). In so doing, it retrospectively raises the possibility that cates themselves may be "wild," that there is something unruly, something that must be made to conform, in the commodity form itself. This possibility in turn discovers an ambiguity in Petruchio's "as," which may mean either "as other household cates are conformable" or "as I have brought other household cates into conformity." The conformity of household cates cannot be taken for granted within the play because cates, unlike use-values, are not proper to or born of the domestic sphere but are produced outside the home by the market. They are by definition extra-domestic or to-be-domesticated. Yet insofar as cates obey the logic of exchange and of the market, they may be said to resist such domestication. Petruchio cannot restrict the movement of cates in his utterance, cannot set all "chat" aside and speak "in plain terms," because commodities, like words, tend to resist all attempts to restrict their circulation and exchange.

The latter assertion finds support—quite literally—in Petruchio's own chat. The term *chat*, as Brian Morris points out in a note to his Arden edition, was itself a variant spelling of *cate* in the early modern period (both forms descend from *achat*). The term *chat* thus instantiates, literally performs, the impossibility of restricting the semantic excess proper to language in general and epitomized by Kate's speech in particular. In so doing, however, it also links lin-

guistic excess—via its etymological link with the signifier *cate*—to
the economic excess associated with the commodity form in general and with cates, or luxury goods, in particular. Within the play,
the term *chat* may thus be said to name both material and linguistic forms of excess as they converge on the figure of the shrew. It
refers at once to Kate's "chattering tongue" [4.2.59] and to her untamed consumption of cates.

*** My argument thus departs from traditional accounts of the
commodification of or traffic in women which maintain that
women "throughout history" have been passive objects of exchange
circulating between men. Such accounts do little to explain the
specific historical forms the domination of woman assume with the
rise of capitalism and development of the commodity form. They do
not, for example, explain the housewife's emerging role as a manip-
ulator of status objects, or household cates.

I would like to question as well the viability, in the present context, of Veblen's assertion that the housewife's "manipulation of the
household paraphernalia" does not render her any less a commodity, "chattel," of her husband. The housewife's consumption of
cates, which Veblen views as thoroughly domesticated, was in the
early modern period thought to be something wild, unruly, and in
urgent need of taming.[2] If *Shrew*'s taming narrative positions Kate
as a "vicarious consumer" to ensure that her consumption and manipulation of household cates conforms to her husband's economic
interests, it nevertheless points to a historical moment when the
housewife's management of household property becomes poten-

2. Thorstein Veblen, *The Theory of the Leisure Class* (1899: rpt. New York: Penguin Books,
1983), 57–58. Domestic manuals of the period manifest anxiety over the limits of a
woman's right to dispose of household property. William Gouge's *Of Domesticall Duties*
(London, 1622), for example, devotes some fifteen chapters to defining the precise limits of the housewife's managerial role with respect to household goods. While it is the responsibility of the "godly, wise, faithfull, and industrious woman," he maintains, to
"ordereth all the things of the house," he goes on to specify that this power must never
exceed the scope of her husband's authority. In the dedicatory epistle of Gouge's treatise,
however, we find that his attempt to limit the housewife's governance of household property was not overly popular with his parishioners: "I remember that when these *Domesticall Duties* were first uttered out of the pulpit, much exception was taken against the
application of a wiues subiection to the restraining of her from disposing the common
goods of the family without, or against her husbands consent." Gouge defends himself
as follows:

> But surely they that made those exceptions did not well thinke of the *Cautions* and
> *Limitations* which were then deliuered, and are now againe expresly noted: which are,
> that the foresaid restraint be not extended to the *proper goods of a wife*, no nor over-
> strictly to such *goods as are set apart for the use of the family*, nor to *extraordinary cases*,
> nor alwaies to an *expresse consent*, nor to the *consent of such husbands as are impotent,
> or farre and long absent*. If any other warrantable caution shall be shewed me, I will be
> as willing to admit it, as any of these. Now that my meaning may not still be peruerted,
> I pray you, in reading the restraint of wiues power in disposing the goods of the family,
> euer beare in minde those Cautions.

Gouge proffers so many mitigating exceptions to his own rule that perhaps it was more
often honored in the breach than in the observance.

tially threatening to the symbolic order of things. Before attending to the ways in which the shrew-taming comedy seeks to elide this threat, we should take the threat itself seriously; only then will we be able to chart with any clarity Kate's passage from "chat" (i.e., from the material and linguistic forms of excess characteristic of the shrew) to "chattel."

At the start of the play, as Newman asserts, Kate's fretting is represented as an obstacle to her successful commodification on the marriage market. When Baptista finally arranges Kate's match to the madcap Petruchio, Tranio remarks: "'Twas a commodity lay fretting by you, / 'Twill bring you gain, or perish on the seas" [2.1.320–21], Baptista's response, "The gain I seek is quiet in the match" [2.1.322], underscores the economic dilemma posed by Kate's speech: her linguistic surplus translates into his financial lack and, consequently, her "quiet" into his "gain." Yet Kate's fretting refers not only to what comes out of her mouth (to her excessive verbal fretting) but to what goes into it as well (to her excessive consumption). The verb *to fret*, which derives from the same root as the modern German *fressen*, means "to eat, devour [of animals]; . . . to gnaw, to consume, . . . or wear away by gnawing" or, reflexively, "to waste or wear away; to decay."[3] Kate's untamed, animal-like consumption, Tranio's remark implies, wears away both at her father's resources and at her own value as well. In describing Kate as a "fretting commodity," as a commodity that not only consumes but consumes itself, Tranio emphasizes the tension between her position as a cate, or object of exchange, between men and her role as a consumer of cates.

To grasp the threat posed by the early modern housewife's consumption of cates, as this threat is embodied by Kate, however, we must first consider more closely what Baudrillard terms the "relative social class configurations" at work within the play. For the discourse of objects in *The Taming of the Shrew* becomes intelligible only if read in the context of its "class grammar"—that is to say, as it is inflected by the contradictions inherent in its appropriation by a particular social class or group.[4] In general terms *The Taming of the Shrew* represents an *embourgeoisement* of the traditional shrew-taming narrative: Petruchio is not a humble tradesman but an upwardly mobile landowner. Unlike the cooper's wife, Kate is not of "gentle kin"; she is a wealthy merchant's daughter. The play casts the marriage of Petruchio and Kate as an alliance between the gentry and mercantile classes and thus between land and money, status and wealth, or what Bourdieu identifies as symbolic and economic capital.

3. *OED*, 6:185.
4. Baudrillard, 37.

Petruchio is straightforward about his mercenary motives for marrying Kate: "Left solely heir to all his [father's] lands and goods," which he boastfully claims to "have better'd rather than decreas'd" [2.1.115–16], Petruchio ventures into the "maze" of mercantile Padua hoping to "wive it wealthily . . . / If wealthily, then happily in Padua" [1.2.72–3], Likening his mission to a merchant voyage, he claims to have been blown in by "such wind as scatters young men through the world / To seek their fortunes farther than at home" [1.2.47]. Petruchio's fortune-hunting bombast, together with his claim to have "better'd" his inheritance, marks him as one of the new gentry, who continually sought to improve their estates through commerce, forays into business or overseas trade, or by contracting wealthy marriage.[5] If Petruchio seeks to obtain from his marriage to Baptista's mercantile household what is lacking in his own domestic economy, however, the same can be said of Baptista, who seeks to marry off his daughter to a member of the landed gentry. The nuptial bond between the two families promises a mutually beneficial exchange of values for the domestic economies of each: Petruchio hopes to obtain surplus capital (a dowry of "twenty thousand crowns"), and Baptista the status or symbolic capital that comes with land (the jointure Petruchio offers in return) [2.1.120].[6]

Kate's commodification as a marriage-market cate thus proves beneficial to both her father's and her future husband's households. But it is also the case that her consumption of cates is represented, at least initially, as mutually detrimental. At the start of the play, as we have seen, Kate's excessive consumption renders her an unvendible commodity. Baptista is unable to "rid the house" [1.1.139] of Kate and is consequently unwilling to wed his younger daughter, Bianca, to any of her many suitors. Kate's fretting represents perhaps an even greater threat to Petruchio's household, however, although one of a different order. To comprehend this difference, one must comprehend the place occupied by cates within the two domestic economies. Petruchio's parsimonious attitude toward cates, evidenced by the disrepair of his country house and the "ragged, old, and beggarly" condition of his servants [4.1.117], stands in stark contrast to the conspicuous consumption that characterizes

5. Carol F. Heffernan, "*The Taming of the Shrew*: The Bourgeoisie in Love," *Essays in Literature* 12 (1985); 3–14, esp. 5. On the gentry's increasing reliance on commerce in the period, see Lawrence Stone and Jeanne C. Fawtier Stone, *An Open Elite? England 1540–1880* (Oxford: Clarendon Press, 1984).

6. On the "economic and cultural symbiosis of land and money" in the period, see Stone and Stone, 26. The Stones conclude that the perceived symbiotic relation between the landed and merchant classes was more a "question of values and attitudes" than of "the facts of social mobility" (211).

Padua's mercantile class.[7] Gremio, a wealthy Paduan merchant and suitor to Bianca, for example, describes his "house within the city" as "richly furnished with plate and gold" [2.1.338]:

> My hangings all of Tyrian tapestry.
> In ivory coffers I have stuff'd my crowns,
> In cypress chests my arras counterpoints,
> Costly apparel, tents, and canopies,
> Fine linen, Turkey cushions boss'd with pearl,
> Valance of Venice gold in needlework,
> Pewter and brass, and all things that belongs
> To house or housekeeping.
>
> [2.1.342–48]

If housekeeping at Petruchio's country estate involves little more than keeping the "rushes strewed" and the "cobwebs swept" [4.1.38], in Gremio's description of his city dwelling, it is an enterprise that centers on the elaborate arrangement and display of cates. Each of Gremio's "things" bears testimony to his ability to afford superfluous expenditure and to his taste for imported luxuries: his tapestries are from Tyre (famous for its scarlet and purple dyes), his apparel "costly," his linen "fine," his "Turkey cushions boss'd with pearl." His household is invested, literally "stuff'd," with capital.

The marked difference between the two men's respective notions of the "things that belongs/To house or housekeeping" underscores the differing attitudes held by the minor gentry and mercantile classes in the period toward "household cates." For the mercantile classes conspicuous consumption served to compensate for what, borrowing Baudrillard's terminology, we might call a "true social recognition" that otherwise evaded them; the accumulation of status objects served to supplement their "thwarted legitimacy" in the social domain.[8] As Lawrence and Jeanne Fawtier Stone observe, however, for the upwardly mobile gentry "the obligation to spend generously, even lavishly," as part of their newly acquired social status "implied a radical break with the habits of frugality which had played an essential part in the[ir] . . . upward climb."[9] The lesser gentry could make it into the ranks of the elite only by being "cautious, thrifty, canny, and grasping, creeping slowly, generation after generation, up the ladder of social and economic progress, and

7. Cf. William Harrison's description of the "great provision of tapestry, Turkey work, pewter, brass, fine linen, and thereto costly cupboards of plate" found in the houses of "gentlemen, merchantmen, and some other wealthy citizens" (200).
8. Baudrillard, 40.
9. Stone and Stone, 185. On taste as a category of social distinction, see Bourdieu, *Distinction*, passim.

even at the end only barely indulging in a life-style and housing suitable to their dignity and income."[1] For the mercantile classes conspicuous consumption functioned as a necessary (though not always sufficient) means to elite status; for the lesser gentry it was an unwished-for consequence of it.

Arriving at their wedding in tattered apparel and astride an old, diseased horse, Petruchio proclaims: "To me she's married, not unto my clothes. / Could I repair what she will wear in me / As I can change these poor accoutrements, / 'Twere well for Kate and better for myself" [3.2.110–13]. As if to prove his point that Kate's extravagance will leave him a pauper, his self-consuming costume seems to wear itself out before our eyes: his "old breeches" are "thrice turned" (l. 42); his boots have been used as "candle-cases" (l. 43); his "old rusty sword" has a "broken hilt" (ll. 44–45). As for his horse: it is "begnawn with the bots [parasitical worms or maggots]" (ll. 52–53) and, even more appropriately, "infected"—as, he insinuates, is his future wife—"with the fashions" (l. 50). The term *fashions* (or *farcin*, as it was more commonly spelled), which derives from the Latin *farcire*, meaning "to stuff," denotes a contagious equine disease characterized by a swelling of the jaw. Kate's taste for fashionable cates is likened to this disease of excessive consumption, which threatens to gnaw away at her husband's estate.

Following the wedding ceremony, Kate's excessive consumption seems to result in her swift reduction to the status of "chattel." Petruchio whisks his bride away after announcing to the stunned onlookers:

> I will be master of what is mine own.
> She is my goods, my chattels, she is my house,
> My household stuff, my field, my barn,
> My horse, my ox, my ass, my any thing,
> And here she stands.
>
> [3.2.221–25]

Petruchio's blunt assertion of property rights over Kate performs the very act of domestication it declares; reduced to an object of exchange ("goods" and "chattels"), Kate is abruptly yanked out of circulation and sequestered within the home, literally turned into a piece of furniture or "household stuff." The speech follows a domesticating trajectory not unlike that outlined by housework theory: it circumscribes Kate within a matrix of use-value production. The relationship between household stuff and household cates may be described as that between mere use-values and exchange-values, or commodities, properly speaking. The *OED* defines *stuff* as "the

---

1. Stone and Stone, 187.

substance or 'material'. . . . of which a thing is formed or consists, or out of which a thing may be fashioned."[2] As such, it may be identified with the use-value of the object.[3] Entering into the process of exchange, commodities, "ungilded and unsweetened, retaining their original home-grown shape," are split into the twofold form of use-value and value proper, a process Marx calls "*Stoffwechsel*"—literally, the act of (ex)change (*Wechsel*) that transforms mere stuff (*Stoff*) into values, or cates.[4] In transforming Kate from an object of exchange into the home-grown materiality of mere stuff, into a thing defined by its sheer utility, a beast of burden ("my horse, my ox, my ass"), Petruchio's speech reverses the processes of commodification. Reducing Kate to a series of increasingly homely things, it finally strips her down to a seemingly irreducible substance whose static immobility ("here she stands") puts a stop to the slippage of exchange evoked by his list of goods. Her deictic presence seems to stand as the guarantee of an underlying, enduring use-value.

As a member of the gentry, Petruchio stands for the residual, land-based values of a domestic economy that purports to be "all in all sufficient" (*Othello*, 4.1.265). The trajectory traced by his index of goods moves not only from exchange-value to use-value but from liquid capital, or "movables,"[5] to the more secure form of landed property ("house . . . field . . . barn"). Yet Petruchio's portrait of an ideally self-sufficient household economy, in which the value of things is taken to be self-evident and not subject to (ex)change, is belied by the straightforwardly mercenary motives he avows for marrying Kate. Paradoxically, in order to maintain his land-based values, Petruchio must embrace those of the marketplace.[6] In seeking to arrest the slippage of exchange, his speech implicates its speaker in an expanding network or maze of equivalent value-forms ("goods . . . any thing") whose slide threatens to destabilize the hierarchy of values he would uphold. If Petruchio succeeds in mastering Kate, his position as master is nevertheless qualified by his own subjection to the exigencies and uncertainties of the new mar-

---

2. *OED*, 16:983. Note that this definition dates from the beginning of the sixteenth century.
3. According to Marx, it is "the physical body of the commodity which is the use-value or useful thing" (126).
4. "Commodities first enter into the process of exchange ungilded and unsweetened, retaining their original home-grown shape. Exchange, however, produces a differentiation of the commodity into two elements, commodity and money, an external opposition which expresses the opposition between use-value and value which is inherent in it" (Marx, 198–99).
5. The term *chattel* derives from the Latin *capitale* and in the sixteenth century meant either "capital, principal," or, more commonly, "a movable possession; any possession or piece of property other than real estate or a freehold" (*OED*, 3:59).
6. By the late sixteenth century the landed gentry had to a large extent adopted an emergent-market view of land and labor, though their view of their own society was still governed by residual concepts of feudal entitlement; see Stone and Stone, 181–210.

ket economy. In his endeavor to domesticate the commodity form, one might say, Petruchio is himself commodified, himself subjected to the logic of commodity exchange. As Gremio so eloquently puts it: in taming Kate, Petruchio is himself "Kated" [3.2.237]

The contradictions inherent in Petruchio's class status make his task as shrew-tamer a complex one: he must restrict his wife's consumption without abolishing it entirely, must ensure that it adequately bears testimony to his own elite status without simultaneously leading him to financial ruin. The urgent requirement to maintain a proper balance between expenditure and thrift in the elite (or would-be elite) household and the perceived danger of delegating this task to the housewife are described in the following mid-seventeenth-century letter of advice, written by the Marquis of Halifax to his daughter:

> The Art of laying out Money wisely, is not attained to without a great deal of thought; and it is yet more difficult in the Case of a *Wife*, who is accountable to her *Husband* for her mistakes in it: It is not only his *Money*, his *Credit* too is at Stake, if what lyeth under the *Wife's* Care is managed, either with undecent *Thrift*, or too loose *Profusion*; you are therefore to keep the *Mean* between these two *Extreams*, . . . when you once break through those bounds, you launch into a wide Sea of *Extravagance*.[7]

At stake in the housewife's proper management of money or economic capital, Halifax suggests, is her husband's credit, or symbolic capital. "Symbolic capital," Bourdieu maintains, "is always *credit*, in the widest sense of the word, i.e. a sort of advance which the group alone can grant those who give it the best material and symbolic *guarantees*."[8] It is not simply that economic capital serves to buttress symbolic capital when it is spent on "material and symbolic guarantees" such as status objects. Symbolic capital in turn attracts economic capital: "the exhibition of symbolic capital (which is always very expensive in economic terms) is one of the mechanisms which (no doubt universally) make capital go to capital."[9] Yet symbolic and economic capital are not always mutually reinforcing. Indeed, insofar as "symbolic capital can only be accumulated at the expense of the accumulation of economic capital," the two are often at odds.[1] In the case of the upwardly mobile gentry in early modern England, as the Stones make clear, the effort to balance the two was an ongoing struggle.

---

7. [George Savile, Marquis of Halifax], *The Lady's New-years Gift: or, Advice to a Daughter*, 3d ed. (London: M. Gillyflower and J. Partridge, 1688), 86–90.
8. Bourdieu, *Outline*, 181.
9. Bourdieu, *Outline*, 181.
1. Bourdieu, *Outline*, 180.

In this context the early modern housewife's new role in the symbolic ordering of household cates takes on its full importance. She was made responsible for maintaining the proper balance of economic and symbolic capital within the household economy. The early modern housewife had to learn to spend enough to ensure her husband's status or cultural credit without overspending his income or economic credit.

* * *

* * * It becomes the ideological burden of Kate's final speech to conceal the economic underpinnings of her symbolic labor, to render them culturally invisible. The speech accomplishes this task by defining the housewife's (nonproductive) activity as a form of leisure rather than labor:

> Thy husband is thy lord, thy life, thy keeper,
> Thy head, thy sovereign; one that cares for thee,
> And for thy maintenance; commits his body
> To painful labour both by sea and land,
> To watch the night in storms, the day in cold,
> Whilst thou liest warm at home, secure and safe;
> And craves no other tribute at thy hands
> But love, fair looks, and true obedience;
> Too little payment for so great a debt.
>   [5.2.150–158]

Kate's speech inaugurates a new gendered division of labor, according to which husbands "labour both by sea and land" while their wives luxuriate at home, their "soft," "weak" bodies being "unapt to toil and trouble in the world" (ll. 166–67). It is this new division of labor that produces the economic invisibility and unremunerated status of housework described by housework theory. In erasing the status of housework as work, separate-sphere ideology renders the housewife perpetually indebted to her husband insofar as her "love, fair looks, and true obedience" are insufficient "payment" for the material comfort in which she is "kept."

Within the terms of the play, however, the unremunerated status of housework derives not from its circumscription within a matrix of use-value production but from the cultural necessity of concealing the economic origins of the housewife's symbolic labor. If *The Taming of the Shrew* may be said to map the market's infiltration of the household through the commodity form in late-sixteenth-century England, it also marks the emergence of the ideological separation of feminine and masculine spheres of labor (and with it the separation of home/market and housework/work), which masked this infiltration by constructing the household as a refuge *from* the market. Ironically, Kate's final speech renders invisible the

housewife's managerial role as a consumer and caretaker of household cates—the very role for which Petruchio's "taming-school"
(4.2.54) seeks to prepare her. At the end of the play, she herself appears to stand idle, frozen within the domestic sphere, like a use-
less household cate.

* * *

FRANCES E. DOLAN

Household Chastisements:
Gender, Authority, and "Domestic Violence"[†]

Recently a number of critics have described sixteenth- and seventeenth-century English culture as a "culture of violence." Those who
do so tend to assume that such a culture is invariably dialectical:
Francis Barker, for instance, discusses "the dialectical relation between the coercive violence of the authorities on the one hand, and
the various forces which attempt to oppose, block or mitigate that violence on the other."[1] The evidence that early modern England was
a "culture of violence" comes most obviously, then, in its reliance on
public whippings, mutilations, burnings, hangings, and beheadings
to punish crime and maintain order, and in the occasional violent rebellions against state power. In such a culture, violence is not inevitably transgressive; it can assert authority or impose discipline as
well as betray a lack of control.[2] If violence is a pervasive means of
wielding power, preserving order, controlling behavior, and resolving
conflicts, then it must extend beyond the scaffold to less visible
sites, such as the household, in which relations are less clearly or
stably dialectical, violence takes on a subtler range of meanings,
and the line between acceptable and unacceptable, everyday and
transgressive violence must constantly be negotiated and redrawn.

The decorums shaping household discipline in early modern
England, and distinguishing between its legitimate and illegitimate
manifestations, suggest that many members of the domestic culture of violence were multiply positioned. The violence that subordinates learn, for instance, is not inevitably, as in Barker's dynamic,
turned against their oppressors; instead, a person who is the victim

---

† From *Renaissance Culture and Everyday Life*, ed. Patricia Fumerton and Simon Hunt
  (Philadelphia: University of Pennsylvania Press, 1999). Reprinted by permission of University of Pennsylvania Press.
1. Francis Barker, *The Culture of Violence: Essays on Tragedy and History* (Chicago: University of Chicago Press, 1993), p. 189.
2. Susan Dwyer Amussen, "Punishment, Discipline, and Power: The Social Meanings of
  Violence in Early Modern England," *Journal of British Studies* 34, 1 (1995): 1–34.

of violence in one location, or in relation to one person or group, may strive for dominance elsewhere (especially where the odds are better). Because of the wife and mistress's contradictory position in the early modern household—as both her husband's partner and his subordinate—I will scrutinize her relation to the culture of domestic violence in early modern England, hoping thereby to problematize the sharp dichotomy between the dominant and the subordinate, the violent and the victims. I am most interested here in the processes by which early modern culture attempted to distinguish between acceptable and unacceptable forms, targets, and occasions of violence in the household. Under what conditions were women licensed to discipline others? I am less interested in evidence of the extent to which women actually harmed, coerced, or threatened others than in a range of representations, including books on personal conduct, ballads, and plays such as *The Taming of the Shrew*, in which women's verbal and physical domination of others is constructed positively.

If, as Derek Cohen argues, "acts of violence belong to patriarchy as surely as fathers do," the violence in patriarchal households is not perpetrated only by fathers.[3] While marriage was widely represented in the early modern period as a struggle for dominance in which violence was, according to Joy Wiltenburg, "the fundamental arbiter," wives were not imagined to be violent only when resisting their husbands, despite the fact that such violent resistance was feared and frequently represented.[4] Elsewhere I have examined the disparity between assize court records, which tend to depict women more often as the victims of domestic *murder* than its perpetrators, and legal statutes, pamphlets, plays, and ballads, which invert this pattern by depicting women as the dangerous, rather than endangered, murderers of their intimates.[5] This sharp opposition—between the representation of women as casualties in court records and as killers in a range of legal and literary representations—collapses when the focus shifts from murder to non-lethal forms of violence. So does the sharp opposition between court records and other kinds of evidence. Prosecution rates are an unreliable gauge of the extent of any kind of legally prohibited conduct; they are even less helpful in assessing acceptable conduct. Non-lethal physical and verbal abuse is difficult to document through legal records

3. Derek Cohen, *Shakespeare's Culture of Violence* (New York: St. Martin's, 1993), p. 1. The assumption that men were the only or the primary disciplinarians in households is widely shared.
4. Joy Wiltenburg, *Disorderly Women and Female Power in the Street Literature of Early Modern England and Germany* (Charlottesville: University of Virginia Press, 1992), p. 137.
5. Frances E. Dolan, *Dangerous Familiars: Representations of Domestic Crime in England, 1550–1700* (Ithaca, N.Y.: Cornell University Press, 1994).

because, for the most part, it was not illegal; as a result, it is impossible to quantify how common or how severe domestic violence was in the early modern period. Indeed, "domestic violence" seems an inadequate category for describing a whole range of behaviors, some of which were considered transgressive at the time and many others of which were not. The category elides the very distinctions that gave meaning to the use of physical force in early modern households, and obscures the rules by which that force was applied.

Those forms of violence that were censured in the early modern period as transgressive or disorderly, and were therefore scrutinized and regulated, are the most visible now. Legal records, and subsequent scholarship, focus on those assaults by subordinate women against their social superiors which can be understood as acts of resistance—for instance, the transgressive speech of "scolds" and "witches." Verbal or physical assaults on one's social *inferiors* left few traces precisely because they were not seen as transgressive. Furthermore, men's and women's non-criminal uses of violence were not of particular interest to those who documented sensational crimes. Obscured because it is assumed to be acceptable and unremarkable, non-lethal violence against acceptable targets (that is, obvious subordinates) tends to appear in comedies rather than tragedies, in subplots rather than mainplots, in folktales, ballads, and jokes, and woven through the prescriptions in books on personal conduct. In the absence of any unmediated access to what actually happened in early modern households, such discourses offer valuable insight into the available constructions of acceptable modes of domestic discipline. Such constructions, while not necessarily descriptions of lived experience, would have informed that experience, shaping its conditions of possibility.

The Taming of the Shrew provides a useful focus because it is increasingly labelled a "problem" comedy, in part because many readers and viewers find the taming process so disturbing. But where is the violence in the households the play depicts? If asked, most students of the play will focus on the relationship between Katharine and Petruchio, then immediately become confused. For the most expected form of domestic violence—wife-beating—does *not* occur here. Yet in looking for Petruchio to hit Katharine, and being unsettlingly disappointed that he does not, it is easy to miss the other forms of violence through which they negotiate their relationship, as well as the most prominent kind of violence in the play—the beating of servants by both masters and mistresses.

The shrew-taming tradition, which includes jokes, ballads, stories, and plays such as *The Taming of the Shrew*, and which thrives throughout the early modern period, assumes a gendered domestic hierarchy—man in charge, woman his subordinate—which is over-turned by the shrew and righted by her tamer. The tradition is or-ganized around a double standard for domestic violence. The shrews in folktales and ballads routinely encroach on their hus-band's authority and usurp their power by beating, as well as scold-ing, them. The frequent pun on "baiting" and "beating" reinforces this association; in *The Winter's Tale*, for instance, Leontes calls Paulina "a callat [scold] / Of boundless tongue, who late hath beat her husband,/ And now baits me" (2.3.91–93).[6] The "patient" hus-bands whose laments are recorded in ballads often complain about their wives' violence: in "The Patient Husband and the Scolding Wife" (c. 1660–80), the husband complains that his wife broke his nose with a ladle and beat him until he "bepist" himself; in "The Cruel Shrew: Or, The Patient Man's Woe" (c. 1600–50), the hus-band describes how his wife "takes up a cudgel's end,/ and breaks my head full sore."[7] In striking the first (and only) blow in her con-flict with her husband, Katharine is thus typical of the physically and verbally abusive "shrew." Although this tradition depicts shrews as initiating, even monopolizing, domestic violence, it also suggests that the shrew's self-assertions, no matter how angry and violent, are temporary.[8]

The patient husband can regain his appropriate mastery through his own show of violence, a violence provoked and justified by his wife's conduct. Although some husbands lament their inability to rise to the challenge—the husband in "My Wife Will Be My Mas-ter" (c. 1640), for instance, regrets that he is not "a lusty man, and able for to baste" his wife—most husbands in these stories respond to their wives' insults and blows with maximum force.[9] The most fa-mous example of this is the lengthy verse tale *A Merry Jest of a Shrewd and Curst Wife Lapped in Morel's Skin* (c. 1550), often considered a source for *The Taming of the Shrew*, in which a hus-band locks his wife in the cellar, beats her senseless with rods, then wraps her raw, bleeding body in a salted horsehide until she sub-mits to him. As this example shows, the husband's violence—depicted as discipline more than as retaliation—is excessive. This is

6. Citations of all Shakespeare plays other than *The Taming of the Shrew* are from *The Complete Works of Shakespeare*, ed. David Bevington, 4th ed. (New York: Harper Collins, 1994).
7. *Roxburghe Ballads*, vols. 1–3 ed. William Chappell; vols. 4–9 ed. J. Woodfall Ebsworth (Hertford: Ballad Society, 1872–99), rpt. 9 vols. (New York: AMS, 1966), 7: 182–84, 1: 94–98.
8. On the shrew-taming tradition, see Lynda E. Boose, "Scolding Brides and Bridling Scolds: Taming the Woman's Unruly Member," *Shakespeare Quarterly* 42, 2 (1991): 179–213; Valerie Wayne, "Refashioning the Shrew," *Shakespeare Studies* 17 (1985): 159–87; Wiltenburg, *Disorderly Women*; and Linda Woodbridge, *Women and the English Renaissance: Literature and the Nature of Womankind, 1540–1620* (Urbana: University of Illinois Press, 1984).
9. *Roxburghe Ballads* 7: 188–89.

hardly a prescription for actual conduct, especially since most wives would not have survived such treatment. What interests me here is the double standard governing the violence in the shrew-taming tradition: women's violence is depicted as disorderly and transgressive; men's violence is depicted as a legitimate way of restoring the order that women have overturned. Violence thus seems to be a masculine prerogative that shrews usurp; when they insist on wearing the breeches, they also seize the rod.

But outside the supposedly comic shrew-taming tradition the gendering of domestic violence is considerably more complicated. Men's use of violence was not always endorsed, nor was women's use of violence always censured or ridiculed. During this period, as various scholars have shown, men's use of violence in the house-hold was being questioned and monitored. Wife-beating had an ambiguous status in the early modern culture of violence precisely because of the wife's double position as an "authoritative mistress who is also a subjected wife."[1] Although a wife's misbehavior might sometimes require that she be treated like a child, that is, beaten, in most cases "that small disparity which . . . is betwixt man and wife," according to divine William Gouge, "permitteth not so high a power in an husband, and so low a servitude in a wife, as for him to beate her."[2] Wife-beating was not illegal, and within limits—that is, if it did not kill, maim, or make too much noise—neighbors and courts did not intervene to stop it. Yet prescriptive texts urged men not to abuse their right to "correct" and discipline their wives, not because it was immoral or unfair, but because it was counterpro-ductive.[3]

While the comic tradition of violent spousal antagonism rollicked on, prescriptive literature articulated an emergent sense that the

1. Catherine Belsey, *The Subject of Tragedy: Identity and Difference in Renaissance Drama* (London: Methuen, 1985), p. 154. See also, among many others, Lena Cowen Orlin, *Private Matters and Public Culture in Post-Reformation England* (Ithaca, N.Y.: Cornell University Press, 1994), pp. 98–104. While the wife's double position has been much discussed, her relation to the complex dynamics of domestic discipline has not.
2. William Gouge, *Of Domesticall Duties: Eight Treatises* (London, 1634), p. 395. Modern-ized and standardized versions of many of the primary texts discussed here are included in William Shakespeare, *The Taming of the Shrew: Texts and Contexts*, ed. Frances E. Dolan (Boston: Bedford Books, 1996); references to the play will be to David Beving-ton's edition, included in that volume. Line numbers in brackets refer to this Norton Critical Edition.
3. On changing attitudes toward domestic violence, see Susan Dwyer Amussen, " 'Being stirred to much unquietness': Violence and Domestic Violence in Early Modern En-gland," *Journal of Women's History* 6.2 (1994): 70–89; Emily Detmer, "Civilizing Subor-dination: Domestic Violence and *The Taming of the Shrew*," *Shakespeare Quarterly* 48, 3 (1997): 273–94; Anthony Fletcher, *Gender, Sex, and Subordination in England 1500–1800* (New Haven and London: Yale University Press, 1995), chaps. 10 and 11; Laura Gowing, *Domestic Dangers: Women, Words, and Sex in Early Modern London* (Ox-ford: Clarendon Press, 1996), chap. 6; and Margaret Hunt, "Wife Beating, Domesticity and Women's Independence in Eighteenth-Century London," *Gender and History* 4.1 (1992): 10–33.

household, at least for husband and wife, should not be a site of physical contests. William Gouge even goes so far as to argue that a particularly recalcitrant wife who will not respond to "forceable meanes" other than beating, which might include being "restrained of liberty, [and] denied such things as she most affecteth," should be handed over to a magistrate to be beaten so that "shee may feare the Magistrate, and feele his hand, rather then her husbands."[4] Although William Whately argues that "even blows," when they are provoked, deserved, and judiciously administered as a last resort, "may well stand with the dearest kindnesses of matrimony," blows and marriage were increasingly being viewed as incompatible.[5] It is impossible to tell whether men were actually hitting their wives less frequently or less hard. But prescriptive literature was constructing wife-beating as a failure of control, a lapse in good household government. Although violence became a less acceptable solution to spousal strife, if not a less common one, the alternative, offered in *The Taming of the Shrew* as well as in prescriptions for domestic conduct, is not a nonviolent household. Instead, a happy ending involves ingenious forms of coercion which can be called "policy" rather than "force" and the redirection of both spouses' violence away from one another and toward more acceptable, that is, unambiguously subordinate, targets.

The focus on Petruchio's methods of taming Katharine, as well as the assumption that domestic violence is always and only enacted by husbands against wives, can obscure who hits whom and why in the play. As I have mentioned, Petruchio never strikes Katharine, despite the fact that she strikes him. Yet, as part of his "politic" regime for taming her, he relies on physical violence, directed at those near her and enacted before her eyes. The first instance of violence we see in the play occurs when Petruchio wrings Grumio's ears (1.2). At the wedding, Petruchio cuffs the priest and throws winesops in the sexton's face (3.2). We hear that on their way home, he beats Grumio because Katharine's horse stumbled (4.1); once at home, he kicks, strikes, and throws food at his servants (4.1). Many critics emphasize that Petruchio's violence "is not aimed at Kate."[6] But whether we believe that Petruchio routinely acts this way, or that this is a performance in which he and his servants collaborate (a favorite justification of his conduct by critics, for which there is little evidence), he directs his violence at his subordinates—at those over whom he has power—to remind Katharine that she, too, is his subordinate and that he could beat

4. Gouge, *Of Domesticall Duties*, p. 397.
5. William Whately, *A Bride-Bush* (London, 1623), p. 108.
6. Wayne, "Refashioning the Shrew," p. 171.

her if he chose. At the wedding, we are told that Katharine "trembled and shook" [3.2.160]; when Petruchio abuses his servants, she intervenes to stop or reprimand him (4.1). She responds as if the violence *is* "aimed at" and threatening to her.

Just as Petruchio simultaneously espouses a "politic regime" that distinguishes him from other shrew-tamers and engages in extremely violent behavior, so Katharine is simultaneously tamed and domineering. Katharine, like Petruchio, uses violence to assert mastery over those to whom she feels superior. She threatens to hit Hortensio on the head with a three-legged stool [1.1.64–5]; she ties up Bianca and strikes her; she breaks Hortensio's/Litio's head with the lute; and she strikes Petruchio (2.1). Petruchio's servants assume that Katharine will be violent toward them. Grumio warns Curtis that he will "soon feel" their new mistress's hand, "she being now at hand" [4.1.26]. Indeed, later at Petruchio's house, Katharine beats Grumio for refusing to feed her (4.2).

Katharine's violence toward characters other than Petruchio is not necessarily, or not only, "shrewish." That is, it is not invariably depicted as something she must learn not to do. For if the blow she strikes at Petruchio allies her to the shrew tradition, some of her other outbursts place her in the tradition of spirited English lasses or, as Petruchio says admiringly, "lusty wench[es]" [2.1.158]. In this tradition, in which women's violence is celebrated as helpful and fun, women assault others (usually men) in the interests of English nationalism, sexual probity, and social order. In the ballad "Couragious Betty of Chick-Lane," Betty beats up two tailors who "provoke" her—"She bang'd 'em, and bruis'd 'em, and bitterly us'd 'em"—thus reforming them; in "The Coy Cook-Maid," the far from coy maid brains, kicks, and threatens her Irish, Welsh, Spanish, French, and Dutch suitors, holding out for the poor English tailor, to whom she submits.[7]

*   *   *

In all of these cases, women vent their spleen only against those who have no authority over them, and who are stout antagonists rather than dependents; the spectacle is therefore entertaining rather than threatening. In the last scene of *The Taming of the Shrew*, Petruchio urges Katharine to play the role of lusty wench in her verbal sparring match with the widow: "To her, Kate!" [5.2.34].

But Katharine is not only a "lusty wench," but a wife and mistress; her characterization participates in yet another discourse constructing women's violence positively. Prescriptive texts on personal conduct suggest that, under certain circumstances, women's

7. *Roxburghe Ballads* 3: 641–44; 3: 627–30.

use of violence was acceptable and unremarkable. In those relations in which women had authority—over servants and children,
for instance—they were licensed to use violence. In fact, they were
empowered to use violence to the same extent that they were construed as inappropriate targets of it. William Gouge's claim, for instance, that "God hath not ranked wives among those in the family
who are to be corrected" depends upon the assumption that God
has ranked others, children and servants, "among those in the family who are to be corrected."[8] The distinction made between wife-
beating and servant-beating relied on the assumption that servants
(like children, but unlike wives) were unambiguously subordinate
to their masters. Even as prescriptive literature censured blows between spouses as disorderly, it defended the corporal punishment
of servants as crucial to the maintenance of order. As Dod and
Cleaver argue: "God hath put the rod of correction in the hands of
the Governors of the family, by punishments to save them from de-
struction which, if the bridle were let loose unto them, they would
run unto"; "household chastisement is agreeable to God's will, [as]
is evident out of the Proverbs."[9] The wife asserts and maintains her
status as "a joynt governour of the family" by administering "correction," especially corporal punishment.[1] To see women only as
victims or resisters is to ignore those locations and relations in
which women had authority; it also oversimplifies women's position
in the household. While the household was an arena in which
women were subordinate, it was also the arena in which they could
most readily and legitimately exercise authority. Thus it was not just
masculinity that was associated with violence—usurped by the
shrew, then reasserted in the taming—but authority.

If some evidence suggests that the household was a dangerous
place for women, in which they could be starved, overworked, sexually preyed upon, or beaten with little recourse, other kinds of evidence depict the household as a place in which women were
dangerously powerful and likely to injure others. Assize court
records, for instance, cast women in significant roles as the murderers of children and servants, who were more likely than any
other members of the household to be murdered by family members. According to J. A. Sharpe, women constituted 7% of those accused of non-domestic killing, but 42% of those accused of killing a
relative, and 41% of those accused of killing servants or apprentices, in Essex assizes, 1560–1709; women also figured importantly

---

8. Gouge, *Of Domesticall Duties*, p. 395.
9. John Dod and Robert Cleaver, *A Godly Forme of Household Government* (London,
   1612), sigs. D5ᵛ, D4ᵛ.
1. Gouge, *Of Domesticall Duties*, p. 395.

in prosecutions for the murder of children, especially newborns.[2] The high acquittal rate for murders of servants suggests a reluctance to punish discipline that gets out of hand, that is, to criminalize household chastisement. Of 44 persons accused at these assizes of killing servants or apprentices, only 5 were found guilty (3 men, 2 women).[3] While these assize records would seem to suggest that women were more likely to murder their servants or their children than anyone else, they also represent only those outbreaks of violence in the family that ended in death, and that were discovered and prosecuted. As J. S. Cockburn has argued, "the true dimensions of domestic violence in earlier times are irretrievably lost behind a veil of domestic privacy, societal reticence and the common-law doctrine which sanctioned the 'moderate' correction of wives, children and servants by heads of households."[4] This veil was designed to protect the authority and privacy of *male* heads of household; but it also obscures the role of women in correcting servants and children.

Advice on running households and governing families often confers on women not only the right but the responsibility to use force. * * * Although household chastisement was an obligation, it was not a license to lash out in anger. Instead, domestic discipline was expected to operate within carefully delineated rules.[5]

Again, the issue is that peers may not hit peers or subordinates their superiors.[6] Striking a subordinate counts as a transgression only when it disregards the rules.

* * *

In *The Taming of the Shrew*, we begin with the familiar spectacle of a woman who abuses authority—Katharine binding and striking her younger sister—and then watch the process by which she learns the complex etiquette for domestic violence. Obviously, Petruchio teaches other husbands how to tame their unruly wives. Under his instruction, Katharine also learns not only how to be an obedient wife, but how to use violence to assert dominance in more socially acceptable ways. Although many critics argue that, as actress Fiona Shaw puts it, "Petruchio abuses a servant to teach her that the abuse of servants isn't right," I would argue that Petruchio inducts Katharine into a more complex moral universe and network of power

---

2. J. A. Sharpe, "Domestic Homicide in Early Modern England," *The Historical Journal* 24, 1 (1981): 29–48, esp. pp. 37, 36; J. S. Cockburn, "Patterns of Violence in English Society: Homicide in Kent, 1560–1985," *Past and Present* 130 (February 1991): 70–106, esp. pp. 95–97.
3. Sharpe, "Domestic Homicide," pp. 38–39.
4. Cockburn, "Patterns of Violence," pp. 93–95.
5. Amussen, " 'Being Stirred'," p. 82, and "Punishment," pp. 12–18.
6. On why servants should not hit their fellows, see Thomas Carter, *Carters Christian Commonwealth; or, Domesticall Dutyes Deciphered* (London, 1627), sigs. S4–S5.

relations than this.[7] This is especially clear in *The Taming of a Shrew*, in which the violence progresses differently. In this "alternate version" of the play, printed in 1594, the first violent act we witness is Ferando (the husband and master, or Petruchio figure) beating his servants in front of Kate; as a stage direction explains, "He beates them all."[8] Kate's first act of violence is not to beat her tutor, her suitor, or her sister (none of whom she ever hits in this version), but to beat her husband's servant, *after* she has watched him do so repeatedly. In this version of the play, she observes and emulates violence toward servants as an acceptable form of unruliness, which purports to maintain rather than disrupt household order.

Throughout *The Taming of the Shrew*, Katharine attempts to instruct others in obedience and subordination by means of both physical violence (from torturing her sister to "swingeing" Bianca and the widow "soundly forth unto their husbands" [5.2.108]) and of assertive speech (from her first complaint to her father to her final sermon to other wives). What Katharine learns is not to be less aggressive, but to redirect her violence toward more appropriate targets; that Bianca becomes an acceptable target by the end of the play—a "breeching scholar"—suggests how the balance of power has shifted between the sisters. When Katharine uses violence to dominate servants and other women rather than to resist her father and husband, her conduct is presented as acceptable, even admirable.

While it is true that Katharine often resorts to violence "because of provocation or intimidation resulting from her status as a woman," as Coppèlia Kahn has argued, she also acts out of an empowerment resulting from her status as a *gentle*woman.[9] She acts simultaneously out of gender subordination and class (or age) privilege. It is not just that class is displaced onto gender * * *, but also

---

7. Carol Rutter, *Clamorous Voices: Shakespeare's Women Today* (London: Women's Press, 1988), p. 18. In her recent essay on the play, Natasha Korda also emphasizes an educational process, in this case one in which Petruchio "seeks to educate Kate in her new role as a consumer of household cates" (Natasha Korda, "Household Kates: Domesticating Commodities in *The Taming of the Shrew*," *Shakespeare Quarterly* 47, 2 [1996]: 109–31, esp. p. 112). As I do here, Korda emphasizes the authority conferred on the housewife in prescriptive literature, and in the play, but she focuses on the authority to oversee and manage status objects, rather than to discipline servants.

8. *A Pleasant Conceited History, Called The Taming of a Shrew*, ed. Graham Holderness and Bryan Loughrey (Lanham, Md.: Barnes and Noble, 1992), sig. D3. Compared to *The Shrew, A Shrew* also makes it more clear that, in the "wager scene," Kate "brings her sisters forth by force . . . thrusting [them] before her." *The Taming of a Shrew* was published in 1594; *The Taming of the Shrew* was not published until 1623, in Shakespeare's First Folio. Critics have long debated the relationship between the two versions. See Graham Holderness, "Introduction," to his facsimile edition, p. 34; Brian Morris, "Introduction," *The Taming of the Shrew*, by William Shakespeare, ed. Morris (London: Methuen, 1981), pp. 12–50.

9. Coppèlia Kahn, *Man's Estate: Masculine Identity in Shakespeare* (Berkeley: University of California Press, 1981), pp. 104–18, p. 108.

that attention to gender alone can obscure conflicts of class in which Katharine is a privileged participant.

*   *   *

I am *not* arguing here that Katharine and Petruchio are "equals" in the culture of domestic violence. He clearly has the upper hand, because he controls Katharine's access to material resources (like food), he is stronger, he has more lines, he addresses the audience directly and when he is alone (we never see Katharine alone), and, as the husband, he is assumed to be the one who should be "on top." Indeed, he rewards Katharine's submission to him by authorizing her to domineer over others. Furthermore, in early modern England, men and women use different forms of violence, choose different targets, and act violently in different contexts. Gender shapes how the culture perceives and responds to their violence. All of the representations I have discussed, from conduct books to plays, are to some extent prescriptive, instructing men and women in these complexly gendered decorums of violence.

*   *   *

LYNDA E. BOOSE

Scolding Brides and Bridling Scolds: Taming the Woman's Unruly Member[†]

For feminist scholars, the irreplaceable value if not pleasure to be realized by an historicized confrontation with Shakespeare's *The Taming of the Shrew* lies in the unequivocality with which the play locates both women's abjected position in the social order of early modern England and the costs exacted for resistance. For romantic comedy to "work" normatively in *Shrew*'s concluding scene and allow the audience the happy ending it demands, the cost is, simply put, the construction of a woman's speech that must unspeak its own resistance and reconstitute female subjectivity into the self-abnegating rhetoric of Kate's famous disquisition on obedience. The cost is Kate's self-deposition, where—in a performance not unlike Richard II's—she moves centerstage to dramatize her own similarly theatrical rendition of "Mark, how I will undo myself."

Apparently from the play's inception its sexual politics have inspired controversy. Within Shakespeare's own lifetime it elicited John Fletcher's sequel, *The Woman's Prize, or The Tamer Tam'd,*

† *Shakespeare Quarterly* 42.2 (Summer 1991): 179–213. © The John Hopkins University Press. Reprinted with permission of the Johns Hopkins University Press.

which features Petruchio marrying a second, untamable wife after his household tyranny has sent poor Kate to an early grave. As the title itself announces, Fletcher's play ends with Petruchio a reclaimed and newly lovable husband—"a woman's prize"—and, needless to say, a prize who still has the last words of the drama. Yet Fletcher's response may in itself suggest the kind of discomfort that *Shrew* has characteristically provoked in men and why its many revisions since 1594 have repeatedly contrived ways of softening the edges, especially in the concluding scene, of the play's vision of male supremacy. Ironically enough, if *The Taming of the Shrew* presents a problem to male viewers, the problem lies in its representation of a male authority so successful that it nearly destabilizes the very discourse it so blatantly confirms. Witness George Bernard Shaw's distress:

> No man with any decency of feeling can sit it out in the company of a woman without being extremely ashamed of the lord-of-creation moral implied in the wager and the speech put into the woman's own mouth.[1]

Yet the anxiety that provokes Shaw's reaction hardly compares with what the play's conclusion would, by that same logic, produce in women viewers. For Kate's final *pièce de non résistance* is constructed not as the speech of a discrete character speaking her role within the expressly marked-out boundaries of a play frame; it is a textual moment in which, in Althusserian terms, the play quite overtly "interpellates," or hails, its women viewers into an imaginary relationship with the ideology of the discourse being played out onstage by their counterparts.[2] Having "fetched hither" the emblematic pair of offstage wives who have declined to participate in this game of patriarchal legitimation, Kate shifts into an address targeted at some presumptive Everywoman. Within that address women viewers suddenly find themselves universal conscripts, trapped within the rhetorical co-options of a discourse that dissolves all difference between the "I" and "you" of Kate and her reluctant sisters. Kate vacates the space of subjectivity in

> I am ashamed that women are so simple
> To offer war where they should kneel for peace,
> Or seek for rule, supremacy and sway,
> When they are bound to serve, love and obey. . . .
> Come, come, you froward and unable worms,

1. *Saturday Review*, 6 November 1897, as quoted in editor Ann Thompson's introduction to the New Cambridge Shakespeare *The Taming of the Shrew* (Cambridge: Cambridge Univ. Press, 1984), p. 21. Line numbers in brackets refer to this Norton Critical Edition.
2. Louis Althusser, "Ideology and Ideological State Apparatuses" in *Lenin and Philosophy and Other Essays*, trans. Ben Brewster (London: New Left Books, 1971).

My mind hath been as big as one of yours,
My heart as great, my reason haply more,
To bandy word for word and frown for frown.
But now I see our lances are but straws,
Our strength as weak, our weakness past compare,
That seeming to be most which we indeed least are.
Then vail your stomachs, for it is no boot,
And place your hands below your husband's foot.

[5.2.174–81 ff]

In doing so, she rhetorically pushes everyone marked as "woman" out of that space along with her. And it is perhaps precisely because women's relationships to this particular comedy are so ineluctably bound up in such a theatricalized appropriation of feminine choice that Shakespeare's play ultimately becomes a kind of primary text within which each woman reader of successive eras must renegotiate a (her) narrative.

Inevitably, it is from the site/sight of the subjected and thoroughly spectacularized woman that virtually all critiques of *The Taming of the Shrew* have felt compelled to begin. For when Kate literally prostrates herself in her final lines of the play and thus rearranges the sexual space onstage, she reconfigures the iconography of heterosexual relationship not merely for herself but for all of those "froward and unable worms" inscribed within her interpellating discourse. Not surprisingly, the discomforts of such a position have produced an investment even greater in female than in male viewers in reimagining an ending that will at once liberate Kate from meaning what she says and simultaneously reconstruct the social space into a vision of so-called "mutuality"—an ending that will satisfy the "illusion of a potentially pleasureable, even subversive space for Kate."[3] Thus, the critical history of *Shrew* reflects a tradition in which such revisionism has become a kind of orthodoxy. For albeit in response to a play which itself depends upon the exaggerations of gender difference, the desires of directors, players, audiences, and literary critics of both sexes have been curiously appeased by a similar representation: whether for reasons of wishing to save Kate from her abjection or Petruchio from the embarrassment of having coerced it, almost everyone, it seems, wants this play to emphasize "Kate's and Petruchio's mutual sexual attraction, affection, and satisfaction [and] deemphasize her coerced submission to him."[4] Ultimately, what is under covert recuperation and

---

3. The phrase comes from Barbara Hodgdon's essay, forthcoming in PMLA, "Katherina Bound, or Pla(k)ating the Strictures of Everyday Life," which offers an insightful assessment of the visual pleasures that performance of this play makes available to the female spectator.
4. Carol Thomas Neely, *Broken Nuptials in Shakespeare's Plays* (New Haven: Yale Univ. Press, 1985), p. 218.

imagined as tacitly at stake is the institution of heterosexual marriage.

*   *   *

For what transpires onstage turns out to be a virtual representation of the ceremony that women were required to perform in most pre-Reformation marriage services throughout Europe. In England this performance was in force as early as the mid-fifteenth century and perhaps earlier; and it may well have continued in local practice even after Archbishop Cranmer had reformed the Book of Common Prayer in 1549 and excised just such ritual excesses.[5] Kate's prostration before her husband and the placing of her hand beneath his foot follow the ceremonial directions that accompany the Sarum (Salisbury) Manual, the York Manual, the Scottish Rathen Manual, and the French Martène (*Ordo IV*) for the response the bride was to produce when she received the wedding ring and her husband's all-important vow of endowment.

According to the Use of Sarum, after the bridegroom had given the vow, "With this rynge I wedde the, and with this golde and siluer I honoure the, and with this gyft I dowe thee," the priest next "asks the dower of the woman." If "land is given her in the dower," the bride "prostrates herself at the feet of the bridegroom." In one manuscript of the Sarum Rite, the bride is directed to "kiss the right foot" of her spouse, which she is to do "whether there is land in the doury or not."[6] The York, Rathen, and Martène manuals, however, direct "this courtesying to take place only when the bride has received land as her dower." As Shakespeare's audience knows, Petruchio has indeed promised Baptista that he will settle on his wife an apparently substantial jointure of land. And while Kate offers to place her hands below her husband's foot rather than kiss it, the stage action seems clearly enough to allude to a ritual that probably had a number of national and local variants. Thus Giles Fletcher, Queen Elizabeth's ambassador to Russia, writes of a Russian wedding:

> the Bride commeth to the Bridegroome (standing at the end of the altar or table) and falleth downe at his feete, knocking her head upon his shooe, in token of her subjection and obedi-

---

5. J. Wickham Legg, *Ecclesiological Essays* (London: de la More Press, 1903), p. 190.
6. George Elliott Howard, *A History of Matrimonial Institutions,* 2 vols. (London: T. Fisher Unwin, 1904), Vol. 1, pp. 306–7. *"Tunc procidat sposa ante pedes ejus, et deosculetur pedem ejus dextrum; tunc erigat eam sponsus"* (Surtees Society Publications, 63, 20 n.). See also J. Wickham Legg, pp. 189–90, and *The Rathen Manual: Catholic Church, Liturgy and Ritual,* ed. Duncan MacGregor (Aberdeen: Aberdeen Ecclesiological Society, 1905), p. 36. In comments on the wedding-ritual structure that underwrites the scene of Lear, Cordelia, and her suitors, I had earlier suggested the possibility of such a literal, ceremonial basis to the line "I take up what's cast away" (1.1.253) that France speaks to Cordelia ("The Father and the Bride in Shakespeare," *PMLA,* 97 [1982] 325–47, esp. pp. 333–34).

ence. And the Bridegroom again casteth the cappe of his gowne or upper garment over the Bride, in token of his duetie to protect and cherish her.[7]

Within the multi-vocal ritual logic of Christian marriage discourse, the moment in which the woman was raised up probably dramatized her rebirth into a new identity, the only one in which she could legally participate in property rights. Yet the representation of such a public performance obviously exceeds the religious and social significances it enacts. Giles Fletcher, for instance, reads the Russian ceremony through its political meanings. In its political iconography the enactment confirms hierarchy and male rule. And yet in its performance both in church and onstage, the woman's prostration—which is dictated by the unvoiced rubrics of the patriarchal script—is staged to seem as if it were an act of spontaneous gratitude arising out of choice.

From the perspective of twentieth-century feminist resistance, it is hardly possible to imagine this scene outside the context of feminine shame. Yet is it necessarily ahistorical to presume the validity of such a reading? Absent any surviving commentaries from sixteenth-century women who performed these rituals, perhaps we can nonetheless indirectly recover something about such women's reactions. In 1903 the Anglican church historian J. Wickham Legg transcribed the French Roman Catholic cleric J. B. Thiers's discussion of the ways that eighteenth-century French women had come to restage this ceremony:

> the bride was accustomed to let the ring fall from her finger as soon as it was put on. Necessarily she would stoop to pick up the ring, or make some attempt at this, and so a reason would be given for her bending or courtesying at her husband's feet, and the appearance of worship paid to him would be got rid of.[8]

What seems at work in the women's behavior is the same impulse that motivates certain feminist *Shrew* criticism—the creation of explanatory scenarios that will justify Kate's actions. Confronted by a ritual of self-debasement, the women strive to construct another narrative that will rationalize their stooping.

---

7. *Of the Russe Common Wealth*, chap. 24, fol. 101, as quoted in Legg, p. 190.
8. Legg, p. 190. See also J. B. Thiers, *Traité des Superstitions qui regardent les Sacremens*, 4th ed. (Avignon, 1777), Book 10, chap. 11, p. 457. Although the "falling at the feet of the husband" had been banished from the Anglican Rite for some 350 years by the time Legg wrote, his recognition of the women's resistance in the French text prompts him to decry "innovators in their slack teaching on the subject of matrimony" and comment acerbically that "the modern upholders of the rights of women would never endure this ceremony for one moment." As stays against such "modern ideas," he then invokes Augustine and Paul and digresses from his topic (marriage customs) to include Augustine's definition of a "good *materfamilias*" as a woman who "is not ashamed to call herself the servant (*ancilla*) of her husband" (pp. 190–91).

To locate the staging of *The Taming of the Shrew*'s final scene inside of the pre-Reformation English marriage ceremony may provide the missing historical analogue, but it hardly explains why Shakespeare chose to use it. For the wedding ceremony that Shakespeare's text alludes to, while almost certainly recognizable to an audience of the 1590s, was itself an anachronistic form outlawed by the Act of Uniformity over forty years earlier. Embedding the Kate and Petruchio marriage inside of a performance understood as prohibited inscribes the play's vision of male dominance as anachronism; but the very act of inscription collocates the anachronistic paradigm with the romantically idealized one and thus also recuperates the vision into a golden-age lament for a world gone by—a world signified by a ceremony that publicly confirmed such shows of male dominance. On the other hand, through just that collocation, the play has situated the volatile social issue of the politics of marriage on top of the equally volatile contemporary political schism over the authority of liturgical form. By means of constructing so precarious and controversial a resolution, the play works ever so slightly to unsettle its own ending and mark the return to so extremely patriarchal a marriage as a formula inseparable from a perilously divisive politics.

Thus it seems appropriate to perceive both *Shrew* and the world that produced it as texts in which gender is foregrounded through the model of a layered social fabric, with crisis stacked upon social crisis. According to David Underdown, the sense of impending breakdown in the social order was never "more widespread, or more intense, than in early modern England"; moreover, the breakdown was one that Underdown sees as having developed out of a "period of strained gender relations" that "lay at the heart of the 'crisis of order'."[9] The particular impact of this crisis in gender speaks through records that document a sudden upsurge in witchcraft trials and other court accusations against women, the "gendering" of various available forms of punishment, and the invention in these years of additional punishments specifically designated for women. As the forms of punishment and the assumptions about what officially constituted "crime" became progressively polarized by gender, there emerged a corresponding significant increase in instances of crime defined as exclusively female: "scolding," "witchcraft," and "whoring." But what is striking is that the punishments meted out to women are much more frequently targeted at suppressing women's speech than they are at controlling their sexual transgres-

9. "The Taming of the Scold: the Enforcement of Patriarchal Authority in Early Modern England" in *Order and Disorder in Early Modern England*, Anthony Fletcher and John Stevenson, eds. (Cambridge: Cambridge Univ. Press, 1985), pp. 116–36, esp. pp. 116, 136.

sions. In terms of available court records that document the lives of the "middling sort" in England's towns and larger villages, the chief social offenses seem to have been "scolding," "brawling," and dominating one's husband. The veritable prototype of the female offender of this era seems to be, in fact, the woman marked out as a "scold" or "shrew."

* * *

In *The Taming of the Shrew* Kate is the archetypal scold whose crime against society is her refusal to accept the so-called natural order of patriarchal hierarchy. But since Kate cannot be socially controlled by gender inversions that would treat her like a man, she * * * is instead treated to ritual humiliation inside the space of the feminine. In Shakespeare's play the shaming rites begin at the famous wedding.

* * *

Because shame is already a gendered piece of cultural capital, Petruchio can transgress norms of social custom and instigate the production of shame without it ever redounding upon him. He politicly begins his reign, in fact, by doing so. By inverting the wedding rite in such a way that compels its redoing and simultaneously depriving Kate of her renown as the "veriest shrew" in Padua, he seizes unquestioned control of the male space of authority. Of course, all the woman-shaming and overt male dominance here are dramatically arranged so as to make Kate's humiliation seem wildly comic and to festoon Petruchio's domination with an aura of romantic bravado bound up with the mock chivalry with which he "saves" Kate by carrying her away from the guests in a ritual capture, shouting, "Fear not, sweet wench, they shall not touch thee, Kate" [3.2.230–31]. But what is being staged so uproariously here is what we might call the benevolent version of the shaming of a scold. Kate is not being encouraged to enjoy even what pleasures may have attended the narrowly constructed space of womanhood. She is being shamed inside it. For, as Petruchio says in 4.1, she must be made, like a tamed falcon, to stoop to her lure—to come to know her keeper's call, and to come with gratitude and loving obedience into the social containment called wifehood. But she will do so only when she realizes that there are no other spaces for her to occupy, which is no doubt why Petruchio feels such urgency to shunt her away from the bridal feast and its space of honor in Padua and lead her off to the isolation defined by "her" new home, the space over which Petruchio has total mastery. Petruchio's politic reign is to construct womanhood for Kate as a site of seeming contradiction, the juncture where she occupies the positions of both shamed object and chivalric ideal. But it is between and inside those contradictions that the dependencies of "wifehood" can be constructed. When Kate realizes that there are no other socially available spaces, and when she furthermore realizes that Petruchio controls access to all sustenance, material possession, personal comfort, and spatial mobility, she will rationally choose to please him and encourage his generosity rather than, as he says, continue ever more crossing him in futile imitation of birds whose wings have been clipped—birds that are already enclosed but nonetheless continue to try to fly free: "these kites"—or kates—"That bate and beat and will not be obedient" [4.1.176]. Ultimately, in her final speech, Kate does, literally, "stoop" to her lure.

Kate is denied her bridal feast. Nonetheless, the bridal feast that is absent the bride acts as a particularly apt metaphor for the entire play, for the space of the feminine is actually the space under constant avoidance throughout. Even Bianca, who has seemed to occupy the space with relish, bolts out of it in the surprise role reversal at the end of the play. But in a world where gender has been constructed as a binary opposition, someone is going to be pushed into that space. Inside the pressures of such a binary, if the wife refuses or escapes this occupation, the husband loses his manhood. And thus, as Kate is being "gentled" and manipulated to enter the feminine enclosure of the sex-and-gender system, the audience is also being strategically manipulated to applaud her for embracing that fate and to resent Bianca for impelling poor adoring Lucentio into the site of nonmanhood. Through Bianca's refusal to compete in the contest of wifely subordination, Lucentio is left positioned as the play's symbolically castrated husband whose purse was cut off by a wife's rebellion. Since someone must occupy the abjected space of a binary—and since doing so is so much more humiliating for men—better (we say) in the interest of protecting the heterosexual bond that women should accept their inferiorization. By dramatizing Kate's resignation as her joyous acceptance of a world to which we recognize no alternatives exist, Shakespeare reinscribes the comfortingly familiar order inside of a dialogue that challenges the social distributions of power but concludes in a formula that invites us to applaud the reinstatement of the status quo.

* * *

For Tudor-Stuart England, in village and town, an obsessive energy was invested in exerting control over the unruly woman—the woman who was exercising either her sexuality or her tongue under her own control rather than under the rule of a man.[1]

---

1. John Webster Spargo, *Juridical Folklore in England: Illustrated by the Cucking-stool* (Durham, N.C.: Duke Univ. Press, 1944). Spargo devotes considerable time to examining this and other etymological questions; see esp. pp. 3–75. An exchange in Middleton's

*   *   *

* * *By being imagined as a defense of all the important institutions upon which the community depends, such a project could, in the minds of the magistrates and other local authorities, probably rationalize even such extreme measures as the strange instrument known as the "scold's bridle" or "brank."* * *Because records are so scarce, we have no precise idea of how widespread the use of the bridle really was. What we can know is that during the early modern era this device of containment was first invented—or, more accurately, adapted—as a punishment for the scolding woman. It is a device that today we would call an instrument of torture, despite the fact—as English legal history is proud to boast—that in England torture was never legal. Thus, whereas the instrument openly shows up in the Glasgow court records of 1574 as a punishment meted out to two quarreling women, if the item shows up at all in official English transactions, it is usually through an innocuous entry such as the one in the 1658 Worcester Corporation Records, which show that four shillings were "Paid for mending the bridle for bridleinge of scoulds, and two cords for the same."[2]

*   *   *

In Mr. T. N. Brushfield's Cheshire County alone he was able to discover thirteen of these 200–250-year-old artifacts still lying about the county plus an appallingly large number of references to their use. In fact some eighteen months after he had presented his initial count in 1858, Mr. Brushfield, with a dogged empiricism we can now be grateful for, informed the Society that he had come across three more specimens. There are, furthermore, apparently a number of extant bridles in various other parts of England, besides those in Chester County that Brushfield drew and wrote about,[3] and each one very likely carries with it its own detailed, local history. Nonetheless, so little has been written about them that had the industrious T. N. Brushfield not set about to report so exhaustively on scolds' bridles and female torture, we would have known almost nothing about these instruments except for an improbable-sounding story or two. As it is, whenever the common metaphor of "bridling a wife's tongue"

The Family of Love depends on the equation. In response to her husband's threat, "I say you are a scold, and beware the cucking-stool." Mistress Glister snaps back, "I say you are a ninnihammer, and beware the cuckoo" (The Works of Thomas Middleton, ed. A. H. Bullen, 8 vols. [London: Nimmo, 1885], 5.1.25–28). My thanks to Sarah Lyons for this reference.

2. T. N. Brushfield, "On Obsolete Punishments, with particular reference to those of Cheshire," in Chester Archaeological and Historic Society Journal, 2 (1855–62), 35 n.

3. I am particularly indebted to Susan Warren for her invaluable research in Cheshire County into this issue. Not only was she able to locate the whereabouts of several of these items, but she discovered from an overheard conversation between two women that the notion of a woman "needing to be bridled" was apparently still alive in the local phrasing.

turns up in the literature of this era, the evidence should make us uncomfortably aware of a practice lurking behind that phrase that an original audience could well have heard as literal.

Scolds' bridles are not directly mentioned as a means for taming the scold of Shakespeare's *Shrew*—and such a practice onstage would have been wholly antithetical to the play's desired romantic union as well as to the model of benevolent patriarchy that is insisted on here and elsewhere in Shakespeare.[4] What Shakespeare seems to have been doing in *Shrew* * * * is conscientiously modelling a series of humane but effective methods for behavioral modification. The methods employed determinedly exclude the more brutal patriarchal practices that were circulating within popular jokes, village rituals, and in such ballads as "A Merry Jest of a Shrewde and Curste Wyfe, Lapped in Morrelles Skin, for Her Good Behavyour," in which the husband tames his wife by first beating her and then wrapping her in the salted skin of the dead horse, "Morel." In 1594 or thereabout Shakespeare effectively pushes these practices off his stage. And in many ways his "shrew" takes over the cultural discourse from this point on, transforming the taming story from scenarios of physical brutality and reshaping the trope of the shrew/scold from an old, usually poor woman or a nagging wife into the newly romanticized vision of a beautiful, rich, and spirited young woman. But the sheer fact that the excluded brutalities lie suppressed in the margins of the shrew material also means that they travel, as unseen partners, inside the more benevolent taming discourse that Shakespeare's play helps to mold. And, as Ann Thompson's synopsis of *Shrew*'s production history clearly demonstrates, such woman-battering, although not part of Shakespeare's script, repeatedly leaks back in from the margins and turns up in subsequent productions and adaptations (including, for instance, the Burton-Taylor film version, to which director Franco Zefferelli added a spanking scene):

> In the late seventeenth century, John Lacey's *Sauny the Scott, or The Taming of the Shrew* (c. 1667), which supplanted Shakespeare's text on stage until it was replaced in 1754 by David Garrick's version called *Catherine and Petruchio*, inserts an additional scene in which the husband pretends to think that his wife's refusal to speak to him is due to toothache and sends for a surgeon to have her teeth drawn. This episode is repeated with relish in the eighteenth century in James Worsdale's adaptation, *A Cure for a Scold* (1735).[5]

4. See especially Peter Erickson, *Patriarchal Structures in Shakespeare's Drama* (Berkeley: Univ. of California Press, 1985).
5. pp. 18–19.

What turns up as the means to control rebellious women imagined by the play's seventeenth- and eighteenth-century versions is, essentially, the same form of violence as that suppressed in Shakespeare's playscript but available in the surrounding culture: the maiming/disfiguring of the mouth.

The scold's bridle is a practice tangled up in the cultural discourse about shrews. And while it is not materially present in the narrative of Shakespeare's play, horse references or horse representations—which are, oddly enough, an almost standard component of English folklore about unruly women—pervade the play.[6] The underlying literary "low culture" trope of unruly horse/unruly woman seems likely to have been the connection that led first to a metaphoric idea of bridling women's tongues and eventually to the literal social practice. Inside that connection, even the verbs "reign" and "rein" come together in a fortuitous pun that reinforces male dominance. And there would no doubt have been additional metaphoric reinforcement for bridling from the bawdier use of the horse/rider metaphor and its connotations of male dominance. In this trope, to "mount" and "ride" a woman works both literally and metaphorically to exert control over the imagined disorder presumed to result from the "woman on top." Furthermore, the horse and rider are not only the standard components of the shrew-taming folk stories but are likewise the key feature of "riding skimmington," which, unlike the French charivari customs of which it is a version, was intended to satirize marriages in which the wife was reputed to have beaten her husband (or was, in any case, considered the dominant partner).[7]

In shrew-taming folktale plots in general, the taming of the unruly wife is frequently coincident with the wedding trip home on

6. See especially Joan Hartwig, "Horses and Women in *The Taming of the Shrew*," *Huntington Library Quarterly*, 45 (1982), 285–94 and Jeanne Addison Roberts, "Horses and Hermaphrodites: Metamorphoses in *The Taming of the Shrew*," *Shakespeare Quarterly*, 34 (1983); 159–71, as well as Linda Woodbridge, *Women and the English Renaissance: Literature and the Nature of Womankind, 1540–1620* (Urbana: Univ. of Illinois Press, 1984).

7. Antiquarian folklorist C.R.B. Barrett notes, the first recorded skimmington at Charing Cross in 1562. See Barrett " 'Riding Skimmington' and 'Riding the Stang'," *Journal of the British Archaeological Association*, 1 (1895), 58–68, esp. p. 63. Barrett discusses the way that a skimmington usually involved not the presentation of the erring couple themselves but the representation of them acted out by their next-door neighbors, other substitutes, or even effigies. Thomas Lupton's *Too Good to be True* (1580) includes a dialogue that comments acerbically upon the use of neighbors rather than principles.

As Martin Ingram, "Ridings, Rough Music, and Mocking Rhymes in Early Modern England," *Popular Culture in Seventeenth-Century England*, Barry Reay, ed. (New York: St. Martin's Press, 1985), pp. 166–97 notes, "the characteristic pretext" for such ridings "was when a wife beat her husband or in some other noteworthy way proved that she wore the breeches" (p. 168). The skimmington derisions frequently incorporated the symbolics of cuckoldry—antlers, or animal horned heads, once again collapsing the two most pervasively fetishized signs of female disorder into a collocation by which female dominance means male cuckoldry.

horseback.[8] The trip, which is itself the traditional final stage to the "bridal," is already the site of an unspoken pun on "bridle" that gets foregrounded in Grumio's horse-heavy description of the journey home and the ruination of Kate's "bridal"—"how her horse fell, and she under her horse; . . . how the horses ran away, how her bridle was burst" (4.1.) [61–7]. By means of the syntactical elision of "horse's," the phrase quite literally puts the bridle on Kate rather than her horse. What this suggests is that the scold's bridal/horse bridle/scold's bridle associations were available for resonant recall through the interaction of linguistic structures with narrative ones. The scold's bridle that Shakespeare did not literally include in his play is ultimately a form of violence that lives in the same location as the many offstage horses that are crowded into its non-representational space. The bridle is an artifact that exists in *Shrew's* offstage margins—along with the fist-in-the-face that Petruchio does not use and the rape he does not enact in the offstage bedroom we do not see.

*　*　*

Around 1640 the proverbial scold seems virtually to disappear from court documents. As Susan Amussen informs us, the "formal mechanisms of control were rarely used after the Restoration."[9]

> The prosecution of scolds was most common before 1640; while accusations of scolding, abusing neighbours, brawling in church and other forms of quarrelling usually make up between a tenth and a quarter of the offences in sample Act Books of the Archdeacons of Norwich and Norfolk before 1640, they do not appear in the samplebooks after 1660.[1]

Why did "scolds" apparently disappear? Were they always just the projections of an order-obsessed culture, who disappeared when life became more orderly? Or is the difference real and the behavior of women in the early modern era indeed different from the norms of a later one? Did they really brawl, curse, scold, riot, and behave so abusively? Brushfield clearly assumes that they did, and thus is able to rationalize the otherwise disturbing fact that so many of these illegal instruments of torture turned up in good old Cheshire County, his own home space. As he says, "if such a number of tongue-repressing Bridles were required," then they were so because the women must have been so disorderly as to have turned Cheshire into "a riotous County indeed." Benevolently, however, he

8. See Thompson, introduction to the New Cambridge Shakespeare *The Taming of the Shrew*, p. 12.
9. *An Ordered Society: Gender and Class in Early Modern England* (London: Basil Blackwell, 1988), p. 130.
1. p. 122.

then continues, forgiving England its disruptive foremothers and invoking the authority of the Bard himself to authorize his beatific vision of silent women:

> Suffice it, however, for us to say,—and I speak altogether on behalf of [all] the gentlemen,—that whatever it may have been in times gone by, yet it is certain that the gentleness and amiability of the ladies of the present generation make more than ample amends for the past; and Shakespeare, when he wrote those beautiful words,
> "Her voice was ever soft, / Gentle and low; an excellent thing in woman," unintentionally, of course, yet fully anticipated the attributes of our modern Cheshire ladies.[2]

And it well may be that in his work on scolds' bridles, T. N. Brushfield may unwittingly have described the silent process of how gender is historicized. He may have recorded the social process by which the women of one generation—perhaps as rowdy, brawling, voluble, and outspoken as men have always been authorized to be—were shamed, tamed, and reconstituted by instruments like cucking stools and scolds' bridles, into the meek and amiable, softspoken ladies he so admires in his own time.[3] Perhaps the gentle and pleasing Stepford Wives of mid-nineteenth-century Chester are precisely the products that such a searing socialization into gender would produce—and would continue to reproduce even long after the immediate agony of being bridled or of watching a daughter, mother, or sister being paraded through the streets and forced to endure that experience had passed from personal and recorded memory. The history of silencing is a history of internalizing the literal, of erasing the signifier and interiorizing a signified. The iron bridle is a part of that history. Its appropriate epigraph is a couplet from Andrew Marvell's "Last Instructions to a Painter"[4]—a couplet that could in fact have been written at exactly the moment that some curst and clamorous Kate in some English town was being bridled:

> Prudent Antiquity, that knew by Shame
> Better than Law, Domestic Crimes to tame.

2. p. 47. The Shakespeare lines Brushfield quotes are, of course, King Lear's words as he bends over the dead—and very silent—Cordelia.
3. Such a progress would complement the transformation Margaret George defines as "From 'Goodwife' to 'Mistress': the transformation of the female in bourgeois culture," *Science and Society*, 37 (1973), 152–77.
4. I defer to David Underdown, who earlier used these lines as an epigraph to "The Taming of the Scold."

HAROLD BLOOM

The Taming of the Shrew[†]

The Taming of the Shrew begins with the very odd two scenes of the Induction, in which a noble practical joker gulls the drunken tinker, Christopher Sly, into the delusion that he is a great lord about to see a performance of Kate and Petruchio's drama. That makes their comedy, the rest of *The Taming of the Shrew*, a play-within-a-play, which does not seem at all appropriate to its representational effect upon an audience. Though skillfully written, the Induction would serve half a dozen other comedies by Shakespeare as well or as badly as it coheres with the *Shrew*. Critical ingenuity has proposed several schemes creating analogies between Christopher Sly and Petruchio, but I am one of the unpersuaded. And yet Shakespeare had some dramatic purpose in his Induction, even if we have not yet surmised it. Sly is not brought back at the conclusion of Shakespeare's *Shrew*, perhaps because his disenchantment necessarily would be cruel, and would disturb the mutual triumph of Kate and Petruchio, who rather clearly are going to be the happiest married couple in Shakespeare (short of the Macbeths, who end separately but each badly). Two points can be accepted as generally cogent about the Induction: it somewhat distances us from the performance of the *Shrew*, and it also hints that social dislocation is a form of madness. Sly, aspiring above his social station, becomes as insane as Malvolio in *Twelfth Night*.

Since Kate and Petruchio are social equals, their own dislocation may be their shared, quite violent forms of expression, which Petruchio "cures" in Kate at the high cost of augmenting his own boisterousness to an extreme where it hardly can be distinguished from a paranoid mania. Who cures, and who is cured, remains a disturbing matter in this marriage, which doubtless will maintain itself against a cowed world by a common front of formidable pugnacity (much more cunning in Kate than in her roaring boy of a husband). We all know one or two marriages like theirs; we can admire what works, and we resolve also to keep away from a couple so closed in upon itself, so little concerned with others or with otherness.

It may be that Shakespeare, endlessly subtle, hints at an analogy between Christopher Sly and the happily married couple, each in a dream of its own from which we will not see Sly wake, and which

† From Harold Bloom, *Shakespeare: The Invention of the Human* (New York: Riverhead Books, 1998), pp. 28–35. Copyright © 1998. Used by permission of Riverhead Books, an imprint of Penguin Group (USA) Inc. Line numbers in parentheses for *The Taming of the Shrew* reference this Norton Critical Edition.

Kate and Petruchio need never abandon. Their final shared reality is a kind of conspiracy against the rest of us: Petruchio gets to swagger, and Kate will rule him and the household, perpetually acting her role as the reformed shrew. Several feminist critics have asserted that Kate marries Petruchio against her will, which is simply untrue. Though you have to read carefully to see it, Petruchio is accurate when he insists that Kate fell in love with him at first sight. How could she not? Badgered into violence and vehemence by her dreadful father Baptista, who vastly prefers the authentic shrew, his insipid younger daughter Bianca, the high-spirited Kate desperately needs rescue. The swaggering Petruchio provokes a double reaction in her: outwardly furious, inwardly smitten. The perpetual popularity of the *Shrew* does not derive from male sadism in the audience but from the sexual excitation of women and men alike.

The *Shrew* is as much a romantic comedy as it is a farce. The mutual roughness of Kate and Petruchio makes a primal appeal, and yet the humor of their relationship is highly sophisticated. The amiable ruffian Petruchio is actually an ideal—that is to say an overdetermined—choice for Kate in her quest to free herself from a household situation far more maddening than Petruchio's antic zaniness. Roaring on the outside, Petruchio is something else within, as Kate gets to see, understand, and control, with his final approval. Their rhetorical war begins as mutual sexual provocation, which Petruchio replaces, after marriage, with his hyperbolical game of childish tantrums. It is surely worth remarking that Kate, whatever her initial sufferings as to food, costume, and so on, has only one true moment of agony, when Petruchio's deliberately tardy arrival for the wedding makes her fear she has been jilted.

No one enjoys being jilted, but this is not the anxiety of an unwilling bride. Kate, authentically in love, nevertheless is unnerved by the madcap Petruchio, lest he turn out to be an obsessive practical joker, betrothed to half of Italy. When, after the ceremony, Petruchio refuses to allow his bride to attend her own wedding feast, he crushes what she calls her "spirit to resist" with a possessive diatribe firmly founded upon the doubtless highly patriarchal Tenth Commandment:[1]

> They shall go forward, Kate, at thy command.
> Obey the bride, you that attend on her.
> Go to the feast, revel and domineer,
> Carouse full measure to her maidenhead,
> Be mad and merry, or go hang yourselves.
> But for my bonny Kate, she must with me.

1. The Tenth Commandment: "Thou shalt not covet thy neighbor's house, thou shalt not covet thy neighbor's wife . . ."

Nay, look not big, nor stamp, nor stare, nor fret;
I will be master of what is mine own.
She is my goods, my chattels, she is my house,
My household stuff, my field, my barn,
My horse, my ox, my ass, my any thing,
And here she stands. Touch her whoever dare!
I'll bring mine action on the proudest he
That stops my way in Padua. Grumio,
Draw forth thy weapon, we are beset with thieves,
Rescue thy mistress if thou be a man.
Fear not, sweet wench, they shall not touch thee, Kate.
I'll buckler thee against a million.
Exeunt PETRUCHIO, KATHARINA [*and* GRUMIO]
[3.2.214–31]

This histrionic departure, with Petruchio and Grumio brandishing drawn swords, is a symbolic carrying-off, and begins Petruchio's almost phantasmagoric "cure" of poor Kate, which will continue until at last she discovers how to tame the swaggerer:

PET   Come on, a God's name, once more toward our father's.
       Good Lord, how bright and goodly shines the moon!
KATH   The moon? the sun! It is not moonlight now.
PET   I say it is the moon that shines so bright.
KATH   I know it is the sun that shines so bright.
PET   Now by my mother's son, and that's myself,
       It shall be moon, or star, or what I list,
       Or e'er I journey to your father's house.—
       [*To Servants.*] Go on, and fetch our horses back again.—
       Evermore cross'd and cross'd; nothing but cross'd.
HOR   Say as he says, or we shall never go.
KATH   Forward, I pray, since we have come so far,
       And be it moon, or sun, or what you please.
       And if you please to call it a rush-candle,
       Henceforth I vow it shall be so for me.
PET   I say it is the moon.
KATH   I know it is the moon.
PET   Nay, then you lie. It is the blessed sun.
KATH   Then, God be blest, it is the blessed sun.
       But sun it is not, when you say it is not,
       And the moon changes even as your mind.
       What you will have it nam'd, even that it is,
       And so it shall be so for Katharine.
       [4.5.1–23]

From this moment on, Kate firmly rules while endlessly protesting her obedience to the delighted Petruchio, a marvelous Shakespearean reversal of Petruchio's earlier strategy of proclaiming

Kate's mildness even as she raged on. There is no more charming a scene of married love in all Shakespeare than this little vignette on a street in Padua:

> KATH   Husband, let's follow, to see the end of this ado.
> PET   First kiss me, Kate, and we will.
> KATH   What, in the midst of the street?
> PET   What, art thou ashamed of me?
> KATH   No, sir, God forbid; but ashamed to kiss.
> PET   Why, then, let's home again. Come, sirrah, let's away.
> KATH   Nay, I will give thee a kiss. Now pray thee, love, stay.
> PET   Is not this well? Come, my sweet Kate.
>   Better once than never, for never too late.
>
> *Exeunt.*
>
> [5.1.122–30]

One would have to be tone deaf (or ideologically crazed) not to hear in this a subtly exquisite music of marriage at its happiest. I myself always begin teaching the *Shrew* with this passage, because it is a powerful antidote to all received nonsense, old and new, concerning this play. (One recent edition of the play offers extracts from English Renaissance manuals on wife beating, from which one is edified to learn that, on the whole, such exercise was not recommended. Since Kate does hit Petruchio, and he does not retaliate—though he warns her not to repeat this exuberance—it is unclear to me why wife beating is invoked at all.) Even subtler is Kate's long and famous speech, her advice to women concerning their behavior toward their husbands, just before the play concludes. Again, one would have to be very literal-minded indeed not to hear the delicious irony that is Kate's undersong, centered on the great line "I am asham'd that women are so simple." It requires a very good actress to deliver this set piece properly, and a better director than we tend to have now, if the actress is to be given her full chance, for she is advising women how to rule absolutely, while feigning obedience:

> Fie, fie! Unknit that threatening unkind brow,
> And dart not scornful glances from those eyes,
> To wound thy lord, thy king, thy governor.
> It blots thy beauty as frosts do bite the meads,
> Confounds thy fame as whirlwinds shake fair buds,
> And in no sense is meet or amiable.
> A woman mov'd is like a fountain troubled,
> Muddy, ill-seeming, thick, bereft of beauty,
> And while it is so, none so dry or thirsty
> Will deign to sip or touch one drop of it.

Thy husband is thy lord, thy life, thy keeper,
Thy head, thy sovereign; one that cares for thee,
And for thy maintenance; commits his body
To painful labour both by sea and land,
To watch the night in storms, the day in cold,
Whilst thou liest warm at home, secure and safe;
And craves no other tribute at thy hands
But love, fair looks, and true obedience;
Too little payment for so great a debt.
Such duty as the subject owes the prince
Even such a woman oweth to her husband.
And when she is froward, peevish, sullen, sour,
And not obedient to his honest will,
What is she but a foul contending rebel,
And graceless traitor to her loving lord?
I am asham'd that women are so simple
To offer war where they should kneel for peace,
Or seek for rule, supremacy, and sway,
When they are bound to serve, love, and obey.
Why are our bodies soft, and weak, and smooth,
Unapt to toil and trouble in the world,
But that our soft conditions and our hearts
Should well agree with our external parts?
Come, come, you froward and unable worms,
My mind hath been as big as one of yours,
My heart as great, my reason haply more,
To bandy word for word and frown for frown.
But now I see our lances are but straws,
Our strength as weak, our weakness past compare,
That seeming to be most which we indeed least are.
Then vail your stomachs, for it is no boot,
And place your hands below your husband's foot.
In token of which duty, if he please,
My hand is ready, may it do him ease.

[5.2.140–83]

I have quoted this complete precisely because its redundancy and hyperbolical submissiveness are critical to its nature as a secret language or code now fully shared by Kate and Petruchio. "True obedience" here is considerably less sincere than it purports to be, or even if sexual politics are to be invoked, it is as immemorial as the Garden of Eden. "Strength" and "weakness" interchange their meanings, as Kate teaches not ostensible subservience but the art of her own will, a will considerably more refined than it was at the play's start. The speech's meaning explodes into Petruchio's delighted (and overdetermined) response:

Why, there's a wench! Come on, and kiss me, Kate. [5.2.184]

If you want to hear this line as the culmination of a "problem play," then perhaps you yourself are the problem. Kate does not need to be schooled in "consciousness raising." Shakespeare, who clearly preferred his women characters to his men (always except-ing Falstaff and Hamlet), enlarges the human, from the start, by subtly suggesting that women have the truer sense of reality.

PATRICIA PARKER

Construing Gender: Mastering Bianca in *The Taming of the Shrew*[†]

At the beginning of Act 3 of *The Taming of the Shrew*, Lucentio (disguised as Cambio, master of "letters") and Hortensio (disguised as Litio, master of music) vie as rival "masters" for Bianca, the sis-ter presented up to this point as exhibiting (in contrast to her sister the "shrew") the "Maid's mild behavior and sobriety" [1.1.71], which appears to guarantee that she will be a tractable, obedient, and subordinate wife. As the scene opens, Lucentio accuses Hor-tensio the "fiddler" of being too "forward" in putting music *before* letters or "philosophy" rather than the other way round, in lines that curiously echo the descriptions of the "frowardness" and for-wardness of Kate the "shrew" herself:

> LUCENTIO   Fiddler, forbear, you grow too forward, sir,
> Have you so soon forgot the entertainment
> Her sister Katherine welcom'd you withal?
> HORTENSIO   But, wrangling pedant, this is
> The patroness of heavenly harmony.
> Then give me leave to have prerogative,
> And when in music we have spent an hour,
> Your lecture shall have leisure for as much.
> LUCENTIO   Preposterous ass, that never read so far
> To know the cause why music was ordain'd!
> Was it not to refresh the mind of man
> After his studies or his usual pain?
> Then give me leave to read philosophy,
> And while I pause, serve in your harmony.
>   [3.1.1–14]

[†] From *The Impact of Feminism in English Renaissance Studies*, ed. Dympna Callaghan (Basingstoke: Palgrave Macmillan, 2007), pp. 193–209. Reprinted by permission of Pal-grave Macmillan.

"Preposterous" here is usually glossed by editors of the play as "reversing the natural order of things" or putting "the cart before the horse," the form of *hysteron proteron* or preposterous placing that was routinely available in the period for the inversion of allegedly natural orders of all kinds.[1]

This inversion or exchange of place is introduced in a contest between two rival masters which appears, at least initially, to be simply wrangling over which of the arts should have "prerogative," or come first. There is, however, much more at stake in the staging here of competing arts, in a scene in which the "preposterous" becomes the marker of much broader issues of order at work within the play as a whole. This prominently includes the "cambio," or exchange, within the Lucentio–Bianca subplot itself, whereby Bianca becomes the master of both of her potential masters in this pivotal scene and finally emerges as an anything but a tamed wife by the play's post-marital end.

That the proper ordering of rival arts appears to be the subject of the debate in this scene is consistent with the emphasis on arts and learning that pervades *The Taming of the Shrew*—though it has often been easy to forget this emphasis in a play so often characterized as simply an early Shakespearean farce. It might even be said that its combination of such traditionally elevated with lower (and lower bodily) registers is part of the cambio of preposterous inversions it foregrounds. Lucentio opens the taming play proper by speaking of "the great desire I had/To see Padua, nursery of arts" [1.1.1–2], a reminder that Padua's university was famous throughout Europe. As the subsequent rhyming of "arts" and "hearts" and the competition of rival suitors for Bianca makes clear, however, the *ars amatoria* is the principal *ars* it pursues, however loftily disguised. Even the following of an "art" or *ars* itself within the play becomes part of the preposterous bodily reversals it both echoes and compounds. In a play that features a "tongue" in a "tail," and in ways crucial for the Latin lesson used in this scene by Lucentio as a cover for his wooing of Bianca, Latin *ars* from the venerable

1. The edition used for quotations throughout is *The Riverside Shakespeare*, ed. G. Blakemore Evans (Boston, MA: Houghton Mifflin, 1975). Line numbers in brackets reference this Norton Critical Edition. For sample glosses on "preposterous" here, see G. R. Hibbard, ed., *The Taming of the Shrew* (Harmondsworth: Penguin, 1968), "one who inverts the natural order of things, one who puts the cart before the horse"; Brian Morris, ed. *The Taming of the Shrew* (London: Methuen, 1981): *Preposterous* literally, placing last that which should be first (OED, a.1)"; Ann Thompson, *The Taming of the Shrew* (Cambridge: Cambridge University Press, 1984): "*Preposterous*: Used literally to mean that Hortensio puts things first which should come later"; The Signet Classic Shakespeare, ed. Robert B. Heilman (New York: New American Library, 1966), "putting later things (*post-*) first (*pre-*)." As noted in H. J. Oliver, ed., *The Taming of the Shrew* (Oxford: Clarendon Press, 1982), "preposterous" is used by Lucentio here in "the literal meaning 'having last that which should be first', but the more general meaning 'perverse' or 'unreasonable' was already common" as well by the time of the play (57).

sermo patrius or "father" tongue already came compounded with inverted, preposterous or lower bodily senses. Lyly's *Endymion* famously rhymes "I am all Mars and Ars" with "Nay, you are all mass and ass," but it is only one of the many translations from father to mother tongue that mingled high and low in the period. Nashe's lines on the "excrements of Arts" even more explicitly exploit the bodily and bawdy potential in any discussion of the learned *artes* or *ars*.[2] Within *The Taming of the Shrew*, Grumio's "O this woodcock, what an ass it is"—in response to Gremio's "O this learning, what a thing it is!" [1.2.153]—is comically underwritten by such vernacular slippages, but so is Lucentio's "Preposterous ass" as an insult to a master of music who insists on the right of his particular *ars* to come first or before. Lucentio-Cambio's accusation against his "forward" rival—that he is "preposterous" for desiring to put *before* what should come behind—resonates with the scatalogy that from as early as Augustine identified the *ars musica* with the lower bodily or hindparts, as well as the literal sense of *preposterous* as arsy-versy which gives Hortensio's placing of music first the stigma of turning back-to-front. In a scene that will soon suggest the lower bodily counterparts of this "fiddler" teaching Bianca "fingering" and of the *re* (or "thing") as a double-meaning part of the musical gamut, it is impossible to separate the apparently high discourses of learning and the arts from the lower bodily and all it implies.[3] As modern readers or audiences, we are distanced from the full implications of such preposterous play in *The Taming of the Shrew* by what Norbert Elias has characterized as the historically intervening "civilizing process," or what Pierre Bourdieu has described as later developments of "distinction" between high and low. But as with the scatalogical overtones of apparently learned or mock-learned scenes of *Loves Labours Lost*, another early Shakespeare play, we

2. See Lyly's *Endymion* 1.3; and Thomas Nashe *The Anatomie of Absurditie*, with chapter 1 of my *Shakespeare from the Margins* (Chicago: University of Chicago Press, 1996) on the posterior implications of the "preposterous" in the bodily sense, including what was known as "preposterous venery."

3. In the slang of the period, "fiddler" connoted among other things a "sexual partner," and "fiddle" and "fiddle-case" (Aretino's double-meaning "cassa de la viola") various kinds of sexual instruments, both back and front. In *A Young Man's Tryal* (1655), a later "Kate" is anxious "for one to play on her Fiddle," while in Fletcher's *The Woman's Prize* (c.1611), the play that rewrites *The Taming of the Shrew*, Petruchio comments on how some husbands are deprived of their conjugal rights while others "fall with too much stringing of the Fiddles." See Gordon Williams, *A Dictionary of Sexual Language and Imagery in Shakespearean and Stuart Literature* 3 vols. (London and Atlantic Highlands, NJ: Athlone Press, 1994), vol. 1 under "fiddle" for these citations as well as Aretino's *Ragionamenti* I.ii.48 ("cassa de la viola") and the "fiddlestick" and "consort" of *Romeo and Juliet* (3.1). Williams also cites *Comforts of Whoreing* (1694) 29 on a prostitute satisfying her client "with her various Motions and Activity, that his Breech Dances, Capers and Firks it in as good Time as if she had a Fidle in her Commodity." *Commodity*, in this sexually double-meaning sense, is the term that Sly substitutes for "comedy" in the Induction to *The Taming of the Shrew*. For more examples of the sexual senses of "fiddling," see *The Oxford English Dictionary* under "minikin."

need to take time to learn this historical vernacular in order to see what is at stake in the dramatic *mise-en-scène* of preposterous or arsy-versy exchanges of place and position in *The Taming of the Shrew*, not only in relation to gender but also for the other kinds of order and hierarchy it both stages and disrupts.[4]

The sense of reversal introduced into this subplot scene by Lucentio's "preposterous ass" soon involves subtle and not so subtle over-turnings at the level of gender, but ones that we are able to track only if we become aware of the gender and other hierarchies already at work within contemporary discussions of the arts and of what was at stake in the Latin texts used by Lucentio as Bianca's would-be "master," both pedagogically and maritally. Debate over the hierarchy of rival "arts" was a preoccupation not only in Castiglione's *The Courtier* (translated by Thomas Hoby in 1561 and published in no fewer than four London editions by 1603), but also in the spate of books directed at upwardly mobile bourgeois families like Bianca's (and Kate's) in *The Taming of the Shrew*, concerned with what their merchant father Baptista calls "good bringing-up" [1.1.99]. Such manuals offered the aspiring merchant class the promise of access to the more gentle arts, while simultaneously foregrounding the cultural capital of such markers of distinction as something that (like clothing) could be acquired—as the tutoring of Bianca by hired masters suggests.

Maureen Quilligan (whose reading of the play is attentive to its emphasis on "class" as well as on hierarchies of gender) notes that the Induction to the play—where Sly is schooled in how to address his Lady ("SLY: Ali'ce madam, or Joan madam? / LORD: Madam, and nothing else: so lords call ladies")—draws "a quick conduct-book lesson in how to 'lord it,'" in a period when social identity itself was being shaped by these models of fashioning and "'self-fashioning,'" thus staging in the process "the same social premise that underlies the courtesy books," that "social behavior is not a natural, biologically determined fact" but "can be learned (and unlearned)."[5] As so much feminist work over the past two decades

---

4. I refer here to Norbert Elias, *The History of Manners* (1939), vol. 1 of *The Civilizing Process*, trans. Edmund Jephcott (New York: Pantheon, 1978); and Pierre Bourdieu, *Distinction: A Social Critique of the Judgement of Taste*, trans. Richard Nice (Cambridge, MA: Harvard University Press, 1984). See also Gail Kern Paster, *The Body Embarrassed: Drama and the Disciplines of Shame in Early Modern England* (Ithaca, NY: Cornell University Press, 1993), which draws on the opposition between the closed and the open grotesque body from Mikhail Bakhtin, *Rabelais and His World*, trans. Helene Iswolsky (Bloomington, IN: Indiana University Press, 1984). For an analysis of *Loves Labours Lost* in this regard, see my "Preposterous Reversals: *Loves Labours Lost*," *Modern Language Quarterly* 54.4 (December 1993): 435–82. For the whole of *The Taming of the Shrew* in relation to these broader cultural and historical contexts, see my *Preposterous Shakespeare*, forthcoming.
5. See Maureen Quilligan, "Staging Gender: William Shakespeare and Elizabeth Cary," in

has taught us, this same vogue for conduct literature was simultaneously schooling young women on how to be "chaste, silent, and obedient," alongside a sprinkling of learning in music and other arts.
The conduct book culture that the scene of rival "masters" and
"arts" evokes in Shakespeare's *Shrew* should not, therefore, be unexpected in a play that repeatedly underscores the markers of upward
mobility—or social hierarchies in a state of transition—including
the double-meaning "titles" and "deeds" that hover between their
older chivalric or aristocratic meanings and the new world of property transfers and marriage markets. In this sense, the "preposterous" (as a marker of the unnatural as well as the reversed),
introduced into this scene of tutors hired by Bianca's upwardly mobile father, was itself a cultural keyword for all such "unnatural" ac-
quisitions, as well as for social and gender reversals in the period.

In the scene that begins with the contest between Lucentio and
Hortensio as supposed masters of arts who are simultaneously rival
masters for Bianca on the marriage market, Lucentio's "Preposterous ass, that never read so far / To know the cause why music was
ordain'd" directly evokes such contemporary reading. At the same
time, the gendered invocation of "heavenly harmony" in these
opening lines recalls contemporary debates over what should come
first and what follow after, in a pivotal scene in which what seems
to be simply a learned or mock-learned discussion of the priority of
different arts has implications for the corresponding order of first
and second, or subordinate, in the hierarchy of gender and social
place. Hortensio (or Litio), in advancing music's "prerogative" or
right to come *first*, invokes the Neoplatonic and Pythagorean tradition of "heavenly harmony," music as the cosmic *arche* or beginning
of the world. Lucentio/Cambio, who reverses Hortensio's status
and claim by denigrating this master of music, in social terms, as a
mere "fiddler," champions the inverse tradition in which music itself was characterized as subordinate or second, upbraiding his rival for not having "read" enough to know that music was to come
only *after* more exalted studies. His "Preposterous ass, that never
read so far / To know the cause why music was ordain'd! / 'Was it
not to refresh the mind of man / *After* his studies or his usual
pain?" [3.1.9–12] thus recalls texts such as *The Courtier* itself,
where music is cast in a subordinate or secondary role, as "a most
sweete lightning of our travailes and vexations" or "a verie great refreshing of all worldlye paines and griefes." In Castiglione's influen-

---

James Grantham Turner, ed., *Sexuality and Gender in Early Modern Europe* (Cambridge:
Cambridge University Press, 1993), esp. 216 and 219. I put "class" in scare quotes here
to underscore that both in Quilligan and here the term is used not in the classical Marx-
ist sense but rather as a current critical shorthand for position within a social hierarchy.

tial text, which also had a major impact on conduct books for upwardly mobile or not yet gentle readers, the frequent or unsolicited
performance of music by members of the aristocracy is rigorously
condemned because such a pursuit would break down the distinctions between a nobleman and his music-performing servant (much
less "fiddlers," or mechanical practictioners of the art).[6]

Sir Thomas Elyot's *The Boke named the Governour*—in its description of the "order" to be followed in "the bringing up of . . .
children"—similarly counsels that music should come after more
serious study, emphasizing that music "only serveth for recreation
after tedious or laborious affairs." In ways that make clear the multiple hierarchies at stake in texts that have a noble audience in
view, Elyot too warns that aristocratic practitioners of music risk
being held "in the similitude of a common servant or minstrel," a
term of opprobrium not unlike Lucentio's depiction of the music
master as a "fiddler" here. But even Thomas Morley's *Plain and
Easy Introduction to Practical Music*—directed to a readership of
the middling sort—makes clear that music is meant to "recreate"
scholars only "*after* [their] more serious studies."[7]

Music in such guides to "good bringing up" was thus understood
as a diversion or form of recreation, not primary or first but subordinate or second. By contrast, to put music *first*—as Hortensio
seeks to do, before he is called down by Lucentio as a "fiddler" as
well as a "forward" and a "preposterous ass"—would be simultaneously preposterous in other senses, since it would involve a reversal
of first and second, higher and lower on the social hierarchy reflected by the hierarchy of the arts themselves. "Fiddler" here
evokes several of these subordinate positions at once. Contempt for
musicians as practitioners of a "mechanical" art ranged from complaints such as Stephen Gosson's in *The Schoole of Abuse* against
beggar companies of "fiddlers," to the use of the term "fiddler" itself
both for the player of the violin (considered a rather vulgar instrument) and for the lower social status of musicians in the period.
John Ferne, in *The Blazon of Gentrie*, treats of these "mechanicall
practicioners" of "so base a profession" that the laws of the "Countrey . . . have determined them for roages and vagabonds, enemies
to the publique good of our Countrey" and contrasts them to the

---

6. On music as primary in creation, see Joseph Barnes's *The Praise of Musicke* (Oxford
   1586): "time cannot say that hee was before [Music], or nature that she wrought without her. To prove this looke upon the frame & workmanship of the whole worlde,
   whether there be not above, an harmony between the spheres." For Castiglione's *Il
   Cortegiano* (published in Venice in 1528), see *The Courtier*, trans. Thomas Hoby,
   Book I, 75–7.

7. See Morley's *A Plain and Easy Introduction to Practical Music*, 2nd edition, ed. R. Alex
   Harman (New York: W. W. Norton, 1963) 298; Sir Thomas Elyot, *The Book Named Governor* (New York: Dutton Everyman's Library, 1962), 15, 20, 22.

"learned professor of that Science" commended by Pythagoras, Plato, Aristotle, and others, a social bias reflected in Thomas Morley's reference to "ignorant *Asses*, who take upon them to lead others, being more blind than themselves."[8] As is well known, derogatory references to such musical "roages and vagabonds" in the period join contemporary sneers at players and other practitioners of "mechanic" arts. Hortensio complains that even Katherine had branded him with this class sneer when he attempted to teach her music in an earlier scene. There, having had the "lute" broken on his head in her resistant "frets," he complains that "she did call me rascal fiddler / And twangling Jack, with twenty such vild terms, / As had she studied to misuse me so" [2.1.155–7].

Lucentio's ridicule of his rival tutor as ignorant of the proper order of the arts is thus a pedantic putdown grounded in one of the multiple indices of upward mobility in the period, reflected in texts such as Castiglione's *Courtier* and its bourgeois counterparts. Treatises such as Elyot's *The Governour* were directed to the governing classes broadly conceived, but handbooks such as Morley's joined the demand for tutors in the households of upwardly mobile merchants like Baptista who "had made fortunes . . . and who modelled their households on those of the social strata immediately above them."[9] At the level of contested social hierarchies, *The Taming of the Shrew*—which already calls such sustained attention to the marriage-market "cambio" or exchange between landed gentry and merchant money—simultaneously reflects in this contest between Bianca's rival masters the market for schooling in the "arts" of proper "bringing up."

Lucentio's "preposterous" is pronounced as a judgment on his rival's ignorance of this required reading. But even more importantly for the place of this Bianca scene within the larger taming plot, what appears to be simply a pedantic discussion of the priority and ordering of the arts comes with important implications for the hierarchy of gender, in a scene in which Bianca will soon preposterously overturn the hierarchy of mastery itself. The casting of music as a diversion or recreation—to follow only after more serious pursuits—had its parallel in the subordination of music, as handmaiden, to letters, philosophy and the *logos* of words, the patroness of "heavenly harmony" not as *arche* or first but as literally ancillary (the etymological resonance of its "handmaiden" status). In this re-

8. In addition to Morley, see Stephen Gosson, *The School of Abuse* (London, 1587); and John Ferne, *The Blazon of Gentrie* (London, 1586).
9. See the editor's introduction to Morley's *Practical Music*, p. viii. On the differentiation between music as heavenly harmony (or the music of the spheres) and practical music in the period, see John Hollander's classic study *The Untuning of the Sky* (Princeton, NJ: Princeton University Press, 1961).

spect, the subordination of music was frequently described in the period of *The Taming of the Shrew* in explicitly gendered terms. If Wagner, much later, could make music female in the scale of gender—noting that "Music is the handmaid of Poetry [and] in the wedding of the two arts, Poetry is the man, music the woman; Poetry leads and Music follows"—the more contemporary witness of early modern texts such as *The Passionate Pilgrim* (1599) invoked the gendering of music and poetry as "sister" and "brother" ("If Music and sweet Poetry agree, / As they must needs, the Sister and the Brother . . ."). Music is directly associated with women in *The Courtier*, which advises its readers that music is "meete to be practised in the presence of women" because their "sights sweeten the mindes of the hearers, and make them the more apt to bee pierced with the pleasantnesse of musicke, and also they quicken the spirits of the very doers" (Book II, 101). At the same time, music was feminized as something seductive that must be kept subordinate or under control. The same *Boke named the Governour* that counsels that male children should be "taken from the company of women" at age seven, lest they be imperiled by "sparks of voluptuosity which, nourished by any occasion or object, increase often times into so terrible a fire that therewith all virtue and reason is consumed" (Book I, ch. vi, 19), warns in its chapter on music that its "pleasant" diversion must not "allure" to "so much delectation" that it lead to "wantonness," "inordinate delight," or the "abandoning [of] gravity" and more serious pursuits (Book I, ch. vii, 21–2).

As a "thing to passe the time withall," music is simultaneously associated in *The Courtier* and other contemporary texts with the making of womanish or effeminate men, along with "other vanities" that are "meet for women, and peradventure for some also that have the likeness of men, but not for them that be men in deede: who ought not with such delicacies to womanish their mindes." Ascham writes that "The minstrelsie of lutes, pipes, harps, and all other that standeth by such nice, fine, minikin fingering is farre more fit for the wommanishnesse of it to dwell in the courte among ladies."[1] Music is thus not only associated *with* women but is cast as able to turn men *into* women, a transformation highlighted explicitly in *The Taming of the Shrew* in multiple forms, not only in the transvestism that makes its first apparently tractable wife the Induction's scripted transvestite page, but also in the later scene on

---

1. See Castiglione's *The Courtier* (Hoby trans. Book I, 75) with Book II, p. 101 on music as " "meete to be practised in the presence of women"; Roger Ascham, *The Schoolmaster*, ed. John E. B. Mayor (1863; rpt. New York: AMS Press, 1967), Book I, which also includes the warning that "Moch Musick marreth mens maners." Music in relation to gender is also the subject of the analysis of the play in Linda Phyllis Austern, " 'Sing Againe Syren': The Female Musician and Sexual Enchantment in Elizabethan Life and Literature," *Renaissance Quarterly* 42 (1989): 420–48.

the "sun" and the "moon" (already highly gendered figures), where the patriarch Vincentio is pronounced a "maid" and Hortensio comments "twould make a man mad to make a woman of him" [4.5.36].

But there is an even more striking echo in the lines in which Lucentio claims that music should be not "forward" or first but subordinate or second, and that to invert this order would be "preposterous"—an echo that comes with direct implications for the gendering of this hierarchy through even more authoritative contemporary forms. The scene's invocation of the "preposterous" as a culturally loaded term that already foregrounds the issue of what should have "prerogative" or precedence thus simultaneously calls for even closer scrutiny in relation to the marriage market and the hierarchy of male and female within it. Lucentio's "Preposterous ass, that never read so far / To know *the cause why music was ordain'd*" directly echoes the "causes for which *Matrimonie* was ordeyned" from the marriage ceremony in the Boke of Common Prayer (1552), the text that enjoins the woman as the "weaker vessell" to be "subject" unto her husband as a "milde and quiet wife" in "quietnes, sobrietie & peace," or in other words precisely what Bianca is assumed to be potentially when the play begins, in contrast to her sister, the "shrew."[2] This unmistakable echo of the Ceremony of Matrimony here—and with it the Pauline and other biblical assumptions of male prerogative and female subordination from the Genesis 2 order of Adam *before* Eve—has momentous implications for this pivotal scene in which Bianca will master both of her would-be "masters" in turn, extending the sense of preposterous overturning from the initial context of the ordering of the arts to a reconstructing at the level of gender.

Such a direct echo of the Ceremony of Matrimony sets up even further reverberations between this Bianca subplot scene and the larger shrew-taming play, which repeatedly recalls that ceremony (foundation of the Elizabethan homiletic tradition that counseled the subordination of women) and famously ends with Kate's apparent iteration of the Pauline figure of the man as "head" [5.2.151]. The Ceremony itself invokes the prescribed sequence of the genders among the "things set in ordre" in Genesis, and other biblical texts from which this order of priority was derived: man made in God's "owne ymage and similitude," and woman, secondarily and "out of man." If music as handmaiden or subordinate is "ordain'd" to "refresh the mind of man / *After* his studies or his usual pain"— in the hierarchy of primary and secondary in which its "harmony" is to be "serve[d] in" only *following* the "prerogative" of "philosophy"

2. See Brian Morris's gloss in the Arden 2 edition, 218.

or "letters"—then in the order derived from Genesis 2, matrimony is "ordained" to be similarly refreshing ("for the mutuall societie, helpe & comfort, that ye one ought to have of the other, both in prosperitie and adversitie"), with the helpmeet wife, or "weaker vessel," a clearly subordinate second.[3]

That there should be an echo of the Ceremony of Matrimony in the very lines that evoke a "preposterous" reversal at the opening of Act 3 thus gives to the question of order in this first major Bianca scene a much greater resonance than mere wrangling over rival arts, one with implications not only for the play as a whole but also for the portrayal of the apparently tractable Bianca within it. By the end of the play, as already noted, Bianca herself will be anything but subordinate or submissive, but will be chastised instead, like Kate before her, for being too "forward" as well as "froward" [5.2.161], a synonym for the "preposterous" that was routinely used for unruly wives). In this pivotal Act 3 scene, the echo of the Ceremony of Matrimony and with it, of the ordaining of matrimony in Genesis, is sounded in opening lines devoted ostensibly to a contest only between men, with Bianca the apparently passive object of their rivalry. But in this first major scene of the play to feature the supposedly submissive younger sister, this unmistakable echo invokes the Ceremony's strictures on the hierarchy of the genders at the very moment when Bianca will overturn it and manipulate it, becoming not a submissive female but director of both masters.

Textual editors from Theobald (1733) and Malone (1790) onwards have emended what they see in this opening as a truncated line—"this is / The patroness of heavenly harmony"—to a formulation that identifies this "patroness" of "harmony" as Bianca herself, as distinguished from the discordant "frets" of her shrewish sister, Kate. Bianca in this scene, however, far from providing a contrast to her elder sister, proves to be less tractable than her alignment with music as either handmaiden or heavenly harmony suggests. The scene's initial discussion of the proper order of the arts is cut short by Bianca herself. She refuses to be a "breeching scholar" [3.1.18] to either of her rival tutors, rejecting the master–pupil relationship of "following" or imitation prescribed in school texts such as Mulcaster's *Positions* and the following of appointed "hours" and "times," in ways that pointedly recall the earlier rejection of "appointed hours" [1.1.103] by Kate the *designated* shrew, in the scene that had contrasted Bianca's "mild behavior and sobriety" [1.1.71] to her more "froward" sister [1.1.69]. Bianca puts an end

---

3. For the impact of this Genesis 2 creation story, combined with Aristotle on the female as a secondary or defective male, see the final chapter of my *Literary Fat Ladies: Rhetoric, Gender, Property* (London and New York: Methuen, 1987).

to the wrangling of her would-be masters by reminding them of *her* prerogative:

> Why, gentlemen, you do me double wrong
> To strive for that which resteth in *my* choice.
> I am no breeching scholar in the schools,
> I'll not be tied to hours, nor 'pointed times,
> But learn the lessons *as I please myself* . . .
> [3.i.16–20; emphasis mine]

The scene that invokes the "preposterous" in relation to the appropriate sequence of the arts thus not only summons echoes of the proper order of the genders from the Ceremony of Matrimony (where women, like music, are to be secondary or subordinate), but already undercuts the taming plot's ostensible contrast between a "fretful" shrew and her apparently obedient younger sister, long before the final scene. This overturning is even clearer when this scene in Act 3 turns (after Bianca asks "Cambio" to "conster" or construe some Latin lines) into a lesson in translation—or what was known in early modern English as construing or construction. For this kind of linguistic construction was dominated by the very discipline of subordination, or obedient following of a "master," that Lucentio proceeds to assume.[4]

In a play that is literally filled with tags from grammar school texts—including the *Grammar* of Lilly and Colet whose "Masculine gender is more worthy than the Feminine" was already a watchword for more than simply grammatical gender in the period—the lesson offered by the would-be "master" Lucentio/Cambio to Bianca as his intended pupil is based on precisely this contemporary order of following after, the pedagogical counterpart to the later textual description of Bianca as a supposed wifely "appendix" [4.4.88–9] and the printing metaphors of the husband's' "ad imprimendum solum" or exclusive "right to print." This scene's actual staging, however, of the formula for such pedagogical construing or construction—a student's supposedly faithful following of a master's script—simultaneously evokes a "construction" that is exploited elsewhere in Shakespeare with different and much more suggestive implications: from the impossibility of reading the "mind's construction in the face" (*Macbeth*) and the ambiguous "merciful construction of old women" (*Henry VIII*) to the adulterously "shrewd construction" to be made of Mistress Ford, in the scene where her husband "prescribes" to himself "preposterously" (*Merry Wives* II.ii.223), and the "illegitimate construction" of

---

4. For the master-schoolboy form of translation from Latin to English and back again, see chapter 4 of my *Shakespeare from the Margins* on Ascham's *The Scholemaster* and the translation scene of *The Merry Wives of Windsor*.

women in *Much Ado About Nothing* (III.iv.50). "Illegitimate construction" itself turns as a *double entendre* on the connection between the infidelity of translations or constructions and the feared infidelity of women, the cultural anxiety evoked in *The Taming of the Shrew* when the Pedant responds: "Ay, sir, so his mother says, if I may believe her" to the question of whether Lucentio is his legitimate son [5.1.29]. Though it may be as foreign to us as modern readers as the multiple early modern implications of the "preposterous," this interconnection between the fidelity of translations and the fidelity of women was commonplace in Shakespeare and other contemporary texts. In *Merry Wives*, for example, Mistress Quickly translates into ever-more promiscuous vernacular constructions the Latin of the *sermo patrius* she fails to understand, in a play that makes clear that words, like wives, can be both diverting and unfaithful.[5]

In *The Taming of the Shrew*, the disguised Lucentio/Cambio, who argues for the "prerogative" of going *first*, begins by expecting that his Latin lesson will unfold according to his own agenda and construing:

> 'Hic ibat,' as I told you before, 'Simois,' I am Lucentio, 'hic est,' son unto Vincentio of Pisa, '[Sigeia] tellus,' disguis'ed thus to get your love, 'Hic steterat,' and that Lucentio that comes a-wooing, 'Priami,' is my man Tranio, 'regia,' bearing my port, 'celsa senis,' that we might beguile the old pantaloon.
>
> [3.1.31–6]

But in contrast to the schoolboy or "breeching scholar" who might be expected to follow the construction of a "master," Bianca produces her own, very different construction, no more seconding or repeating his words than she consents to yield to "appointed times" or "hours." If from the perspective of the master's script, the role of the schoolboy is to follow after, this is precisely the subordinate or second position that Bianca here eschews. Instead of iterating the translation of her would-be master (in both the pedagogical and the marital sense), then, Bianca provides her own very different, and more ambiguous, construing:

> Now let me see if I can conster it: 'Hic ibat Simois,' I know you not, 'hic est [Sigeia] tellus,' I trust you not, 'Hic steterat Priami,' take heed he hear us not, 'regia,' presume not, 'celsa senis,' despair not.
>
> [3.1.31–36]

---

5. See chapter 4 of my *Shakespeare from the Margins*, with the reading of this translation lesson in the opening chapter of *Literary Fat Ladies: Rhetoric, Gender, Property* (London and New York: Methuen, 1987).

Editors have argued that Bianca's very different translation here is simply a way of raising her price in the marriage market, by withholding immediate assent from a suitor at the same time as adding that he should not "despair." But the implications of this translation lesson—and of Bianca's more ambiguous as well as divergent construings—are actually much more subtle and far-reaching than any such culturally commonplace reading of her demurring might suggest. Bianca turns the tables here by providing a very different translation of the same Latin text that Lucentio or "Cambio" is attempting to make serve his turn with her. But strikingly, even feminist critics have missed the female complaint that provides the very basis of this Latin lesson—as well as the inter-textuality that makes Bianca's doubts about Lucentio's constructions both more resistant and more complex.[6]

Such intertextual markets frequently go unnoticed in *The Taming of the Shrew*, perhaps because of the longstanding critical fiction that it is part of a supposedly naive or simple "early Shakespeare." Once again, even feminist critics have concurred with Lucentio's constructions, or read Bianca as simply repeating the words of her "master" here, making this scene continuous with (rather than a striking departure from) the Bianca described by others earlier in the play as the tractably chaste, silent, and obedient woman of the conduct books. However, the actual text that provides the basis for this translation lesson—from Ovid's *Heroides*, familiar to schoolboys including Shakespeare in Latin, and already translated into English by Turberville in 1567—is Penelope's anything but submissive or silent complaint against her own husband and master for taking so long to return home, a complaint that Shakespeare puts into the mouth not of a mild and tractable but rather of a "shrewish" wife in *The Comedy of Errors*, another early play.[7] The particular Latin lines presented for translation in this

6. Ann Thompson's New Cambridge edition of the play (p. 106) compares "Bianca's skill at 'holding off' " to that of "Cressida, who knows all about such techniques." Like other editors of the play, she does not pick up on the complaint of Penelope that forms the basis of the Latin lesson; curiously, she also supports Lucentio's "sure" translation of "Aeacides" as "Ajax," though, as other editors point out, this is a highly doubtful translation. Thompson's edition was first published in 1984, when it was rare to have a female editor in such a prestigious series. Since then, however, she has published pioneering work on feminist editing and become a General Editor of the Arden Shakespeare Third Series. On possibilities for feminist editing, see also Laurie Maguire in Dympna C. Callaghan, *A Feminist Companion to Shakespeare* (Malden, MA: Blackwell, 2000).

7. In *The Comedy of Errors*, the complaints of Adriana against her absent husband echo Penelope's in the first epistle of the *Heroides*, including the suspicion that her husband's delayed return means that he has been unfaithful; and are contrasted to her sister Luciana's iteration of the familiar Pauline counsel to wives. For the English translation of the *Heroides* already in print well before *The Taming of the Shrew*, see George Turberville, trans., *The Heroycall Epistles of the learned Poet Publius Ouidius Naso* (London, 1567). On the importance of the *Heroides* for Shakespeare and others, see Elizabeth D. Harvey, *Ventriloquized Voices: Feminist Theory and English Renaissance Texts* (New York: Routledge, 1992). Harvey (personal communication) notes that Turberville's

scene are from Penelope's complaining that other wives have heard
the Troy story directly from their already returned husbands, while
she has had to get the story herself, and only at second hand, by
sending her son to find his father. But Bianca's "Where left we
last?" [3.1.26] makes clear that Penelope's much longer female
complaint—which initiates the entire series of female complaints
that make up the *Heroides* and includes her anger at being left
alone for twenty years as well as her justified suspicion that Ulysses
has been unfaithful—had already provided the text for a lesson begun even before this scene. The choice of the particular lines for
translation here—on the siege of Troy before the ultimate guileful
breaching of its "walls" (or in Turberville's translation "walles which
you by breach haue brought to utter spoyle and sacke")—may
themselves be part of the sotto voce commentary here; for the disguised Lucentio has himself gained entry to Bianca's house only
through guile and the wooers in the sources for this subplot of Lucentio's wooing use their disguised entry to breach the walls of the
corresponding female figures, in a sexual sense.[8]

The text chosen by Shakespeare for Lucentio's supposed instruction of Bianca here thus provides a highly suggestive commentary
indeed, though the implications of this striking choice have been
passed over by feminist as well as other editors and critics. The implications of such well known subtexts for Bianca's resistance to
Lucentio's instruction-construction in this scene become even
more telling when the lesson moves on to the next line of the *Heroides* text, which Lucentio presents in a translation he offers as authoritative or "sure":

> *Bianca*: In time I may believe, yet I mistrust.
> *Lucentio*: Mistrust it not, for sure Aeacides
> Was Ajax, call'd so from his grandfather.
> *Bianca*: I must believe my master, else I promise you,
> I should be arguing still upon that doubt.
> But let it rest. Now, Litio, to you . . . .
>
> [3.1.49–54]

---

text continues the Renaissance practice—and tradition ascribed to Aulus Sabinus,
Ovid's contemporary and friend, but not reflected in Ovid's own text—of providing male
responses to the charges in three of the female complaints: Ulysses to Penelope,
Demophon to Phyllis, and Paris to Oenone.

8. Lucentio's counterpart in Gascoigne's *Supposes*, the immediate source for the Bianca
subplot, uses his entry into the household as a tutor to lie with his pupil, not just instruct her. For the line of transmission through Ariosto's *I Suppositi* and the disguised
lover of Terence's *Eunuch*, see Keir Elam, "The Fertile Eunuch: Twelfth Night, Early
Modern Intercourse, and the Fruits of Castration," *Shakespeare Quarterly* 47: 1 (Spring
1996): 1–36. The breaching of walls identified by Shakespeare with "maiden walls" (as
in *Henry V*) is similarly identified with entry into Troy through the disguise of the Trojan
horse in *Cymbeline*, where Iachimo gains entry into Innogen's bedroom hidden inside a
trunk.

This next line of the *Heroides* text, which Lucentio's "sure Aeacides / Was Ajax" appears to be translating, is *"illic Aeacides, illic tendebat Ulixes."* But—contrary to the translation of "Aeacides" (or descendant of Aeacus) that Lucentio presses Bianca to believe is "Ajax"—both Turberville and modern translations of the *Heroides* agree that "Aeacides" in this line from Penelope's complaint is not Ajax at all, but Achilles. Turberville translates this as "There fierce Achilles pight his Tents, / there wise Vlysses lay," while the modern Loeb translation has no index entry for Ajax at all, since *Aeacides* designates Achilles every time this phrase appears, even in its other female complaints.[9]

In ways equally suggestive for a subplot in which closing the marriage-market deal with Bianca's father requires Lucentio's patrimony or inheritance from a "supposed" father is so crucial, Lucentio or "Cambio" here assures Bianca that his construction is "sure" by appealing to the male lineage for this connection ("for sure Aeacides / Was Ajax, call'd so *from his grandfather*").[1] But his attempt to assure as well as instruct in answer to Bianca's "yet I mistrust" is even at the level of purely textual translation a construction that is simply not to be trusted. In mistrusting the assurance of her would-be "master," in the pedagogical as well as the wooing sense here, Bianca not only takes over the direction of that wooing but proves to be clearly the better scholar, since what he tells her to believe—on his assurance—is like other supposes in this play of supposes, only his own very doubtful construction. As part of an in-joke that those with grammar schooling might be expected to appreciate, there is already every reason to mistrust this master's translation from Penelope's well-known *Heroides* complaint. But even more tellingly, Lucentio/Cambio's insistence that "Aeacides" is "Ajax" here actually abandons the *Heroides* text of justifiably complaining women for a different text altogether, one where there are no women present but only rival men competing for possession of a property or prize that is both passive and inert, as before she intervened, Bianca herself might have been supposed to be. In this very different text—from the famous rivalry between Ajax and Ulysses over who will inherit Achilles' armor in *Metamorphoses* 13 (a debate that Shakespeare would later write large in

9. In Ovid, *Heroides and Amores*, with an English translation by Grant Showerman (Cambridge, MA: Harvard University Press; London: W. Heinemann, 1977), *Aeacides* is translated as "Achilles" every time it appears in the *Heroides* text (I.35; III.87; VIII.7, 33, 55). Turberville (1567) likewise renders *Aeacides* in Penelope's complaint as "Achylles," as he also does consistently elsewhere.

1. The provision of "assurance" for Lucentio's own required patrimony or male inheritance as a rival suitor for Bianca is stressed in relation to his "supposed" father in the scene just before this translation lesson, where the plot is hatched to invent a "supposed Vincentio" [2.1.400] to underwrite the patrimony or "assurance" promised to Bianca's father [2.1.379; 388] as part of the deal.

Troilus and Cressida as well as echoing in *Hamlet*)—Ajax's claim that he is "Aeacides" or male kinsman to Achilles and hence legitimate heir to this prize, bases his dubious right to inherit it as his property on a patriarchal line of descent and "title," while arguing that his rival can only by a "forged pedigree" ally himself to the "Aeacyds" (as Golding translated it) because Ulysses himself is a bastard—not his supposed father Laertes' son but offspring of his mother's coupling with another.[2] The text that the wooing "Cambio" here exchanges or substitutes for Penelope's introduction to the litany of complaints against men that fill the *Heroides* is, in other words, not only a rivalry exclusively between men for possession of a purely passive object but a text that once again draws attention to the very issues of property, patrimony, supposed fathers, or "illegitimate constructions" that pervade *The Taming of the Shrew* itself.[3] Ajax, of course, also famously loses the debate, with even his own claim to be "Aeacides" left open to question.

In a scene that begins with such a clear echo of the Ceremony of Matrimony and its supposed "weaker vessell" who is to be "subject" to her husband, Bianca not only intervenes but takes over the lessons offered by both "masters." And there is in her bringing of an end to the lesson in translation or construction a comment that is even more suggestive for the apparent shrew-taming trajectory of the play as a whole. When Bianca moves from "In time I may believe, yet I mistrust" to "I *must* believe my master" (in a line that may at first *appear* to signal her tractability or submission), it is not because Lucentio's is a "sure" construction or one she actually ac-

---

2. See *Ovid's Metamorphoses: The Arthur Golding Translation 1567*, ed. John Frederick Nims, with a new essay "Shakespeare's Ovid" by Jonathan Bate (Philadelphia: Paul Dry Books, 2000), 320, for Book 13, lines 27–41, where the Latin title *Aeacides* is claimed by Ajax, who also claims that Ulysses was fathered adulterously by Sisyphus rather than his supposed father Laertes. While it might be expected that Lucentio would present himself as the successful Ulysses—rather than the traditionally blockish Ajax (man of deeds not words)—it is ultimately Bianca who wins the debate. The original Arden edition, edited by R. Warwick Bond (London: Methuen and Co., 1904), 73, traces editorial awareness of this other Ovidian intertext back to Steevens' eighteenth-century glosses on Lucentio's "Aeacides" with Golding's translation of *Metamorphoses* XIII.27–8 ("The highest Jove of all / Acknowledgeth this AEacus, and dooth his sonne him call. / Thus am I Ajax third from Jove") and comments that "The application of the patronymic by Ovid to Peleus, Telamon, and Phocas, AEcus' sons; by Homer and Virgil to Achilles, another grandson; and by Virgil to Pyrrhus, his great-grandson, might justify Bianca's professed 'doubt,' line 55." Though this Bianca translation scene recalls other mock translation lessons cited in Bond's edition (71–2)—including one in Lyly's *Mother Bombie* (III.i.139), where "Candius translates Ovid to Livia while their fathers overhear, 'I am no Latinist, Candius, you must conster it. *Can.* So I will, and pace (parse) it too'." Bianca by contrast not only provides her own construing or translation, but proves a better Latinist than her tutor of "letters."

3. The complexity of the larger shrew-taming plot's presentation of women as only ostensibly passive objects is analyzed in relation to Petruchio's pun on "Kate" and "cates" (etymologically connected to "chattel" and the mercantile context of purchases or "achats") in Natasha Korda's "Household Kates: Domesticating Commodities in *The Taming of the Shrew*," *Shakespeare Quarterly*, vol. 47, no. 2 (Summer, 1996): 109–31.

cepts. As this anything but passive female quickly makes clear, it is only a practical way of putting an end to what otherwise might continue interminably here: "else I promise you / I should be arguing still upon that doubt. / But let it rest. Now, Litio, to you."

Bianca's bringing Lucentio's proffered "lesson" to an end—in ways that make good on her promise to "learn the lessons as I please myself"—thus conveys something very different from acceptance of the conclusion that Lucentio himself presents as "sure," in a scene that forecasts the much less tractable Bianca of the play's post-marital end. It may even provide a suggestive advance gloss on her sister Katherine's apparent seconding of *her* master's constructions, when she makes the decision to iterate but also to transform Petruchio's aberrant designations of the "sun" and "moon," and delivers what appears to be her apparently submissive final speech. In a play full of such dramatic cross-references, as well as such "counterfeit supposes" (5.1.99)—beginning with the *sotto voce* witness of the Induction, where the play's first and perhaps only tractably obedient wife is a transvestite page following his master's script—perhaps Katherine's own apparent iteration of a culturally proffered script or construction is simply a way of bringing an otherwise endless debate to an at least temporary end, and nothing so straightforward as assumed assent.

Whatever the larger implications of this pivotal subplot scene—which begins by invoking the "preposterous" in the context of what should come *first* and what subordinately *second*—it is crucial in relation to the trajectory of Bianca within the play. Both Bianca's putative masters here find the orthodox teacher–pupil relationship unexpectedly overturned. The evocation of Penelope not in her patient but in her complaining mode joins the echoing of the Ceremony of Matrimony from the lines on the preposterous overturning of other orders with which this scene begins, yielding not the simple subordinate Penelope, but one used elsewhere in early Shakespeare for the speeches of a "shrew." And Bianca herself—described at the opening of the taming play as the wifely ideal so often represented by the more submissive Penelope—emerges through her own constructions of the *sermo patrius* or Latin text as a much less tractable figure, even while she continues to be described by others, who see her from the outside as a wifely subordinate or "appendix" [4.4.98].

My reading of this pivotal subplot scene is thus that Bianca is revealed to be neither a submissive Penelope nor the subordinate "weaker vessel" of the biblical texts on which the Ceremony of Matrimony itself depended. Characterizations of Bianca as only much later turning into a surprisingly "froward" wife—in the play's final, post-marital scene—miss the implications of the "preposterous" overturning displayed in this much earlier scene of a putative master's construing. Even a feminist critic as prescient as Karen Newman falls into this conventional reading of Bianca when she asserts of this language lesson that "Far from the imaginative use of language and linguistic play we find in Kate, Bianca repeats verbatim the Latin words Lucentio 'construes' to reveal his identity and his love. Her revelation of her feelings through a repetition of the Latin lines he quotes from Ovid are as close as possible to the silence we have come to expect from her." What, on the contrary, we encounter in this scene of putative instruction is a very different Bianca from either the representations of her the play has already cast up, as the potentially chaste, silent, and obedient future wife, or the assumptions and constructions of otherwise astute feminist readings.

SHIRLEY NELSON GARNER

The Taming of the Shrew: Inside or Outside of the Joke?[†]

If you had grown up hearing that Shakespeare is the greatest writer in the English language (or at least one of the two or three greatest) and that he is a "universal" poet, who speaks across time and national (even cultural) boundaries, you—especially if you were a woman student—would be shocked to study him in a college or university in the 1980s and to read *The Taming of the Shrew* for the first time. My own students—particularly my women students, though sometimes the men in my classes as well—often exclaim in dismay, "I can't *believe* Shakespeare wrote this!" A graduate student, rereading the play with only a faded memory of having read it before, commented that it was commonly her experience now to read something that she had once enjoyed only to find it disappointing. That was what happened when she read *Taming of the Shrew,* and it gave her a sense of loss. Reading the play from a woman's perspective, she could not help but be a "resisting reader."[1] Even if teachers of literature offer an ingenious reading of the play, their students will probably not be seduced into a very

† From *"Bad" Shakespeare: Revaluations of the Shakespeare Canon,* ed. Maurice Charney (Rutherford, N.J.: *Fairleigh Dickinson University Press,* 1988). Reprinted by permission of the Associated University Presses.
1. I use Judith Fetterley's term because it so aptly names the common position of the woman reader (*The Resisting Reader: A Feminist Approach to American Fiction* [Bloomington: University of Indiana Press, 1978]).

happy view of it. They will know in their hearts that—at the least—
there is something wrong with the way Kate is treated. And they
will be right.[2]

I am not sure that anyone except academics who have invested
much—perhaps all—of their professional lives in studying Shakespeare would need to debate whether *Taming of the Shrew* is good
or bad. The best that can be said for the play is just what Peter
Berek concludes in his essay * * * that it shows Shakespeare had
suppler attitudes toward gender than his contemporaries and that
it "may have been a valuable, even necessary, stage in moving toward his astonishing expansion of the possibilities of gender roles."
This argument makes the play *interesting*, but it does not make it
good.

* * *

The Induction makes immediately clear the assumptions about
women and sexuality that are at the core of *Taming*. When a Lord,
a character named only according to his rank, imagines and creates
for Christopher Sly a world like his own (though more romantic),
the "woman" he peoples it with suggests a sixteenth-century ideal:
gentle, dutiful, utterly devoted to her husband. He directs his servingman to tell Bartholomew, his page, how to play the part of Sly's
wife:

> Such duty to the drunkard let him do
> With soft low tongue and lowly courtesy,
> And say, "What is't your honor will command
> Wherein your lady and your humble wife
> May show her duty and make known her love?"
> And then, with kind embracements, tempting kisses,
> And with declining head into his bosom,
> Bid him shed tears, as being overjoyed
> To see her noble lord restored to health
> Who for this seven years hath esteemed him
> No better than a poor and loathsome beggar.[3]
> [Ind. 1.109–19]

Surface manner, "With soft low tongue and lowly courtesy," defines
inner character, marks the "lady" as "feminine." The importance of

---

2. Students recognizing the misogyny of *Taming* may encounter a response similar to that
   which, according to Leslie Fiedler, a Jewish child may meet when he confronts the anti-
   Semitism of *The Merchant of Venice*: "A Jewish child, even now, reading the play in a
   class of Gentiles, feels this [the full horror of anti-Semitism] in shame and fear, though
   the experts, Gentile and Jewish alike, will hasten to assure him that his responses are irrelevant, even pathological, since 'Shakespeare rarely "takes sides" and it is certainly
   rash to assume that he here takes an unambiguous stand "for" Antonio and "against"
   Shylock'" (Leslie A. Fiedler, *The Stranger In Shakespeare* [New York: Stein and Day,
   1972], 98–99.
3. This and subsequent quotations from Shakespeare's plays are from *The Complete Signet
   Classic Shakespeare*, ed. Sylvan Barnet (New York: Harcourt, 1963). Line numbers in
   brackets for *The Taming of the Shrew* reference this Norton Critical Edition.

soft-spokenness as an essential attribute of femininity is suggested by King Lear's lament over his dead Cordelia: "Her voice was ever soft, / Gentle and low, an excellent thing in woman" (5.3.274–75). In a culture that tended to see things in opposition, to split mind and body, virgin and whore, the quiet woman represented the positive side of the opposition. The woman who spoke up or out, the angry woman, represented the negative side. At a moment when Hamlet feels the greatest contempt for himself, he mourns that he "must, like a whore, unpack . . . [his] heart with words / And fall a-cursing like a very drab" (2.2.592–93). When Bartholomew appears dressed as a lady and Christopher Sly wonders why the page addresses him as "lord" rather than "husband," Bartholomew answers:

> My husband and my lord, my lord and husband,
> I am your wife in all obedience.
>
> [Ind. 2.103–4]

The male fantasy that underlies this exchange is that a wife will be subject, even subservient, to her husband in all matters.

More subtly suggested as attractive in the Induction is a notion of sexuality associated with the violent, the predatory, the sadistic. The Lord immediately directs that the drunken Christopher Sly be carried to bed in his "fairest chamber," which is to be hung round with all his "wanton pictures" [Ind. 1.42–3]). After Sly is promised all the requisites for hunting, including hawks that "will soar / Above the morning lark" and greyhounds "as swift / As breathèd stags, . . . fleeter than the roe" [Ind. 2.41–6]), he is offered the most desirable paintings. The movement from hunting to the predatory sexuality imaged in the pictures makes obvious the association between hunting and the sexual chase. Sly is promised by the Second Servingman:

> Adonis painted by a running brook
> And Cytherea all in sedges hid,
> Which seem to move and wanton with her breath
> Even as the waving sedges play with wind.

And the other men join in the game, revealing their own erotic fantasies:

> LORD   We'll show thee Io as she was a maid
> And how she was beguiled and surprised,
> As lively painted as the deed was done.
> THIRD SERVINGMAN   Or Daphne roaming through a thorny wood,
> Scratching her legs that one shall swear she bleeds,
> And at that sight shall sad Apollo weep,
> So workmanly the blood and tears are drawn.
>
> (Ind. 2.52–8]

Suggestions of violence, particularly of rape, underlie all of these images. The figures the paintings depict are among the familiar ones in Ovid's *Metamorphoses*: Adonis, the beautiful, androgynous youth gored to death on a wild boar's tusks; Io, a maid Zeus transformed into a heifer in order to take her; and Daphne, who was changed into a laurel tree to prevent Apollo's raping her. The images of violence intensify, as though each character's imagination sets off a darker dream in another. Interestingly enough, the story of Adonis is drawn the least bloody though it is inherently more so. It is Daphne, the innocent virgin, who bleeds. It would seem that the most predatory and sadistic impulse calls forth the most compelling eroticism for those who participate in the shared creation of these fantasies.

It is appropriate that *The Taming of the Shrew* is acted for the male characters of the Induction, for its view of women and sexuality is attuned to their pleasure. Underlying the notion of heterosexual relationships in *Taming*, especially marriage, is that one partner must dominate. There can be no mutuality. The male fantasy that the play defends against is the fear that a man will not be able to control his woman. Unlike many of Shakespeare's comedies, *Taming* does not project the fear of cuckoldry (though perhaps it is implicit), but rather a more pervasive anxiety and need to dominate and subject. In taming Kate, Petruchio seems to give comfort to all the other men in the play. Before Hortensio marries the Widow, he goes to visit Petruchio, to see his "taming school," which Tranio describes to Bianca:

> Petruchio is the master,
> That teacheth tricks eleven and twenty long
> To tame a shrew and charm her chattering tongue.
> [4.2.57–9]

However pleasant the idea of a "taming school" may be for men, the attitude it implies toward women is appalling.

*   *   *

Shakespeare also allows Kate to claim her anger and gives her a moving explanation of her outspokenness:

> My tongue will tell the anger of my heart,
> Or else my heart, concealing it, will break,
> And rather than it shall I will be free
> Even to the uttermost, as I please, in words.
> [4.3.77–80]

Yet what is said or shown to extenuate Kate does not weigh heavily enough to balance the condemnation of her, which is an effort to prepare us to accept Petruchio's humiliation of her as a necessity, or "for her own good."

Kate and Petruchio are both strong-willed and high spirited, and one of Petruchio's admirable qualities is that he has the good sense to see Kate's passion and energy as attractive. When he hears of her tempestuous encounter with Hortensio, he exclaims:

> Now, by the world, it [sic] is a lusty wench!
> I love her ten times more than e'er I did.
> O how I long to have some chat with her!
>   [2.1.158–60]

Presumably Petruchio puts on an act to tame Kate; he pretends to be more shrew than she [4.1.70]. As one of his servants says, "He kills her in her own humor" [4.1.160]. But Kate's "shrewishness" only allows Petruchio to bring to the surface and exaggerate something that is in him to begin with.[4] When we first see him, he is bullying his servant—wringing him by the ears, the stage direction tells us—so that Grumio cries, "Help, masters, help! My master is mad" [1.2.18]. It surprises only a little that he later hits the priest who marries him, throws sops in the sexton's face, beats his servants, and throws the food and dishes—behaves so that Gremio can exclaim, "Why, he's a devil, a devil, a very fiend" [3.2.148]. When he appears for his wedding "a very monster in apparel," we learn that his dress is not wholly out of character; Tranio tells Biondello:

> 'Tis some odd humor pricks him to this fashion,
> Yet oftentimes he goes but mean-appareled.
>   [3.2.65–6]

The strategy of the plot allows Petruchio "shrewish" behavior; but even when it is shown as latent in his character and not a result of his effort to "tame" Kate, it is more or less acceptable. Dramatically, then, Kate and Petruchio are not treated equally.

In general, whatever is problematic in Petruchio is played down; whereas Kate's "faults" are played up. For example, we tend to forget how crassly Petruchio puts money before love at the beginning of the play since he becomes attracted to Kate for other reasons. He speaks frankly:

> I come to wive it wealthily in Padua;
> If wealthily, then happily in Padua.
>   (1.2.[72–3])

---

4. Joel Fineman is either reading wishfully or perversely when he argues that Petruchio's "lunatic behavior" is "a derivative example" of Kate's shrewishness; see "The Turn of the Shrew" in *Shakespeare and the Question of Theory*, eds. Geoffrey Hartman and Patricia Parker (London: Methuen, 1986), 142.

And Grumio assures Hortensio in the most negative terms that money will be Petruchio's basic requirement in a wife:

> Nay, look you sir, he tells you flatly what his mind is. Why, give him gold enough and marry him to a puppet or an aglet-baby or an old trot with ne'er a tooth in her head, though she have as many diseases as two-and-fifty horses. Why, nothing comes amiss so money comes withal.
>
> [1.2.74–8]

No one in the play speaks against this kind of materialism; indeed, it seems to be the order of the day.

Kate's humbling begins from the moment Petruchio meets her. Petruchio immediately denies a part of her *self*, her identity as an angry woman. Just as the Lord of the Induction will make Christopher Sly "no less than what we say he is" [Ind. 1.67], so Petruchio will begin to turn Kate into his notion of her. Yet because her will and spirit meet his, the absurdity of his finding Kate "passing gentle" [2.1.235–49]) and his elaboration of that idea is more humorous than not. It is when Petruchio begins to give Kate ultimatums, which I know he can and will enforce, that the play begins to give me a sinking feeling:

> Setting all this chat aside,
> Thus in plain terms: your father hath consented
> That you shall be my wife, your dowry 'greed on,
> And will you, nill you, I will marry you.
>
> . . . .
>
> For I am he am born to tame you, Kate,
> And bring you from a wild Kate to a Kate
> Conformable as other household Kates.
>
> [2.1.260–70]

The reason I begin to lose heart at this point is that I am certain Kate will not be able to hold her own against Petruchio. The lack of suspense is crucial to my response. I know that an angry woman cannot survive here. When I read or see *Macbeth* or *The Merchant of Venice*, though I know the witches' prophecies will come true to defeat Macbeth and that Portia will trick Shylock out of his pound of flesh, I always feel the power of the contest. But not in *Taming*.

After Kate and Petruchio are married and go to Petruchio's house in act 4, the play loses its humor for me. The change in tone follows partly from the fact that Petruchio's control over Kate becomes mainly physical. In Padua, the pair fights mainly through language, a weapon that Kate can wield as well as Petruchio. When Kate strikes Petruchio in the city, he swears he will hit her back if she does it again [2.1.216]. Though he deserves slapping in the country, she cannot risk that there. While Petruchio never strikes her, he tries to intimidate her by hitting the servants and throwing food and dishes at them. The implication is that if she does not behave, he will do the same to her. Petruchio's physical taming of Kate is objectionable in itself; it is particularly humiliating because it is "appropriate" for animals, not people. Petruchio's description of his plan to tame Kate has no humor in it; related in soliloquy, it has the sound of simple explanation.

Kate's isolation in the country among Petruchio and men who are bound to do his bidding creates an ominous atmosphere. Her aloneness is heightened by the fact that even Grumio is allowed to tease her, and her plight becomes the gossip of Petruchio's servants. Her humiliation has a sexually sadistic tinge since there is always the possibility that Petruchio will rape her, as he threatens earlier:

> For I will board her though she chide as loud
> As thunder when the clouds in autumn crack.
>   (1.2.91–2]

Petruchio's notion of sexual relations here is worthy of Iago, who says of Othello's elopement, "Faith, he tonight hath boarded a land carack" (*Othello* 1.2.49). Grumio immediately tells Hortensio, " 'A my word and she knew him as well as I do, she would think scolding would do little good upon him. . . . I'll tell you what, sir, and she stand him but a little, he will throw a figure in her face and so disfigure her with it that she will have no more eyes to see withal than a cat" [1.2.104–10]. He suggests that Petruchio can out-scold and outwit Kate, but he also implies, through particularly violent imagery, that Petruchio will use force if necessary. Petruchio even tells Baptista, "I am rough and woo not like a babe" [2.1.135].

When we hear that Petruchio is in Kate's bedroom "making a sermon of continency to her" [4.1.165]. I imagine that he is obviously acting contrary (his favorite mode), preaching abstinence when he might be expected to want to consummate his marriage. I have also wondered whether we are supposed to imagine that Kate has hoped to please him by offering herself sexually. Or does she actually desire him? Is the play reinforcing the male fantasy that the more a man beats and abuses a woman the more she will fawn on him?[5] But the episode is probably related mainly to assure us that Petruchio does not rape Kate, since we have been led to think he might. A play within a play, *The Taming of the Shrew* is enacted to crown Christopher Sly's evening. I think it is intended to have the same salacious appeal as are the paintings proposed for his enjoyment.

---

5. Niccolò Machiavelli, *The Prince*, trans. and ed. Robert M. Adams (New York: Norton, 1977), 72.

Kate and Petruchio's accord is possible only because Kate is finally willing to give up or pretend to give up her sense of reality—
which *is* reality—for Petruchio's whimsy. He will do nothing to
please Kate until she becomes willing to go along with him in
everything, including agreeing that the sun is the moon. When she
will not, he stages a temper tantrum: "Evermore crossed and
crossed, nothing but crossed!" (4.5.10). Eager to visit Padua, she
gives over to him in lines that can only be rendered with weariness:

> Forward, I pray, since we have come so far,
> And be it moon or sun or what you please.
> And if you please to call it a rush-candle,
> Henceforth I vow it shall be so for me.
>   [4.5.12–15]

What follows is one instance after another of Petruchio's testing
Kate's subjection to him.

One of the most difficult aspects of the play for me is the way the
women are set against each other at the end. Kate and Bianca have
been enemies from the beginning, but now the Widow takes sides
against Kate, calling her a "shrew" [5.2.29]). Kate's famous speech
on wifely duty is addressed to the widow as a reproach. The men
use their wives to compete with each other:

> PETRUCHIO   To her, Kate!
> HORTENSIO   To her, widow!
>
>   [5.2.34–5]

Betting on whose wife is the most obedient, the men stake their
masculinity on their wives' compliance. A friendly voice will be
raised against this kind of wager in *Cymbeline*, but not here. Only
the Widow and Bianca, who will subsequently become "shrews,"
demur. When Kate throws her cap under foot at Petruchio's direction, the Widow remarks, "Lord, let me never have a cause to sigh /
Till I be brought to such a silly pass"; and Bianca queries, "Duty
call you this?" When Lucentio reproaches Bianca for costing him
five hundred crowns, she replies, "The more fool you for laying on
my duty" [5.2.133]. Though the Widow and Bianca are hateful
characters, I find myself in sympathy with them. The ending of the
play simply goes awry for me.

Kate's final speech may be taken straight, as a sign that she has
"reformed"; or it may be taken ironically, as though she mocks
Petruchio. The happiest view of it is that Kate and Petruchio perform this final act together, to confound those around them and
win the bet. Even if we accept this last interpretation, I cannot take
pleasure in Kate's losing her voice. In order to prosper, she must
speak patriarchal language. The Kate we saw at the beginning of

the play has been silenced. In one sense, it does not matter whether she believes what she is saying, is being ironical, or is acting: her words are those that satisfy men who are bent on maintaining patriarchal power and hierarchy. For them, Kate's obedience, in Petruchio's words, bodes

> peace . . . and love, and quiet life,
> An awful rule and right supremacy;
> And . . . what not that's sweet and happy.
>
> [5.2.112–14]

For Kate, it means speaking someone else's language, losing a part of her identity. She no longer engages in the high-spirited play of wit that was characteristic of her when Petruchio first met her [2.1.181–259].

If I stand farther back from the play, it seems even less comic. It is significant that *Taming* is a play within a play: "not a comontie a Christmas gambold or a tumbling trick" or "household stuff," but "a kind of history" [Ind. 2.132–5]. It seems to carry the same weight as *The Murder of Gonzago* in *Hamlet* or the rustics' dramatization of *Pyramus and Thisbe* in *A Midsummer Night's Dream*. The pithy truth that *Taming* contains implies a kind of heterosexual agony. It is noticeable that just before the play begins, the Induction calls attention to the fact that the Page, though pretending to be a woman, is actually a man. Convinced that he is a lord and that the Page is his wife, Sly wants to take his "wife" to bed. The Page begs off, claiming the physicians have said that lovemaking would be dangerous for Sly, and adds: "I hope this reason stands for my excuse." Picking up the double meaning attendant on the similarity of pronunciation between "reason" and "raising," Sly continues the phallic pun: "Ay, it stands so that I may hardly tarry so long" [Ind. 2.121]. The source of Sly's desire is ambiguous: Is it the woman the Page pretends to be, or is it the man the Page reveals he is? Perhaps they are the same: a man in drag. In any case, the breaking of aesthetic distance here asks us to recognize that we are watching a homosexual couple watch the play. From their angle of vision, *Taming* affirms how problematic heterosexual relations are, especially marriage. The fault would seem to lie with women, who are all "shrews" at heart. If a man aspires to live in harmony with a woman, he must be like Petruchio (a comic version of Hotspur) and able to "tame" her. If he is gentle, like Lucentio, he will undoubtedly become the victim of a shrewish wife. This is not a happy view of women; it is an equally unhopeful vision of love and marriage.

Even though there may be ambiguities at the conclusion of Shakespeare's comedies, they are most joyous when couples join with the prospect of a happy marriage before them. In order for marriage to be hopeful in Shakespeare, women's power must be contained or channeled to serve and nurture men. When it is—in *As You Like It*, *Twelfth Night*, or *A Midsummer Night's Dream*—the comic ending is celebratory. When it is not, in *The Merchant of Venice* or *Love's Labor's Lost*, the tone of the ending is less buoyant, even discordant. In *Love's Labor Lost*, when women remain in power and set the terms of marriage, it is implied that something is not right. Berowne comments:

> Our wooing doth not end like an old play;
> Jack hath not Jill. These ladies' courtesy
> Might well have made our sport a comedy.
> [5.2.872–74]

When the King insists that it will end in "a twelvemonth and a day," after the men have performed the penances their ladies have stipulated, Berowne replies, "That's too long for a play." The final songs contain references to cuckoldry, and their closing note is on "greasy Joan" stirring the pot.[6] What is different about the movement toward a comic ending in *Taming*, is that women are set ruthlessly against each other, Kate's spirit is repressed, and marriage is made to seem warfare or surrender at too high a price.

Taming is responsive to men's psychological needs, desires, and fantasies at the expense of women. It plays to an audience who shares its patriarchal assumptions: men and also women who internalize patriarchal values. As someone who does not share those values, I find much of the play humorless. Rather than making me laugh, it makes me sad or angry. Its intended effect is spoiled. It is not only that I do not share the play's values, but also that I respond as a woman viewer and reader and do not simply respond according to my sense of Shakespeare's intention or try to adopt an Elizabethan perspective (assuming I *could*). I stand outside of the community the joke is intended to amuse; I sympathize with those on whom the joke is played.

I understand that within the tradition of shrew stories, Shakespeare's version is more generous of spirit and more complex than other such stories. But *Taming* seems dated. I think that it is interesting historically—in tracing a tradition, in understanding sixteenth-century attitudes toward women—and that it is significant as part of Shakespeare's canon, as any work of his is. But limiting its importance this way, I imply that I find it less good than many of his comedies. And I do. If I went to see it, it would be out of curiosity, to find out how someone in our time would direct it.

6. Shirley Nelson Garner, "*A Midsummer's Night's Dream*: 'Jack shall have Jill / Nought shall go ill,' " *Women's Studies: An Interdisciplinary Journal* 9 (1981): 47–63.

Shakespeare continually depicts in comedy an infertile world in which lovers are separated; the task of the play is to restore the world by bringing lovers together. In several instances, he presents characters who are "man-haters" or "woman-haters" and unites them. Benedick and Beatrice, Hippolyta and Theseus are examples; Kate and Petruchio are forerunners of these couples. Interestingly enough, Shakespeare never again shows a woman treated so harshly as Kate except in tragedy. I think that Shakespeare either began to see the world differently or that he recognized the story of Kate and Petruchio did not quite work. Most significantly, he obviously enjoyed portraying witty women characters, and he must have seen that it was preferable to leave their spirits untamed.

JULIET DUSINBERRE

The Taming of the Shrew: Women, Acting, and Power[†]

The opening of *The Taming of the Shrew* is strikingly different from that of the related play *The Taming of a Shrew* in offering the audience in the first ten lines a battle between the sexes. The Beggar, who calls himself Christopher Sly, threatens to "pheeze" the Hostess who throws him out of her inn, not just for drunkenness, but for not paying for broken glasses. Threatening Sly with the stocks, the Hostess exits, determining to send for the constable. In *A Shrew*, the innkeeper is a Tapster, and Slie's offence simply inebriation. Shakespeare's Sly defies the Hostess in a strange little speech: "Ile not budge an inch boy. Let him come, and kindly." He has in the course of eleven lines quoted Kyd's *Spanish Tragedy* and challenged her abuse of him as a rogue: "Y'are a baggage, the Slies are no rogues. Look in the Chronicles, we came in with Richard Conqueror: therefore *paucas pallabris*, let the world slide: Sessa" (*First Folio*). He sounds momentarily like John Durbeyfield in Hardy's *Tess*, claiming an ancient and declining stock. The little interchange offers a vignette in which a man and woman engage in a power struggle: she, only a woman, but with a trade and a function which give her access to authority over him: he a beggar with illusions of grandeur, ancestral memories of great men, culture, a power he no longer possesses. But why does he call her "boy"?

I want to argue that he calls her boy because she is a boy. The

† Originally published in *Studies in the Literary Imagination* 26.1 (Spring 1993): 67–84. Copyright © 1993, Department of English, Georgia State University. Reproduced by permission.

Hostess must, in Shakespeare's theatre, have been played by a boy actor. But if Sly addresses her as a boy, then a new dimension is added to the interchange. In his drunkenness he seems momentarily to refuse to enter the play: to be, not a drunken beggar, but a drunken actor, who forgets that his dialogue is with a Hostess, and thinks that the boy actor is getting above himself. In other words, the theatrical illusion seems to be tested before it is even under way. Is Sly a beggar, or is he an actor who must play a beggar?

In *The Taming of the Shrew*, more than in any other play, Shakespeare uses the relationships between actors as a commentary on the social relationships represented in the self-contained world of the play, the drama of *The Shrew* which is performed before the Beggar (persuaded to believe that he is a lord) at the request of the "real" Lord of the Induction who enters from hunting to refresh himself at the inn and is visited by a company of players. The audience in the theatre is required to react to two competing dramas: a stage representation of a traditional courtship and taming drama; and a more covert drama which constantly interrupts and comments on the taming drama, one generated by the actual structures of relationship present in the company which performs the piece. Sly's use of the term "boy" to the boy actor is only one of many oddities which suggest to the audience the presence in the play itself of actors, not just impersonators of characters. I want to demonstrate how this works in a number of interchanges in the play, and to reinterpret Kate's role in the light of its original theatrical provenance: that Kate would have been played, like the Hostess, Bianca, the Widow, and the young Biondello, by a boy. How would this material condition of Shakespeare's theatre have modified audience perception of the power structures represented in the fiction of *The Taming of the Shrew*?[1]

If Kate is played by a boy in the position of apprentice, then the dynamic between Kate and other players on stage, and between Kate and women in the audience, is altered from what it is in the modern theatre. The boys stood in the position of apprentice towards the adult sharers in the company.[2] It was not a guild apprenticeship, but more of a personal arrangement, such as that between Pepys and his boy Tom Edwards in the 1660s, a child whom he employed as his attendant from the Chapel Royal: well-educated and a

---

1. The valuable edition of *The Taming of a Shrew* by Graham Holderness and Bryan Loughrey has stimulated a number of questions in this paper, although I disagree with some of the editors' conclusions, and find it surprising that in a cultural materialist edition there should be no specific analysis of the effect on the play of the theatrical condition that Kate would have been played by a boy.

2. Bentley (1984) argues that although there was no player's guild to which boys were officially apprenticed, there is plenty of evidence that boys were attached as apprentices to particular adults in the company. Rastall (1985) finds no evidence that post-pubertal youths played Shakespeare's women.

good singer (Pepys 1971, V [1664], 228, 234 n.1, 255). The boys in Shakespeare's company would each have had a particular master; Burbage was master to Nicholas Tooley, and Augustine Phillips—another boy in the company—spoke in his will of Tooley as his "fellow" in the company (Greg 1931, I: 47). The master-pupil relationship between the apprentices and the adult actors and sharers in the company is a highly significant one in the dynamics of the company and can be seen to be in operation in *The Shrew*. The Lord sends instructions to his page on how to play the lady, as any master might have instructed his apprentice on how to play Kate. Furthermore, the apprentice's role in the company creates for him a special relationship with the women in the theatre audience. He must, when the play is done, return to a position of dependency. But great ladies enjoyed a position of social superiority to that of apprentices (Howard 1989, 31–40). The apprentice has within the world of the play access not only to that momentary social superiority but also access to the stage power of the female heroine. Women in the theatre audience may return to the subservient lives of women in Elizabethan social structures, but they too have been allowed within the theatre the fantasy of different kinds of power which link them in sympathy with the boy himself as he represents women on stage. Sly, as an actor refusing to play his part—there was, after all, an actor in Shakespeare's company called William Sly—defies his inferior in the company, the boy playing the Hostess. But the play gives the Hostess authority over him: she demands that he pay for the broken glasses and sends for the constable.

The Taming of the Shrew creates for the audience images of power in the male world in the roles of Petruchio, Baptista, Lucentio, but it also undermines them with a different kind of power, generated by the counterpointing of the actor with the role he plays. This special energy enters the play through the ambiguous medium of Sly, but is sustained throughout the drama by the covert juxtaposing in Kate's role of the heroine and the boy apprentice who must act her. Similarly, the actor who plays Tranio with histrionic virtuosity oscillates between the subservience of his social role and the dominance of his acting role as Lucentio.

Curiously, various snippets of information back up a theory that the Induction of *The Shrew* deliberately places before the theatre audience not a fiction, but a group of players whom they may identify as actors, rather than as characters, as a modern audience might identify repertory players or particular actors and actresses in a number of different roles. Two actors who appear in the Induction set this line of enquiry in motion. *The Taming of the Shrew* contains a number of prefixes in the text which refer directly to the names of actors: possibly Sly himself, and certainly Sincklo: named as the Second Player in the Induction. This seems to be more than accident as the play constantly obliges the audience to remember that behind the character in the play is an actor who has his own reality and his own relation to the other figures on the stage, a relation forged in the acting company, not in the Italian society world in which he plays a part.

Shakespeare's Sly may in fact have been played by William Sly, a member of both the Pembroke's men in the early 1590s (McMillin 1972) and subsequently of Shakespeare's company, the Chamberlain's men, later the King's men. His name is on the list of Shakespeare's company at the beginning of the 1623 Folio. In 1604, William Sly appears in the new induction which the playwright John Marston wrote for *The Malcontent*. He is named in the *Dramatis Personae* under a special heading: "*Actors of the King's Men, at the Globe Theatre, who appear in the Induction*: WILLIAM SLY, JOHN SINKLO, RICHARD BURBAGE, HENRY CONDELL, JOHN LOWIN." In this Induction, Sly pretends to be a member of the audience with social pretensions who has come to sit on the stage as if he were a gallant. The Tire-man, realising that he is not a gentleman, tries to shoo him off: "Sir, the gentlemen will be angry if you sit there." Sly calls for the other actors, saying that he has seen the play often and "can give them intelligence for their action." When the actor John Sincklo enters, he greets Sly familiarly: "Save you, coz." They gossip, and call for the players, Burbage, Condell and Lowin. At a certain point, Sly seems to be rambling and one of the actors begs him to leave the stage, this time successfully. The part is a curiosity in its transparent disguising of two actors for audience members, while on the page they remain simply actors.

Odder still, Sincklo appears in *The Shrew*, just seventy lines after Sly has fallen into a drunken sleep. The Players enter and the Lord turns to the second player, named in the Folio prefix, probably on Shakespeare's own authority, Sincklo. Sincklo was distinguished in Shakespeare's company by his appearance: he was extremely thin and cadaverous-looking, and he played parts which suited this physiognomy. He is named in *2 Henry IV* as the Beadle who arrests Mistress Quickly and Doll. He played the forester in *3 Henry VI* who arrests the King. He probably played the emaciated Apothecary who supplies Romeo with poison, and Robert Faulconbridge in *King John*, mocked by the Bastard for his lack of sex appeal (Gaw 1926, 289–303; Wentersdorf 1980; McMillin 1972, 155, 157). The Lord remembers him in a particular part:

> This fellow I remember
> Since once he played a farmer's eldest son—
> 'Twas where you wooed the gentlewoman so well—

I have forgot your name, but sure that part
Was aptly fitted and naturally performed.[3]

This passage is always taken straight: Shakespeare made a friendly gesture towards an actor for a good performance. But its jests seem to me to huddle in upon each other. The Lord cannot remember his name, although Shakespeare names him in his text: he is John Sincklo. You were a wonderful lover, remarks the Lord to someone who looks like a jailer or a supplier of poison. It is a theatre company's joke, but it becomes much funnier if the audience has seen the actor in other parts and can share the joke. They would have been able to share the joke if they had just seen 2 Henry IV; The Shrew was certainly performed in these years.

But one must perhaps also ask whether Shakespeare's play was written sometime in 1595–1597, not in the earlier period. Sincklo's presence in the Induction to The Shrew, together with the possible references to his other roles, particularly in 2 Henry IV, might imply a later date for Shakespeare's play than is usually suggested.[4] The Shrew would then enter the constellation of plays in which Shakespeare probably used Sincklo: Romeo and Juliet, and King John. The interchanges between Sly and the Hostess at the beginning of The Shrew are rich partly because they recall the interchanges in the two parts of Henry IV between Mistress Quickly and Falstaff.

Sincklo's name for the Second Player immediately raises the question of doubling. The Elizabethan custom of theatrical doubling would have made it possible for The Shrew to be acted with only thirteen players (nine adults and four boys), excluding hired men.[5] It has been suggested that the absence of a return to the Sly plot at the end, and of the interventions in the play made by Slie in A Shrew, result from a theatrical exigency when the Players were touring at the time of theatre closures because of the plague. With his talent for making a virtue out of necessity, Shakespeare seems

---

3. [Ind. 1.79–83] The Taming of the Shrew. All quotations from Shakespeare's Shrew are from this edition unless otherwise stated. Line numbers in brackets reference this Norton Critical Edition.
4. Leeds Barroll's argument for the bunching of plays in the Jacobean period when Shakespeare could foresee performance in the public theatre, if taken back to the earlier decade, must oblige scholars to rethink the dating of the plays in relation to outbreaks of plague in the 1590s. The Shrew on this reckoning might have been written after the 1592–1594 outbreaks which would put it in the same period as the plays discussed in my text, although of course this speculation would force a reconsideration of the memorial reconstruction theory in relation to A Shrew.
5. I am indebted to Wentersdorf's (1978) analysis of the ending of The Shrew although my conclusions differ from his, as he believes that Shakespeare did provide a "Sly" ending to the play. Wentersdorf remarks that its absence in the Folio may be because the Folio editors "believed the revision to have been carried out with Shakespeare's approval and therefore that the shortened text constituted an authentic if artistically less satisfactory version" (215).

often to have constructed his plays with doubling written into their artistic conception. Hippolyta may have been doubled with Titania, and often is so on the modern stage; In *Pericles*, it is almost certain that the incestuous Princess at the beginning doubles with Marina, the virtuous and chaste Princess at the end. Many correspondences in structure and language make doubling part of the play's emotional impact. If Shakespeare used an economical touring cast of only thirteen actors, all the players who appear in the Induction to *The Shrew* must originally have played parts in the drama presented to Sly. Did Shakespeare, as was his custom, consider the artistic implications of doubling in relation to the fiction he was creating in the main body of the play, and if so, how did that theatrical necessity affect the construction of the action? Sincklo as Second Player must have acted a part in the main action of *The Shrew*. But which part?

The question can be answered by returning to the peculiar partnership between Sly and Sincklo, in theatrical terms, in both the Induction to *The Shrew*, and later in Marston's *The Malcontent*. The doubling process seems in *The Shrew* to create a special line of communication with the audience particularly evident in the scene in which Lucentio's father Vincentio is brought face to face with the Pedant who pretends to be the father. The scene acquires a special point of Sly doubles with Vincentio. Artistically, Sly makes an ideal Vincentio. The Beggar took little convincing (although much more than in the quarto play) that he was a lord; he is doubled with a wealthy man incapable of entering a world of illusion, whether created by drink or disguise, a man of solid single identity, the antithesis of an actor. Vincentio is a "sober ancient gentleman" who is presented with a tale about his own identity: that he is an imposter.

This is not Vincentio's first encounter with a challenge to his own self-perception. Kate has greeted him on the road to her father's house:

> Young budding virgin, fair and fresh and sweet,
> Whither away, or where is thy abode?
> Happy the parents of so fair a child!
> Happier the man whom favourable stars
> Allots thee for his lovely bedfellow. [4.5.38–43]

Vincentio is gentleman enough to take it all in good part as a merry joke between gentlefolk. But the habits of sobriety which determine his good-humoured acceptance of a joke at his expense threaten to turn the second comic denial of his identity into a scene more tragic than comic. Turning on Tranio, disguised as Lucentio, he cries: "O, he hath murdered his master! Lay hold on him, I charge you in the Duke's name. O my son, my son!" [5.1.73–5]. In *The*

Taming of the Shrew, where everyone tries his or her hand at playing a part, Vincentio's rugged adherence to a God-given role is both a weakness and a strength. It underlines Vincentio's social reality as a man of wealth and position but heralds in the play itself the end of the play-acting, by defining the limits of theatricality for both actors and audience. Vincentio's distress provides a necessary agent between the brilliant carnivalesque of the sun and moon scene on which he enters, and the sobering domestic closures of the obedience speech. Sly may not re-enter Shakespeare's scene, but the world in which he is a beggar is reasserted in Vincentio, the rich man who refuses even for one moment to play another part.

At the height of Vincentio's alarm about his son, in the anonymous *The Taming of a Shrew*, Slie intervenes: "I say wele have no sending to prison" (Holderness and Loughrey 1992, 80). In Shakespeare's play, the intervention is made by Gremio, the unsuccessful suitor to Bianca, billed in the stage direction as a "pantaloon" (the shrunken old man from the Italian *commedia del'arte*): "Take heed, Signor Baptista, lest you be cony-catched in this business. I dare swear this is the right Vincentio" [5.1.74–5]. Gremio has a curious part in *The Shrew* not paralleled by anything in the quarto. He is old and rich and unsuccessful. His suit is the source of an interchange between Katherina and Bianca in 2.1. Kate tries to find out which of the suitors Bianca affects. Bianca denies Hortensio, and the following exchange ensues:

> KAT   O then, belike, you fancy riches more:
> You will have Gremio to keep you fair.
> BIA   Is it for him you do envy me so?
> Nay then, you jest. [2.1.16–19]

You *must* be joking, remarks Bianca, in the confident tone of a woman who can choose, which infuriates her suitorless sister more than anything. Gremio at the end does not get a wife either to obey him or not. But he has one important moment in the play. He protests against sending Vincentio to prison and declares that he is sure this is the right Vincentio.

That Slie intervenes in *A Shrew* but Gremio intervenes in Shakespeare's version is odd. Shakespeare's Hostess threatened Sly with the constable; in his drunken apprehension of the play this episode could plausibly have reminded him that he might go to prison for not paying for the broken glasses. A possible ending for the play would indeed be the return of the Hostess with the officer, perhaps played by John Sincklo, who played the Beadle who arrested Mistress Quickly in *2 Henry IV*, an inversion of roles which would have its own theatrical irony for audiences who had seen both plays. But

the Slie who intervenes and prevents Vincentio's arrest is the *other*
Slie, the one in *A Shrew* where there is no Hostess, and no threat
of prison (although, confusingly, there may have been the same
John Sincklo acting in the play). Why did Shakespeare give the intervention to Gremio when it would have been much more appropriate in the drama he had himself written, to give it—as in the
anonymous text—to Sly?

The easy answer is of course that Sly was needed for the part of
Vincentio. But another answer based on theatrical realities suggests itself. Gremio, old shrunken and unsuccessful suitor to
Bianca, must have been doubled with the Second Player of the Induction, the man called Sincklo, whom the Lord praised for acting
the lover so well. Skinny, cadaverous, with a stage history of ar-
resting people, Sincklo, having failed yet again to be a good ladies'
man, steps forward to protest against sending people to prison. It
is a joke based on the acting company and aimed at a repertory audience. Beneath the role of Gremio is the reality of Sincklo, the
actor who looked like a jailor. Beneath Vincentio, a man who resists the denial of his identity, is Sly, willing to apprehend being a
Lord. Almost, the two parts coalesce: Sly as Vincentio is momentarily in danger of going to prison after all, and possibly Vincentio's
acting should register, however fleetingly, his own double role as
rich man and Beggar, until he is returned to singular identity by
Sincklo, protesting that in this play he is not a jailor but a man
who plays the (albeit unsuccessful) lover. *The Taming of the Shrew*
never completely conceals the presence of the actor behind the
mask, showing the audience two competing power structures, one
social, the other theatrical.

One of the peculiarities of the anonymous *The Taming of a Shrew*
is that instead of Slie's rising in status under the influence of the
trick, he stays the same, and the Lord descends to his level, the level
of good fellows. Slie in this play only recognises his new state
through his clothes: "Jesus, what fine apparell I have got" (Holderness and Loughrey 1992, 46). He is easily persuaded, where Shakespeare's beggar resists: he would much rather drink beer than sherry;
he doesn't want to wear a doublet, and he accuses his attendants, as
Vincentio accuses the Pedant and his accolade, of trying to make him
mad. He is ultimately convinced not by clothes but by poetry, and responds—as Sebastian responds to the equally unexpected raptures of
Olivia in *Twelfth Night*—by adopting the poetic idiom:

> Am I a lord, and have I such a lady?
> Or do I dream? Or have I dreamed till now?

He is still asking for beer, but he tries to translate it into an
aristocratic idiom: "And once again a pot o'th' smallest ale"

[Ind. 2.66–7; 74]. Shakespeare's Sly unwillingly becomes an actor in an aristocratic show. The Slie of *A Shrew* remains himself, but brings the actors into his orbit. The Lord remains with him all the time, and has become "Sim," a good fellow. But oddly, this name also seems, like Sincklo's name, to link the Lord with a particular player, because at the very beginning of the play-within-a-play the direction reads: "Enter *Simon, Alphonsus*, and his three daughters" (Holderness and Loughrey 1992, 48). Simon, the Lord who gulls Slie, is already on stage, however. Possibly the actor who played Alphonsus was one Simon Jewell, a player in the Queen's or Pembroke's Men, who died of the plague in August 1592.[6] But it is also possible that, as in the 1960 John Barton production (Holderness 1989, 31), an actor playing in the play stepped out of it to address Sly, when he intervened, about the prison, and also during the negotiating with Alfonso. Simon, the Lord, never seems, even when he comes from hunting, remotely like a lord. He is much more like an actor, one of the boys.

In Shakespeare's play, the Lord is emphatically never one of the boys: he is an instructor of boys, both those he would call boy because they are his social inferiors, Sly, the player who must not spoil the show by laughing—and those who really are boys—Bartholomew the page who must play Sly's lady; he calls to one of his men:

> Sirrah, go you to Barthol'mew my page
> And see him dressed in all suits like a lady
> That done, conduct him to the drunkard's chamber,
> And call him "madam", do him obeisance.
> Tell him from me—as he will win my love—
> He bear himself with honourable action
> Such as he hath observed in noble ladies
> Unto their lords, by them accomplished.

He not only advises on the idiom, how the boy is to behave and speak, but on practical matters, how he is to produce tears:

> And if the boy have not a woman's gift
> To rain a shower of commanded tears,
> An onion will do well for such a shift,
> Which in a napkin being close conveyed
> Shall in despite enforce a watery eye.

He is confident that all will be satisfactorily performed: [Ind 1.120–24];

---

6. Thompson 1984, 3. This would put early 1592 as the last possible date for the composition of *A Shrew*.

I know the boy will well usurp the grace.
Voice, gait and action of a gentlewoman. [Ind. 1.127–28]

In the next scene he instructs Sly: to be a lord requires a mind stocked with poetry and luxury, hawking and hunting, the arts and music, and the ideal. Sly is beguiled by the language of birth, the imaginative world which opens before him: "I smell sweet savours and I feel soft things" [Ind. 2.67]. When the Lady enters, she plays her part to perfection:

My husband and my lord, my lord and husband,
I am your wife in all obedience.

Does she, one might ask, overplay it a little? Sly announces that he seems to have slept fifteen years, and the Lady responds:

Ay, and the time seems thirty unto me,
Being all this time abandoned from your bed.

The effect is instantaneous:

SLY   'Tis much. Servants, leave me and her alone.
Madam, undress you and come now to bed. [Ind. 2.103–13]

If this is a page acting, one suspects that he willfully overplayed his part to make the onlookers laugh. The moment has the zest of purest amateurism: a naughty boy let loose in a woman's clothes, pushing his luck as far as it will go.

Ben Johnson's play *Cynthia's Revels*, which was acted by a children's company at court, opens with an Induction in which three children in the company quarrel about who is to speak the prologue:

2 CHILD   I thinke I have most right to it:
I am sure I studied it first.
3 CHILD   That's all one, if the Author thinke
I can speake it better.
1 CHILD   I pleade possession of the cloake.

This child appeals, brandishing his costume, to the audience: "Gentles, your suffrages I pray you." A voice [*within*] calls out angrily: "Why, *Children*, are you not asham'd? Come in there" (4.35). Admittedly this is a company of children (of the Chapel Royal); but the apprentices could be as young as ten and most people would feel it is not only children who are capable of such speeches. Bottom is more genial, but he still wants the best part: indeed he wants every part.

The sense of the power invested in the actual part which is played is not confined to the apprentice boy actor in *The Taming of the Shrew*. A parallel can be drawn with the role of Tranio, servant to Lucentio, who gets to play the master. One presumes that the less proficient actor was given what seems on the face of it to be a side-lined part, until one realises that he is in fact required to take over from Lucentio, who thus becomes an onlooker, and a subordinate: the schoolmaster of Bianca, not the acknowledged wealthy lover. Presumably the more skilled actor actually took the part of Tranio. But the servant, Tranio, is almost too convincing in his role of master, Lucentio. It seems to me false to play Tranio as a man who transports into the role of master the commonness of a servant.[7] He plays Lucentio, as the Page is to play Sly's lady, as one who knows how, if necessary, to imitate a good actor and thus become one; this is an Elizabethan view of education even if not ours. The reason for Tranio's success in the part of Lucentio is his command of a noble language, the language of Petrarch in Petrarch's city, Padua. When Lucentio devises the disguise, Tranio accepts in these terms:

> In a brief, sir, sith it your pleasure is
> And I am tied to be obedient—
> . . . I am content to be Lucentio. [1.1.205–209]

The servant must obey the master, but the actor is jumping for joy that he is to play the bigger part, the part of the master, not the servant. His first speech is to his rival suitors to Bianca, defending his right to enter the competition:

> And were his daughter fairer than she is,
> She may more suitors have, and me for one.
> Fair Leda's daughter had a thousand wooers;
> Then well one more may fair Bianca have.
> And so she shall: Lucentio shall make one,
> Though Paris came in hope to speed alone.

Gremio is as startled as we are: "What, this gentleman will out-talk us all!" Lucentio, newly demoted, is sour: "Sir, give him head. I know he'll prove a jade" [1.2.238–45]. Access to the language of class which Tranio as actor can command as easily as he can play his previous role of obedient servant, gives him stage power.

By the end of the play, Tranio has also acquired some social power within its structures. When he sits at the wedding feast and sees the brides already squalling, he is locked into a fellowship with Petruchio, Baptista, Lucentio and Hortensio which seems to offer no cognizance of his renewed status as servant. It is as if, from

7. In the 1992 Royal Shakespeare Theatre production at the main house in Stratford-upon-Avon, directed by William Alexander, Tranio almost succeeded in wooing Bianca, and the tension between his performance as Lucentio and the subservient role the real Lucentio was forced to play became a notable part of the drama.

playing the master, he has acquired the manners of a master and now sits in easy fellowship with the real masters. But equally one could say that fellowship is resolved into actors playing a new kind of role, that of audience. As they share the comradeship of actors watching their fellows play a scene, social distinctions in the world of the play are momentarily forgotten in the theatrical climax. Actors, amateur and professional, will recognise the special comradeship between performers in a particular production and how relationships off-stage intertwine with relationships on stage. This is the stuff of *The Taming of the Shrew*, and more so than in the anonymous *A Shrew*, which is a play dominated by class conflict: them and us, or the workers and the toffs, as Holderness puts it in his edition of the play (Holderness and Loughrey 1992, 18–19). In Shakespeare's play, class is a necessary element of the drama.[8] But its centre of vitality is acting and theatre: the relation of the players beneath the masks to the parts they play, and the special power generated from a sense of interweaving relationships within the theatrical world which comment on the relationships impersonated in the social world of the play.

The Shrew may have been written with particular actors in mind for other parts besides those of Sincklo and Sly. This early comedy, oddly enough, though apparently dating from the early 1590s, reminds one of *Hamlet*. The arrival of the company of professional players, their sophistication: no one is going to laugh at the antics of the mad lord watching the play; the respect with which the hunting Lord of the Induction treats them and above all, that Lord himself, all invoke the world of *Hamlet*. The Lord, like Hamlet, fancies himself as a playwright and has already constructed his own little drama of deceiving Sly before the Players arrive, which then becomes more complex when he has more actors, and more professional actors ready to hand. Hamlet instructs the Player to insert a speech of his own writing into *The Murder of Gonzago* and holds forth about acting. The Lord in *The Shrew*, spurred on by the arrival of the Players, still plans his own amateur show in which his page will play the lady. His speech of instruction is not, to my mind, an instruction on marriage but an instruction on how to act an obedient well-born lady, and the incentive given is that the page will win the Lord's love, or one could say, that the apprentice will win the master's love. Hamlet was played by Burbage. Did that remarkable actor, who joined the newly formed Chamberlain's men at the same time as Shakespeare

---

8. The Victorian William Cory (1865) wrote in his journal: "I have formerly thought I should like to see gentlefolks act *Taming of the Shrew*, of course as a mere trifle" (398). His wish might have been fulfilled in the RSC 1992 *Shrew*, which rewrote the Induction in order to emphasize its modern upper-class equivalents and forced these genteel persons then to play the parts of Petruchio's servants.

in 1594–1595, perhaps also play Petruchio? Did Shakespeare
rewrite the early play in order that it would provide a fit vehicle for
this actor? If so, the memorial construction theory must go out of
the window, and so must the attendant—and far from convincing—
very early date for *The Shrew*. Be that as it may, the possibility that
Petruchio and the Lord were played by Burbage seems worth entertaining from the evidence of the play itself.

Burbage was no doubt a fascinating actor to be apprenticed to,
and probably very demanding. Shakespeare seems to have written
scenes for Burbage which allowed both actor and dramatist to in-
corporate into the play the rehearsing of how it should be acted. An
elegiac tribute to Burbage in Thomas May's *The Heir*, written in
1620, the year after his death (Gurr 1987, 44), recalls that when
he acted:

> . . . Ladies in the boxes
> Kept time with sighs, and teares to his sad accents
> As he had truely been the man he seem'd.

Hamlet's advice to the players to hold the mirror up to nature is
tailor-made for such an actor. It is not only the Lord's interest in
acting in *The Taming of the Shrew* which seems to link him with
the roles which Shakespeare created for Burbage in the mid-1590s.
Another inhabitant of Shakespeare's stage in the mid-1590s is con-
jured up by Petruchio's dedication to the wooing of Kate:

> Think you a little din can daunt mine ears?
> . . . Have I not in a pitched battle heard
> Loud 'larums, neighing steeds and trumpets' clang?
> And do you tell me of a woman's tongue,
> That gives not half so great a blow to hear
> As will a chestnut in a farmer's fire?
> Tush, tush, fear boys with bugs! [1.2.194–205]

Petruchio here sounds like Hotspur in *1 Henry IV*, whose troubled
dreams of battle alarm another Kate. Both men, Petruchio and
Hotspur, share a rhetoric of sport: Hotspur is as much a huntsman
on the battlefield as the hawking Petruchio is a warrior in wooing.
But they share their love with someone else: the Lord in the Induction, who enters praising his hounds as enthusiastically as Theseus
in *A Midsummer Night's Dream*. I want to suggest that the Lord in
the Induction was played by the same actor as Petruchio (Burns
1986, 51) and that that actor was Richard Burbage, who joined
the Chamberlain's men in 1595, along with Shakespeare himself.
Burbage's theatrical career begins, in our records, with a sensational stage brawl (Greg 1931, I:44) not too dissimilar to the first
scene between Petruchio and Kate. Hotspur himself, of course, is

in Shakespeare's play boisterously matched with Kate (in defiance of history).

Many of Kate's lines carry a Dionysiac charge for most women, of things thought but never said, as when she bursts out to Petruchio, over the business of the cap:

> Why, sir, I trust I may have leave to speak?
> And speak I will. I am no child, no babe.
> Your betters have endured me say my mind,
> And if you cannot, best you stop your ears. [4.3.73–6]

Oddly, these lines have found their way into the first Quarto of *Hamlet* (1603), which precedes the more usually authenticated 1604 Quarto 2. Hamlet says of the Players, about to enter:

> The clowne shall make them laugh
> That are tickled in the lungs, or the blanke verse shall halt for't,
> *And the Lady shall have leave to speake her minde freely.*
> (my italics)

In both the 1604 text and the Folio, the link with *The Shrew* passage has been obscured by a slight re-wording: "The Clown shall make those laugh whose lungs are tickled o'th'sear, and the Lady shall say her mind freely, or the blank verse shall halt for't" (*Complete Works* 2.2.324–26). The implications are obvious. The line stuck in the theatre audience's mind, and perhaps was the key moment of Burbage's stage performance with his apprentice. Natalie Zemon Davis has written of the unruly woman on top in European culture: Kate is anarchic. She seems to obey not only no social conventions but no theatrical ones either, speaking when she is supposed to be silent, according to everyone else's rules. This includes the ending of the play too, where she is supposed finally, after a play of speaking her mind, not to speak her obedience. Her final rejection of the heroine's giving way gracefully is marked by her wonderful long outburst. If it is about obedience, its provenance is marked by an apprentice's joyful sense not of the social, but of the theatrical arena, in which, like Tranio, he is a free citizen chosen on merit. The play creates within the comic context a charge of anarchic delight comparable in intensity and verve to the tragic energy of Hamlet himself. It is as though the reality of the boy beneath the role speaks to the reality of the women in the audience, allowing them stage power even as he proclaims social submission.[9]

The incentive offered to the apprentice who plays Kate is not just

---

9. Fineman's argument for the restoration of patriarchal modes at the end of the play ignores this vital dimension of underlying theatrical interchange between audience and player, which creates its own dynamic of difference.

the winning of his master's love—and the satisfaction of an actor like Burbage must have been worth winning—but his own pride of place in the play. Stage power appears here, even if the price of it is a speech on social submission. Furthermore, behind the text of Kate's obedience speech is the powerful evocation of manhood: dangerous, challenging, adventurous, painful (Burns 1986, 46–47). As the apprentice enters the woman's discourse, the dramatist has seen to it that he conjures up a vision of his own entry into the position of master: the one who takes the risks.[1] But this is also mirrored in his stage situation, because the play stands or falls on the apprentice's performance in the last scene, just as Petruchio's wager stands or falls, and as the husbands gather round to witness their wives' performance, so the masters gather round to see whose apprentice will play the big part: the one with the cloak, the one who studied it first, or the one that the author thought would speak it best. One of the reasons why *The Shrew*, with its apparently timebound folk-origin conservative dogmas about women, has not simply died a quiet death like all the other Elizabethan plays in the taming genre, is that it releases into the auditorium an energy created through a dialectic of opposed wills, command versus obedience, and power versus powerlessness, which is polarised in the utterance of the boy actor playing the woman.

In *The Taming of the Shrew*, the apprentice has virtually the last word. As the stage heroine mouths obedience, the apprentice eyes his female audience, both the querulous wives on the stage and the women in the audience. Did the women in the audience register the exhilaration of the apprentice actor seizing his chance to be master, to realise stage power even if the price of it was a recognition of the submission to which he and they would have to return once the play was over? The triumph of *The Shrew* is the triumph of art over life, of making a beggar believe that he is part of the play, or of making a drunken actor enter an illusory world and use its language. Men and women in the theatre audience in Shakespeare's play become the watcher, Sly, and take his place as witnesses of the play, but also become seduced, as the Beggar is, into entering the play world, believing it to be real, as the ladies believed Burbage's acting to be real. In this play, Shakespeare has allowed the apprentice to upstage the master, perhaps originally Burbage himself. No one bothers much about Petruchio's reality because

1. My argument is based on a theatrical exigency: the ways in which the playwright has written into the part the realities of the player's own situation in order to facilitate his representation of the woman he plays. The effect in this speech is not to present the woman as a construction of "masculine self-differentiation" (Greenblatt 1986, 51) but to draw out of the woman's own role an energy implicit in the creation of Kate herself, and related to Zemon Davis's (1978) perception of "unruliness" discussed earlier.

they are so busy talking about Kate's. Her speech steals the show.
Beneath an ostensible message of humility it generates the suppressed exhilaration of its stage power: the seizing of mastery by the
apprentice even as he proclaims a master's doctrine of subjection.

What did Shakespeare's contemporaries make of it? I maintain
that they were not all out ducking their wives in the pond.[2] Sir John
Harington, who owned a copy of *The Taming of a Shrew* (given that
Shakespeare's contemporaries made no distinction between their
title, which *Shrew*?) wrote in 1596 in *The Metamorphosis of Ajax*:
"For the shrewd wife, read the booke of taming of a shrew, which
hath made a number of us so perfect, that now every one can rule
a shrew in our countrey, save he that hath her. But indeed there are
but two good rules. One is, let them never have their willes; the
other differs but a letter, let them ever have their willes, the first is
the wiser, but the second is more in request, and therefore I make
choice of it" (153–55). A year later, in 1597, Harington wrote his
wife a poem on their fourteenth wedding anniversary, entitled "To
his wife after they had been married 14 years":

> Two prentiships with thee I now have been
> Mad times, sad times, glad times, our life hath seen.
> Souls we have wrought four payr, since our first meeting.
> Of which two souls, sweet souls were to to fleeting.
> My workmanship so well doth please thee still
> thou wouldst not graunt me freedom by thy will,
> And Ile confess such usage I have found
> Mine hart yet nere desir'd to bee unbound.
> But though my self am thus thy Prentice vowd,
> My dearest Mall, yet thereof bee not proud,
> Nor claym no rewl thereby, there's no such cause,
> For Plowden who was father of the laws,
> which yet are read and ruld by his indytings,
> doth name himself apprentice in his Writings.
> And I, if you should challenge undew place,
> could learn of him to alter so the case.
> I playn would prove I still kept dew priority,
> and that good wives are still in their minority,
> But far from thee my Deare bee such audacity,
> I doubt more thou dost blame my dull capacity,
> That though I travaile true in my vocation,
> I grow yet worse and worse at th'occupation. (14–15)

In this remarkable poem the husband is the apprentice to his wife
and has served two seven-year terms, which have given him such

---

2. This is not to underestimate the importance of Boose's (1991) fascinating research into
the treatment of scolds in Elizabethan England, although I do find it more relevant to
the world of *The Taming of a Shrew*, with its much more popular frame of reference,
than to Shakespeare's (to my mind) very courtly play.

content that he prefers bondage to freedom. In Harington's *Epigrams*, printed after his death, the compositor has either made an error, or failed to understand the significance of the fourteen years: that the apprentice's bonds were up. In this poem Harington, who always claimed that his poems were not fiction, but truth, warns his wife that if she should prove proud, he could prove in law that the situation might be reversed, and she would find that she was the one who was still in her minority, in the apprentice position. However, he is not afraid that that boldness will be taken by her, but rather that he will fail her in his vocation.

The sexual intimacy of this poem within a domestic context makes it most extraordinary, yet the sustained image of the apprentice suggests that it was not only in the theatre that apprentices and women shared a common minority status, but also that the equality which the apprentice boy might gain as heroine, might have its counterpart in the true interchange between apprentice and master which is created in the delight of Petruchio at the end of the play in the boy's performance. Harington, who was fond enough of Shakespeare's plays to possess fifteen of them in quarto, and three duplicates (Furnivall 1890, 283–93), may have felt that for his own wife and for himself, the witty jesting godson of the queen, the play had much to say. But that that message is a humiliating one for women, however much it may be so in a theatre where women actresses play Kate, seems to me in Shakespeare's theatre to be belied by the realities of the theatrical world in which the boy actor earns his momentary supremacy by means of a brilliant performance of a speech proclaiming subjection. If the boy actor winked at Petruchio, he might also have winked at the women watching him in the theatre. Did the women in the audience hear words which send them back to domestic drudgery, or did they share the heady sensation of mastery which the boy actor infuses into one of the longest and most exciting parts he has ever played, in which, in the end, he silences with his eloquence the greatest actor in Shakespeare's company, and surpasses even that actor's wildest expectations of good performance? The boy actor invites women in the audience to participate not in what he says, but in the theatrical power which orchestrates the act of speaking.

WORKS CITED

Barroll, Leeds. 1991. *Politics, Plague and Shakespeare's Theater: The Stuart Years*. Ithaca: Cornell University Press.

Bentley, Gerald Eades. 1984. *The Profession of Player in Shakespeare's Time 1590–1642*. Princeton: Princeton University Press.

Boose, Lynda. 1991. "Scolding Brides and Bridling Scolds: Taming the Woman's Unruly Member." *Shakespeare Quarterly* 42: 179–213.

Burns, Margie. 1986. "The Ending of *The Shrew*." *Shakespeare Studies* 18: 41–64.

Cory, William. 1865. *Extracts from the Letters and Journals*. Edited by Francis Warre Cornish. Oxford, n.p.

Duthie, G. I. 1943. *"The Taming of a Shrew* and *The Taming of the Shrew." The Review of English Studies* 19: 337–56.

Fineman, Joel. 1985. "The Turn of the Shrew." *Shakespeare and the Question of Theory.* Edited by Patricia Parker and Geoffrey Hartman. London: Methuen.

Furnivall, F. J. 1890. "Sir John Harington's Shakespeare Quartos." *Notes and Queries,* 7th Series, 9 (May 17): 382–83.

Gaw, Alison. 1926. "John Sincklo as One of Shakespeare's Actors." *Anglia* 49: 289–303.

Greenblatt, Stephen. 1986. "Fiction and Friction." *Reconstructing Individualism.* Ed. Thomas Heller, Morton Sosna, and David E. Wellbery. Stanford: Stanford University Press, 1986.

Greg, W. W. 1931. *Dramatic Documents for the Elizabethan Playhouses.* Oxford: Clarendon.

Gurr, Andrew. 1987. *Playgoing in Shakespeare's London.* Cambridge: Cambridge University Press.

Harington, Sir John. 1591. *Epigrams.* Bound into the *Orlando Furioso, in English Heroical Verse.* London: Richard Field.

———. 1962. *Sir John Harington's A New Discourse of a Stale Subject, called The Metamorphosis of Ajax.* Edited by Elizabeth Story Donno. London: Routledge.

Hinman, Charlton, ed. 1968. *The First Folio of Shakespeare: The Norton Facsimile.* London: Hamlyn.

Holderness, Graham. 1989. *The Taming of the Shrew: Shakespeare in Performance.* Manchester: Manchester University Press.

Holderness, Graham, and Bryan Loughrey, eds. 1992. *The Taming of a Shrew.* Memel Hempstead: Harvester Wheatsheaf.

Howard, Jean E. 1989. "Scripts and/versus Playhouses: Ideological Production and the Renaissance Public Stage." *Renaissance Drama* 20 (1989): 31–40.

Jonson, Ben. 1966. *Cynthia's Revels. Ben Jonson.* Edited by C.H. Herford and Percy Simpson. Oxford: Clarendon.

Marston, John. 1967. *The Malconient.* Edited by Bernard Harris. London: The New Mermaids, Benn.

McLuskie, Kathleen. 1987. "The Act, the Role, and the Actor: Boy Actresses on the Elizabethan Stage." *New Theatre Quarterly* 3: 120–30.

McMillin, Scott. 1972. "Casting for Pembroke's Men: The *Henry VI* Quartos and *The Taming of A Shrew.*" *Shakespeare Quarterly* 23: 141–59.

———. 1976. "Simon Jewell and the Queen's Men." *Review of English Studies* 27: 174–77.

Moore, William. 1964. "An Allusion in 1593 to *The Taming of the Shrew?*" *Shakespeare Quarterly* 15: 55–60.

Pepys, Samuel. 1971. *The Diary of Samuel Pepys.* Edited by Robert Latham and William Matthews. London: Bell.

Rastall, Richard. 1985. "Female Roles in All-Male Casts." *Medieval English Theatre* 7: 21–51.

Shakesepeare, William. 1968. *The First Folio of Shakespeare: The Norton Facsimile.* Edited by Charlton Hinman. London: Hamlyn.

———. 1984. *The Taming of the Shrew.* Edited by Ann Thompson. Cambridge: Cambridge University Press.

———. 1986. *The Complete Works.* Edited by Stanley Wells and Gary Taylor. Oxford: Clarendon.

———. 1992. *The Tragicall Historie of Hamlet Prince of Denmarke.* Edited by Graham Holderness and Bryan Loughrey. Hemel Hempstead: Harvester Wheatsheaf.

Taming of a Shrew, The. 1992. Edited by Graham Holderness and Bryan Loughrey. Hemel Hempstead: Harvester Wheatsheaf.

Thompson, Ann. 1982. "Dating Evidence for *The Taming of the Shrew." Notes and Queries* 29: 108–9.

———, ed. *The Taming of the Shrew* Cambridge: Cambridge University Press, 1984.

Trewin, J. C. 1978. *Going to Shakespeare.* London: Allen and Unwin.

Wentersdorf, Karl P. 1978. "The Original Ending of *The Taming of the Shrew*: A Reconsideration." *Studies in English Literature* 18: 201–15.

————. 1980. "Actors' Names in Shakespearean Texts." *Theatre Studies* 23: 18–30.
Zemon Davis, Natalie. 1978. "Women on Top: Symbolic Sexual Inversion and
   Political Disorder in Early Modern Europe." *The Reversible World.* Edited by
   Barbara A. Babcock. Ithaca and London: Cornell University Press, 1978.

MAREA MITCHELL

Performing Sexual Politics in
The Taming of the Shrew†

Performance is central to *The Taming of the Shrew*. All three
strands of the sixteenth-century play (the gulling of Sly, the wooing
of Bianca and the taming of Katherina) involve pretence, deception
and the acting out of roles to achieve particular ends. The Sly-
frame scenes directly invite the audience to focus on the business
of acting and performance while in the plot relating to the wooing
of Bianca various kinds of performances are put on by and for her
suitors, and Petruchio's strategy for taming Katherina entails pretending to be a bigger bully than Katherina. By focusing on performance in and of *Shrew* we can also rehearse key shifts in
understanding sexual politics, or the way that gender and sexuality
are treated as relations of power, in a Shakespearian comedy that
remains surprisingly popular even in the twenty-first century.

Critics have often asked why *The Taming of the Shrew* remains
popular when its main story is one that in modern terms might be
said to be sexist in depicting a relationship that includes a woman
being coerced into various kinds of behaviour and into submission
to her husband's will. Certain power relations are implied in the title where Petruchio is the tamer or "the active agent and Kate, or
rather a category that is said to include her, is only the object."[1]
From this kind of modern analysis of power relations, Kate is acted
upon while Petruchio does the acting. Tori Haring-Smith suggests,
for example, that the Petruchio-Katherina plot relies on the treatment of a woman that "appears to be downright sadistic and thoroughly offensive" to modern eyes and ears, but that "performers
and directors have found a variety of ways to avoid this offense and
to adjust the play to the sensibilities of their age."[2] While dis-

---

† This essay was written especially for this Norton Critical Edition. Printed by permission
   of the author.
1. Susan Snyder, *Shakespeare: A Wayward Journey* (Newark: University of Delaware Press,
   2002), p. 129.
2. Tori Haring-Smith, *From Farce to Metadrama: A Stage History of* The Taming of the
   Shrew (Westport, Connecticut: Greenwood Press, 1985) p. 3. See also Joel Fineman
   "The Turn of the Shrew," in *Shakespeare and the Question of Theory,* ed. Patricia Parker
   and Geoffrey Hartman (New York and London: Methuen, 1985), p. 138, who analyzes
   the play in terms of its use of and inability to escape from a language of patriarchy, and

cussing the play in relation to sexual politics might seem a particularly modern way to understand it, an interest in relationships between people and the power that these relationships involve is
evident from the outset of *Shrew*.

The Induction focuses on the issue of players and playing, and
the production of a performance that encompasses *Shrew* itself. It
is easy to forget as the play unfolds that the main plots of the play,
the taming and the wooing, according to the Sly-frame, are all part
of the performance mounted by the hirelings of the Lord. While
critics have argued that production issues account for the frequent
absence of the Sly-frame[3] it also simplifies the experience of the
play if we are not given the Induction. One layer of perspective,
one point of view from which to see the actions, is stripped away if
the play-within-the play is removed. To consider how the presence
or absence of the Induction alters how we think of the main events
of the play is to reflect on the significance of frames. A frame may
not determine how the following events are received but a frame
can set up expectations and trigger a way of anticipating those
events. Whether or not to include the Induction is then a conundrum that a producer might consider. To include it facilitates one
way of setting up the play itself, so that it becomes a drunken man's
fantasy, that will surely last no longer than the Lord chooses to
carry on the joke, after which Sly will presumably return to the rig-
ors of the Hostess's pursuit of his debt. But including it also leaves
the problem of what to do with those actors after the first scene,
given that no further dialogue is scripted for them, and no stage directions include them. Do you silently elide them or perhaps write
in an epilogue? The theme of performance, thus begins early in this
particular play, and is very closely tied to issues of interpretation
and meaning.[4]

If thinking about the frame is one literal and interpretive way
into the play, the question of whether or not to use the frame also
raises key issues in relation to the representation of character. Diana E. Henderson links the decision about the frame with

---

Diana E. Henderson "A Shrew for the Times," in *Shakespeare the Movie: Popularizing the Plays on Film, TV, and Video*, ed. Lynda E. Boose and Richard Burt (London and New York: Routledge, 1997), p. 148. Miriam Gilbert has an interesting section on *Shrew* in *Shakespeare: An Oxford Companion*, ed. Stanley Wells and Lena Cowen Orlin (Oxford: Oxford University Press, 2003), pp. 560–67, including a brief but useful bibliography.

3. Given the absence of an epilogue that returns the audience to the Sly frame with which the play begins, what are the actors playing Sly and the Lord's followers to do given that they have no dialogue after the end of the first scene in the first act?

4. One of the most influential films of *Shrew*, Zeffirelli's 1966 version starring Richard Burton and Elizabeth Taylor finds another way of setting up the events, without using the Sly frame. Deborah Cartmell suggests that the "carnival atmosphere of the film's opening functions like the Induction, to announce that this is a world of trickery, mock-ery, and artificiality," "Franco Zeffirelli and Shakespeare," in *The Cambridge Companion to Shakespeare on Film*, ed. Russell Jackson (Cambridge: Cambridge University Press, 2000), p. 217.

other obvious shifts in performance values in *Shrew*: the medium through which it is performed and the inclusion of women actors. "In choosing to erase the Sly frame and use actresses for the female roles," she argues, "the filmmakers increase the inset story's claims to social reality, already abetted by the transfer to a normatively realist medium."[5]

Henderson's first point here addresses the key shift from the use of boy actors to play female roles in Elizabethan England to the employment of female actors. There has been much debate about the implications of the fact that women would not have played the female characters on the Elizabethan stage,[6] and there has been much speculation as to what difference this makes, and how we might think about Elizabethan drama with this information. It is rather easier to see how women's playing female roles in modern stage and film adaptations of Shakespeare's play promotes what Henderson calls "modern culture's enshrining of the heterosexual love plot and the presumed link between love and marriage."[7] We may not know how the tensions between all-male casts played out on stage in any particular sixteenth- or seventeenth-century production, but it seems clear that the illusions involved in watching boys play women calls upon a different kind of viewing response. Again, early modern productions might very well have relied on a much more direct focus on performance and performing by nature of the restrictions against women being on the stage.

Different technology, media, and cultural and aesthetic values invite different kinds of responses, particularly given a shift from representational to naturalistic modes of performance. Put simply, late twentieth- and twenty-first century performance values, particularly in terms of television and film, rely on portrayal of characters that is realistic. The commercial success of so-called reality television is the embodiment of the interest in real people's real lives unfolding before the audience in real time.

We cannot reconstruct a production and an audience that is authentically Shakesperian, given that we cannot unknow what we know, nor rebuild sensibilities. What we can do, however, is be aware of the kinds of changes that have occurred from the writing and staging of one of Shakespeare's earliest plays, and its moments of reception now. Fundamental shifts in the representation of Shakespearian drama have occurred, as Robert Weimann explains:

5. Diana E. Henderson, "A Shrew for the Times," in *Shakespeare the Movie*, ed. Boose and Burt, p. 150.
6. See, for example, Juliet Dusinberre, "*The Taming of the Shrew*: Women, Acting, and Power," *Studies in the Literary Imagination* 26 (1993), pp. 67–84, and *The Weyward Sisters: Shakespeare and Feminist Politics*, ed. Dympna Callaghan, Lorraine Helms, and Jyotsna Singh (Oxford: Blackwell, 1994).
7. Henderson, p. 149.

> For a significant, and significantly increasing, majority of peo-
> ple the encounter with Shakespeare is not through reading
> what he wrote but through watching certain electronically
> processed images of filmed performance. To acknowledge this
> major shift is to take cognizance not simply of deep-going
> changes in the media of access; no less important, the shifting
> mode of reception significantly affects the meaning of what is
> received. The parameters of what now authorizes and ener-
> gizes the uses of his plays are themselves in flux. What we see
> emerging before our eyes is a new poetics of cultural response
> that has its own demands and gratifications different from
> those of predominantly textual assimilation of the classic.[8]

Weimann draws attention here to the extra-textual dimensions of
performance or those aspects that cannot be decided directly by
even the closest attention to the words on the page. The Sly frame
provides one kind of entry point to the play, an entry point that
flags performance, deception, and trickery involving impersonation
and role-play in a play whose conventions relied on role-play in the
most obvious ways where adult male or boy actors took on female
parts.

Modern versions also tend to strip away so-called sub-plots and
minor characters to focus on the central relationship between
Katherina and Petruchio, so that emphasis falls not so much on
story "as upon personality, with identification encouraged through
fast-paced yet intimate camera work."[9] Originally, in Shakespeare's
comedies characters "tend to the typical rather than the individuated and require settings that are neither wholly exterior nor wholly
individuated,"[1] making *commedia dell'arte* a useful way of produc-
ing *Shrew* because that style and practice of production is "so arti-
ficial that its characters can easily become acrobats—interesting
for their skill, but not engaging for their emotions."[2] With production values that focus on types rather than personalities, audiences
are not encouraged to deal with the more troubling issues of bullying and intimidation that seems to make Katherina a cowed subservient when in Act IV scene V she says: "[I]t is the blessed
sun./But sun it is not, when you say it is not." Put simply, stagings

8. Robert Weimann, *Author's Pen and Actor's Voice: Playing and Writing in Shakespeare's
   Theatre*, ed. Helen Higbee and William West (Cambridge: Cambridge University Press,
   2000), pp. 2–3.
9. Ramona Wray, "Shakespeare and the Singletons, or, Beatrice Meets Bridget Jones: Post-
   Feminism, Popular Culture and 'Shakespe(Re)-Told,' " in *Screening Shakespeare in the
   Twenty-First Century*, ed. Mark Thornton Burnett and Ramona Wray (Edinburgh: Edinburgh University Press, 2006), p. 187. This must have been particularly true for audiences of productions such as Zeffirelli's *Shrew* and Sam Taylor's 1929 *Shrew*, who were
   aware of the real-life relationships between Burton and Taylor, and Douglas Fairbanks,
   Sr. and Mary Pickford.
1. Michael Hattaway, "The Comedies on Film," in *The Cambridge Companion to Shakespeare on Film*, ed. Jackson, p. 86.
2. Haring-Smith, p. 111.

of the play that use stereotypes such as the shrew, the obedient daughter, and the buffoon go some way to removing the play from modern concerns about equality, in either class or gender terms. Audiences confronted with clearly "unreal" representations are likely to be less taxed with concerns as to how this translates into everyday personal relationships.

In this context Haring-Smith's *From Farce to Metadrama: A Stage History of* The Taming of the Shrew 1594–1983 usefully describes transformations of the play from its earliest known productions. She examines the significance, for example, of David Garrick's 1754 production of *Catherine and Petruchio* and its influence on the eighteenth- and nineteenth-century stage histories of the play. As its name suggests, this adaptation strips away the other elements of Shakespeare's play to focus on two characters. Whereas traditional ways of analyzing Shakespearean drama often rely on relationships between strands of the narrative, Garrick's version proved congenial to modern interest in individuals and emotional relationships, and the representation of psychologically plausible characters. The problems of unifying a play that seems driven through three different, if connected, stories also disappear if two (the Sly and Bianca lines) are either played down or dropped altogether.

Gil Junger's 1999 film *Ten Things I Hate about You* builds on the long tradition started by Garrick in focusing on the Kate/Petruchio relationship, shifting the attention to Kate and her attempts to deal with the pressures on young women as well as the tensions between academic achievement and popularity. Interestingly enough this film version also shows an interest in the anxieties of masculinity, with Bianca's "suitor" uncertain how to perform in his role. It also utilizes popular cultural stereotypes by casting the Australian actor Heath Ledger as the "kangaroo boy" Petruchio figure, thus enabling an audience for a U.S. based film to read in all sorts of expectations about Australian masculinity, including perhaps the oldest one in the book that refers back to Australia's convict history.[3] Perhaps most significantly of all, though, this version explains Kate's "shrewishness" by adding in a sexual experience with a character now courting her sister Bianca, who is portrayed in the film as a vain sexual predator. In adding one character the Junger film provides a way of understanding Kate's antipathy toward boys and her reluctance to be taken in by them again, and her antipathy toward her sister who has fallen for the boy who mistreated Kate. Kate is thus explained and the film given a particular set of moral values about the dangers of early sexual experience. Given that Kate and

---

3. The BBC's 2005 production of *Shrew* also associates Petruchio with Australia through having him just return from there. Both Junger's film and the BBC version would bear closer scrutiny for their use of cultural codes that provide audiences with shorthand ways of identifying types.

Bianca's mother is also an absent presence in the film, having left her family before the film begins, and that their father is comically obsessed with the threat of his daughters' pregnancy, twenty-first century values clearly color this particular adaptation of the sixteenth-century text. In particular, Kate's behavious is portrayed as understandably and credibly assertive. If Kate comes to see that not all men are sexual predators, then her sister has a parallel conversion in understanding that compliance with particular male values of female beauty and sexual availability is not ideal either.

More recently again, the BBC's "Shakespeare Re-Told" (2005) took *Shrew* as one of four plays produced in modern settings for British television.[4] This version translates Kate into a political leader for the opposition to the existing government, and presents her as ruthless, ambitious, and rude. She directly views the possibility of marriage in self-interested terms, as a way of gaining social credibility and off-setting questions about her sexuality. Her representation seems firmly located in the stereotype of the shrew, and less time is given on her portrayal as a character than is given to Petruchio. The contest at the end of this version centers on the signing of prenuptual contracts. The production clearly gestures back to its origins with direct quotations from Shakespeare, but also explicitly flags its twenty-first century context with references to Petruchio's transvestism, work/home relationships, and female sexual desire. It works against a naturalist or realist trend, however, in its tendency to treat Kate as a caricature and in the deliberately excessive end that sees Kate pregnant with triplets.[5]

Whatever differences may be seen in productions of the play since Shakespeare's time, some elements seem relatively constant. Take, for example, the verbal wordplay that characterizes so much of Shakespeare's comedy. Verbal dexterity, misunderstandings, puns, and linguistic game-playing are crucial parts of Shakespeare's comedies and the comic strands in his other plays. In particular, the use of stichomythia is a characteristic of many comic scenes. This use of dialogue where characters are given alternate lines in which they argue, dispute, and repeat and turn upside down their opponents' words is a staple of scenes from *Hamlet* to *Love's Labour's Lost*. A battle of wits, probably drawn from the influence of classical Greek drama, stichomythia does not always or necessarily involve different genders. In *Shrew* itself, for example, the first scene in which we see the male protagonist Petruchio, Act 1, scene 2, begins with his interchanges with Grumio centered on puns

4. The other three were *Macbeth, Much Ado about Nothing* and *A Midsummer Night's Dream.*
5. See Wray, "Shakespeare and the Singletons," in *Screening Shakespeare in the Twenty-First Century,* ed. Burnett and Wray (2006), pp. 185–205.

about knocking on a door. In Act 2, scene 1, a more heightened verbal debate directly employs stichomythia as Kate and Petruchio battle over control, where verbal control implies power in other dimensions, specifically here over the right to choose a marriage partner.

Russ McDonald argues that the splitting of lines between characters, "dividing," for example, "a line of iambic pentameter between two speakers" creates a feeling that "characters seem to be talking with one another, not just at one another." "As characters trade off phrases in a rhythmic fashion, the listener may intuit a growing agitation or increasingly intimate engagement."[6] Here, I think, we have the connection between argument and intimacy that goes a long way to explaining the continued success of rhetorical sparring as a device associated with courtship or emotional intimacy.

It is Kate's rhetorical skills, her ability to use language to make persuasive points, which encourage audiences to be interested in her and to have sympathy for her. In *Shrew* there is a sense that Baptista, her father, is not totally oblivious to his daughter's well-being, difficult daughter though he finds her. When Petruchio is establishing his credentials and dowry for Kate in Act 2, scene 1, Baptista also insists that the arrangement will only take place "when that special thing is obtain'd,/That is, her love" (2.1.126–7). Similarly, earlier in Act 1, scene 1, Baptista prefaces his encouragement to Gremio and Hortensio to court Kate with the statement that he does so "Because I know you well and love you well" (1.1.53). Yet in spite of this, Kate's objection that she is being held up for auction by the highest bidder, and worse, that her father is in effect prostituting her, resonates very powerfully in the line "I pray you, sir, is it your will/To make a *stale* of me among these mates?" (1.1.57–58, my emphasis). The connotations of the word stale (prostitute, decoy, foil for another, dead end) reflect poignantly on the character of Kate, and her self-awareness. They suggest her sense that she is seen to have no virtue or meaning in herself, and introduce a note of pathos into her position. Shrew she may seem, but Shakespeare's printed text has its own way of providing explanation for some of Kate's sharp words.

Putting character, language, and acting style aside, another important aspect of performing *Shrew*, as in any other play, involves the uses of *locus* and *platea*. Coventionally, *platea* has been taken to refer to action that takes place downstage, close to and including the audience, whereas *locus* refers to action that takes place fully in

---

6. Russ McDonald, "Shakespeare's Verse," in *Shakespeare: An Oxford Guide* (Oxford: Oxford University Press, 2003), p. 84.

the stage or play world, upstage, farthest away from the audience. As Robert Weimann puts it, "the *locus* invariably privileges the authority of what and who is presented in the world of the play,"[7] which *platea* may challenge by letting the audience into knowledge not shared by the other characters, giving them an insight into a character's thoughts or motivations. Soliloquies and asides are key examples of using *platea*. Hamlet often uses this convention to explore his reflections, while Claudius's attempt at repentance, thwarted by the realization that he cannot give up the things he has won, might also use *platea*. Both *locus* and *platea* are, again in Weimann's terms, conventional "modes," and while it is traditional to think of them in terms of physical space, downstage and upstage, and in terms of their relations of proximity to the audience, it is as much a matter of representational space as physical space that is at stake.

Let's take, for example, a very important speech assigned to Petruchio, the performance of which will have much to do with an audience's interpretation of his character. In Act 2, scene 1, before Petruchio meets Kate, he announces his strategy to the audience in his intention to counter Kate's words by thwarting her expectations and praising her regardless of her behavior. Thus will he turn her railing into songs of a nightingale, and her frowns into expressions "clear/As morning roses newly wash'd with dew" (2.1.170–71). Alone on the stage, perhaps physically downstage, confiding in the audience, Petruchio's speech may not offset the mercenary inclinations clearly expressed by him at the outset of the play where he declares his intention "Happily to wive and thrive as best I may" (1.2.53). What it might do, however, depending on how it is performed, is suggest an approach to the wooing that is at least not malicious.

This is one way in which the convention of *platea* might be employed. If this convention is seen as involving not simply physical but also representational space, then other possibilities for performance come in to play. Take here as an example one of the most comically ambiguous scenes in the play, Act 4, scene 5, where Petruchio and Kate are traveling back to her father's house. In terms of the words on the page, this scene requires Kate to follow whatever her husband says. The moon becomes the sun, or as Kate puts it "a rush-candle," if Petruchio will have it so, and an old man becomes a "young, budding virgin, fair, and fresh, and sweet," and then a "reverend father" again as Petruchio dictates (4.5.14, 38, 49). Yet this scene could employ the convention of *platea* in its use of space and time that focuses not on the finished "self-contained

7. Robert Wiemann, *Author's Pen*, p. 184.

. . . picture of the performed" but "the process of the performer performing."[8] Kate's words here clearly suggest not that she actually believes the moon to be the sun, or an old man to be a young girl, but that she knows what to do to get where she wants: in this case, home to visit her father and sister. There is a searingly practical acknowledgment evident in her behavior. The scene also creates a relationship of some intimacy between Kate and Petruchio. If the old man Vincentio is completely bamboozled by his sudden insertion into some one else's story (as he will be again later when he falls foul of his son's tricks to gain Bianca), then the audience knows quite well what is going on and is, in a sense, in on the joke with the protagonists. The self-consciousness of this scene and the literal foregrounding of the idea of performance and fulfilling roles, one's own and those to fit the expectations of other people, might provide key interpretive indicators for broader issues in the play.

This might also become the case in the play's final and, from a modern perspective, most controversial scene. Some versions or adaptations of *Shrew* simply avoid the issues this scene raises by dropping the speech altogether. *Ten Things*, for example, shows sisterly solidarity and revenge on the sexual predator Joey, Kate's acceptance of her love for "Petruchio," and her resolution still to attend college, away from home, and by implication, from boyfriend. Elizabeth Taylor in Zeffirelli's film performs the speech straight, without irony, in a declaration of unquestioning love that is simultaneously confirmed and undercut by the knowledge of Taylor's high-profile real-life marriage with Richard Burton and her ambitions as an independent, professional actor. Other versions, such as that produced by Australia's flagship Shakespeare Company, the Bell Shakespeare Company, let Kate's words hang in the air as an indictment of the chauvinist values that they imply.[9]

It is also instructive to consider how *platea* might be used to provide interpretive hooks for key scenes in the play. A focus on *platea* encourages thinking about the relationship between Kate and Petruchio with an emphasis on performance and role-playing. The success that Petruchio enjoys in the final scene of the play relies, after all, on a very public demonstration by Petruchio and Kate that they function as husband and wife, where her role entails compliance but also the performance of, or acting out, the role of the ideal wife.[1] This may be unpalatable to modern ears and eyes in

8. Ibid.
9. *The Taming of the Shrew*, The Bell Shakespeare Company, directed John Bell, Civic Theatre Newcastle, New South Wales, April 1994.
1. The plethora of conduct books and educational guides, such as Richard Brathwait's *The English Gentlewoman* (1631) and Gervase Markham's *The English Housewife* (1615), indicates how keen an interest there was in these issues. These books, and others like them, also make clear how much work has to go into the production and demonstration

terms of the words that sit on the page, but the notion that gender can be seen as performance, as Judith Butler has argued, is an insightful and provocative one. That gender might be considered in terms of performance suggests that these roles might be put down, picked up, changed, and reversed. The notion that gender includes roles might also suggest that what lies behind what it means to be a wife or husband is not set in concrete. How these roles are fulfilled and by whom, then, might also be seen as neither natural nor predetermined.[2] Writing from a different critical perspective, Jonathan Gil Harris suggests that these scenes can also be read in terms of an alienation effect, disclosing "how both nobility and femininity are not natural identities, but socially scripted roles."[3]

The intimacy of the relationship between Katherina and Petruchio in this final scene also effectively marginalizes and excludes, for better or worse, all the other characters in the scene. The final lines of the play, Hortensio's "Now go thy ways, thou hast tam'd a curst shrew," and Lucio's " 'Tis a wonder, by your leave, she will be tam'd so," suggest that the departure of Kate and Petruchio ends the interest in the play, while Lucio's line may also draw attention to the idea that not all may be as it seems. Either way, it is clearly the relationship between this particular husband and wife that works.

What a play means at any particular time relies heavily on how it is performed, perhaps more with *The Taming of the Shrew* than many other plays, but perhaps this play has always been provocative. There is a tendency to think that the twenty-first century is a more complex site of understanding and interpretation than previous periods. It is impossible to ignore the concern that aspects of this play, along with others by Shakespeare, among other early modern writers, simply will not sit comfortably in cultures influenced by feminism and a belief in the rights of all individuals regardless of color, race, gender, and class. But perhaps as Graham Holderness argues, this is to simplify how texts in these earlier periods were received. Perhaps the *Shrew* was always capable of being seen as "provocative and polernical rather than persuasive,"[4] as

---

of virtues that had been naturalized as feminine by the nineteenth century. It is part of the point of Virginia Woolf's *Orlando* to throw a comic light on the idea that feminine virtues are natural through depicting a central character that shifts from male to female and has to achieve, with some difficulty, the behavior to go alongside those changes in anatomy.

2. See, for example, Judith Butler, *Gender Trouble: Feminism and the Subversion of Identity* (New York: Routledge, 1999), especially pp. 171–90. Historical differences are clearly important in thinking about the construction of gendered behavior but the metaphor of performance as used by Butler has been very productive.

3. Jonathan Gil Harris, "Materialist Criticisms," in *Shakespeare: An Oxford Guide* (2003), p. 475.

4. Graham Holderness, *The Taming of the Shrew* (Manchester: Manchester University Press, 1989), p. 24.

something more than requiring apology or that has itself to be tamed for modern consumption.[5]

A focus on the ending and the now notorious "submission" speech by Katherina may also detract from the energy that precedes it, as Donald K. Hedrick argues: "The controversial submission of Kate at the end of *Taming of the Shrew*, repeatedly the object of political and ideological investigation, may have much less ultimate force than the preceding representation of her refusal to be the conventional mistress or wife at the beginning."[6] Nor, we might add, does it necessarily diminish the sense of what the successful performance of such roles costs.

Any analysis of Shakespearean drama has to engage with issues raised by its performance, which it is useful to remember, given that it is primarily studied as a print text that we read rather than watch and experience in more multidimensional ways. In a sense, this turns us back to Shakespeare's works in their original mode, through returning us to performance. This is a point well made by Graham Holderness:

> The play itself, in its given textual form, cannot provide us with a definition of its own sexual politics. The pluralistic meanings that can be provoked by the text lie outside it, in the contradictory evidence of social history, and in the dialectic of theatrical performance.[7]

KAREN NEWMAN

Renaissance Family Politics and Shakespeare's *Taming of the Shrew*[†]

A quarrel may end wi' the whip, but it begins wi' the tongue, and it's the women have got the most o' that.

George Eliot, *Daniel Deronda*

Wetherden, Suffolk. Plough Monday, 1604. A drunken tanner, Nicholas Rosyer, staggers home from the alehouse. On arriving at his door, he is greeted by his wife with "dronken dogg, pisspott and other unseemly names." When Rosyer tried to come to bed to her,

---

5. Henderson, p. 148.
6. Donald K. Hedrick, "War Is Mud: Branagh's Dirty Harry and the Types of Political Ambiguity," in *Shakespeare the Movie*, ed. Boose and Burt, p. 60.
7. Holderness, p. 25.
† From Karen Newman, *Fashioning Femininity and English Renaissance Drama* (Chicago: University of Chicago Press, 1991), pp. 35–50. Reprinted by permission of Blackwell Publishing.

she "still raged against him and badd him out dronken dog dronken pisspott." She struck him several times, clawed his face and arms, spit at him, and beat him out of bed. Rosyer retreated, returned to the alehouse, and drank until he could hardly stand up. Shortly thereafter, Thomas Quarry and others met and "agreed amongest themselfs that the said Thomas Quarry who dwelt at the next howse . . . should . . . ryde abowt the towne upon a cowlstaff whereby not onley the woman which had offended might be shunned for her misdemeanors towards her husband but other women also by her shame might be admonished to offence in like sort."[1] Domestic violence, far from being contained in the family, spills out into the neighborhood, and the response of the community is an "old country ceremony used in merriment upon such accidents."

Quarry, wearing a kirtle or gown and apron, "was carried to diverse places and as he rode did admonishe all wiefs to take heede how they did beate their husbands." The Rosyers' neighbors reenacted their troubled gender relations: the beating was repeated, with Quarry in woman's clothes playing Rosyer's wife, the neighbors standing in for the "abused" husband, and a rough music procession to the house of the transgressors. The result of this "merriment" suggests its darker purpose and the anxiety about gender relations its displays: the offending couple left the village in shame. The skimmington served its purpose by its ritual scapegoating of the tanner and more particularly his wife. Rosyer vented his anger by bringing charges against his neighbors in which he complained not only of scandal and disgrace to himself, "his wief and kyndred," but also of seditious "tumult and discention in the said towne."[2]

The entire incident figures the social anxiety about gender and power that characterizes Elizabethan culture. * * * The community's ritual action against the couple who transgress prevailing codes of gender behavior seeks to reestablish those conventional modes of behavior—it seeks to sanction a patriarchal order. But at the same time, this "old country ceremony" subverts, by its representation, its masquerade of the very events it criticizes, by forcing the offending couple to recognize their transgression through its dramatic enactment. The skimmington seeks "in merriment" to

---

1. This would seem to be Rosyer's neighbor's duty. The *Oxford English Dictionary* cites Lupton's *Sivgila*, 50 (1580), as an early use of cowlstaff: "If a woman beat hir husbande, the man that dwell next unto hir sha ride a cowlstaff." Thomas Platter claimed a neighbor rode cowlstaff dressed as a woman as a punishment for failing to assist the husband being beaten. Certainly Quarry seems more perpetrator than victim here. See *Thomas Platter's Travels in England, 1599*, trans. Clare Williams (London: Cape, 1937), 182.
2. PRO STAC 8, 249/19. I am grateful to Susan Amussen for sharing her transcription of this case and to David Underdown for the original reference. The result of Rosyer's complaint is unknown; only the testimony, not the judgement, is preserved.

reassert traditional gender behaviors that are naturalized in Elizabethan culture as divinely ordained; but it also deconstructs that
"naturalization" by its foregrounding of what is a humanly constructed cultural product: the displacement of gender roles in a
dramatic representation.[3]

Family Politics

The events of Plough Monday 1604 have an uncanny relation to
Shakespeare's *Taming of the Shrew*, which might well be read as a
theatrical realization of such a community fantasy, the shaming and
subjection of a shrewish wife. The so-called induction opens with
the hostess railing at the drunken tinker Sly, and their interchange
figures him as the inebriated tanner from Wetherden.[4] Sly is presented with two "dreams," the dream he is a lord—a fantasy enact-
ing traditional Elizabethan hierarchical and gender relations—and
the "dream" of Petruchio taming Kate. The first fantasy is a series
of artificially constructed power relationships figured first in terms
of class, then in terms of gender. The lord exhorts his servingmen
to offer Sly "low submissive reverence" and traditional lordly prerogatives and pursuits: music, painting, handwashing, rich apparel,
hunting, and finally a theatrical entertainment. In the longer, more
detailed speech that follows in the induction at *1*.100ff., he exhorts
his page to "bear himself with honourable action/Such as he hath
observ'd in noble ladies/Unto their lords." Significantly, Sly is only
convinced of his lordly identity when he is told of his "wife." His realization of this newly discovered self involves calling for the lady,
demanding from her submission to his authority, and finally seeking
to exert his new power through his husbandly sexual prerogative:
"Madam, undress you and come now to bed" [Ind. 2.113]. By en-
acting Sly's identity as a lord through his wife's social and sexual (if
deferred) submission, the induction suggests ironically how in this
androcentric culture men depended on women to authorize their
sexual and social masculine identities.[5] The lord's fantasy takes the
drunken Sly who brawls with the hostess and by means of a "play"
brings him into line with traditional conceptions of gender
relations. But in the induction, these relationships of power and
gender, which in Elizabethan treatises, sermons, homilies, and be-

---

3. See Natalie Zemon Davis, "Women on Top," in *Society and Culture in Early Modern France* (Stanford: Stanford University Press, 1975); E. P. Thompson, " 'Rough Music': le Charivari Anglais," *Annales ESC* 27 (1972): 285–312.
4. In *The Taming of a Shrew* the frame tale closes the action; Sly must return home after his "bravest dreame" to a wife who "will course you for dreaming here tonight," but he claims: "Ile to my/Wife presently and tame her too." See Geoffrey Bullough, Narrative and Dramatic Sources of Shakespeare (London: Routledge and Kegan Paul, 1957), I,: 108.
5. See Montrose's discussion of the Amazonian myth in "Shaping Fantasies," 66–67.

havioral handbooks were figured as natural and divinely ordained, are subverted by the metatheatrical foregrounding of such roles and relations as culturally constructed.

The analogy between the events at Wetherden and Shakespeare's play suggests a tempting homology between history and cultural artifacts. It figures patriarchy as a master narrative, the key to understanding certain historical events and dramatic plots. But as Fredric Jameson points out, "history is not a narrative, master or otherwise, but . . . an absent cause . . . inaccessible to us except in textual form, and . . . our approach to it and to the Real itself necessarily passes through its prior textualization, its narrativization in the political unconscious."[6] If we return to Nicholas Rosyer's complaint against his neighbors and consider its textualization—how it is made accessible to us through narrative—we can make several observations. We notice immediately that Rosyer's wife, the subject of the complaint, lacks the status of a speaking subject. She is unnamed and referred to only as the "wief." Rosyer's testimony, in fact, begins with a defense not of his wife but of his patrimony, an account of his background and history in the village in terms of male lineage. His wife has no voice; typically, she never speaks in the complaint at all. Her husband brings charges against his neighbors presumably to clear his name and to affirm his identity as patriarch, which the incident itself, from his wife's "abuse" to the transvestite skimmington, endangers.

From the account of this case, we also get a powerful sense of life in early modern England, the close proximity of neighbors and the way intimate sexual relations present a scene before an audience. Quarry and the neighbors recount Rosyer's attempted assertion of his sexual "prerogatives" over his wife and her vehement refusal: "she struck him several times, clawed his face and arms, spit at him and beat him out of bed." There is evidently no place in the late Elizabethan sex/gender system for Rosyer's wife to complain of her husband's mistreatment, drunkenness, and abuse, or even to give voice to her point of view, her side of the story. The binary opposition between male and female in the Wetherden case and its figuration of patriarchy in early modern England generates the possible contradictions logically available to both terms: Rosyer speaks, his wife is silent; Rosyer is recognized as a subject before the law, his wife is solely its object; Rosyer's family must be defended against the insults of his neighbors, his wife has no family but has become part of his. In turning to *The Taming of the Shrew*, our task is to articulate the particular sexual/political fantasy, or, in

6. Fredric Jameson, *The Political Unconscious* (Ithaca: Cornell University Press, 1981), 35.

Jameson's Althusserian formulation, the "libidinal apparatus" the play projects as an imaginary resolution of contradictions that are never resolved in the Wetherden case, but which the formal structures of dramatic plot and character in Shakespeare's play present as seemingly reconciled.

A Shrew's History

Many readers of Shakespeare's *Shrew* have noted that both in the induction and the play, language is an index of identity. Sly is convinced of his lordly identity by language, by the lord's obsequious words and recital of his false history. Significantly, when he believes himself a lord, his language changes and he begins to speak the blank verse of his retainers. But in the opening scene of the play proper, Shakespeare emphasizes not just the relationship between language and identity but that between control over language and fatherly authority. Kate's linguistic protest is against the role in patriarchal culture to which women are assigned, that of wife and object of exchange in the circulation of male desire. Her very first words make this point aggressively: she asks of her father, "I pray you, sir, is it your will/To make a stale of me amongst these mates?"[7] Punning on the meaning of stale as laughing stock and prostitute, on "stalemate," and on mate as husband, Kate refuses her erotic destiny by exercising a linguistic willfulness. Her shrewishness testifies to her exclusion from social and political power. Bianca, by contrast, is throughout the play associated with silence [1.1.70–1].

Kate's prayer to her father is motivated by Gremio's threat "to cart her rather. She's too rough for me" [1.1.55]. Although this line is usually glossed as "drive around in an open cart (a punishment for prostitutes)," the case of Nicholas Rosyer and his unnamed wife provides a more complex commentary. During the period from 1560 until the English Civil War, in which many historians have recognized a "crisis of order" in early modern England, the fear that women were rebelling against their traditional subservient role in patriarchal culture was widespread.[8] Popular works such as *The Two Angry Women of Abington* (1598), Middleton's *The Roaring Girl* (1611), *Hic Mulier*, or *The Man-Woman* (1620), and Joseph Swetnam's *Arraignment of lewd idle froward and inconstant women*

---

7. [1.1.157–58]; all references are to the Arden edition ed. Brian Morris (London: Methuen, 1981). Line numbers in brackets reference this Norton Critical Edition.
8. See, among others, Lawrence Stone, *The Crisis of the Aristocracy 1558–1680* (Oxford: Oxford University Press, 1965) and Keith Wrightson, *English Society 1580–1680* (New Brunswick: Rutgers University Press, 1982), esp. chaps. 5 and 6.

(which went through ten editions between 1616 and 1634), all testify to a preoccupation with rebellious women.[9] What literary historians have recognized in late Elizabethan and Jacobean writers as a preoccupation with female rebellion and independence, social historians have also noted in historical records. As David Underdown has observed, the period was fraught with anxiety about rebellious women and particularly their rebellion through language.[1] Although men were occasionally charged with scolding, it was predominately a female offense usually associated with class as well as gender issues and revolt: "women who were poor, social outcasts, widows, or otherwise, lacking in the protection of a family . . . were the most common offenders."[2] Underdown points out that in a few examples after the Restoration, social disapproval shifts to "mismatched couples, sexual offenders, and eventually . . . husbands who beat their wives."[3] Punishment for such offenses and related ones involving "domineering" wives who "beat" or "abused" their husbands often involved public shaming or charivari of the sort employed at Wetherden and Callne. The accused woman or her surrogate was put in a scold's collar or ridden in a cart accompanied by a rough musical procession of villagers banging pots and pans.

Louis Montrose attributes the incidence of troubled gender relations to female rule since "all forms of public and domestic authority in Elizabethan England were vested in men: in fathers, husbands, masters, teachers, magistrates, lords. It was inevitable that the rule of a woman would generate peculiar tensions within such a patriarchal society."[4] Historians point to the social and economic factors that contributed to these troubled gender relations. Underdown observes a breakdown of community in fast-growing urban centers and scattered pasture/dairy parishes where effective means of social control such as compact nucleated village centers, resident squires, and strong manorial institutions were weak or nonexistent. He observes the higher incidence of troubled gender relations in such communities as opposed to the arable parishes, which "tended to retain strong habits of neighborhood and cooperation." Both Montrose's reading of the Elizabethan sex/gender system in terms of the "pervasive cultural presence" of the queen and Underdown's analysis of economic and social factors help to explain this proliferation of accusations of witchcraft, shrewishness, and husband domination. Both demonstrate the clear connection between women's indepen-

9. David Underdown, "The Taming of the Scold: the enforcement of patriarchal authority in Early Modern England," *Order and Disorder in Early Modern England*, ed. Anthony Fletcher and John Stevenson (Cambridge: Cambridge University Press, 1985), 116–36.
1. See Newman Introduction, xviii.
2. Underdown, 120.
3. Underdown, 121, citing E. P. Thompson.
4. Montrose, 64–65.

dent appropriation of speech and a conceived threat to patriarchal authority contained through public shaming or spectacle—the ducking stool, usually called the cucking stool, or carting.[5]

From the outset of Shakespeare's play, Katherine's threat to male authority is posed through language; it is perceived as such by others and is linked to a claim larger than shrewishness—witchcraft—through the constant allusions to Katherine's kinship with the devil.[6] Control of women and particularly of Kate's revolt is from the outset attempted by inscribing women in a scopic economy.[7] Woman is represented as spectacle (Kate) or object to be desired and admired, a vision of beauty (Bianca). She is the site of visual pleasure, whether on the public stage, the village green, or the fantasy "cart" with which Hortensio threatens Kate. The threat of being made a spectacle, here by carting or later in the wedding scene by Petruchio's "mad-brain rudesby," is an important aspect of shrew-taming.[8] Given the evidence of social history and of the play itself, language is power, both in Elizabethan and Jacobean England and in the fictional space of the *Shrew*.

The *Shrew* both demonstrated and helped produce the patriarchal social formation that characterized Elizabethan England, but representation gives us a perspective on that system that subverts its status as natural. The theatrically constructed frame in which Sly exercises patriarchal power and the dream in which Kate is tamed undermine the seemingly eternal nature of those structures by calling attention to the constructed character of the representation rather than veiling it through mimesis. The foregrounded female protagonist of the action and her powerful annexation of traditionally male discursive domains distances us from that system by exposing and displaying its contradictions. Representation undermines the ideology about women that the play presents and produces, both in the induction and in the Kate/Petruchio plot: Sly disappears as lord, but Kate keeps talking.

5. Montrose, 64–65. See also Davis and Thompson, cited above.
6. E.g., I, i, 65, 105, 121, 123; II, i, 26, 151; for the social context of English witchcraft, see Alan Macfarlane, *Witchcraft in Tudor and Stuart England* (New York: Harper & Row, 1970) and Keith Thomas, *Religion and the Decline of Magic* (London: Weidenfeld & Nicolson, 1971).
7. For carting as a means of social control, see Robert Ashton, "Popular Entertainment and Social Control in Later Elizabethan and Jacobean England," *The London Journal* 9 (1983): 13–15. On the importance of the gaze in managing human behavior, see Michel Foucault, *Surveiller et Punir* (Paris: Gallimard, 1975) and Irigaray, *Speculum de l'autre femme* (Paris: Editions de Minuit, 1974); see also Laura Mulvey's discussion of scopophilia in "Visual Pleasure and Narrative Cinema," *Screen* 16 (1975): 6–18.
8. Kate's speech at III, ii, makes clear this function of his lateness and his "mad-brain rudesby." She recognizes that shame falls not on her family, but on her alone: "No shame but mine . . . /Now must the world point at poor Katherine/And say, 'Lo, there is mad Petruchio's wife,/If it would please him come and marry her' " (8, 18–20). Although Katherine to herself, she recognizes that for others she is already "Petruchio's wife."

The Price of Silence

At II, i, in the spat between Bianca and Kate, the relationship between silence and women's place in the marriage market is made
clear. Kate questions Bianca about her suitors, inquiring as to her
preferences. Some critics have read her questions and her abuse of
Bianca (in less than thirty lines, Kate binds her sister's hands behind her back, strikes her, and chases after her calling for revenge)
as revealing her secret desire for marriage and for the praise and
recognition afforded her sister.[9] Kate's behavior may invite such an
interpretation, but her questions and badgering also expose the relationship between Bianca's sweet sobriety and her success with
men. Kate's abuse may begin as a jest, but her feelings are aroused
to a different and more serious pitch when her father enters, taking
as usual Bianca's part against her sister. Baptista emphasizes both
Bianca's silence, "When did she cross thee with a bitter word?" and
Katherine's link with the devil, "thou hilding of a devilish spirit"
[2.1.28.26]. We should bear in mind here Underdown's observation
that shrewishness is a class as well as gender issue, that women
"lacking in the protection of a family . . . were the most common
offenders."[1] Kate is motherless, and virtually fatherless as well, for
Baptista consistently rejects her and favors her obedient sister.
Kate's threat that follows, "Her silence flouts me, and I'll be reveng'd" [2.1.29] reveals that silence has insured Bianca's place in
the male economy of desire and exchange to which Kate pointedly
refers in her last lines:

> What, will you not suffer me? Nay, now I see
> She is your treasure, she must have a husband,
> I must dance barefoot on her wedding day,
> And, for your love to her lead apes in hell.
> [2.1.31–4]

Throughout the play, Bianca is a treasure, a jewel, an object of desire and possession. Although much has been made of the animal
analogies between Kate and beasts, the metaphorical death of the
courtly imagery associated with Bianca has been ignored as too
conventional, if not natural, to warrant comment.[2] At issue here is
not so much Kate's lack of a husband, or indeed her desire for a
marriage partner, but rather her distaste at those folk customs that

---

9. See Marianne Novy's discussion of the importance of the father and paternity, "Patriarchy and Play in *The Taming of the Shrew*," *English Literary Renaissance* 9 (1979):
   273–74.
1. Underdown, 120.
2. See Novy's detailed discussion of Kate's puns, animal imagery, and sexual innuendoes in
   this scene, 264, and Martha Andreson-Thom's "Shrew-taming and Other Rituals of Aggression: Baiting and Bonding on the Stage and in the Wild," *Women's Studies* 9 (1982):
   121–43.

make her otherness, her place outside the sex/gender system, a public fact, a spectacle for all to see and mock.

In the battle of words between Kate and Petruchio at [2.1.180ff], it is Kate who gets the best of her suitor. She takes the lead through puns that allow her to criticize Petruchio and patriarchal practices of wooing and marriage. Her sexual puns make explicit to the audience not so much her secret preoccupation with sex and marriage but what is implicit in Petruchio's wooing: the marriage is a sexual exchange in which women are exploited for their use-value as producers. Significantly, Petruchio's language is linguistically similar to Kate's in its puns and wordplay. He also presents her, as many commentators have noted, with an imagined vision that makes her conform to the very order against which she rebels: he makes her a Bianca with words, shaping an identity for her that confirms the social expectations of the sex/gender system that informs the play.

In the altercation over staying for the wedding feast after their marriage, Kate again claims the importance of language and her use of it to women's place and independence in the world. But here it is Petruchio who controls language, who has the final word, for he creates through words a situation to justify his actions: he claims to be rescuing Kate from thieves. More precisely, he claims she asks for the rescue. Kate's annexation of speech does not work unless her audience, and particularly her husband, accepts what she says as independent rebellion. By deliberately misunderstanding and reinterpreting her words to suit his own ends, Petruchio effectively refuses her the freedom of speech identified in the play with her independence. Such is his strategy throughout this central portion of the action, in their arrival at his house, and in the interchange with the tailor. Kate is figuratively killed with kindness, by her husband's rule over her not so much in material terms—the withholding of food, clothing and sleep—but in the withholding of linguistic understanding. As the receiver of her messages, he simply refuses their meaning; since he also has material power to enforce his interpretations, it is his power over language that wins.

In the exchange between Petruchio and Kate with the tailor, Kate makes her strongest bid yet for linguistic freedom:

> Why, sir, I trust I may have leave to speak,
> And speak I will. I am no child, no babe.
> Your betters have endur'd me say my mind,
> And if you cannot, best you stop your ears.
> My tongue will tell the anger of my heart,
> Or else my heart concealing it will break,
> And rather than it shall, I will be free
> Even to the uttermost, as I please, in words.
> [4.3.73–80]

When we next encounter Kate, however, on the journey to Padua, she finally admits to Petruchio: "What you will have it nam'd, even that it is,/And so it shall be so for Katherine" [4.5.22–3]. On this journey Kate calls the sun the moon, an old man a budding virgin, and makes the world conform to the topsy-turvy of Petruchio's patriarchal whimsy. But we should look carefully at this scene before acquiescing in too easy a view of Kate's submission. Certainly she gives in to Petruchio's demands literally; but her playfulness and irony here are indisputable. As she says at [4.5.46–50].

> Pardon, old father, my mistaking eyes,
> That have been so bedazzled with the sun
> That everything I look on seemeth green.
> Now I perceive thou art a reverend father.
> Pardon, I pray thee, for my mad mistaking.

Given Kate's talent for puns, we must understand her line, "bedazzled with the sun," as a pun on son and as play with Petruchio's line earlier in the scene "Now by my mother's son, and that's myself,/It shall be moon, or star, or what I list" [4.5.6–7]. "Petruchio's bedazzlement" is exactly that, and Kate here makes clear the playfulness of their linguistic games.

In his paper "Hysterical Phantasies and Their Relation to Bi-Sexuality" (1908), Freud observes that neurotic symptoms, particularly the hysterical symptom, have their origins in the daydreams of adolescence.[3] "In girls and women," Freud claims, "they are invariably of an erotic nature, in men they may be either erotic or ambitious."[4] A feminist characterological rereading of Freud might suggest that Kate's ambitious fantasies, which her culture allows her to express only in erotic directions, motivate her shrewishness.[5] Such behavior, which in a man would not be problematic, her family and peers interpret as "hysterical," diabolic, or both. Her "masculine" behavior saves her, at least for a time, from her feminine erotic destiny.

Freud goes on to claim that hysterical symptoms are always bisexual, "the expression of both a masculine and a feminine unconscious sexual phantasy."[6] The example he gives is a patient who "pressed her dress to her body with one hand (as the woman) while trying to tear it off with the other (as the man)."[7] To continue our "analysis" in the scene we are considering, we might claim that

---

3. Sigmund Freud, *Collected Papers*, tr. Joan Rivière (London: International Psychoanalytic Press, 1948), II, 51–59.
4. Freud, II, 51.
5. For a discussion of female fantasy, see Nancy K. Miller, "Emphasis Added? Plots and Plausibilities in Women's Fiction," *PMLA* 97 (1981): 36–48.
6. Freud, II, 57.
7. Freud, II, 58.

Kate's female masquerade obscures her continuing ambitious fantasies, now only manifest in the puns and ironic wordplay that suggest the distance between her character and the role she plays.[8] Even though she gives up her shrewishness and acquiesces to Petruchio's whims, she persists in her characteristic "masculine" linguistic exuberance while masquerading as an obedient wife.[9]

Instead of using Freud to analyze Kate's character, a critical move of debatable interpretive power, we might consider the Freudian text instead as a reading of ideological or cultural patterns. The process Freud describes is suggestive for analyzing the workings not of character but of Shakespeare's text itself. No speech in the play has been more variously interpreted than Kate's final speech of women's submission. In a useful essay on the *Shrew*, John Bean has conveniently assigned to the two prevailing views the terms "revisionist" for those who would take Kate's speech as ironic and her subservience as pretense—a way of living peaceably in patriarchal culture but with an unregenerate spirit— and "anti-revisionist" for those who argue that farce is the play's governing genre and that Kate's response to Petruchio's taming is that of an animal responding to "the devices of a skilled trainer."[1] Bean himself argues convincingly for a compromise position that admits the "background of depersonalizing farce unassimilated from the play's fabliau sources" but suggests that Kate's taming needs to be seen in terms of romantic comedy, as a spontaneous change of heart such as those of the later romantic comedies "where characters lose themselves in chaos and emerge, as if from a dream, liberated into the bonds of love."[2] Bean rightly points out the liberal aspects of the final speech in which marriage is seen as a partnership as well as a hierarchy, citing the humanist writers on marriage and juxtaposing Kate's speech with corresponding, and remarkably more misogynist, lines in *The Taming of a Shrew* and other taming tales.[3]

Keeping in mind Bean's arguments for the content of the speech and its place at the intersection of farce and romantic love plot, I would like to turn to its significance as representation. What we

---

8. See Joan Rivière's essay on female masquerade in *Psychoanalysis and Female Sexuality*, ed. H. Ruitenbeek (New Haven: Yale University Press, 1966); also of interest is Sir Thomas Elyot's *Defense of Good Women* in which Zenobia is allowed autonomy in relation to her husband but exhorted to dissemble her disobedience; Constance Jordan, "Feminism and the Humanists: The Case of Thomas Elyot's *Defence of Good Women*," *Renaissance Quarterly* 36 (1983): 195.
9. Freud describes a similar strategy of evasion in II, 58.
1. John Bean, "Comic Structure and the Humanizing of Kate in *The Taming of the Shrew*," In *The Woman's Part*, ed. Carolyn Ruth Swift Lenz, Gayle Greene, and Carol Thomas Neely (Urbana: University of Illinois Press, 1980).
2. Bean, 66.
3. Ibid., 67–70.

find is Katherine as a strong, energetic female protagonist represented before us addressing not the onstage male audience, only
too aware of its articulation of patriarchal power, but Bianca and
the Widow, associated with silence throughout the play and finally
arriving by means, as Petruchio calls it, of Kate's "womanly persuasion" [5.2.124].

Unlike any other of Shakespeare's comedies, we have here represented not simply marriage, with the final curtain a veiled mystification of the sexual and social results of that ritual, but a view,
however brief and condensed, of that marriage over time.[4] And what
we see is not a quiet and submissive wife but the same energetic and
linguistically active Kate with which the play began. We know, then,
in a way we never know about the other comedies—except perhaps
The Merchant of Venice, and there our knowledge is complicated by
Portia's male disguise—that Kate has continued to speak. She has
not, of course, continued to speak her earlier language of revolt and
anger. Instead she has adopted another strategy, a strategy the
French psychoanalyst Luce Irigaray calls mimeticism.[5] Irigaray argues that women are cut off from language by the patriarchal order
in which they live, by their entry into the Symbolic, which the Father represents in a Freudian-Lacanian model.[6] Women's only possible relation to the dominant discourse is mimetic:

> To play with mimesis is . . . for a woman to try to recover the
> place of her exploitation by language, without allowing herself
> to be simply reduced to it. It is to resubmit herself . . . to
> ideas—notably about her—elaborated in and through a mascu-
> line logic, but to "bring out" by an effect of playful repetition
> what was to remain hidden: the recovery of a possible opera-
> tion of the feminine in language. It is also to unveil the fact
> that if women mime so well they are not simply reabsorbed in
> this function. They also remain elsewhere.[7]

Whereas Irigaray goes on to locate this "elsewhere" in sexual pleasure (*jouissance*), Nancy Miller has elaborated on this notion of
"mimeticism," describing it as a "form of emphasis: an italicized version of what passes for the neutral. . . . Spoken or written, italics are
a modality of intensity and stress; a way of marking what has already

---

4. See Nancy K. Miller's discussion of the mystification of defloration and marriage in
   "Writing (from) the Feminine: George Sand and the Novel of Female Pastoral," in *The
   Representation of Women: English Institute Essays* (Baltimore: Johns Hopkins University
   Press, 1983), 125–51.
5. Luce Irigaray, *Ce sexe qui n' en est pas un* (Paris: Editions de Minuit, 1977), 134ff. Also
   available in English translation, *This Sex Which Is Not One,* trans. Catherine Porter with
   Carolyn Burke (Ithaca: Cornell University Press, 1985).
6. Irigaray, *Speculum de l'autre femme,* particularly 282–98.
7. Irigaray, *Ce sexe,* 74, quoted and translated by Nancy Miller, "Emphasis Added?" 38.

been said, of making a common text one's own."[8] Interestingly it is Bianca, revealed once married as herself a "shrew," who perhaps most memorably appropriates dominant discourse and italicizes it in the conventional wooing scene at 3.1. There Lucentio construes lines from Ovid's *Heroides* to reveal his identity and love; Bianca playfully repeats them to discover her own anxieties and feelings.

Joel Fineman has observed the difficulty in distinguishing between man's and woman's speech in the *Shrew* by demonstrating how the rhetorical strategies Kate deploys are like Petruchio's.[9] But Kate's self-consciousness about the power of language, her punning and irony, and her techniques of linguistic masquerade, are strategies of italics—mimetics strategies, in Irigaray's sense of mimeticism. Instead of figuring an essentialized woman's speech, they deform language by subverting it, that is, by turning it inside out so that metaphors, puns, and other forms of wordplay manifest their veiled equivalences: the meaning of woman as treasure, of wooing as a civilized and acceptable disguise for sexual exploitation, of the objectification and exchange of women. Kate's speech contradicts the very sentiments she affirms; rather than resolve the play's action, her monologue simply displays the fundamental contradiction presented by a female dramatic protagonist, between woman as a sexually desirable silent object and women of words, women with power over language who disrupt, or at least italicize, women's place and part in Elizabethan culture.

To dramatize action involving linguistically powerful women characters militates against Tudor and Stuart ideologies of women's silence. To maintain their status as desirable, Shakespeare's heroines frequently must don male attire in order to speak: Rosalind, Portia, even the passive Viola. The conflict between the explicitly repressive content of Kate's speech and the implicit message of independence communicated by representing a powerful female protagonist speaking the play's longest speech at a moment of emphatic suspense is not unlike Freud's female patient who "pressed her dress to her body with one hand (as the woman) while trying to tear it off with the other (as the man)." We might even say that this conflict shares the bisexuality Freud claims for the hysterical symptom, that the text itself is sexually ambivalent, a view in keeping with the opposed readings of the play in which it is either conservative farce or subversive irony. Such a representation of gender, what might be termed the "female dramatizable,"[1] is always

---

8. Miller, "Emphasis Added?" 38.
9. Joel Fineman, "The Turn of the *Shrew*," in *Shakespeare and the Question of Theory*, ed. Patricia Parker and Geoffrey Hartman (London: Methuen, 1985), 141–44.
1. D. A. Miller in his discussion of Jane Austen describes the "narratable" in *Narrative and Its Discontents* (Princeton: Princeton University Press, 1981).

at once patriarchally suspect and sexually ambivalent, clinging to Elizabethan patriarchal ideology and at the same time tearing it away by foregrounding or italicizing its constructed character.

Missing Frames and Female Spectacles

Kate's final speech exemplifies what Jameson describes as "imaginary or formal 'solutions' to unresolvable social contradictions," but the appearance of resolution is an "ideological mirage."[2] On the level of plot, as many readers have noted, if one shrew is tamed, two more reveal themselves. Bianca and the widow refuse to do their husbands' bidding, thereby undoing the sense of closure Kate's "acquiescence" produces. By articulating the contradiction manifested in the scene's formal organization and its social "content"—between the "headstrong women," now Bianca and the widow who refuse their duty, and Kate and her praise of women's submission—the seeming resolution of the play's ending is exploded and its heterogeneity rather than its unity is foregrounded. But can a staged transgression of the law of women's silence be subversive? It is, after all, a theoretical commonplace to argue that transgression presupposes norms or taboos. Anthropologists have claimed that such ritual transgression insures order and stability; and literary critics, influenced by anthropology and a fashionable cultural pessimism that skirts the reactionary, argue that such subversion is always already contained.[3] The "female dramatizable," then, would be no more than a means of managing troubled gender relations, the fabled safety valve. By transgressing the law of women's silence, far from subverting it, the *Shrew* reconfirms the law, if we remember that Kate, Bianca, and the widow remain the object of the audience's gaze, specular images, represented female bodies on display, as on the cucking stool or in the cart. Representation contains female rebellion. And because the play has no final framing scene, no return to Sly, it could be argued that its artifice is relaxed, that the final scene is experienced naturalistically. The missing frame allows the audience to forget that Petruchio's taming of Kate is presented as a fiction.

Yet even with its missing frame and management of woman through spectacle, the *Shrew* deconstructs its own mimetic effect if we remember the bisexual aspect of the representation of women

2. Jameson, 79, 56.
3. For the anthropological argument, see Barbara Babcock, ed., *The Reversible World: Symbolic Inversion in Art and Society* (Ithaca: Cornell University Press, 1978), 13–36, and more recently, Peter Stallybrass and Allon White, *The Politics and Poetics of Transgression* (London: Methuen, 1986). For a brief survey of the educational theorists, see Margaret Ferguson, "Afterword," in *Shakespeare Reproduced*, ed. Jean E. Howard and Marion F. O'Connor (New York: Methuen, 1987), 273–83.

on the Elizabethan and Jacobean stage. In the early modern period, when women's behavior was closely circumscribed, containing operations such as generic closure—the tamings in shrew tales, the weddings that end other of Shakespeare's comedies, the convention of the boy actor—might be understood as enabling conditions for the foregrounding of transgression. Such operations, however, can never "retrospectively guarantee ideological erasure" of contestatory voices.[4] Kate would have been played by a boy whose transvestism, like Thomas Quarry's in the Wetherden skimmington, emblematically embodied the sexual contradictions manifest both in the play and Elizabethan culture. The very indeterminateness of the actor's sexuality, of the woman/man's body, the supplementarity of its titillating homoerotic play (Sly's desire for the page boy disguised as a woman, Petruchio's "Come Kate, we'll to bed"), foregrounds its artifice and therefore subverts the play's patriarchal master narrative by exposing it as neither natural nor divinely ordained, but culturally constructed.

E. M. W. TILLYARD

The Fairy-Tale Element in *The Taming of the Shrew*[†]

That the induction and the main plot of *The Taming of the Shrew* go back to folk themes has long been known. Christopher Sly, picked up dead drunk, clothed in fine clothing, and made to wake up in a lordly setting corresponding to his clothes, has an ancestry going back to the *Arabian Nights*. Petruchio dealing with Katherina is only one of a long succession of wife-tamers. I shall have nothing to do with the first motif except later to point to an odd instance of its being combined with the second. But distinguishing between two different versions of the immemorial theme of the taming of the shrew, the second of which has been almost ignored, may help with an understanding of Shakespeare's play.

Petruchio's whirlwind wooing and subsequent cure of his newly wedded wife have usually been connected with the crudities of the fabliau tradition; and the latest study of Shakespeare's sources does not depart from this habit. Geoffrey Bullough writes as follows:

> The Petruchio-Katharina story . . . is a variant of the Shrew theme common in fabliaux from classical times. . . . Humorous

---

4. Jonathan Dollimore, *Radical Tragedy* (Chicago: University of Chicago Press, 1984), 61.
† From *Shakespeare 1564–1964: A Collection of Modern Essays,* Ed. Edward A. Bloom. (Providence, R.I.: Brown University Press, 1964), pp. 110–114. © 1964 by Brown University Press. Reprinted by permission of University Press of New England.

discussions about mastery in marriage had enlivened the road to Canterbury in Chaucer, and the Jest Books of the Tudor age contained many stories of battle between the sexes. . . . French folk-literature was peculiarly rich in stories of this nature. Their interest often depends on the methods adopted by the husband or wife to win supremacy. In a crude specimen, *Sire Hain et Dame Anieuse*, the husband and wife actually fight for a pair of breeches until the husband knocks the wife into a tub of water and she has to beg for mercy. . . . Nearer to Shakespeare's theme are the tales in which the husband takes the initiative.[1]

And Bullough gives an example of the tales where the husband kills his domestic animals to show what happens to them when they are disobedient and what will happen to his bride if she offends in the same way. Among the resemblances, the one closest to Shakespeare is a Danish tale which not only gives this theme but includes the husband's teaching his wife to follow him in misnaming objects, and the wager on who has the most tractable wife. The story was first recounted by Svend Grundtvig and first related to the *Shrew* by Reinhold Köhler.[2] The characters are three sisters (as in the *Shrew*), who are all shrewish, and the worst of whom is tamed into a model wife as her sisters are not. It is a pity that Bullough did not include this tale in his analogues: analogues, for it can hardly rank as a source.

In all these tales it is the taming of the *wife* that is the main thing;[3] how the wife behaved before marriage is hardly touched on. But Shakespeare dwells as emphatically on the unapproachableness of the maiden as on the contrariness of the wife. It was through taking this truth into account that Peter Alexander conjectured that the Petruchio-Katherina story might be "a version of one of the great themes of literature, a comic treatment of the perilous maiden theme, where the lady is death to any suitor who woos her except the hero, in whose hands her apparent vices turn to virtues."[4] Alexander may be right, but I think Simrock takes us farther when he cites (I, 351–52) the legend of *König Drosselbart* or *King Thrushbeard*. But Simrock hardly develops his citation, on the ground that in this story the trials the shrewish wife is made to undergo duplicate those of the patient Griselda. I do not see what difference this makes, provided the resemblances to Shakespeare's

1. *Narrative and Dramatic Sources of Shakespeare* (London and New York, 1957), I, 61–62.
2. In "Zu Shakespeare's *The Taming of the Shrew*," *Jahrbuch der Deutschen Shakespeare-Gesellschaft* (1868), pp. 397–401.
3. An exception is in a story in the Spanish *Conde Lucanor* of Don Juan Manuel, where all the men keep off the shrew, except one who is poor and wishes to better himself. See Karl Simrock, *Die Quellen des Shakespeare in Novellen, Märchen und Sagen* (2nd ed.; Bonn, 1870), I, 343.
4. *Shakespeare's Life and Art* (London, 1939), p. 71.

play are close; and I find them close enough to wish to plead that more should be made of the story of King Thrushbeard as an analogue of *The Taming of the Shrew.*

The best-known version of the story is in the *Kinder- und Hausmärchen* of the brothers Grimm;[5] and here is a summary of it. A king had a daughter who was lovely but so proud that she would not look at any of her many suitors. In a last effort to get her married he organized a muster of all the eligible young men from a great distance round, lined them up according to their rank, and ordered his daughter to make her choice. With every suitor she had a fault to find; she singled out one of the kings for special rudeness, saying that his chin (which had a slight irregularity) was like a thrush's beak, whereupon her victim was nicknamed King Thrushbeard. Finally, she refused them all. Whereupon her father came to the end of his patience and swore that he would marry her to the first beggar who presented himself. A few days after, a fiddler in ragged clothes appeared at the king's palace, was admitted, and pleased the king with his music. For a reward the fiddler received the princess as his bride, and they were married then and there. At once he took her to his house, a hovel with no servants, and set her to do menial work. She did it badly and in the end her husband procured her a place in the kitchen of the palace of the land in which they lived. Here she did the humblest work and used to take home the scraps she picked up in the kitchen. One day a wedding was to be celebrated, and as she was standing at the door a finely dressed young man caught hold of her and dragged her into the hall where there was to be dancing. Here she dropped the pot in which she had hoarded some soup and scraps, and these, to her utter confusion, were scattered on the floor. As she tried to escape, the fine young man caught her, and she saw it was King Thrushbeard, who told her that her trials were ended: that he was the fiddler and that the wedding in course of celebration was theirs. All her trials had been to punish her proud spirit. She duly admitted her faults. Finally, she was clothed richly, her father and his court joined the celebrations, and all ended happily.

There are many versions of the story,[6] and these are spread over a large area, including Ireland. The version collected by the brothers Grimm differs from most of the others in making the king force his daughter to marry. Usually the rejected prince, arriving in disguise, attracts the girl by some charm, for instance an entrancing voice, or by some tempting object, which she must have at all costs.

5. For an English translation, see *Grimm's Household Tales*, by Margaret Hunt (London, 1884), I, 203–7.
6. See J. Bolte and G. Polívka, *Anmerkungen zu den Kinder- und Hausmärchen der Brüder Grimm* (Leipzig, 1913), I, 443–49.

Often, the bride's humiliation is made worse by her husband's compelling her to steal and then seeing to it that she is caught. But all the versions have these differences from the wife-taming fabliau: they treat of the girl before as well as after marriage, and she is always a princess. They do not subject her to personal violence or sheer terror, but they cause her to be humbled, one might say educated, by a way of life the remotest possible from the one she has hitherto experienced and has finally abused. They present a sudden marriage uncelebrated at the time but celebrated with the utmost splendor after the girl has been tamed into repentance.

With respect to Shakespeare's *Taming of the Shrew*, scholars have been right in seeing traces of the fabliau treatment of the wife-taming theme. Katherina strikes Petruchio in the wooing scene, and even if he does not strike back he is coarse-mouthed to a degree. Further, the hawk-taming motive, so prominent in the scenes at Petruchio's country house, is in keeping with the violence of the fabliau treatment. Before any training was possible, a hawk's will had to be broken in a sheer head-on battle. There was no question of giving the bird a job. Nevertheless, if you take the whole play into account, its resemblances with *King Thrushbeard* are more than those with the fabliau. True, Katherina is not a princess, but her shrewishness before marriage figures largely. Her lover appears at the wedding in rags, as the fiddler did when he came to get his bride; and if in so doing he did not disguise his identity at least he disguised his inner nature. Both King Thrushbeard and Petruchio take their brides to their homes (pretended or actual) immediately after the wedding ceremony. The tasks set the princess were educative as well as humiliating; and Petruchio, while proceeding to tame his hawk, pursues simultaneously a more kindly and educative method, trying to make Katherina see for herself the error of her ways. And finally the wedding, uncelebrated at the time, is celebrated in the last scene of the play, after the shrew has been tamed.

What with Chaucer and the Jest Books it is certain that Shakespeare knew the fabliau treatment of the shrewish wife. That he knew a version of the King Thrushbeard story cannot be proved; yet the resemblances between it and his play are so strong that it is likely he did. If, as is accepted, he used the Teutonic version of *Snow White* for parts of *Cymbeline*, there is not the least improbability about his knowing the other story.

I cannot pretend that by taking this new source into account we are better enabled to decide the literary nature of the *Taming of the Shrew*. That decision remains in doubt. A Mark van Doren finds the play quite satisfactory as a hearty farce, a Hardin Craig as a comedy where the farcical elements are remotely vestigial and need not trouble us. For myself I can neither ignore nor reconcile the

two components—the farcical and comic—and am forced to conclude that the play fails insofar as it misses such a reconciliation.
But however little bearing the sources may have on literary criticism, it is an interesting possibility that in framing his play Shakespeare resorted to both fabliau and fairy tale and that in his loyalty
to both he was cheated of the unity at which surely he must have
aimed.

Lastly I must point to a version of the King Thrushbeard story[7]
that includes the theme of a person waking in alien surroundings
and coming to think that the past has been a dream. It comes from
Corsica and was collected by Julie Filippi. The beginning is on familiar lines but with the addition that the princess's pride caused
her to be hated by her people. There is the usual muster of suitors,
but the story differs from the norm in that the successful suitor is a
late-comer reaching the palace after the rest have been dismissed.
The princess likes him but is too proud to accept him without criticism. So she says she might have had him but for a twisted hair in
his beard. Her father suggests that she can pull it out in fun after
the wedding, but the suitor feigns meekness, goes down on his
knees, and begs her to pull out the offending hair then and there.
She pulls out a single hair at random and consents to the match.
They are married at once but without the full religious ceremony.

Meanwhile the father and the husband of the bride have a private talk together and among other things fix the date of the church
wedding, which is to take place in the bridegroom's country. Bride
and bridegroom leave immediately and travel to the bridegroom's
palace. The bride goes to sleep and in her sleep she is conveyed to
a shepherd's hut where mean clothing is set out by her bedside.
When she wakes she finds she is in a room along with sheep, dogs,
and three white-bearded old men. She is terrified and asks where
she is. In answer the youngest of the three, calling her daughter,
expresses wonder that she no longer recognizes her home but
dreams she is a king's daughter and a prince's wife. They all laugh
when she protests, and her apparent father tells her to get up and
go with her grandfather to take the beasts out into the fields, where
he and her uncle will join them. She has to obey and before long
gets used to the country life and really believes that her old life was
a dream. After three months, when the church wedding was due,
she is conveyed in her sleep to the palace and wakes up in rich surroundings and attended by four maids. At first she cannot believe in
the new setting, and when the three old men come in and bow to
her she calls them father, uncle, and grandfather. And so in a way
they are, for that is their true relationship to her husband. Then

7. Published in *La Revue des Traditions Populaires* (1907), pp. 321–23.

her father appears, the wedding is celebrated, and the princess, now cured of her pride, becomes in due course a model queen.

I do not suggest that Shakespeare derived his own combination of the two themes used in his induction and main plot from a version of this Corsican story but think that the duplication is fortuitous. And yet there is just the chance I may be wrong. That Shakespeare knew some version of the King Thrushbeard story is probable; and in one detail at least the Corsican version is closer to Shakespeare than the others. Only in it does the proud girl want to marry the bridegroom for his own sake. Shakespeare does not tell us explicitly that Katherina wants from the first to marry Petruchio; but when it comes to the point, she does not oppose the betrothal, and when the bridegroom is late she gets into a passion of grief. Moreover, in the *Shrew* Kate in a soliloquy confesses she is ready to marry Ferando. There is nothing improbable in Shakespeare's transferring the appearance and reality theme from the princess in the Corsican story to the drunkard in his own induction. So I think there is just an off chance of derivation. But even if there were none, it is diverting to see the master dramatist and a humble teller of tales in wild Corsica hitting on the same conflation.

JAN HAROLD BRUNVAND

The Folktale Origin of *The Taming of the Shrew*†

I

The title "The Taming of the Shrew", apart from Shakespeare's comedy, has been applied to many literary creations, subliterary pieces, and folktales in which a bad wife is improved. By folklorists, however, this designation has been reserved for Tale Type 901 in the Aarne-Thompson *Types of the Folk-Tale*, where it is summarized as follows: "The youngest of three sisters is a shrew. For their disobedience the husband shoots his dog and his horse. Brings his wife to submission. Wager: whose wife is the most obedient."[1]

Similar to Type 901 is Tale Type 1370, *The Lazy Cat*, in which a husband beats his cat for not working and simultaneously punishes his wife, who must hold the cat during the beating.[2] In both tales a

---

† *Shakespeare Quarterly* 17.4 (Autumn 1966): 345–59. © The Johns Hopkins University Press. Reprinted with permission of The Johns Hopkins University Press.
1. Antti Aarne and Stith Thompson, *The Types of the Folk-Tale: A Classification and Bibliography*, FF Communications No. 74 (Helsinki, 1928), p. 136.
2. Closer investigation reveals that there are actually three subtypes of Type 1370. In most texts a cat is beaten, but in another group of versions an animal hide is beaten on the wife's back. In a few versions some other object is punished. Two English texts fall into

man cures his bad wife by administering cruel and irrational punishment to a recalcitrant animal; also, the texts of both types frequently share further traits, such as the wager on the wives'
obedience. Other similar devices to tame a bad wife are sometimes
found in folktales, and all of these stories involving some kind of violent trick by a husband make up an interrelated group of oral nar-
ratives which may be called "The Taming of the Shrew Complex".

Considering the broad distribution of these tales and the evident
relationship Shakespeare's play has to them, it is surprising that no
lengthy study of the complex has been attempted. Although a few
folklorists have commented upon individual texts of Types 901,
1370, and related tales, none has produced a definitive analysis of
them.[3] Shakespearian scholars have concerned themselves very little with folktale analogues of the play, but rather have concentrated
upon the possible literary influences.

I have attempted to fill this gap with a comprehensive study of all
available versions of the shrew-taming stories.[4] I have assembled
more than 400 literary and oral texts belonging to the Taming of
the Shrew Complex in thirty different nations from India to Ireland
in the Old World, and from Canada, the United States, and Mexico
in the New. Three hundred and eight of these versions are of Type
901 itself and come from the following sources:[5] literary texts, 12;
Iceland, 3; Norway, 1; Sweden, 6; Swedish-Finland, 3; Denmark,
20; Germany, 5; The Netherlands, 1; United States, 31; Scotland,
1; Ireland, 130; Finland, 36; Estonia, 16; Lithuania, 6; White Russia, 2; The Ukraine, 1; Russia, 10; Yugoslavia, 7; France, 1;
Canada, 4; Portugal, 1; Spain, 3; Spanish-America, 2; Greece, 3;
Persia, 1; and India, 2.

---

the second class; in "A Merry Jeste of a Shrewde and curste Wyfe lapped in Morrelles
Skin", reprinted in W. C. Hazlitt, *Remains of the Early Popular Poetry of England* (London, 1866), a horse hide is beaten. In the ballad "The Wife Wrapt in Wether's Skin"
(Child 277) a sheep's hide is put on the wife's back and beaten. The "object-beaten subtype" in folktales contains such motifs as a knapsack, basket, or picture of a servant that
is commanded to work and then beaten on the wife's back.

3. Besides the studies of Köhler and Boggs mentioned below, the following lengthy annota-
tions of texts have been published: Waldemar Liungman, *Sveriges Samtliga Folksagor i
Ord ach Bild*, I (Stockholm, 1949), 361–363, 454, II (Stockholm, 1950), 452, and III
(Djursholm, 1952), 288, 494–497; Aurelio Macedonio Espinosa, *Cuentos populares es-
pañoles*, II (Madrid, 1947), 351–355.

4. *"The Taming of the Shrew:* A Comparative Study of Oral and Literary Versions" (diss., Indiana University, 1961). My study followed the Historic-Geographic method set forth in
such works as Antti Aarne, *Leitfaden der vergleichenden Märchenforschung*, FF Communications No. 13 (Helsinki, 1913); Kaarle Krohn, *Die Folkloristische Arbeitsmethode*
(Oslo, 1926); Walter Anderson, "Geographische-historische Methode", in Johannes
Bolte and Lutz Mackensen, edd., *Handwörterbuch des deutschen Märchens*, II (Berlin,
1934–40), 508–522; and Stith Thompson, "The Life History of a Folktale", in *The Folktale* (New York, 1946), pp. 428–448.

5. Most of these texts are unpublished and were secured by direct application to folklore
archives. For a brief discussion of the problems involved and for addresses of archives,
see my note "Sources of Texts for Comparative Studies of Tales", *The Folklore and Folk
Music Archivist*, III (Summer, 1960), 2f.

Type 901, which proved to be the nucleus of the whole complex, seems to have originated in the east, possibly in India. It had entered southeastern Europe by the Middle Ages, after which it underwent certain changes and thereafter spread both orally and by means of print throughout Northern Europe; later it came by several routes to the New World, where it may still be collected from oral tradition. The purpose of this essay is to demonstrate that examination of the background of this folktale tradition coupled with study of a few key texts can prove quite conclusively that Shakespeare's taming plot, which has not been traced successfully in its entirety to any known printed version, must have come ultimately from oral tradition.

II

The main plot, or "taming plot", of Shakespeare's play may be summarized as follows:

> A wealthy man has two daughters, the elder a shrew. The father insists that the shrew be married before her sister. A young man, despite the father's warning and warnings by his friends, decides to marry her. He arrives late for the wedding, riding on an old decrepit nag and dressed in outlandish clothing. He insists upon leaving, with his bride also mounted on horseback, immediately after the ceremonies. On the way home the bride's horse throws her off into a muddy bog, and the bridegroom beats one of his servants for this. At home the husband continues to outdo his wife in shrewishness. Later they travel back to visit the bride's father, and on the trip, as a condition of continuing it, the man forces his wife to agree that the sun is the moon, that the time of day is different from what it really is, and that an old man they meet is a young girl. After dinner three husbands lay a wager on which has the most obedient wife; the husband of the reformed shrew easily wins, for his wife comes when called, throws her cap to the floor, brings in the other wives, lectures them on obedience, and finally kisses her husband.

In broad outlines, as well as in most details, the taming plot of the play matches Type 901 as it is known orally in the Indo-European folktales. The wealthy father with good and bad daughters, the warnings to the suitor about the shrew, the bizarre wedding behavior, the trip home on horseback, the taming, and the later return trip to the father's home where a wager is laid are all traits commonly found in the folktales. As a matter of fact, if one were to read several hundred miscellaneous versions of Type 901 and then for the first time come upon Shakespeare's play, he would probably assume either that the playwright had constructed his plot from details in different oral versions or that he had found an especially full text to rework. Closer comparison with the folktales reveals a device which might have been used to adapt certain unstageable actions from oral tradition for the play. The treatment of the pivot point of the Taming of the Shrew stories illustrates this device.

In all versions of Type 901 the secret of the successful taming is the husband's trick of administering excessively severe punishment to an animal in order to frighten his bad wife. In texts of the tale from India and Persia (and in allusions to the story from Burma and Turkey) a cat has its neck wrung when it meows out of turn in the bridal chambers. Traces of this "cat-killed" tale are found in fourteenth-century Spanish literature and in contemporary oral tales from Greece, Yugoslavia, Russia, Estonia, Lithuania, Swedish-Finland, and Ireland.[6] Sometimes a parrot, falcon, cock, hen, or dog is also killed to frighten the wife, but in nearly all of the northwestern European texts a horse or mule is killed when it disobeys, balks, stumbles, splashes its rider, or does something similar. (A horse becomes stuck in a muddy bog, just as in Shakespeare's play, in three tales from Iceland, nine from Ireland, and one each from Estonia and Lithuania.)

Shakespeare must have been exposed to some "horse-killed" version of the tale, for in his play he alluded to this episode, though, of necessity, he put the action into dialogue. The standard folktale scene is employed in the comedy. The characters in the play, however, could hardly be required to ride horses on stage and to shoot one; instead Grumio, the servant, describes to another servant how on the trip home one horse fell in a mire, the bride's clothes spoiling, and how his master whipped *him* for the mishap while both horses ran off and the bride had to pull her furious husband away.[7] That Shakespeare did not have his hero shoot the horse does not spoil the parallel to Type 901 since the pattern of traits in the rest of the plot identifies it clearly as the same tale. However, as a matter of fact, there is one version of Type 901 from northwestern Russia in which a servant is mistreated by his master when horses refuse to start pulling a carriage. Thus even this detail, although

6. The significance of such "peripheral distribution" of tale traits has been noted by Warren E. Roberts in *The Tale of the Kind and the Unkind Girls* [Type 480], Fabula Supplement, Serie B: Untersuchungen, No. 1 (Berlin, 1958). It is more likely for a tale to have been known over a wide area and to have died out everywhere except on the periphery of this area than for it to have been transmitted in a circle and never to have been known in the middle at all. Therefore, peripheral traits belong with much older forms of tales than do traits commonly known in the middle of the distribution area. Other data normally bear out the validity of this line of reasoning.

7. *Shr.* 4.1. 50–70.

certainly it is an accidental correspondence, may be found in folk-lore.[8]

It seems reasonable to suggest that Shakespeare might have worked this way with oral material to adapt it to the formal requirements of the stage.[9] To support the contention that this is truly what he did, we must show first that the play itself could not have given rise to the folktales, and secondly that Shakespeare could not have derived his plot independently from any known earlier printed source.

*   *   *

IV

Further support for the theory of *The Shrew*'s dependence upon the traditional tale complex is furnished by the comparative study of all versions. Shakespeare's play *** belong[s] to a special sub-type of Type 901 which is found throughout northern Europe and distinguished by the following elaborations on the basic plot: several details about the bridegroom's arrival at the wedding (riding a nag, wearing old clothes, etc.), the absurd statements to which the wife must agree, the incident with the bent green branch, and a wager on the wives' obedience. Shakespeare's play, lacking the bent-branch motif, is actually less elaborated than four Danish, one Swedish, and one German version which contain full references to all four of the distinguishing traits. *A Shrew* is even more deficient in not containing even a reference to the horse and its punishment. A total of thirty-seven variants of the folktale contain enough details of these traits to be classified in the subtype; the numbers by countries are Denmark, 15; Sweden, 4; Germany, 2; Ireland, 13;

8. The Russian tale is in M. K. Azadovskij, *Russkije Skazki v Karelii* (Petrozavodsk, 1947), pp. 131–133. A similar example of the means by which such action may be handled in drama is in a play by the Spaniard Alejandro Casona based on Chapter XXXV of *El Conde Lucanor*. (See "Entremes del Mancebo que Caso con Mujer Brava", *Retablo Jovial* [Buenos Aires, 1949].) The original in this instance calls for a horse, dog, and cat to be slain. In the play the dog is dragged offstage and howls of fear and pain are heard after which the hero returns and wipes his knife clean on a table cloth. The cat is chased offstage, and the hero comes back with a stuffed cat impaled on his sword. Finally a prop horse head appears at the window and the hero shoots it down with a pistol.
   In modern productions dialogue from old plays is often restaged as action. Thus in a television production of *The Taming of the Shrew* on "Hallmark Hall of Fame", March 18, 1956, according to a review, the trip home was staged as a ride out to a ranch in a covered wagon. On the way Petruchio killed a bear. The reviewer comments, "Nichols [the director, William Nichols] never forewent the chance to dramatize episodes that Shakespeare had chosen merely to narrate." See Paul A. Jorgensen, *"The Taming of the Shrew*: Entertainment for Television", *The Quarterly of Film, Radio and Television*, X (1956), 395.
9. Besides numerous folk sayings, superstitions and allusions to traditional ballads found in Shakespeare's plays which help to establish his awareness of folklore, there are several direct parallels to other folktales. The wager on the wife's chastity in *Cymbeline* is Tale Type 882, and the pound of flesh tale in *The Merchant of Venice* is Type 890. *King Lear* corresponds in part to Type 923, while *As You Like It* is essentially a fairy tale about an underdog younger brother who overcomes obstacles and wins a princess and half a kingdom.

and French-Canada, 3.[1] Examples of these traits are scattered in versions of Type 901 from the same area and somewhat beyond it, but the heart of the tradition is Denmark; three-fourths of the collected Danish texts are pure examples of the subtype. There the most detailed texts have been recorded and, as will be seen, the subtype traits are freely found in all versions and their geographic center may most clearly be plotted.

What we find in oral tradition is just what our preliminary reasoning has led us to expect; namely that localized in an area encompassing Great Britain there is a subtype of the widely-known folktale in which all basic elements of Shakespeare's main plot are contained in generally the same form as in the play. The broad features of the taming plot are found widely in tradition, as we have seen, but these details belong more specifically to the northern European subtype. Reviewing the plot of the play against this background establishes the interrelationship.

The traits concerned with the bridegroom's arrival at the wedding are a good example of the affinity of Shakespeare's plot to the folk tradition. The Old High German poem mentioned the nag upon which the man rode, as well as a falcon, a dog, and a gun which he had with him. The *fabliau* text contained a reference to his refusal to stay for a celebration. Both of these old texts state that the couple rode away mounted double on the old horse. Shakespeare's hero has no dog and gun with him; however, he is described as wearing old and outlandish clothing. He also leaves at once after the wedding accompanied by his bride, mounted, in this instance, on separate horses.

In the folktales of northern Europe we find motifs corresponding more closely to the scene. The late arrival is in Danish (10), Swedish (1), and German (1) tales; the nag is mentioned in Danish (4), Icelandic (1), German (6), American (1), Irish (13), and Canadian (1) tales; the poor clothes are in Danish (2), German (1), Irish (1), and Canadian (2) versions; and the insistence upon leaving early is in Swedish (1), Danish (11), and German (1) oral texts. The couple ride double in Swedish (2), Danish (12), German (2), American (7), Irish (23), Scottish (1), and two Spanish folktales.[2] (In

1. Although the majority of these texts are not printed, the following representative versions in print may be referred to as samples: Denmark, see note 17 above; Sweden, see Liungman collection (note 3 above), I, 361–363; Germany, Gustav Fr. Meyer, *Plattdeutsche Volksmärchen und Schwänke* (Neumünster, 1925), pp. 214–217; Ireland, Éamonn ÓTuathail, "Sgéal Na Dtrí Slat", *Béaloideas*, I (1927), 345–348, and a text in *Ireland's Own* (June 3, 1933), p. 710—the only two Irish versions of this subtype in print. All of the French-Canadian texts are in manuscript at the Archives de Folklore de l'Université Laval in Québec.

2. The following bit of byplay in Shakespeare's play may be an allusion to this motif: Grumio says, ". . . my master riding behind my mistress", and Curtis interrupts, "Both of one horse?" (*Shr.* IV. i. 56–57). But Grumio clarifies the point—they are mounted separately.

eastern Europe the couple generally ride in a sleigh or buggy pulled by their horse.) These details are found in roughly one-third of the versions of Type 901, most commonly in tales from Scandinavia, less frequently in Ireland, and only in altered or fragmentary form in southern and eastern Europe.

The absurd statements with which the husband forces his wife to agree further indicate the closeness of Shakespeare's play to the northern tradition. The trait has been found in two Spanish versions of Type 901, suggesting that Don Juan Manuel may have split such a folktale to create the two chapters in *El Conde Lucanor*. But it is only in northern Europe that we find the *necessity* of the wife's agreeing before she is allowed to continue the trip to her father's home, as in Shakespeare's plot. Absurd statements are found in folktales of Norway (1), Sweden (3), Denmark (5), Germany (2) and in a single Estonian tale.[3] In most of the texts the color or species of birds is miscalled by the husband—ravens are called doves, geese are called blackbirds, and so forth. In a few texts other animals are mentioned, and in one Swedish tale a sunny day is referred to as rainy. Nowhere in folktales are the specific errors of Petruchio found—sun called moon, time of day mistaken, and old age called youth. But the reason for this variance is not hard to discern. Like the horse-killing scene, the identification of birds or animals is unstageable action. In place of it the playwright substituted what could easily be handled on stage with dialogue or by means of a gesture towards the open sky above or to an actor.

The motif of the bent green branch is not found in Shakespeare, but, it is worth noting, is present in most Danish texts, in Sweden, Finland, Germany and Estonia and in three Irish texts. The distribution of our subtype is further established by the spread of this motif.

The wager scene in the story has developed somewhat separately in Scandinavia, where often the father-in-law proposes a contest on the obedience of wives and sets up a canister of money or another prize for the winner. Shakespeare's version follows the motif more generally known, common, for instance, in Irish texts, with the wife-testing coming after dinner (93 versions ranging from Ireland to Russia), and a cash wager being laid (123 versions from Ireland through Russia and in Canada). Everywhere the wives are called in successively and further demands are made on them. Often in the tales the wives must either enter in some stage of undress or re-

---

3. "A Contrary Wife, A Folk Tale", in Andres Pranspill, comp. and tr., *Estonian Anthology* (Milford, Conn., 1956), pp. 211–215. This version describes a husband calling wild geese swans and demanding that his wife agree. She will not until he puts her in a grave and has dirt shoveled down upon her. Similar motifs in separate folktales suggest that here an element of Type 901 has joined part of another folktale type.

move some clothing in front of the men, just as in Shakespeare's play Kate must remove her cap and throw it to the floor. (In two Irish texts the wife must burn her cap in the fireplace.)

Quite clearly, Shakespeare's play may now be regarded as a good literary version of the northern-European subtype of Tale Type 901—the kernel narrative of the Taming of the Shrew Complex of traditional Indo-European folktales.

* * *

VI

We have seen that there is an old and widespread oral tradition of Tale Type 901 and that Shakespeare's *The Taming of the Shrew* is a relatively late literary variant belonging to a northern-European subtype. It is clearly impossible either to derive the folktales out of Shakespeare's play or to attribute the play solely to previous literary versions, including *A Shrew* and *El Conde Lucanor*. It is unlikely that Shakespeare independently made up elements of the plot which are widely found in folktales. It follows from the comparative evidence that Shakespeare must have been familiar with the tale as it was developed in oral tradition, and that, whether this familiarity was direct or through printed texts, the ultimate origin of the taming plot was the traditional folktale.

* * *

REWRITINGS AND APPROPRIATIONS

A Pleasant Conceited History, Called
The Taming of a Shrew (1594)

[First published in 1594 and reprinted in 1596 and 1607, the anonymously authored *The Taming of a Shrew* bears structural and thematic
resemblance to Shakespeare's *The Taming of the Shrew*. Both plays begin with Christopher Sly as the spectator of a play in which a "shrewish"
wife is "tamed" and made submissive to her husband. While the obvious
similarities between the two plays have been the impetus for a long history of critical investigation into their relationship, what Shakespeare
scholars have perhaps found most interesting are the differences between the plays, most notably *The Taming of a Shrew's* return to the
Christopher Sly subplot at the end of the play. The excerpts here, modernized from the 1594 quarto reproduced on Early English Books Online, are taken from the beginning and end of *The Taming of a Shrew*.]

Scene 1 *Enter a* TAPSTER, *beating out of his doors* SLY, *drunken*

TAPSTER   You whoreson drunken slave, you had best be gone,
  And empty your drunken paunch somewhere else
  For in this house thou shalt not rest tonight.

Exit TAPSTER.

SLY   Tilly vally! By crisee, Tapster, I'll feeze you anon. Fill's the
  t'other pot and all's paid for, look you I do drink it of my own   5
  instigation. Here I'll lie awhile, why Tapster, I say, fill's a fresh
  cushion here. Heigh ho, here's good warm lying.

Falls asleep.

Enter a LORD *and his men from hunting*

LORD   Now that the gloomy shadow of the night,
  Longing to view Orion's drizzling looks,
  Leaps from th'antarctic world unto the sky   10
  And dims the welkin with her pitchy breath,
  And darksome night o'ershades the crystal heavens,
  Here break we off our hunting for tonight.
  Couple up the hounds and let us hie us home,
  And bid the huntsman see them meated well,   15
  For they have all deserved it well today.
  But soft, what sleepy fellow is this lies here?
  Or is he dead? See one what he doth lack.
SERVINGMAN   My lord, 'tis nothing but a drunken sleep.

---

4. **feeze you**: fix you.

His head is too heavy for his body,   20
And he hath drunk so much that he can go no further.
LORD   Fie, how the slavish villain stinks of drink.
Ho, sirrah, arise! What so sound asleep?
Go, take him up and bear him to my house,
And bear him easily for fear he wake,   25
And in my fairest chamber make a fire,
And set a sumptuous banquet on the board,
And put my richest garments on his back,
Then set him at the table in a chair.
When that is done, against he shall awake,
Let heavenly music play about him still.   30
Go two of you away and bear him hence,
And then I'll tell you what I have devised.
But see in any case you wake him not.

                                              Exit two with SLY.

Now take my cloak and give me one of yours,
All fellows now and see you take me so,   35
For we will wait upon this drunken man,
To see his countenance when he doth awake
And find himself clothed in such attire,
With heavenly music sounding in his ears,
And such a banquet before his eyes,   40
The fellow sure will think he is in heaven.
But we will be about him when he wakes,
And see you call him 'lord' at every word,
And offer thou him his horse to ride abroad,
And thou his hawks and hounds to hunt the deer,   45
And I will ask what suits he means to wear,
And whatsoe'er he saith, see you do not laugh,
But still persuade him that he is a lord.

                Enter MESSENGER.

MESSENGER   And it please your honor your players be come
And do attend your honor's pleasure here.   50
LORD   The fittest time they could have chosen out.
Bid one or two of them come hither straight,
Now will I fit myself accordingly,
For they shall play to him when he awakes.

        Enter two of the players with packs at their backs, and a BOY.

Now sirs, what store of plays have you?   55
SANDER   Marry my lord, you may have a tragical or a
commodity, or what you will.

---

56. a commodity: Sander mistakes commodity for "comedy."

TOM   A comedy thou shouldst say, souns thou shame us all.

LORD   And what's the name of your comedy?

SANDER   Marry my lord 'tis called *The Taming of a Shrew*. 'Tis a
  good lesson for us my lord, for we are married men.   60

LORD   *The Taming of a Shrew*, that's excellent sure.
  Go see that you make you ready straight,
  For you must play before a lord tonight.
  Say you are his men and I your fellow,
  He's something foolish, but whatsoe'er he says,   65
  See that you be not dashed out of countenance.
  [*to* BOY] And sirrah, go you make you ready straight,
  And dress yourself like some lovely lady,
  And when I call see that you come to me,
  For I will say to him thou art his wife.   70
  Dally with him and hug him in thine arms,
  And if he desire to go to bed with thee,
  Then feign some 'scuse and say thou wilt anon.
  Be gone I say, and see thou dost it well.

BOY   Fear not my lord, I'll dandle him well enough,   75
  And make him think I love him mightily.

      Exit BOY.

LORD   Now sirs you go and make you ready too,
  For you must play as soon as he doth wake.

SANDER   Oh brave, sirrah Tom, we must play before a foolish
  lord. Come let's go make us ready, go get a dishclout to make   80
  clean your shoes, and I'll speak for the properties. My lord, we
  must have a shoulder of mutton for a property, and a little
  vinegar to make our devil roar.

LORD   Very well: sirrah, see that they want nothing.

                          Exit all.

Scene 2. *Enter two with a table and a banquet on it, and
two others, with* SLY *asleep in a chair, richly appareled, and
the music playing.*

ONE   So sirrah, now go call my lord and tell him that all things
  are ready as he willed it.

ANOTHER   Set thou some wine upon the board and then I'll go
  fetch my lord presently.

                          Exit.

---

57. souns: a blasphemous oath, "God's wounds."
66. dashed . . . countenance: disconcerted. The lord is ordering his men to keep up the
appearance of the trick they are playing on Sly.
67. sirrah: term of address to a social inferior.
75. dandle: flirt with.

Enter the LORD *and his men.*

LORD   How now, what is all things ready?   5
ONE   Ay, my lord.
LORD   Then sound the music, and I'll wake him
    And see you do as erst I gave in charge.
    My lord, my lord. He sleeps soundly. My lord.
SLY   Tapster, gi's a little small ale. Heigh ho.   10
LORD   Here's wine my lord, the purest of the grape.
SLY   For which lord?
LORD   For your honor, my lord.
SLY   Who I, am I a lord? Jesus what fine apparel have I got.
LORD   More richer far your honor hath to wear,   15
    And if it please you I will fetch them straight.
WILL   And if your honor please to ride abroad,
    I'll fetch you lusty steeds more swift of pace
    Than winged Pegasus in all his pride,
    That ran so swiftly over the Persian plains.   20
TOM   And if your honor please to hunt the deer,
    Your hounds stand ready coupled at the door,
    Who in running will overtake the roe
    And make the long-breathed tiger broken-winded.
SLY   By the Mass, I think I am a lord indeed.   25
    What's thy name?
LORD   Simon, and it please your honor.
SLY   Simon, that's as much to say 'Si mi on,' or Simon put forth
    thy hand and fill the pot. Give
    me thy hand, Sim. Am I a lord indeed?   30
LORD   Ay, my gracious lord, and your lovely lady
    Long time hath mourned for your absence here,
    And now with joy behold where she doth come
    To gratulate your honor's safe return.

Enter the BOY *in woman's attire.*

SLY   Sim, is this she?   35
LORD   Ay, my lord.
SLY   Mass, 'tis a pretty wench. What's her name?
BOY   Oh that my lovely lord would once vouchsafe
    To look on me, and leave these frantic fits,
    Or were I now but half so eloquent   40
    To paint in words what I'll perform in deeds,
    I know your honor then would pity me.
SLY   Hark you mistress, will you eat a piece of bread? Come sit
    down on my knee. Sim, drink to her, Sim, for she and I will go
    to bed anon.   45

10. **gi's:** give us (give me).
25. **By the Mass:** an oath referring to the Eucharist service.

LORD   May it please you, your honor's players be come
   To offer your honor a play.
SLY   A play, Sim, oh brave, be they my players?
LORD   Ay, my lord.
SLY   Is there not a fool in the play?   50
LORD   Yes, my lord.
SLY   When will they play, Sim?
LORD   Even when it please your honor, they be ready.
BOY   My lord, I'll go bid them begin their play.
SLY   Do, but look that you come again.   55
BOY   I warrant you, my lord, I will not leave you thus.

    Exit BOY.

SLY   Come Sim, where be the players? Sim, stand by me and
   we'll flout the players out of their coats.
LORD   I'll call them, my lord. Ho, where are you there?

*

Scene 13. SLY *sleeps.*

LORD   Who's within there?

    Enter BOY *and servingmen.*

Come hither sirs, my lord's asleep again.
Go take him easily up,
And put him in his own apparel again,
And lay him in the place where we did find him,   5
Just underneath the alehouse side below.
But see you wake him not in any case.
BOY   It shall be done, my lord. Come help to bear him hence.

                           Exit.

Scene 14. *Enter* FERANDO, AURELIUS, *and* POLIDOR *and his boy and* VALERIA *and* SANDER.

FERANDO   Come gentlemen, now that supper's done,
   How shall we spend the time till we go to bed?
AURELIUS   Faith, if you will, in trial of our wives,
   Who will come soonest at their husbands' call.
POLIDOR   Nay, then Ferando he must needs sit out,   5
   For he may call I think till he be weary
   Before his wife will come before she list.
FERANDO   'Tis well for you that have such gentle wives,
   Yet in this trial will I not sit out.

------

58. flout . . . coats: mock the players.

It may be that Kate will come as soon as yours.   10
AURELIUS   My wife comes soonest for a hundred pound.
POLIDOR   I take it: I'll lay as much to yours,
  That my wife comes as soon as I do send.
AURELIUS   How now, Ferando, you dare not lay belike.
FERANDO   Why true, I dare not indeed, but how   15
  So little money on so sure a thing?
  A hundred pound? Why, I have laid as much
  Upon my dog, in running at a deer,
  She shall not come so far for such a trifle.
  But will you lay five hundred marks with me,   20
  And whose wife soonest comes when he doth call,
  And shows herself most loving unto him,
  Let him enjoy the wager I have laid.
  Now what say you? Dare you adventure thus?
POLIDOR   I were it a thousand pounds I durst presume   25
  On my wife's love and I will lay with thee.

    Enter ALFONSO.

ALFONSO   How now sons, what in conference so hard?
  May I without offence know whereabouts?
AURELIUS   Faith, father, a weighty cause about our wives
  Five hundred marks already we have laid,   30
  And he whose wife doth show most love to him,
  He must enjoy the wager to himself.
ALFONSO   Why then Ferando he is sure to lose.
  I promise thee, son, thy wife will hardly come,
  And therefore I would not wish thee lay so much.   35
FERANDO   Tush, father, were it ten times more,
  I durst adventure on my lovely Kate,
  But if I lose I'll pay, and so shall you.
AURELIUS   Upon mine honor if I lose I'll pay.
POLIDOR   And so will I upon my faith I vow.   40
FERANDO   Then sit we down and let us send for them.
ALFONSO   I promise thee, Ferando, I am afraid thou wilt lose.
AURELIUS   I'll send for my wife first. Valeria,
  Go bid your mistress come to me.
VALERIA   I will, my lord.   45

    Exit VALERIA.

AURELIUS   Now for my hundred pound.
  Would any lay ten hundred more with me,
  I know I should obtain it by her love.
FERANDO   I pray God you have not laid too much already.
AURELIUS   Trust me, Ferando, I am sure you have,   50
  For you I dare presume have lost it all.

Enter VALERIA *again.*

Now sirrah, what saith your mistress?
VALERIA   She is something busy but she'll come anon.
FERANDO   Why so, did I not tell you this before,
    She is busy and cannot come.   55
AURELIUS   I pray God your wife send you so good an answer.
    She may be busy yet she says she'll come.
FERANDO   Well, well. Polidor, send you for your wife.
POLIDOR   Agreed. Boy, desire your mistress to come hither.
BOY   I will, sir.   60

                                               Exit BOY.

FERANDO   Ay so, so he desires her to come.
ALFONSO   Polidor, I dare presume for thee,
    I think thy wife will not deny to come.
    And I do marvel much, Aurelius,
    That your wife came not when you sent for her.   65

    Enter the BOY *again.*

POLIDOR   Now where's your mistress?
BOY   She bade me tell you that she will not come,
    And you have any business, you must come to her.
FERANDO   Oh, monstrous intolerable presumption,
    Worse than a blazing star or snow at midsummer,   70
    Earthquakes or anything unseasonable.
    She will not come, but he must come to her.
POLIDOR   Well, sir, I pray you let's hear what
    Answer your wife will make.
FERANDO   Sirrah, command your mistress to come to me
    presently.   75

                                          Exit SANDER.

AURELIUS   I think my wife for all she did not come,
    Will prove most kind. For now I have no fear,
    For I am sure Ferando's wife, she will not come.
FERANDO   The more's the pity, then I must lose.

    Enter KATE *and* SANDER.

But I have won, for see where Kate doth come.   80
KATE   Sweet husband, did you send for me?
FERANDO   I did, my love, I sent for thee to come.
    Come hither, Kate, what's that upon thy head?
KATE   Nothing husband but my cap I think.
FERANDO   Pull it off and tread it under thy feet,   85

---

70. blazing star: a comet.

'tis foolish. I will not have thee wear it.

She takes off her cap and treads on it.

POLIDOR   Oh wonderful metamorphosis.

AURELIUS   This is a wonder almost past belief.

FERANDO   This is a token of her true love to me,   90
And yet I'll try her further you shall see.
Come hither, Kate, where are thy sisters?

KATE   They be sitting in the bridal chamber.

FERANDO   Fetch them hither and if they will not come,
Bring them perforce and make them come with thee.   95

KATE   I will.

ALFONSO   I promise thee, Ferando, I would have sworn
Thy wife would ne'er have done so much for thee.

FERANDO   But you shall see she will do more than this,
For see where she brings her sisters forth by force.   100

Enter KATE *thrusting* PHYLEMA *and* EMELIA *before her,*
making them come unto their husbands' call.

KATE   See husband, I have brought them both.

FERANDO   'Tis well done, Kate.

EMELIA   Ay, sure, and like a loving piece! You're worthy
To have great praise for this attempt.

PHYLEMA   Ay, for making a fool of herself and us.   105

AURELIUS   Beshrew thee, Phylema, thou hast
Lost me a hundred pound tonight.
For I did lay that thou wouldst first have come.

POLIDOR   But thou, Emelia, hast lost me a great deal more.

EMELIA   You might have kept it better then.   110
Who bade you lay?

FERANDO   Now lovely Kate, before their husbands here,
I prithee tell unto these headstrong women
What duties wives do owe unto their husbands.

KATE   Then you that live thus by your pampered wills,   115
Now list to me and mark what I shall say:
The eternal power that with his only breath,
Shall cause this end and this beginning frame,
Not in time, nor before time, but with time confused,
For all the course of years, of ages, months,   120
Of seasons temperate, of days and hours,
Are tuned and stopped, by measure of his hand,
The first world was a form without a form,
A heap confused, a mixture all deformed,
A gulf of gulfs, a body bodyless   125

---

95. perforce: by force.

Where all the elements were orderless,
Before the great commander of the world,
The King of kings, the glorious God of heaven
Who in six days did frame his heavenly work
And made all things to stand in perfect course.   130
Then to his image he did make a man,
Old Adam, and from his side asleep
A rib was taken, of which the Lord did make
The woe of man so termed by Adam then,
Woman for that, by her came sin to us,   135
And for her sin was Adam doomed to die,
As Sarah to her husband, so should we,
Obey them, love them, keep, and nourish them,
If they by any means do want our helps,
Laying our hands under their feet to tread,   140
If that by that we, might procure their ease,
And for a precedent I'll first begin,
And lay my hand under my husband's feet.

She lays her hand under her husband's feet.

FERANDO   Enough, sweet, the wager thou hast won,
And they I am sure cannot deny the same.   145
ALFONSO   Ay, Ferando, the wager thou hast won,
And for to show thee how I am pleased in this,
A hundred pounds I freely give thee more,
Another dowry for another daughter,
For she is not the same she was before.   150
FERANDO   Thanks, sweet father, gentlemen, goodnight.
For Kate and I will leave you for tonight,
'Tis Kate and I am wed, and you are sped,
And so farewell, for we will to our beds.

Exit FERANDO *and* KATE *and* SANDER.

ALFONSO   Now, Aurelius, what say you to this?   155
AURELIUS   Believe me father, I rejoice to see
Ferando and his wife so lovingly agree.

Exit AURELIUS *and* PHYLEMA *and* ALFONSO *and* VALERIA.

EMELIA   How now, Polidor, in a dump? What sayst thou man?
POLIDOR   I say thou art a shrew.
EMELIA   That's better than a sheep.   160
POLIDOR   Well, since 'tis done let it go, come let's in.

Exit POLIDOR *and* EMELIA.

Scene 15. *Enter two men bearing* SLY, *dressed in his own apparel, and leaving him where they found him.*

Enter TAPSTER.

TAPSTER Now that the darksome night is overpast,
And dawning day appears in crystal sky,
Now must I haste abroad. But soft, who's this?
What, Sly? Oh wondrous, hath he lain here all night?
I'll wake him. I think he's starved by this,   5
But that his belly was so stuffed with ale.
What now, Sly, awake for shame.

SLY Sim, gi's some more wine. What's all the players gone? Am
I not a lord?

TAPSTER A lord with a murrain! Come, art thou drunken still? 10

SLY Who's this? Tapster, oh lord, sirrah, I have had the bravest
dream tonight, that ever thouhadst in all thy life.

TAPSTER I marry, but you had best get you home,
For your wife will curse you for dreaming here tonight.

SLY Will she? I know now how to tame a shrew,   15
I dreamt upon it all this night till now,
And thou hast waked me out of the best dream
That ever I had in my life.
But I'll to my wife presently and tame her too, and if she 20
anger me.

TAPSTER Nay, tarry Sly, for I'll go home with thee,
And hear the rest that thou hast dreamt tonight.

Exit all.

JOHN FLETCHER

The Tamer Tamed; or, The Woman's Prize[†]

[John Fletcher (1579–1625) is best known as a playwright who wrote
in collaboration most famously with Shakespeare but also with Frances
Beaumont and Philip Massinger. *The Tamer Tamed* (1611) constitutes
a "reply" to Shakespeare's *Shrew* that is of particular interest since it
was written and performed in Shakespeare's own lifetime. In Fletcher's
sequel to Shakespeare's play, Kate is dead and the widower, Petruchio,
has remarried. His new wife, Maria, is no docile maiden, and by the
end of the play, Petruchio is himself tamed. However, this conclusion

---

10. murrain: a pestilence.
† From John Fletcher, *The Tamer Tamed; Or, The Woman's Prize* [1611]. Notes from the
   text by Celia R. Daileader and Gary Taylor (Manchester: Manchester University Press,
   2006).

does not, the play tells us, represent the victory of women over men, but rather urges equality in marriage.]

The Persons Represented in the Play

[*Men:*]

PETRUCCIO, *an Italian gentleman,* [*widowed, and newly remarried;*] *husband to* MARIA.

SOPHOCLES: ⎫
TRANIO: ⎭ *two gentlemen, friends to* PETRUCCIO.

MOROSO, *an old rich doting citizen, suitor to* LIVIA.

ROLAND, *a young gentleman, in love with* LIVIA.

PETRONIUS, *father to* MARIA *and* LIVIA.

JAQUES: ⎫
PEDRO: ⎭ *two witty servants to* PETRUCCIO.

WATCHMEN

[SERVANT to PETRONIUS]

Porters

[Servants]

Women:

MARIA, *a chaste witty lady*: ⎫ *the two daughters*
LIVIA, [*a lady, in love with*] ROLAND: ⎭ *of* PETRONIUS.

BIANCA, [*a lady,*] *their cousin.*

CITY [WIFE], *drunk*: ⎫
COUNTRY [WIFE], *drunk*: ⎬ *to the relief of the ladies.*
[THREE COUNTRY WENCHES]: ⎭

THE SCENE: *London.*

Act 1

1.1

Enter MOROSO, SOPHOCLES, *and* TRANIO *with rosemary as from a wedding.*

MOROSO   God give 'em joy!
TRANIO   Amen.
SOPHOCLES   Amen, say I too.
  The pudding's now i'th' proof. Alas, poor wench,
  Through what a mine of patience must thou work
  Ere thou know'st good hour more!
TRANIO   'Tis too true, certain,
  Methinks her father has dealt harshly with her,   5
  Exceeding harshly, and not like a father,
  To match her to this dragon. I protest
  I pity the poor gentlewoman.
MOROSO   Methinks now
  He's not so terrible as people think him.
SOPHOCLES   [*Aside to Tranio*] This old thief flatters out of mere
  devotion   10
  To please the father for his second daughter.
TRANIO [*Aside to* SOPHOCLES]   But shall he have her?
SOPHOCLES [*Aside to* TRANIO]   Yes, when I have Rome.
  And yet the father's for him.
MOROSO   I'll assure ye,
  I hold him a good man.
SOPHOCLES   Yes sure, a wealthy—
  But whether a good woman's man is doubtful.   15
TRANIO   Would 'twere no worse!
MOROSO   What though his other wife,
  Out of her most abundant stubbornness,

1.1. Between the church and Petronius's house.
1.1.0.1. **rosemary:** a fragrant evergreen herb, used at weddings and funerals as an emblem of memory and immortality.
1. **God:** (Here and occasionally elsewhere the manuscript has been censored, substituting 'heaven' for 'God'.)
2. **The pudding's . . . proof:** (Alluding to the proverb 'The proof of the pudding is in the eating').
wench: (An affectionate, patronizing slang term for a young woman, comparable to the modern 'girl'; referring to Maria.)
3. **mine:** large amount; store.
4. **good hour more:** i.e., another happy moment.
certain: certainly (modifying the preceding and following clauses).
7. **this dragon:** i.e., Petruccio (comparing Maria to Andromeda, whose father sacrificed her to a sea-dragon).
protest: declare.
10. **thief:** unscrupulous greedy person.
11. **for:** in order to win.
12. **when . . . Rome:** i.e., never.
14. **hold:** consider.
16. **his other wife:** Katherine, depicted in Shakespeare's *The Taming of the Shrew*.

Out of her daily hue and cries upon him—
For, sure, she was a rebel—turned his temper
And forced him blow as high as she? Does't follow   20
He must retain that long-since-buried tempest
To this soft maid?

SOPHOCLES   I fear it.

TRANIO   So do I too,
And so far that, if God had made me woman
And his wife that must be—

MOROSO   What would you do, sir?

TRANIO   I would learn to eat coals with an angry cat   25
And spit fire at him. I would, to prevent him,
Do all the ramping roaring tricks a whore,
Being drunk and tumbling-ripe, would tremble at.
There is no safety else, nor moral wisdom,
To be a wife, and his.

SOPHOCLES   So I should think, too.   30

TRANIO   For yet the bare remembrance of his first wife—
I tell ye on my knowledge, and a truth too—
Will make him start in's sleep, and very often
Cry out for cudgels, cowl-staves, anything,
Hiding his breeches, out of fear her ghost   35
Should walk and wear 'em yet. Since his first marriage
He is no more the still Petruccio
Than I am Babylon.

SOPHOCLES   He's a good fellow,
And, by my troth, I love him; but to think
A fit match for this tender soul—   40

TRANIO   Her very sound, if she but say her prayers
Louder than men talk treason, makes him tinder.

---

19. turned his temper: altered his calm temperament.
20. blow . . . she: storm as blusteringly as she, Katherine.
21. long-since-buried: (Petruccio is a widower.)
25. eat . . . cat: (Hot coals in a wet mouth would produce a hissing sound; anger is often associated with heat, and women with cats.)
26. prevent: anticipate.
27. ramping: raging, behaving like a wild animal rearing up on its hind legs.
28. tumbling-ripe: ready to (1) fall prostrate; (2) have sex.
29. else: otherwise.
31. bare: mere.
33. in's: in his.
34. cudgels: (Often associated with Petruccio's wife-taming, like the riding-whip of later stagings of *Shrew*.)
cowl-staves: stout poles used to carry a heavy burden, supported on the shoulders of two bearers. Hence, (1) a common household implement and civilian weapon; (2) a pole used to carry someone derisively through the streets—a popular punishment inflicted on husbands dominated by their wives.
37. still: (1) same; (2) quiet, mild.
38. Babylon: i.e., a violent outlaw. In an old ballad, 'Babylon' kills two sisters before the third identifies him as their long-lost brother, 'baby Lon'.
42. tinder: (1) flammable material, used to kindle fires or ignite gunpowder; (2) punningly opposite to 'tender' and easily lit by a 'match' (line 40).

The motion of a dial, when he's testy,
Is the same trouble to him as a waterwork.
She must do nothing of herself, not eat,   45
Sleep, say 'Sir, how do ye?', make her ready, piss,
Unless he bid her.
SOPHOCLES   He will bury her,
Ten pounds to twenty shillings, within this three weeks.
TRANIO   I'll be your half.
MOROSO   He loves her most extremely,
And so long 'twill be honeymoon.

       Enter JAQUES *with a pot of wine.*

                           Now, Jaques!   50
You are a busy man, I am sure.
JAQUES   Yes, certain,
This old sport must have eggs—
SOPHOCLES   Not yet this ten days.
JAQUES   Sweet gentlemen, with muscatel.
TRANIO   That's right, sir.
MOROSO   This fellow broods his master.—Speed you, Jaques.
SOPHOCLES   We shall be for you presently.
JAQUES   Your Worships   55
Shall have it rich and neat and, o' my conscience,
As welcome as Our Lady Day. Oh, my old sir,
When shall we see Your Worship run at ring?
That hour, a standing were worth money.
MOROSO   So, sir.

---

43. **dial:** hand of a clock.
44. **waterwork:** (noisy) machinery for re-directing river water.
45. **of:** by.
46. **make her ready:** get dressed.
48. **twenty shillings:** one pound sterling (i.e., ten to one) (equivalent to the cost of forty-four loaves of bread at the time).
49. **I'll be your half:** I will put up half the amount you have wagered, in exchange for getting half the winnings. The same phrase occurs at *Shrew* 5.2.84. Fletcher's play begins, as Shakespeare's ends, with a wager on Petruccio's relationship with his new wife.
50. **so long:** i.e., three weeks.
52. **old:** ancient, primitive (but perhaps also alluding to Petruccio's age).
sport: (Often used of sexual activity.)
eggs: (Considered an aphrodisiac.)
53. **muscatel:** a sweet wine. (Wine in general was believed to enhance sexual potency.)
54. **This . . . master:** This servant is solicitous for his master, Petruccio, and hovers protectively over him like a brooding hen.
Speed you: May you have good success.
55. **be for you:** have need of you.
Your Worships: Your Honours, good sirs.
56. **it:** i.e., the wine I will bring you.
neat: straight, not diluted with water.
57. **Our Lady Day:** feast celebrating the Virgin Mary, 25 March, the Feast of the Annunciation (coincident with the beginning of spring).
58. **run at ring:** (1) engage in the chivalric sport in which a tilter, riding on horseback at full speed, tries to thrust the point of the lance through a ring; (2) try to penetrate a woman.
59. **standing:** (1) standing place or room for spectators at the tiltyard (2) erection.

JAQUES   Upon my little honesty, your mistress,   60
    If I have any speculation,
    Must think this single thrumming of a fiddle,
    Without a bow, but even poor sport.
MOROSO   You're merry.
JAQUES   Would I were wise too. So, God bless Your Worships.

                                                        Exit.

TRANIO   [*To* MOROSO]   The fellow tells you true.
SOPHOCLES [*To* MOROSO]   When is the day, man?   65
    Come, come, you'd steal a marriage.
MOROSO   Nay, believe me.
    But when her father pleases, I am ready,
    And all my friends shall know it.
TRANIO   Why not now?
    One charge had served for both.
MOROSO   There's reason in't.
SOPHOCLES   Called Roland.
MOROSO   Will ye walk? They'll think we are lost.   70
    Come, gentlemen.   [*Exit.*]
TRANIO [*To* SOPHOCLES]   You have whipped him now.
SOPHOCLES   So will he never the wench, I hope.
TRANIO   I wish it.   *Exeunt.*

                                1.2

        Enter ROLAND *and* LIVIA.

ROLAND   Nay, Livia, if you'll go away tonight,
    If your affections be not made of words—
LIVIA   I love you, and you know how dearly, Roland.—

60. **your mistress:** the woman to whom you devote your attention as a wooer, Livia.
61. **speculation:** powers of intelligent observation.
62–3. **single . . . bow:** another impotence joke. 'Fiddling' was a euphemism for sexual intercourse: the bow represents the erect penis, the fiddle and its strings the female genitals. Jaques implies that Moroso's bride, lacking a capable 'bow', would have to be content with unmarried ('single') digital stimulation (thrumming).
66. **steal a marriage:** elope.
69. **One . . . both:** It would have been thriftier if you had combined two weddings in one (as a wedding and funeral are huddled together in *Hamlet*).
in't: in it.
70. **Called Roland:** i.e., The reason for the delay is that you have a rival, Roland, for the hand of Livia.
They'll: The rest of the wedding party will.
71. **whipped:** beaten.
72. **So . . . wench:** The 'whipping' Sophocles would prevent here is most likely sexual, playing on the horse-and-rider metaphors which pervade the text (a horse is urged forward by whipping). None the less, the literal sense of whipping the bride is not irrelevant, as it highlights the latent violence and subjugation intrinsic in the notion of wife-taming.
1.2: Petronius's house. Wedding feasts—which could last several days, and include consummation of the marriage—were often held at the home of the bride's father. This places Maria between the lapsed authority of her father and the not-yet-enforced authority of her husband.

Is there none near us?—My affections ever
Have been your servants. With what superstition   5
I have ever sainted you—
ROLAND   Why then, take this way.
LIVIA   'Twill be a childish and less prosperous course
Than his that knows not care. Why should we do
Our honest and our hearty loves such wrong
To over-run our fortunes?
ROLAND   Then you flatter.   10
LIVIA   Alas, you know I cannot.
ROLAND   What hope's left else,
But flying, to enjoy ye?
LIVIA   None so far.
For let it be admitted, we have time
And all things now in other expectation,
My father's bent against us. What but ruin   15
Can such a by-way bring us? If your fears
Would let you look with my eyes, I would show you,
And certain, how our staying here would win us
A course, though somewhat longer, yet far surer.
ROLAND   And then Moroso has ye.
LIVIA   No such matter.   20
For hold this certain: begging, stealing, whoring,
Selling (which is a sin unpardonable)
Of counterfeit cods, or musty English cracus,
Switches, or stones for th' toothache, sooner finds me
Than that drawn fox Moroso.
ROLAND   But his money!   25
If wealth may win you—
LIVIA   If a hog may be
High priest among the Jews! His money, Roland?
O Love forgive me! What a faith hast thou?

---

4. Is . . . us?: Can no one overhear us?
6. take this way: follow the course I've proposed (elopement).
8. his . . . care: the course of someone completely careless.
10. over-run: run beyond.
flatter: deceive.
12. flying: fleeing, escaping.
13–15. For . . . us: Although we have an opportunity and everyone is distracted by other business (Petruccio's wedding), nevertheless my father's opposition remains as an obstacle.
16. by-way: indirect course.
22–4. Selling . . . toothache: (As a member of the gentry class, Livia regards the retail trade in trivial accessories as the ultimate degradation, worse than being a courtesan.)
23. counterfeit cods: (1) small bags resembling testicles, containing spurious or adulterated civet or musk (perfume) (2) codpieces.
cracus: brand of tobacco sold in London c. 1610–16.
24. Switches: riding whips.
stones: testicles of an animal (used for medicinal purposes).
25. drawn: disemboweled; stuffed.
26–7. If . . . Jews!: An impossible condition; orthodox Jews are forbidden to eat pork.

Why, can his money kiss me?
ROLAND   Yes.
LIVIA   Behind,
  Laid out upon a petticoat. Or grasp me,   30
  While I cry, 'Oh, good thank you'? (O' my troth,
  Thou mak'st me merry with thy fear.)—Or lie with me
  As you may do? Alas, what fools you men are!
  His mouldy money? Half a dozen riders
  That cannot sit but stamped fast to their saddles?   35
  No, Roland, no man shall make use of me.
  My beauty was born free, and free I'll give it
  To him that loves, not buys me. You yet doubt me?
ROLAND   I cannot say I doubt ye.
LIVIA   Go thy ways!
  Thou art the prettiest puling piece of passion.   40
  I' faith, I will not fail thee.
ROLAND   I had rather—
LIVIA   Prithee, believe me. If I do not carry it
  For both our goods—
ROLAND   But—
LIVIA   What 'but'?
ROLAND   I would tell you.
LIVIA   I know all you can tell me. All's but this:
  You would have me, and lie with me. Is't not so?   45
ROLAND   Yes.
LIVIA   Why, you shall. Will that content you? Go.
ROLAND   I am very loath to go.

    Enter BIANCA *and* MARIA.

LIVIA   Now, o' my conscience,
  Thou art an honest fellow. Here's my sister.
  Go, prithee, go. This kiss, and credit me: [*They kiss.*]
  Ere I am three nights older I am for thee.   50
  You shall hear what I do.
ROLAND   I had rather feel it.
LIVIA   Farewell.

---

29. Behind: On the posterior.
30. Laid out: (1) spent; (2) placed.
32. lie: have sex.
34. riders: gold coins upon which the figure of a horseman is stamped.
35. cannot sit: (Livia continues the equestrian innuendo: unlike a lover, the coins cannot sit on her or ride her sexually.)
36. make use of me: (1) use me as a sexual object; (2) make a profit from me, as usury accumulates interest on loaned money.
39. Go thy ways: Get on with you.
40. puling: whining.
42. carry it: bring it off.
49. credit: believe.
52. it: him (a diminutive, often used of children).

ROLAND   Farewell.   *Exit* ROLAND.
LIVIA   [*Aside*]   Alas, poor fool, how it looks!
It would e'en hang itself, should I but cross it.
For pure love to the matter, I must hatch it.

[LIVIA *stands apart.*]

BIANCA   Nay, never look for merry hour, Maria,   55
If now ye make it not. Let not your blushes,
Your modesty and tenderness of spirit
Make you continual anvil to his anger.
Believe me, since his first wife set him going,
Nothing can bind his rage. Take your own counsel;   60
You shall not say that I persuaded you.
MARIA   Stay. Shall I do it?
BIANCA   Have you a stomach to't?
MARIA   I never showed it.
BIANCA   'Twill show the rarer and the stranger in you.   65
But do not say I urged you.
MARIA   I'll do it.
Like Curtius, to redeem my country have I
Leaped into this gulf of marriage.
Farewell, all poorer thoughts but spite and anger,
Till I have wrought a miracle upon him!   70
BIANCA   This is brave now,
If you continue it. But your own will lead you.
MARIA   Adieu, all tenderness! I dare continue.
Maids that are made of fears and modest blushes,
View me, and love example!   75
I am no more the gentle, tame Maria.
Mistake me not. I have a new soul in me,
Made of a north wind, nothing but a tempest—

---

53. cross: contradict.
54. matter: (1) business; (2) female genitals.
hatch it: devise and develop a plan.
60–1. Take . . . you: Make up your mind to do the right thing; it should be your decision (even if I am urging it).
62. Stay: (Bianca moves as though to leave.)
63. a stomach to't: the strength or appetite for it.
65. stranger: more extraordinary.
67. Curtius: Marcus Curtius (362 BCE), Roman hero described by the historian Livy (VII:6). When a gap suddenly appeared in the Forum at Rome, an oracle claimed that it could be closed only by the most precious thing Rome possessed. Curtius saved Rome by sacrificing himself, leaping—fully armed—into the gap, which then closed.
71. brave: (1) courageous; (2) excellent.
72. your . . . you: remember that this is your decision.
74. Maids: (1) unmarried women; (2) virgins; (3) female servants.
75. love example: do not simply 'take example' (the usual idiom), but fall in love with an exemplary precedent.
76. tame: (Fletcher's play begins with a woman already tame, thus reversing the narrative of *The Taming of the Shrew*.)

And, like a tempest, shall it make all ruins
Till I have run my will out.

BIANCA   Here is your sister.   80

MARIA   Here is the brave old man's love.

BIANCA   That loves the young man.

MARIA   Ay, and hold thee there, wench. What a grief of
　　　heart is't,
When Paphos' revels should up-rouse old Night,
To sweat against a cork, to lie and tell
The clock o'th' lungs, to rise sport-starved!

LIVIA   Dear sister,   85
Where have you been, you talk thus?

MARIA   Why, at church, wench,
Where I am tied to talk thus. I am a wife now.

LIVIA   It seems so, and a modest.

MARIA   You're an ass.
When thou art married once, thy modesty
Will never buy three pins.

LIVIA   Bless me!

MARIA   From what?   90

BIANCA   From such a tame fool as our cousin Livia.

LIVIA   You are not mad?

MARIA   Yes, wench, and so must you be,
Or none of our acquaintance—mark me, Livia—
Or indeed fit for our sex. 'Tis bedtime.
Pardon me, yellow Hymen, that I mean   95
Thy offerings to protract, and to keep fasting
My valiant bridegroom.

LIVIA   [To BIANCA]   Whither will this woman?

BIANCA   You may perceive her end.

LIVIA   Or rather, fear it.

MARIA   Dare you be partner in't?

---

80. run . . . out: had my way.
81. brave: (1) courageous; (2) gorgeously dressed (ironic, whether applied to Moroso or Livia).
83. Paphos': Paphos was a city in Cyprus sacred to Aphrodite, goddess of love.
old Night: (1) primeval darkness; (2) aged Moroso.
84. sweat against: (1) work hard on; (2) waste bodily fluids on.
cork: (1) cylindrical shape made of dry cork, used as a stopper for a bottle (2) dry penis.
84–5. tell . . . lungs: count the hours by his snoring or coughing.
sport-starved: starved of sex.
87. tied: (1) obligated; (2) bound in marriage.
88. modest: (Said ironically.)
89–90. When . . . pins: Once you are married, your modesty is worth nothing. (Modesty was one of the attributes that made women marriageable; once married, a woman could no longer use this as a bargaining chip.)
92. mad: (Livia means 'crazy', but Maria takes the word in the sense 'angry'.)
95. Hymen: Roman deity of marriage, traditionally yellow-haired and dressed in yellow.
98. end: intent.

LIVIA   Leave it, Maria.
I fear I have marked too much. For goodness, leave it.   100
Divest you with obedient hands: to bed.

MARIA   To bed? No, Livia. There are comets hang
Prodigious over that yet. There's a fellow
Must yet, before I know that heat—ne'er start, wench—
Be made a man, for yet he is a monster.   105
Here must his head be, Livia.

LIVIA   Never hope it.
'Tis as easy with a sieve to scoop the ocean, as
To tame Petruccio.

MARIA   Stay.—Lucina, hear me!
Never unlock the treasure of my womb,
For human fruit to make it capable,   110
Nor never with thy secret hand make brief
A mother's labour to me, if I do
Give way unto my married husband's will,
Or be a wife in anything but hopes,
Till I have made him easy as a child   115
And tame as fear! He shall not win a smile
Or a pleased look from this austerity,
Though it would pull another jointure from him
And make him every day another man;
And when I kiss him, till I have my will,   120
May I be barren of delights, and know
Only what pleasure is in dreams and guesses.

LIVIA   A strange exordium!

BIANCA   [To MARIA]   All the several wrongs

---

100. marked: heard.
101. Divest you: (1) undress yourself; (2) strip yourself of your possessions and legal rights.
102–3. There . . . yet: (Comets were regarded as bad omens.)
103. fellow: (Disrespectful slang, implying Maria's equality with Petruccio.)
104. heat: sexual pleasure.
ne'er start: don't be startled.
106. Here: (There are a number of options for this gesture in performance. Maria might indicate that she will be Petruccio's head, thus reversing the Pauline notion that the husband is the 'head' of the married couple, the wife the 'body'. Or she might indicate a body-part of hers that will be level with his soon-to-be lowered head: her feet, or perhaps, more bawdily, her waist, suggesting cunnilingus.)
108. tame: (Again alluding to the title of Shakespeare's play.)
Stay: (Livia is about to leave.)
Lucina: Roman goddess of childbirth.
112. labour: birth pangs.
113. will: (1) volition; (2) sexual appetite.
115. easy: compliant.
117. this austerity: (Maria refers to her own stern demeanour.)
118. jointure: estate held jointly by a married couple which would be passed to the wife in the event of widowhood.
119. another: a new.
123. exordium: Latin term for the beginning of a discourse; common rhetorical exercise in English grammar schools, and therefore appropriate to men, not women.
several: various.

Done by imperious husbands to their wives
These thousand years and upwards, strengthen thee!   125
Thou hast a brave cause.

MARIA   And I'll do it bravely,
Or may I knit my life out ever after.

LIVIA   In what part of the world got she this spirit?—
Yet pray, Maria, look before you truly:
Besides the disobedience of a wife,   130
Which you will find a heavy imputation
(Which yet I cannot think your own, it shows
So distant from your sweetness)—

MARIA   'Tis, I swear.

LIVIA   Weigh but the person, and the hopes you have
To work this desperate cure.

MARIA   A weaker subject   135
Would shame the end I aim at. Disobedience?
You talk too tamely. By the faith I have
In mine own noble will, that childish woman
That lives a prisoner to her husband's pleasure
Has lost her making, and becomes a beast   140
Created for his use, not fellowship.

LIVIA   His first wife said as much.

MARIA   She was a fool,
And took a scurvy course. Let her be named
'Mongst those that wish for things but dare not do 'em.
I have a new dance for him, and a mad one.   145

LIVIA   [To Bianca] Are you of this faith?

BIANCA   Yes, truly, and will die in't.

LIVIA   Why then, let's all wear breeches.

BIANCA   That's a good wench!

MARIA   Now thou com'st near the nature of a woman.
Hang those tame-hearted eyases that no sooner

127. knit . . . after: spend the rest of my life knitting (a woman's traditional pastime, but also alluding to the female destinies who knit the length of a person's life).
129. look before you: i.e., look to the future.
131. imputation: accusation.
132. shows: appears.
134. Weigh . . . person: Consider the person (Petruccio).
hopes: (slender) means.
135. subject: i.e., challenge.
140. making: true nature.
140-1. a beast . . . fellowship: (Alluding to Genesis: the animals were created for Adam's use, but Eve was created as a companion.)
141. fellowship: partnership, alliance, intimate friendship, union of equals.
143. scurvy: worthless, contemptible. (Scurvy is a disfiguring disease resulting from malnutrition.)
144. 'Mongst: amongst.
145. a new dance: in contrast to Petruccio's 'wooing dance' in Shakespeare's Shrew, 1.2.67.
149–59: Maria here reverses an extended image Shakespeare's Petruccio uses in his soliloquy about 'how to tame a shrew': 'My falcon now is sharp and passing empty, / And till

See the lure out and hear their husbands holler   150
But cry like kites upon 'em! The free haggard
(Which is that woman that has wing and knows it,
Spirit and plume) will make a hundred checks
To show her freedom, sail in every air
And look out every pleasure, not regarding   155
Lure nor quarry till her pitch command
What she desires, making her foundered keeper
Be glad to fling out trains (and golden ones)
To take her down again.

LIVIA   You are learnèd, sister.
Yet I say still, take heed.   160

MARIA   A witty saying!
I'll tell thee, Livia: had this fellow tired
As many wives as horses under him,
With spurring of their patience, had he got
A patent, with an office to reclaim us,
Confirmed by Parliament, had he the malice   165
And subtlety of devils or of us
Or anything that's worse than both—

LIVIA   Hey, hey, boys! This is excellent.

MARIA   Or could he
Cast his wives new again, like bells, to make 'em

---

she stoop she shall not be full-gorged, / For then she never looks upon her lure. / Another
way I have to man my haggard, / To make her come and know her keeper's call' (*Shrew*,
4.1.176–80).
149. eyases: young hawks (compared in *Hamlet* to boy actors, like those who played
women's roles).
150. lure: apparatus used by falconers to train hawks.
151. kites: birds of prey, scavengers. (Term of abuse.)
haggard: female adult hawk, full-plumed. (Shakespeare's Hortensio calls Bianca 'this proud
disdainful haggard', *Shrew*, 4.2.39.)
153. Spirit: (1) vitality; (2) courage; (3) intelligence; (4) wind (under her wings).
plume: full plumage; but also suggesting the crest of a (male) soldier's helmet.
checks: (1) stoopings at game other than the prey her keeper wants her to attack; (2)
taunts; (3) rebukes.
156. quarry: bird flown at by a hawk.
pitch: (1) height to which a falcon soars before swooping down on its prey; (2) fixed opinion; (3) register of voice.
157. foundered: (1) disabled, lamed; (2) stuck in the mire; (3) sent to the bottom (from
the perspective of the bird, high above).
keeper: (1) gamekeeper; (2) guardian, husband; (3) man who keeps a mistress.
158. trains: (1) pieces of meat laid in a line to lure falcons to their keepers; (2) elongated
parts of skirts trailing behind on the ground, worn by women of rank; (3) groups of attendants waiting on a person of importance.
159. take her down: (1) make the bird descend; (2) persuade a woman to lie down for sexual intercourse.
164. patent: licence, monopoly.
office: commission.
166. or: either.
168. boys: (1) Probably mimicking male slang, and comparing Maria and Bianca to 'roaring boys', groups of males who specialized in braggadocio; (2) adolescent male actors, playing the roles of Maria and Bianca.
169. Cast: make in a mould with molten metal.

Sound to his will, or had the fearful name   170
Of the first breaker of wild women, yet,
Yet would I undertake this man, thus single,
And spite of all the freedom he has reached to
Turn him and bend him as I list, and mould him
Into a babe again, that agèd women,   175
Wanting both teeth and spleen, may master him.

BIANCA   Thou wilt be chronicled.

MARIA   That's all I aim at.

LIVIA   I must confess I do with all my heart
Hate an imperious husband, and in time
Might be so wrought upon—

BIANCA   To make him cuckold?   180

MARIA   If he deserve it.

LIVIA   There I'll leave ye, ladies.

BIANCA   Thou hast not so much noble anger in thee.

MARIA   Go sleep, go sleep. What we intend to do
Lies not for such starved souls as thou hast, Livia.

LIVIA   Good night. The bridegroom will be with you
presently   185

MARIA   That's more than you know.

LIVIA   If ye work upon him
As ye have promised, ye may give example,
Which no doubt will be followed.

MARIA   So.

BIANCA   Good night. We'll trouble you no further.

MARIA   If you intend no good, pray do no harm.   190

LIVIA   None, but pray for ye.

                                                        Exit LIVIA.

MARIA   Now, Bianca—

BIANCA   Cheer, wench!

MARIA   Those wits we have, let's wind 'em to the height.
My rest is up, wench, and I pull for that
Will make me ever famous. They that lay

---

170. **fearful name:** fearsome reputation.
172. **undertake:** take on.
single: single-handed.
173. **spite of:** in spite of.
reached to: attained.
174. **list:** wish.
176. **Wanting:** lacking.
spleen: bodily organ associated with irritable moods and aggression.
177. **be chronicled:** make history.
180. **wrought:** prevailed.
187. **give example:** set an example.
193. **rest is up:** stake is laid.
pull: draw a card.
that: that which.

Foundations are half-builders, all men say.   195

    Enter JAQUES.

JAQUES   My master, forsooth—
MARIA   Oh, how does *thy* master?
Prithee, commend me to him.
JAQUES   [*Aside*]   How is this?—
My master stays, forsooth—
MARIA   Why, let him stay.
Who hinders him, forsooth?
JAQUES   [*Aside*]   The revel's ended now.—
To visit you.
MARIA   I am not sick.
JAQUES   I mean,   200
To see his chamber, forsooth.
MARIA   Am I his groom?
Where lay he last night, forsooth?
JAQUES   In the low matted parlour.
MARIA   There lies his way, by the long gallery.
JAQUES   I mean, *your* chamber. You're very merry, mistress.
MARIA   'Tis a good sign I am sound-hearted, Jaques.   205
But, if you'll know where I lie, follow me,
And what thou see'st deliver to thy master.
BIANCA   Do, gentle Jaques.

    Exeunt MARIA *and* BIANCA.

JAQUES   Ha, is the wind in that door?
By'r Lady, we shall have foul weather, then.
I do not like the shuffling of these women.   210
They are mad beasts when they knock their heads together.
I have observed 'em all this day: their whispers
One in another's ear, their signs and pinches,

---

196. **forsooth**: truly. (A mild oath, sarcastically repeated by Maria.)
thy: (Maria emphasizes the fact that Petruccio is Jaques' master, not hers.)
198. **stays**: waits.
199. **revel's ended**: party's over.
200. **visit**: (Maria takes this in the specific sense 'attend on a sick person'.)
201. **his chamber**: Jaques later explains this phrase: 'I mean, *your* chamber' (1.204): Petruccio expects to consummate his marriage in his bride's bedroom. Maria objects to the appropriation (by which her space has suddenly become 'his').
groom: male attendant, one who would help him to bed.
202. **low**: (1) downstairs; (2) low-ceilinged; (3) inferior.
matted: with coarse pleated material strewn on the floor (where he presumably slept).
parlour: small private room.
203. **gallery**: corridor.
207. **deliver**: report.
208. **wind . . . door**: (Proverbial. 'Door' means 'direction, quarter'.)
209. **By'r Lady**: An oath: 'By our Lady', the Virgin Mary.
210. **shuffling**: (1) manner of walking; (2) mixing and dealing of cards; (3) joining together; (4) sneaky behaviour.
211. **knock**: put.

And breaking often into violent laughters,
As if the end they purposed were their own.   215
Call you these weddings? Sure, this is a knavery,
A very rank and dainty knavery,
Marvellous finely carried, that's the comfort.
What would these women do in ways of honour
That are such masters this way? Well, my sir   220
Has been as good at finding out these toys
As any living. If he lose it now,
At his own peril be it! I must follow.

Exit.

*   *   *

Epilogue [spoken by Maria]

The tamer's tamed—but so, as nor the men
Can find one just cause to complain of, when
They fitly do consider, in their lives
They should not reign as tyrants o'er their wives;
Nor can the women from this precedent   91
Insult or triumph, it being aptly meant
To teach both sexes due equality
And, as they stand bound, to love mutually.
If this effect, arising from a cause
Well laid and grounded, may deserve applause,   100
We something more than hope our honest ends
Will keep the men, and women too, our friends.

---

215. as if they were keeping their plans to themselves, i.e., conspiring together.
217. rank: fertile, luxurious, licentious, gross, rancid.
dainty: rare, delicate, fastidious, excellent.
221. toys: tricks.
90.2. spoken by Maria: (Not specified in the 1647 text, but revivals of the play since 1660 have always given the last speech to Maria, and this was probably theatrical practice from the beginning.)
91. nor: neither.
93. consider: consider that.
96. Insult or triumph: vaunt proudly or boast.
98. stand bound: are obligated.
101–2.: We have high hopes that our honest efforts will win over both the men and the women in the audience.

JOHN LACEY

Sauny the Scott; or, the Taming of the Shrew: A Comedy[†]

[Written by John Lacey, *Sauny the Scott* was first performed in 1667, although it was not published until 1698. Unlike *The Taming of the Shrew*, which is set in Italy (with the exception of the Induction), Lacey's adaptation eschews the Sly plot and sets the courtship and taming plot in London. A specifically English identity is important to this play: for instance, the title character Sauny's use of Scottish dialogue throughout the play annoys his master Petruchio, who wishes him to speak proper English. English counties, towns, and landmarks are also a common point of reference. Lacey's "shrew," the strong-willed Margaret, maintains her witty banter and feisty attitude throughout most of the play but is "tamed" at last not by direct action on the part of Petruchio, but by a toothache that almost kills her—a toothache the play suggests she has caught from keeping her mouth constantly open.]

Dramatis Personae

GER: Geraldo
SAUN: Sauny
WOOD: Woodall

WIN: Winlove
PET: Petruchio
MARG: Margaret

BIAN: Biancha
TRAN: Tranio
BEAU: Beaufoy

* * *

Act II

Enter WOODALL *and* WINLOVE *Disguis'd.*

GER 'Tis Mr. *Woodall*, a rich old Citizen, and my Rival: Hark.

SAUN Out, out, What sud an awd Carle[1] do with a young bonny Lass, are ye not an Aud theif, Sir.

WOOD How!

SAUN Are ye not an Aud Man, Sir?

WOOD Yes marry am I, Sir.

SAUN And are not ye to Marry a young Maiden?

WOOD Yes, What then?

SAUN And are not ye troubled with a sear griefe, Sir?

WOOD A sear grief, what sear grief?

SAUN Your troubled with a great weakness i'th' bottome of your Bally, what sid yea dea with a young Maiden? Out, out, out.

WOOD You understand me, your French Books treat most of Love;

---

† From *Sauny the Scott; or, The Taming of the Shrew: A Comedy* [1667] (London: E. Whitlock, 1698).

1. **awd Carle:** old man

those use her too, and now and then you may urge something of my Love and Merit? besides her Fathers bounty, you shall find me Liberal.

WIN   Mounsier, me will tell her the very fine ting of you, me vill make her Love you whether she can or noe?

WOOD   Enough, Peace, here's *Geraldo*, your servant Sir, I am just going to Sir *Nicholas Beaufoy* to carry him this Gentleman, a *Frenchman*, most Eminent for teaching his Country Language.

GER   I have a Master for *Biancha* too, but waving that, I have some news to tell you, I have found out a Friend that will Woo *Margaret*, What will you contribute, for he must be hir'd to't?

WOOD   Why I will give him forty Peeces in hand, and when he has don't, I'll double the Sum.

GER   Done, Sir, I'll undertake it.

SAUN   S'breed Sir, I'se gat it done muckle Cheaper, for twenty Punds I'se dea it my Sel.

GER   Come, down with your Money, and the Bargain's made.

WOOD   But if He shud not do it, I don't care for throwing away so much Money.

GER   If he don't I'll undertake he shall refund.

WOOD   Why then here's ten Pieces, and that Ring I'll pawn to you for 'nother Forty, 'tis worth a Hundred; But doe's the Gentleman know her Qualities?

PET   I Sir, and they are such as I am fond on; I wou'd not be hir'd for any thing, to Woo a person of another Humour.

Enter TRANIO *brave, and* JAMY.

TRAN   Save you Gentlemen; Pray which is the way to Sir *Nicholas Beaufoy's* House?

WOOD   Why Sir, what's your Business there? you pretend not to be a Servant to either of his Daughters, d' ye?

TRAN   You are something blunt in your Questions, perhaps I do.

PET   Not her that Chides, on any hand I pray.

TRAN   I Love no Chiders; come *Jamy*.

GER   Pray stay Sir, Is it the other?

TRAN   May be it is, Is it any offence?

WOOD   Yes 'tis Sir, she is my Mistriss.

GER   I must tell you Sir, she is my Mistriss too.

TRAN   And I must tell you both she is my Mistriss; Will that content you? nay never frown for the Matter.

SAUN   And I mun tell ye all, there's little hopes for *Saundy* then.

WIN   The Rogue does it rarely.

PET   Nay, nay, Gentleman, no Quarrelling, unless it were to the purpose: Have you seen this young Lady Sir?

TRAN   No Sir: but I'm in Love with her Character. They say she has a Sister moves like a Whirlwind.

PET   Pray spare your Description Sir; that Furious Lady is my Mistriss; and till *I* have Married her, *Biancha* is Invisible; her Father has Sworn it, and, till then, you must all move Forty foot off.

TRAN   I thank you for your Admonition; I should have lost my Labour else; and since you are to do all of us the Favour, *I* shall be glad to be numbred among your Servants Sir.

PET   You will honour me to accept of me for yours. But pray Sir let me know who obliges me with this Civility?

TRAN   My Name is *Winlove*, Sir, a *Worstershire*[2] Gentleman; where *I* have something, an Old Man's Death will Intitle me to, not inconsiderable. Come, Gentlemen, let's not fall out, at least till the Fair *Biancha's* at Liberty; Shall we go sit out half an hour at the Tavern, and Drink her Health?

SAUN   Do my Bearns; and I'se Drink with ye to Countenance ye.

PET   I, I, agreed; Come, and then I'll to my Mistriss.

SAUN   Gude these Lades are o' *Saundyes* Mind, they'l lather take a Drink, nor Fight.

Exeunt.

    Enter MARGARET *and* BIANCHA.

MARG   Marry come up Proud Slut, Must you be making your self Fine before your Elder Sister? You are the Favourite you are, but I shall make you know your Distance; Give me that Necklace, and those Pendants, I'll have that Whisk too, there's an old Handkerchief good enough for you.

BIAN   Here, take 'em, Sister, I resign 'em freely, I wou'd give you all I have to Purchase your Kindness.

MARG   You Flattering Gypsie, I cou'd find in my Heart to Slit your Dissembling Tongue; Come, tell me and without Lying, which of your Sutors you Love best? Tell me, or I'll beat you to Clouts, and Pinch thee like a Fary.

BIAN   Believe me, Sister, of all Men alive, I never saw that Particular Face which I cou'd Fancy more than another.

MARG   Huswife you Lye; and I could find in my Heart to Dash thy Teeth down thy Throat; I know thou Lov'st *Geraldo*.

BIAN   If you Affect him Sister, I Vow to plead for you my self, but you shall have him.

MARG   O then belike you fancy Riches more, you Love Old *Woodall*.

BIAN   That Old Fool: Nay now I see you but Jested with me all this while; I know you are not Angry with me.

MARG   If this be Jest, then all the rest is so: I'll make ye tell me e're I have done with you Gossip.

    Enter BEAUFOY.

2. **Worstershire:** Worcestershire county in England.

BEAU   Why now now Dame, Whence grows this Insolence? *Bian-cha* bet thee in my Poor Girle; She Weeps; Fye, *Peg*, put off this Devillish Humour; Why dost thou Cross thy Tender Innocent Sister? When did she Cross thee with a Bitter Word?

MARG   Her Silence Flouts me, and I'll be Reveng'd. [*Flyes at* Bian-cha.

BEAU   What in my sight too? You scurvy I'll-natur'd Thing: Go, poor *Biancha*, get thee out of her way.   [*Exit.*

MARG   What will you not suffer me; nay, now I see she is your Treasure; She must have a Husband; and I Dance Bare-foot on her Wedding-Day: And for your Love to her, lead Apes in Hell. I see your care of me, I'll go and cry till I can find a way to be quit with her.   *Exit*

*   *   *

Enter MARGARET.

PET   Peace Sirrah, here she comes; now for a Rubbers at Cuffs. O Honey Pretty *Peg*, how do'st thou do Wench?

MARG   Marry come up Ragmanners, *Plain Peg*? Where were you bred? *I* am call'd *Mrs. Margaret*.

PET   No, no, thou ly'st *Peg*, thou'rt call'd plain *Peg*, and Bonny *Peg*, and sometimes *Peg the Curst*, take this from me; Hearing thy Wildness prais'd in every Town, thy Virtues Sounded and thy Beauty spoke off: my self am *mov'd* to take thee for my Wife.

MARG   I knew at first you were a *Moveable*.

PET   Why what's a Moveable.

MARG   A Joint Stool.

PET   Thou hast hit it *Peg*, come sit upon me.

MARG   *Asses* were made to bear, and so were you.

PET   Why now *I* see the World has much abus'd thee, 'twas told me thou wert rough and Coy, and Sullen, but *I* do find thee pleasant, Mild and Curteous; Thou can'st not frown, nor Pout, nor bite the Lip as angry wenches do. Thou art all sweetness.

MARG   Do not Provoke me, *I* won't stand still and here my self abus'd.

PET   What a Rogue was that told me thou wert Lame, thou art as streight as an Osier! and as Plyable, O what a rare walk's there! why there's a gate puts down the King of *Frances* best great Horse.

SAUN   And the King of *Scotland*'s tea.

PET   Where did'st thou Learn the grand Paw *Peg*? It becomes thee rarely.

MARG   Doe's it so sawcebox? how will a halter become you with a running knot under one Ear?

PET   Nay, no knot *Peg*, but the knot of Matrimony 'twixt thee and me, we shall be an Excellent *Mad Couple well match'd*.

MARG   *I* match'd to thee? what to such a fellow with such a Grid-iron face; with a Nose set on like a Candels end stuck against a

Mud wall; and a Mouth to eat Milk Porridge with Ladles? Foh, it almost turns my Stomach to look on't.

SAUN   Gud an your Stomach wamble to see his *Face*, What will ye dea when ye see his *Arse* Madam.

MARG   Marry come up *Abberdeen*, take that [*hits him a box on the Ear.*] and speak next when it comes to your turn.

SAUN   S'breed the Deel tak a gripe O yer faw fingers and Driss your Doublat for ye.

PET   Take heed *Peg*, *Sauny's* a Desperate Fellow.

MARG   You'r a couple of Logger heads Master and Man, that *I* can tell you.

PET   Nay, nay, Stay *Peg*, for all this *I* do like thee, and *I* mean to have thee, in truth I am they Servant.

MARG   Aye you, why then I'll give you a favour, and thus I'll tye it on, there's for you.   [*beats him.*]

SAUN   Out, out, *I'se* gea for *Scotland*, Gud an she beat ye *Saundy's* a Dead Man.

PET   *I'll* swear *I'll* cuff you, if you Strike agen.

MARG   That's the way to loose your Armes, if you strike a Woman, you are no Gentleman.

PET   A Herald *Peg*? Prithee Blazon my *Coat*.

MARG   I know not your *Coat*, but your *Crest* is a *Coxcombe*.

[*offers to go away.*]

PET   Stop her Sirrah, stop her.

SAUN   Let her gea her gate Sir, an e'n twa Deels and a Scotch wutch, blaw her weeme full of Wind.

PET   Stay her Sirrah, stay her, *I* say.

SAUN   S'breed Sir, stay her yer sen, but hear ye Sir, an her tale gea as fast as her tang, Gud ye ha meet with a Whupster, Sir.

PET   Prethee *Peg* stay, and *I'll* talk to thee in Earnest.

MARG   You may pump long enough er'e you get out a wise word, get a Night Cap to keep your brains warm.

PET   I mean thou shalt keep me warm in thy Bed *Peg*, What think'st thou of that *Peg*? in plain terms without more ado I have your Fathers Consent, your Portions agreed upon, your Joynture settled, and for your own part, be willing or unwilling all's one, you I will marry, I am resolv'd on't.

MARG   Marry come up Jack a Lent, without my Leave?

PET   A Rush for your Leave, here's a Clutter with a troublesom Woman, rest you contented, I'll have it so.

MARG   You shall be bak'd first, you shall; within there, ha!

PET   Hold, get me a Stick there *Sauny*; by this hand, deny to Promise before your Father, I'll not Leave you a whole rib, I'll make you do't and be glad on't.

MARG   Why you will not Murther me Sirrah? you are a couple of Rascals, *I* don't think, but you have pickt my Pockets.

SAUN I'se sooner pick your tang out O' your head, nor pick your Pocket.

PET Come leave your idle prating, have you I will or no man ever shall, whoever else attempts it his throat will I Cut, before he lyes one night with thee, it may be thine too for company; I am the Man am born to tame thee *Peg*.

Enter BEAUFOY, WOODAL *and* TRANIO.

Here comes your Father, never make denial, if you do, you know what follows.

MARG The Devil's in this fellow, he has beat me at my own Weapon, I have a good mind to marry him to try if he can *Tame* me.

BEAU Now *Petruchio*, how speed you with my Daughter.

PET How but well, it were Impossible I shou'd speed amiss, 'tis the best Naturd'st Lady—

BEAU Why how now Daughter, in your Dumps?

MARG You shew a Fathers care indeed to Match me with this mad Hectoring Fellow.

PET She has been abus'd Father, most unworthily, she is not Curst unless for Pollicy; for Patience, a second Grizel; betwixt us we have so agreed, the Wedding is to be on Thursday next.

SAUN Gud *Saundy's* gea for *Scotland* a Tuesday then.

WOOD Heark *Petruchio*, shee says shee'll see you hang'd first, is this your speeding? I shall make you refund.

PET Pish, that's but a way she has gotten, I have Wood her, Won her, and shee's my own; we have made a bargin that before Company she shall maintain a little of her Extravagant Humour, for she must not seem to fall off from't too soon; when we are alone, we are the kindest, Lovingst, tenderst Chickins to one another! Pray Father provide the Feast, and bid the Guests, I must home to settle some things, and fetch some Writings in order to her Joynture.—Farewel Gallants, give me thy hand *Peg*.

*   *   *

Act V

Enter MARGARET *and* BIANCHA.

BIAN But is't Possible Sister, he shu'd have us'd you thus?

MARG Had I serv'd him as bad as *Eve* did *Adam*, he coud not have us'd me worse; but I am resolv'd now I'm got home again I'll be reveng'd, I'll muster up the Spight of all the Curs'd Women since *Noahs* Flood to do him Mischief, and add new Vigour to my Tongue; I have not par'd my Nails this fortnight, they are long enough to do him some Execution, that's my Comfort.

BIAN Bless me Sister, how you talk.

MARG Thou art a Fool *Biancha*, come Learn of me; thou art Mar-

ried to a Man too, thou dost not know but thou mayst need my
Councel, and make good use on't; Thy Husband bares thee fair
yet, but take heed of going home with him, for when once he has
thee within his verge, 'tis odds he'll have his freaks too; there's no
trusting these Men: Thy temper is soft and easy, thou must Learn
to break him, or he'll break thy Heart.

BIAN   I must Confess I shou'd be Loath to be so us'd, but sure Mr.
Winlove is of a better Disposition.

MARG   Trust him and hang him, they'r all alike; Come thou shalt
be my Schollar, learn to Frown, and cry out for unkindness, but
brave Anger, thou hast a Tongue, make use on't; Scould, Fight,
Scratch, Bite, any thing, still take Exceptions at all he does, if
there be Cause or not, if there be reason for't he'll Laugh at thee.
I'll make *Petruchio* glad to wipe my Shoes, or walk my Horse, ere
I have done with him.

Enter PETRUCHIO, WINLOVE, SAUNY.

BIAN   Peace Sister, our Husbands are both here.

MARG   Thou Child I am glad on't, I'll speak louder,

PET   Well Brother *Winlove* now we are truly happy, never were
Men so blest with two such Wives.

VVIN   I am glad to hear you say so Sir, my own I'm sure I'm blest in.

PET   Yours, why *Biancha*'s a Lyon, and *Margaret* a meer Lamb to
her: I tell thee *Winlove*, there's no Man living tho I say't, (but 'tis
no matter since she does not hear me) that has a Wife so gentle,
and so active and affable, poor thing I durst be sworn she wou'd
walk barefoot a hundred Miles to do me good.

MARG   No but she wou'd not, nor one Mile neither.

SAUN   Now have at your Luggs, Sir.

PET   O *Peg*, art thou there? How dost thou do my Dear?

MARG   You may go look, What's that to you?

SAUN   Stand o' yer guard Sir, Gud *Saundy* will put on his head
Peice.

PET   I am glad to hear thee say thou'rt well introth.

MARG   Never the better for you, which you shall find.

PET   Nay I know thou lov'st me, Prithee take up my Glove *Peg*.

MARG   I take up your Glove; Marry come up, command your Servants, look you there it lyes.

PET   I am glad to see thee merry, poor wanton Rogue.

MARG   'Tis very well, you think you are in the Country but you are
mistaken, the case is alter'd, I am at home now, and my own dis-
poser; Go swagger at your greazy Lubber there, your Patient Wife
will make you no more Sport, she has a Father will allow her Meat
and Lodging, and another gaits Chamber-Maid then a *Highlander*.

SAUN   Gud an ye were a top of *Grantham Steple* that aw the Toon
may hear what a Scauden Queen ye are, out, out.

PET Why what's the matter *Peg*? I never saw thee in so jolly a Humour, sure thou hast been Drinking.

SAUN Gud has she, haud ye tang, ye faw dranken Swine, out, out, out, was ye tak a Drink and nere tak *Saundy* to yee, out, out, out.

MARG 'Tis like I have, I am the sitter to talk to you, for no sober Woman is a Companion for you.

PET Troth thou sayst right, we are excellently Matcht.

MARG Well mark the end on't, *Petruchio* prithee come hither, I have something to say to you.

SAUN De ye nea budge a foot Sir, Deel a my saul bo she'll Scratch your eyn out.

PET Well, your Pleasure Madam.

MARG First thou art a Pittiful fellow, a thing beneath me, which I scorn and Laugh at, ha, ha, ha.

WIN She holds her own yet I see.

MARG I know not what to call thee, thou art no Man, thou coudst not have a Woman to thy Mother, thou paltry, Scurvy, ill condition'd fellow, dost thou not tremble to think how thou hast us'd me; What are you silent Sir? *Biancha* see, Looks he not like a Disbanded Officer, with that hanging dog look there? I must eat nothing because your Cook has Roasted the Mutton dry, as you us'd to have it when your Worship was a Batchellor, I must not go to Bed neither, because the Sheets are Damp.

PET Mark you *Peg*; What a strange Woman are you to Discourse openly the Fault of your Servants in your own Family.

MARG No, no, Sir, this wont serve your turn; your Old Stock of Impudence won't carry you off so: I'll speak your Fame, and tell what a fine Gentleman you are; how Valliantly you, and halfe a Douzen of your Men, got the better of a Single Woman, and made her lose her Supper,

SAUN Gud she Lyes Sir; I wou'd a gin her an awd Boot tull a made Tripes on, and it wod a bin bra Meat with *Mustard*, and she wou'd nea have it.

MARG My Faults? No, good Squire of the Country, you thought to have Tam'd me, I warrant, in good time; why you see I am even with you; Your Quiet Patient Wife, that will go no more in the Country with you, but will stay in Town, to Laugh at your Wife Worship, and wish you more Wit.

PET I shou'd Laugh at that; why we are just now a going; *Sauny* go get the Horses ready quickly.

SAUN Gud will I Sir; I'se Saddle a Highland-Wutch to Carry your Bride; Gud she'll mount your Arse for you Madam.

MARG Sirrah, touch a Horse, and I'll Curry your Coxcomb for you: No Sir, I won't say, Pray let me not go; but boldly, I won't go; you force me if you can or dare: You see I am not Tongue-ty'd, as silent as you thought you made me.

PET   Prithee *Peg*, Peace a little, I know thou canst Speak, leave
now, or thoul't have nothing to say to morrow.

MARG   Yes, I'll say this over again, and something more if I can
think on't, to a poor despised *man of Clouts:* Sister, how he
smoakes now he's off his own Dunghill.

PET   Prithee *Peg* leave making a Noise; I'faith thou'lt make my
Head ach.

MARG   Noise? Why this is Silence to what I intend; I'll talk Louder
than this, every Night in my Sleep.

SAUN   The Dee'l shall be your Bed fellow for *Sawndy* then.

MARG   I will learn to Rail at thee in all Languages; Thunder shall
be soft-musick to my Tongue.

SAUN   The Dee'l a bit Scot's ye gat to brangle in, marry the Dee'l gi
ye a Clap wi a *French* Thunder-bolt.

PET   Very pretty; Prithee go on.

MARG   I'll have a Collection of all the Ill Names that ever was Invented, and call you over by 'em twice a-day.

PET   And have the Catalogue publish'd for the Education of young
Scolds: Proceed *Peg.*

MARG   I'll have you Chain'd to a Stake at *Billingsgate*, and Baited
by the Fish-wives, while I stand to Hiss 'em on.

PET   Ha, ha, ha; Witty *Peg*, forward.

MARG   You shan't dare to Blow your Nose, but when I bid you; you
shall know me to be the Master.

SAUN   Wuns gat her to the Stool of Repantance, Sir.

PET   Nay, I believe, thou wilt go in Breeches shortly; On, on; What
have you no more on't? Ha, ha, ha.

MARG   D'ye Laugh and be Hang'd? I'll spoil your Sport.

   (Flys at him.)

PET   Nay, *Peg,* Hands off; I thought you wou'd not have Disgrac'd
your Good Parts, to come to Blows so soon; Prithee Chide on,
thou can'st not believe what Delight I take to hear thee; It does
become thee so well: What Pumpt dry already? Prithee talk more
and longer, and faster, and sharper, this is nothing.

MARG   I'll see you in the *Indies* before I'll do any thing to please
you; D'ye like it?

PET   Extreamly! On *Peg*, you'll cooll too fast.

MARG   Why then Mark me, if it were to save thee from Drowning,
or Breaking thy Neck, I won't speak one word more to thee these
Two Months.

   (Sits Sullenly)

SAUN   Ah Gud an ye do nea Ly, Madam.

PET   Nay, Good *Peg*, be not so hard-harted. What Melancholly all
o'th' sudden? Come, get up, we'll send for the Fidlers, and have a
Dance; Tho'lt break thy Elbow with Leaning on that hard Table:

Sawny, go get your Mistriss a Cushion; Alas! I doubt she's not well; Look to her Sister.

BIAN   Are you not well, Sister? What ail you? Pray speak Sister: Indeed, Brother, you have so Vext her, she'll be Sick.

PET   Alas, alas! I know what's the matter with her, she has the Tooth-Ach. See how she holds her Cheek; the Wind has gotten into her Teeth, by keeping her Mouth open this Cold Weather.

BIAN   Indeed it may be so Brother, she uses to be troubled with that Pain sometimes.

PET   Without all Question; Poor *Peg*, I pitty thee; Which Tooth is it? Wilt thou have it Drawn, *Peg*? The Tooth-Ach makes Fooles of all the *Physitians*; there is no Cure, but Drawing: What say'st thou? Wilt thou have it pull,d out? Well, thou shalt. *Sauny*, Run, Sirrah, hard by, you know where my Barber Lives that Drew me a Tooth last Week, fetch him quickly; What d'ye stand staring at? Run and fetch him immediately, or I'll cut your Legs off.

SAUN   Gud I'se fetch ean to pull her head off an ye wull.

[*Exit.*]

WIN   This will make her find her Tongue agen, or else for certain she has lost it.

PET   Her Tongue, Brother? Alas! You see her Face is so Swell'd, she cannot speak.

BIAN   You Jest Brother; her Face is not swell'd. Pray let me see, Sister, I can't perceive it.

PET   Not Swell'd? Why you are blind then; Prithee let her alone, you trouble her.

      Enter SAUNY *and* BARBER.

Here, Honest Barber, have you brought your Instruments?

BARBER   Yes Sir; What must I do?

PET   You must Draw that Gentlewoman a Tooth there; Prithee do it neatly, and as gently as thou can'st; And, de hear me, take care you don't tear her Gums.

BARBER   I warrant you Sir.

SAUN   Hear ye Sir, Cou'd not ye Mistake? and pull her Tang out instead of her Teeth.

BIAN   I'll be gone, I can't endure to see her put to so much Pain.

[*Exit.*]

BARB   Pray, Madam, open your Mouth, that I may see which Tooth it is.

      [*She strikes him.*]

Why Sir, Did you send for me to Abuse me.

SAUN   Gud be nea Angry, Ye ha ne aw yer Pay yet Sir. Cud ye not Mistake, and Draw her Tang in stead of her Teeth Sir.

PET   No, no. But it seems now she wo' not have it Drawn. Go, there's something for your Paines however.

      [*Exit* BARBER.]

SAU   Ye sid ha taken my Counsel Sir.

WIN   This will not do, Sir. You cannot raise the Spirit you have laid, with all your Arts.

PET   I'll try; Have at her once more. W*inlove*, you must assist me; I'll make her Stir, if I can't make her Speak. Look, look! alas! How Pale she is! She's gone o'th' sudden; Body O' me, she's stiff too; undone, undone, What an unfortunate Man am I? she's gone! she's gone! never had man so great a Loss as I; O *Winlove*, pity me, my poor *Peg* is Dead, dear *Winlove* call in my Father and the Company that they may share in this sad Spectacle, and help my Sorrows with their joyning Griefs.

                             Exit WINLOVE.

Speak, or by this hand. I'll bury thee alive; *Sauny* thou seest in how sad a condition thy poor Master is in, thy good Mistriss is Dead, hast to the next Church and get the Bier and the Bearers hither, I'll have her buried out of hand; Run *Sauny*.

SAUN   An you'll mack her Dead, we'll bury her deep enough, we'll put her doon intill a Scotch Coalepit, and she shall rise at the Deel's arse o' Peake.

                                        Exit.

PET   I will see that last Pious act Perform'd, and then betake my self to a willing Exile; my own Country's Hell, now my dear *Peg* has left it. Not yet, upon my Life I think thou hast a mind to be buried quick, I hope thou hast.

      Enter WINLOVE, BEAUFOY, *Sir* LYONELL, WOODALL, BIAN-CHA, TRANIO, JAMY, *& c.*

BEAU   Bless me Son *Petruchio*, Is my dear Daughter Dead?

PET   Alas, alas, 'tis but too true, wou'd I had ta'ne her roome.

BEAU   Why methinks she looks brisk, fresh and lively.

PET   So much Beauty as she had must needs leave some wandring remains to hover still about her face.

BEAU   What could her Disease be?

PET   Indeed I grieve to tell it, but truth must out, she Dyed for spight, she was strangely Infected.

BIAN   Fye Sister, for shame speak, Will you let him abuse you thus?

PET   Gentlemen you are my loving Friends and knew the Virtues of my matchless Wife, I hope you will accompany her Body to its long home.

ALL   We'll all wait on you.

BEAU   Thou wilt break her heart indeed.

PET   I warrant you Sir, 'tis tougher then so.

   Enter SAUNY *and* BEARERS *with a* BEIR.

SAUN   I bring you here vera gued Men, an she be nea Dead Sir, for a Croon more they'll bury her quick.

PET   O honest friends, you'r Wellcome, you must take up that Corps, how! hard-hearted, Why de ye not weep? the loss of so much Beauty and goodness, take her up, and lay her upon the Beir.

I BEAR   Why what d'ye mean Sir? She is not Dead.

PET   Rogues, tell me such a Lye to my face? Take her up or I'll swinge ye.

SAUN   Tak her up, tak her up, we'll mak her Dead Billy, ye'st a twa Croons mear, tak her up Man.

I BEAR   Dead or alive all's one to us, let us but have our fees.

PET   There, nay she is stiff, however on with her, Will you not speak yet? So here take these Strings and bind her on the Beir, she had an active stirring body when she Liv'd, she may chance fall off the Hearse now she's Dead. So, now take her up and away, come Gentlemen you'll follow, I mean to carry her through the *Strand* as far as Sr. *James*'s, People shall see what respect I bore her—She shall have so much Ceremony to attend her now she's Dead. There my Coach shall meet her and carry her into the Country, I'll have her laid in the Vault belonging to my Family, she shall have a Monument; some of you inquire me out a good Poet to write her Epitaph suitable to her Birth, Quallity and Conditions, Pitty the remembrance of so many Virtues shou'd be lost; March on, I wou'd say more, but grief Checks my Tongue.

MARG   Father, Sister, Husband, Are you all Mad? Will you expose me to open shame? Rogues set me down you had best.

PET   A Miracle! a Miracle! she Lives! Heaven make me thankful for't, set her down, Liv'st thou my Poor *Peg*?

MARG   Yes that I do, and will to be your Tormentor.

SAUN   Out, out, gea her nea Credit, gud she's as Dead as mine Grannam, talk her, away with her, Sir.

PET   Bless me my hopes are all vanisht agen, 'tis a Demon speaks within her Body; Take her up again, we'll bury 'em together.

MARG   Hold, hold, my dear *Petruchio*, you have overcome me, and I beg your Pardon, henceforth I will not dare to think a thought shall Cross your Pleasure, set me at Liberty, and on my knees I'll make my Recantation.

ALL   Victoria, victoria, the field is won.

PET   Art thou in earnest *Peg*? May I believe thee?

SAUN   You ken very well she was awway's a lying Quean when she was Living, and wull ye believe her now she's Dead?

MARG   By all that's good not truth it self truer.

PET   Then thus I free thee, and make thee Mistriss both of my self
and all I have.

SAUN   S'breed bo ye'l nea gi *Saundy* tull her Sir?

WOOD   Take heed of giving away your Power, Sir.

PET   I'll venture it, nor do I fear I shall repent my bargain.

MARG   I'm sure *I* will not give you Cause, y've taught me now what
'tis to be a Wife, and *I'*ll still shew my self your humble Handmaid.

PET   My best *Peg*, we will change kindness and be each others Servant; Gentlemen why do you not Rejoyce with me?

BEAU   *I* am so full of joy *I* cannot Speak, may you be happy, this is
your Wedding day.

SAUN   Shall *Saundy* get her a Bride-Cake, and Brake o'r her Head
Sir? and wee's gatt us a good Wadding Dunner.

*   *   *

CHARLES JOHNSON

The Cobler of Preston[†]

[Charles Johnson's play *The Cobler of Preston* was one of two plays
based on *The Taming of the Shrew* being performed in London in 1716.
It was performed in London's Drury Lane Theatre. Like *The Taming of
the Shrew*, *The Cobler of Preston* begins with a nobleman playing a trick
on a drunken man of a lower social standing, convincing him that he is
not the poor cobbler Kit but a wealthy lord. As the title suggests, Johnson's play is not about the taming of an unruly wife but the disciplinary
transformation of the cobbler himself, whom the nobleman wishes to
punish for what he considers to be his disorderly social behavior. By
the end of the play, the cobbler has been made to relinquish any aspi-
rations of climbing the social ladder and agrees to be "mannerly to [his]
Superiors."]

From *Act I*

Enter SIR CHARLES BRITON, SQUIRE JOLLY, HUNTSMEN,
SERVANTS, *& c. as from Hunting.*

SIR CHAR   I was never more disappointed in my Life; the Morning
promised us good Sport.

JOLLY   How thick the Mists fell, and puzzled the Scent!

SIR CHAR   And yet, for all that, *Bellman* made it good at yon Hedge
Corner in the coldest Fault.

---

† From *The Cobler of Preston* (London: W. Williams, 1716).

JOLLY I think *Ringwood* is as good a Dog as he, Sir *Charles*; for twice to Day, I observ'd him to pick out the faintest Scent— What's here! one Dead or Drunk! Look—Does the Fellow breathe?—

HUNTS Yes, Sir, he breaths—If he were not well warm'd within, this would be but a cold Bed this hazy Weather—Hah! why, Sir, this is our drunken Neighbour *Kit*—

SIR CHA This Rascal is the greatest Politician, and the great Sot in our Parish, Mr. *Jolly*—His Head is perpetually confounded with the Fumes of Ale and Faction—

JOLLY His Habit shews him a Cobler.

SIR CHA Even so; but he has laid aside cobling of Shoes, to mend our Constitution—

JOLLY Our Constitution has been too much handled by such Fellows as these, who have of late Years been the Journeymen to a Sett of merry Statesmen, that turned all Government into a Jest—

SIR CHAR This Fellow has fancy'd himself of some Consequence a great while, and has been extreamly troublesome and factious; there has been hardly any Iniquity committed in this Country, but this drunken Knave has had a Finger in it—What if we should take this Opportunity to punish him a little, and practice upon him for our Diversion?

JOLLY As how?

SIR CHAR Suppose we should convey him thus drunk and sensless, as he is, to my House, and lodge him in the best Apartment; strip him of his Rags, change his Linnen, put him into a Down-Bed, and order him to be attended in every Respect as a Man of Quality: Will it not strangely amaze him when he awakes, to find his Condition so wonderfully alter'd?

JOLLY It must surprize him, and make his Behaviour entertaining.

SIR CHAR We'll put the Project in execution this instant. *John* and *William*, do you take up that Corpse and beat it into the best Chamber—and do as I have said—I'll follow, and give you farther Directions. (*Ex.*

* * *

From *Act 2*

Enter a SERVANT *running hastily, and in a great Fright— The rest quit the Cobler.*

[Having convinced KIT that he is a lord, his deceivers now tell KIT he has a rebellion on his hands.]

LOREN What's the matter you stare so wildly!

KIT Aye, what's the matter, Friend?

SERV Ah, my good Lord! a whole Troop of Dragoons have sur-

rounded the House, they charge you with Treason, and say, they
have a Warrant to hang you upon one of the highest Elms before
your Palace Gate.—

KIT   High Treason!—Hah!—I have been a little inclin'd to Rebellion, 'tis true, but sure that was when I was a Cobler only. What
shall I do, *Diego*? Cou'd not you clap me into an empty
Hogshead in the Cellar?—Do, *Diego*, do, and throw a *cheshire*
Cheese and a Peck Loaf or two after me; and I'll retire from this
vile World, like a Peace-making Minister, and pass the rest of my
Days in Solitude and Sleep—

DIEGO   Alas, my Lord! they'll put us all to the Torture, who can
keep a Secret when a Sword is at his Throat?

KIT   Good lack!—good lack! This is worse than Senior *Palfrey*'s Re-
ceit. Pray, Friend, what is your King's Name? for I have been in
such Visions, my Memory is absolutely spoil'd.

LOREN   *Alphonso.*

KIT   Oh *Alphonso*! Aye, why if they go to that then, Squire *Blunder*
and I took the Oaths together to his Majesty at the Quarter Ses-
sions.

LOREN   Then you think taking the Oaths absolves you from every
Thing for the future?

KIT   Aye, for when I have sworn I won't be a Rebel, what signifies
what I do after, you know?

LOREN   Right!

KIT   Why aye; there was Squire *Clumsey*, Squire *Blunder*, Nick
Quickset and Sir *Tim. Dodypole*, and I—used to Drink, and
Roar, and talk Treason, it would do your Heart good!—What,
mun one not be Fisky a little bit or so in this Country, Hah!

LOREN   Nay, that I know not: But hark, I fear, my Lord, your Servants have capitulated—Aye, 'tis so! I see the Captain is coming
in: He will take your Confession to be sure.

> *Enter* SQUIRE JOLLY *as a Captain of Dragoons, and* SER-
> VANTS *as Dragoons with him.*

CAPT   My Lord, I am yours—I have a small Affair to dispatch
here——Read this, my Lord, read this—

KIT   I cannot read, an it please your Honour.

CAPT   Read it to him, Slaves.

> (*Diego reads*)

Captain,
When Pedro Lorenzo, *Conde of* Alcantara, *sees this, you are to Ex-*
ecute him forthwith, unless he shows good Reason to the contrary.
                                                            Alphonso.

CAPT   If you have a Prayer or two ready made, huddle it over as
fast as you can; for I am in haste.

KIT   In haste, Sir!

CAPT   Oons Sir———yes, in haste! Come, come, be quick, or I'll
Halter you, and put you out of your Pain in a Moment.

KIT   Give me leave, Sir, to say, I am not the Person you take me
for; I am but a Cobler, Sir.——

CAPT   *Frederico*, do your Office. (*Puts the Halter about his Neck.*

KIT   Ah, dear Sir, my dear Sir, spare me but one Word: Recom-
mend me to my Wife *Joan*; and tell his Majesty, that I ca—not
help—ta—aking it ve—ry i—ill at his Hands.

CAPT   Very well, my Lord! you expect to die like a Man of Qual-
ity—and I'll hold your Lordship a Thousand Pounds now this
Fellow, simply as he looks here———takes off your Head—at one
Blow!—Draw *Pedro*—I warrant you, he nicks the Joint!—Come,
Kneel, kneel———

KIT   Oh, spare my Life, Captain, and I'll Peach; I'll tell you the
whole Plot.

CAPT   Well—you look so penitentially, I'll try you: if what you have
to say will deserve a Reprieve, you shall have it.—Come, begin;
but be very clear and full in your Discovery, without the least
Prevarication.

KIT   Yes indeed, I will make a full and true Discovery.

CAPT   Come then, begin—Was not you concerned in some or all of
the Riots and Rebellions that have been in this Country?

KIT   I do not remember.

CAPT   How came you among the Traitors?

KIT   I do not know.

CAPT   Who sent you thither?

KIT   I cannot tell.

CAPT   What are the Names of your Companions?

KIT   I have quite forgot.

CAPT   Had you any Money or Strong Beer given you?

KIT   My Memory quite fails me of a sudden.

CAPT   How the Rogue prevaricates.! Sirrah, Sirrah, you learnt this
of your Betters: Come, off with his Head; for he can have no farther use for it.

KIT   Ah, dear Sir, do not ye be so hasty, and I'll try to remember.

CAPT   Quickly then, while you have Life to do it.

KIT   *Imprimis* then, I was drawn away, as they sayn, to Drink your
Jacobite Papish Healths; which I did at first for the Love of the
Beer only, as I am a Christian.

CAPT   Well, go on.

KIT   Then, when I was very Boosie, I used to leave my Stall, and go
a Rioting with *Timothy Sprig* the Tythingman, *Edward Belfrey*
our Sexton, *Patrick Quaver* the Clerk, *Dick Marrowbone, John a
Geates, David Bullock.*———

CAPT   Well, and what then?

KIT   Why then we did beat and knock down all People who were soberly disposed? and we did likewise most abominably disuse both the King and the Parliament.

CAPT   Who encourag'd you to do all this?

KIT   The Honourable Sir *Andrew Squib* the Worshipful *Nicholas Quickmatch*, Esq; and the Reverend Mr. *Peter Pinacle*.

CAPT   What Reasons did they give you for it?

KIT   Money and Strong Beer.

CAPT   O my Conscience, I believe thy Confession now is pretty honest—Fear has made thee speak Truth.

KIT   Aye, I have been wheadled and terrify'd too into this Plot, indeed Captain.—Why what cou'd a poor weak Sinner do? Our Parson frighted me with Fire and Brimstone, and the Squire tempted me with Beef and *October*; what could frail Flesh and Blood do in such a case?

CAPT   Do you now promise to amend your Life for the future?

KIT   Most sincerely.

CAPT   Then get thee Home, honest *Kit*; learn to Cobble thy Shoes, and let the Commonwealth alone.—Look upon those *Spaniards*, now their Whiskers are off.—Do you know 'em?

(*The Servants pull off their Wigs and Whiskers.*)

KIT   Hah; what, is not that thy old Friend *Peter Pimpernell?*—and *Diego*, there is my dear Boy *Jack*, the Postilion of *Blossom-Hall*.

CAPT   Aye, and that's your good Master, Sir *Charles Briton*; whose Advice, if you had follow'd, you wou'd never have fall'n into these Scrapes, *Christopher*.

KIT   Ah, good your Worship! I beg your Worship's Pardon for being so free in your House, as they sayn.

DIEGO   There's your Wife below, has seiz'd upon the Butler, and swears she will have him since she has lost her 'tother Husband—

KIT   Why, let her make good her Title, and in Troth I'll serve Sir *Charles* in his stead, if his Honour pleases———A Butler's a snug Thing, as I may say. In troth I am heartily glad this Matter is settled; it is a most perplexing thing not to know who one is— I have been in very whimsical Circumstances in Troth——

SIR CHAR   Aye, and we will transform you again, if you do not keep your Promise to amend your Manners for the future.

KIT   I will, I do promise most faithfully.

SIR CHAR   Upon these Conditions my Cellar Doors shall be always open to you———

KIT   I humbly thank your Honour.

SIR CHAR   Stand aside awhile and attend the Entertainment we prepared for your Lordship. You have a sort of Right to govern here to day.

A Masque.

SIR CHAR   Go, comfort thy Wife. Mend thy Life and thy Shoes. Be
   courteous to thy Customers, and mannerly to thy Superiors. Live
   soberly, and be a good Christian. And remember you are obliged
   to me for bringing you to the Knowledge of your self.

KIT   To be sure I shall never forget your Honour's Kindness. I'll
   from this Hour leave Sir *Andrew Squib*'s Cellar, and be faithful to
   yours, yours, and for the future mix Loyalty with my Liquor.

Our Squire, for Kit, *may by himself Rebel,*
To his mad Politicks I bid Farewel.
Henceforth I'll never Rail against the Crown,
Nor swallow Traytors Healths, in Bumpers down;
Nor sham Pretences of Religion forge,
But with true Protestants cry, Live King GEORGE.

FINIS.

DAVID GARRICK

Catharine and Petruchio[†]

[David Garrick (1717–1779) is arguably the most renowned Shakespearean actor not only of the eighteenth century but of all time. He
was certainly one of the great, shaping influences of English theater,
whose very heart and soul, he felt, lay in the works of Shakespeare. After a sensational debut as Richard III in 1741, Garrick went on to
make his reputation as a great tragedian. He was also a theater manager and playwright who composed original dramas and wrote adaptations of already existing works. Garrick's adaptation, *Catharine
and Petruchio* (1754), supplanted Shakespeare's text until the mid-
nineteenth century.]

Advertisement.

The following PROLOGUE was Spoken to the Dramatic Pastoral,
called the *Winter's Tale*, and this Comedy; both of which are altered
from *Shakespeare*, and were perform'd the same Night.
   Some of the Lines of the PROLOGUE are only relative to the
Winter's Tale, yet as the Publication of that Pastoral is defer'd for
some Time, and as the PROLOGUE has been particularly desir'd,
it is hop'd that it will not be disagreeable to the Reader to see it
prefix'd to this Comedy.

[†] David Garrick, *Catharine and Petruchio: A Comedy, In Three Acts* (London: J. and
   R. Tonson, 1756).

Prologue

to the
Winter's Tale.

and
Catharine and Petruchio.

(Both from SHAKESPEAR.)
Written and Spoken by
Mr. *GARRICK.*

To various Things the Stage has been compar'd,
   As apt Ideas strike each humorous Bard:
This Night, for want of better Simile,
Let this our Theatre a Tavern be:
The Poets Vintners, and the Waiters we.   5
So as the Cant, and Custom of the Trade is,
You're welcome Gem'min, kindly welcome Ladies.
To draw in Customers, our Bills are spread,
You cannot miss the Sign, 'tis Shakespear's Head.
From this same Head, this Fountain-head divine,   10
For different Palates springs a different Wine!
In which no Tricks, to strengthen, or to thin 'em—
Neat as imported—no French Brandy in em'—
Hence for the choicest Spirits flow Champaign;
Whose sparkling Atoms shoot thro' every Vein,   15
Then mount in Magic Vapours to th' enraptur'd Brain!
Hence flow for martial Minds Potations strong,
And sweet Love Potions, for the Fair and Young.
[To the Upper Gallery]
For you my Hearts of Oak, for your Regale,   20
There's good old English Stingo, mild and stale.
For high, luxurious Souls with luscious Smack:
There's Sir John Falstaff, is a Butt of Sack:
And if the stronger Liquors more invite ye;
Bardolph is Gin, and Pistol Aqua Vitæ.   25
But shou'd you call for Falstaff, where to find him,
He's gone—nor left one Cup of Sack behind him.
Sunk in his Elbow-Chair, no more he'll roam;
No more, with merry Wags, to Eastcheap come;
He's gone,—to jest, and laugh, and give his Sack at Home.   30
As for the learned Critics, grave and deep,
Who catch at Words, and catching fall asleep;
Who in the Storms of Passion—hum, —and haw!
For such, our Master will no Liquor draw—
So blindly thoughtful, and so darkly read,   35

They take Tom Durffy's, *for the* Shakespear's *Head.*
   A Vintner once acquir'd both Praise and Gain,
And sold much Perry *for the best* Champaign.
Some Rakes, this precious Stuff did so allure;
They drank whole Nights—what's that—when Wine is pure?   40
"Come fill a Bumper, Jack—, *I will my Lord—*
"Here's Cream! —Damn'd fine!—immense!—upon my Word!"
Sir William, *what say you?—The best, believe me—*
In this—Eh Jack!—*the Devil can't deceive me.*
Thus the wife Critic too, mistakes his Wine,   45
Cries out with lifted Hands, 'tis great!—Divine!
Then jogs his Neighbour, as the Wonders strike him;
This Shakespear! Shakespear!—*oh there's nothing like him!*
In this Night's various, and enchanted Cup,
Some little Perry's *mixt for filling up.*   50
The Five long Acts, from which our Three are taken,
Stretch'd out to *sixteen Years, lay by, forsaken.
Left then this precious Liquor run to waste,
'Tis now confin'd and bottled for your Taste.
'Tis my chief Wish, my joy, my only Plan,   55
To lose no Drop *of that immortal Man!*

Dramatis Personæ

PETRUCHIO	MR. WOODWARD.
BAPTISTA	MR. BURTON.
HORTENSIO	MR. MOZEEN.
GRUMIO	MR. YATES.
MUSIC-MASTER	MR. JEFFERSON.
BIONDELLO	MR. BLAKES.
PEDRO	MR. CLOUGH.
TAYLOR	MR. H. VAUGHAN.
NATHANIEL	MR. W. VAUGHAN.
PETER	MR. ACKMAN.
NICHOLAS	MR. ATKINS.
PHILIP	MR. MARR.
JOSEPH	MR. LEWIS.
CATHARINE	MRS. CLIVE.
BIANCA	MRS. BENNET.
CURTIS	MRS. BRADSHAW.

Scene, *Padua.*

---

* The Action of the *Winter's Tale*, as written by *Shakespear*, comprehends Sixteen Years.

Act I

Scene, BAPTISTA'S *House.*

Enter BAPTISTA, PETRUCHIO *and* GRUMIO.

BAPTISTA   Thus have I, 'gainst my own Self-Interest,
Repeated all the worst you are t'expect
From my shrewd Daughter, *Cath'rine*; if you'll venture,
Maugre my plain and honest Declaration,
You have my free Consent, win her, and wed her.   5
PETRUCHIO   Signior *Baptista*, thus it stands with me.
Anhonio, my Father, is deceased:
You knew him well, and knowing him, know me,
Left solely Heir to all his Lands and Goods,
Which I have better'd, rather than decreas'd.   10
And I have thrust myself into the World,
Haply to wive and thrive as best I may:
My Business asketh Haste, old Signior,
And ev'ry Day I cannot come to wooe.
Let Specialties be therefore drawn between us,   15
That Cov'nants may be kept on either Hand.
BAPTISTA   Yes, when the special Thing is well obtain'd,
My Daughter's Love, for that is all in all.
PETRUCHIO   Why, that is nothing; for I tell you, Father,
I am as peremptory, as she proud-minded;   20
And where two raging Fires meet together,
They do consume the Thing that feeds their Fury.
Tho' little Fire grows great with little Wind,
Yet extreme Gusts will blow out Fire and all;
So I to her, and so she yields to me;   25
For I am rough, and wooe not like a Babe.
GRUMIO   Nay, look you, Sir, he tells you flatly what
his Mind is: Why give him Gold enough and marry him to a
Puppet, or an old Trot with ne'er a Tooth in her Head. Tho'
she have as many Diseases as two and fifty Horses; why noth-   30
ing comes amiss, so Money comes withal.
BAPTISTA   As I have shew'd you, Sir, the coarser Side,
Now let me tell you she is young and beauteous,
Brought up as best becomes a Gentlewoman;
Her only Fault (and that is Fault enough)   35
[i]s that she is intolerably froward;
[o]f that you can away with, she is yours.
GRUMIO   I pray you, Sir, let him see her while the
Humour lasts. O'my Word an' she knew him
as well as I do, she would think Scolding would   40
do little Good upon him. She may perhaps call

him half a Score Knaves, or so; why, that's
nothing; an' he begin once, she'll find her Match.
I'll tell you what, Sir, an' she stand him but a
little, he will throw a Figure in her Face, and so   45
disfigure her with it, that she shall have no more
Eyes to see withal than a Cat—You know him
not, Sir.

BAPTISTA   And will you woo her, Sir?

PETRUCHIO   Why came I hither but to that Intent?   50
Think you a little Din can daunt my Ears?
Have I not, in my Time, heard Lions roar?
Have I not heard the Sea puff'd up with Winds?
Have I not heard great Ord'nance in the Field?
And Heav'n's Artillery thunder in the Skies?   55
Have I not in a pitched Battle heard
Loud 'Larums, neighing Steeds, and Trumpets clangue?
And do you tell me of a Woman's Tongue;
That gives not half so great a Blow to hear,
As will a Chesnut in a Farmer's Fire;   60
Tush, tush! scare Boys with Bugs.

BAPTISTA   Then thou'rt the Man,
The Man for *Cath'rine*, and her Father too:
That shall she know, and know my Mind at once.
I'll portion her above her gentler Sister,   65
New-married to *Hortensio*:
And if with scurril Taunt, and squeamish Pride,
She make a Mouth, and will not taste her Fortune,
I'll turn her forth to seek it in the World;
Nor henceforth shall she know her Father's Doors.   70

PETRUCHIO   Say'st thou me so? Then as your Daughter, Signior,
Is rich enough to be *Petruchio*'s Wife;
Be she as curst as *Socrates' Zantippe*,
She moves me not a Whit—Were she as rough,
As are the swelling *Adriatick* Seas,   75
I come to wive it wealthily in *Padua*;
If wealthily, then happily in *Padua*.

BAPTISTA   Well may'st thou wooe, and happy be thy Speed;
But be thou arm'd for some unhappy Words.

PETRUCHIO   Aye, to the Proof, as Mountains are for Winds, 80
That shake not, tho' they blow perpetually.

CATHARINE *and the* MUSIC-MASTER *make a noise within.*

MUSIC-MASTER   *within.*
Help! help!

CATHARINE   *within.*
—Out of the House, you scraping Fool.

PETRUCHIO   What Noise is that?

BAPTISTA   Oh, nothing; this is nothing—   85
  My Daughter *Catharine*, and her Music-master;
  This is the third I've had within this Month:
  She is an Enemy to Harmony.

     Enter MUSIC-MASTER.

  How now, Friend, why dost look so pale?
MUSIC-MASTER   For Fear, I promise you, if I do look pale.   90
BAPTISTA   What, will my Daughter prove a good Musician?
MUSIC-MASTER   I think she'll sooner prove a Soldier;
  Iron may hold with her, but never Lutes.
BAPTISTA   Why, then, thou canst not break her to the Lute?
MUSIC-MASTER   Why, no; for she hath broke the Lute to me.   95
  I did but tell her she mistook her Frets,
  And bow'd her Hand, to teach her fingering,
  When with a most impatient devilish Spirit,
  Frets call you them? quoth she, I'll fret your Fool's Cap:
  And with that Word, she struck me on the Head,   100
  And through the Instrument my Pate made way,
  And there I stood amazed for awhile,
  As on a Pillory, looking thro' the Lute:
  While she did call me Rascal-fidler,
  And twangling Jack, with twenty such vile Terms,   105
  As she had studied to misuse me so.
PETRUCHIO   Now by the World, it is a lusty Wench,
  I love her ten times more than e'er I did;
  Oh how I long to have a Grapple with her!
MUSIC-MASTER   I wou'd not make another Trial with her,   110
  To purchase *Padua*; for what is past,
  I'm paid sufficiently: If at your Leisure,
  You think my broken Fortunes, Head and Lute
  Deserve some Reparation, you know where
  T'enquire for me; and so good Gentlemen,   115
  I am your much disorder'd humble Servant.

                                         [Exit.]

BAPTISTA   Not yet mov'd, *Petruchio*! do you flinch?
PETRUCHIO   I am more and more impatient, Sir; and long
  To be a Part'ner in these favourite Pleasures.
BAPTISTA   O, by all Means, Sir,—Will you go with me,   120
  Or shall I send my Daughter *Kate* to you?
PETRUCHIO   I pray you do, I will attend her here.

                                   [Exit BAP.]

  Grumio, retire, and wait my Call within.

                                   [Exit GRUM.]

Since that her Father is so resolute,
I'll wooe her with some Spirit when she comes; 125
Say that she rail, why then, I'll tell her plain
She sings as sweetly as a Nightingale:
Say that she frown, I'll say she looks as clear
As Morning Roses, newly wash'd with Dew;
Say she be mute, and will not speak a Word, 130
Then I'll commend her Volubility,
And say she uttereth piercing Eloquence:
If she do bid me pack, I'll give her Thanks,
As tho' she bid me stay by her a Week;
If she deny to wed, I'll crave the Day 135
When I shall ask the Banes, and when be married:
But here she comes, and now, *Petruchio*, speak.

    Enter CATHARINE.

CATHARINE   How! turn'd adrift, nor know my Father's House!
    Reduc'd to this, or none, the Maid's last Prayer;
    Sent to be woo'd like Bear unto the Stake? 140
    Trim wooing like to be!——and he the Bear,
    For I shall bait him—yet the Man's a Man.
PETRUCHIO   *Kate* in a Calm!—Maids must not be Wooers.
    Good Morrow, *Kate*, for that's your Name I hear.
CATHARINE   Well have you heard, but impudently said, 145
    They call me *Catharine*, that do talk of me.
PETRUCHIO   You lie in Faith, for you are call'd plain *Kate*,
    And bonny *Kate*, and sometimes *Kate* the curst,
    But *Kate*—The prettiest *Kate* in *Christendom*.
    Take this of me, *Kate* of my Consolation! 150
    Hearing thy Mildness prais'd in ev'ry Town,
    Thy Virtues spoke of, and thy Beauty sounded,
    Thy Affability, and bashful Modesty,
    (Yet not so deeply as to thee belongs,)
    Myself am mov'd to wooe thee for myself. 155
CATHARINE   Mov'd! in good Time; let him that mov'd you hither,
    Remove you hence! I knew you at the first,
    You were a Moveable.
PETRUCHIO   A Moveable? Why, what's that?
CATHARINE   A Joint-Stool. 160
PETRUCHIO   Thou hast hit it; come, sit on me.
CATHARINE   Asses are made to bear, and so are you.
PETRUCHIO   Women are made to bear, and so are you.
    Alass good *Kate*, I will not burthen thee,
    For knowing thee to be but young and light.— 165
CATHARINE   Too light for such a Swain as you to catch;

                                  [Going.]

PETRUCHIO   Come, come you Wasp; i'faith you are too angry.
CATHARINE   If I be waspish, 'best beware my Sting.
PETRUCHIO   My Remedy, then is to pluck it out.
CATHARINE   Ay, if the Fool cou'd find it where it lies.   170
PETRUCHIO   The Fool knows where the Honey is, sweet *Kate*.

    [*Offers to kiss her.*]

CATHARINE   'Tis not for Drones to taste.
PETRUCHIO   That will I try.

    [*She strikes him.*]

I swear I'll cuff you, if you strike again.—
Nay, come, *Kate*, come; you must not look so sower.   175
CATHARINE   How can I help it, when I see that Face;
But I'll be shock'd no longer with the Sight.

    [*Going.*]

PETRUCHIO   Nay, hear you, *Kate*; in sooth you 'scape not so.
CATHARINE   I chase you, if I tarry, let me go.
PETRUCHIO   No, not a Whit, I find you passing gentle;   180
'Twas told me you were rough, and coy, and sullen,
And now I find Report a very Liar,
For thou art pleasant, gamesome, passing courteous,
But slow in Speech, yet sweet as spring-time Flowers;
Thou can'st not frown, thou can'st not look ascance,   185
Nor bite the Lip as angry Wenches will,
Nor hast thou Pleasure to be cross in Talk:
But thou with Mildness entertain'st thy Wooers,
With gentle Conf'rence, soft and affable.
CATHARINE   This is beyond all Patience; don't provoke me: 190
PETRUCHIO   Why doth the World report that *Kate* doth limp?
Oh sland'rous World! *Kate* like the Hazle Twig,
Is strait, and slender, and as brown in Hue
As Hazle Nuts, and sweeter than the Kernels.
O let me see thee walk, thou do'st not halt.   195
CATHARINE   Go, Fool, and whom thou keep'st command.
PETRUCHIO   Did ever *Dian'* so become a Grove,
As *Kate* this Chamber, with her princely Gaite?
Oh be thou *Dian'*, and let her be *Kate*,
And then let *Kate* be chaste, and *Dian'* sportful.   200
CATHARINE   Where did you Study all this goodly Speech?
PETRUCHIO   It is *extempore*, from my Mother Wit.
CATHARINE   A witty Mother, witless else her Son.
PETRUCHIO   Am I not wife?
CATHARINE   Yes, in your own Conceit,   205
Keep yourself warm with that, or else you'll freeze.

PETRUCHIO   Or rather warm me in thy Arms, my *Kate!*
   And therefore setting all this Chat aside,
   Thus in plain Terms; your Father hath consented
   That you shall be my Wife; your Dowry 'greed on,   210
   And will you, nill you, I will marry you.
CATHARINE   Whether I will or no!—O Fortune's Spite!
PETRUCHIO   Nay, *Kate*, I am a Husband for your Turn;
   For by this Light, whereby I see thy Beauty,
   (Thy Beauty that doth make me like thee well)   215
   Thou must be married to no Man but me:
   For I am he am born to tame you, *Kate*.
CATHARINE   That will admit Dispute, my saucy Groom.
PETRUCHIO   Here comes your Father; never make Denial,
   I must and will have *Catharine* to my Wife.   220

      Enter BAPTISTA.

BAPTISTA   Now, Signior, now, how speed you with my Daughter?
PETRUCHIO   How shou'd I speed but well, Sir? how but well?
   It were impossible I should speed amiss.
BAPTISTA   Why, how now, Daughter *Catharine,* in your Dumps?
CATHARINE   Call you me Daughter? Now I promise you,   225
   You've shew'd a tender Fatherly Regard,
   To wish me wed to one half lunatick;
   A Mad-cap Ruffian, and a swearing Jack,
   That thinks with Oaths to face the Matter out.
BAPTISTA   Better this Jack than starve, and that's your Portion—230
PETRUCHIO   Father, 'tis thus; yourself and all the World
   That talk'd of her, have talk'd amiss of her;
   If she be curst, it is for Policy;
   For she's not froward, but modest as the Dove;
   She is not hot, but temperate as the Morn;   235
   For Patience, she will prove a second *Grissel*,
   And *Roman Lucrece*, for her Chastity;
   And, to conclude, we've 'greed so well together,
   We have fix'd to-morrow for the Wedding-day.
CATHARINE   I'll see thee hang'd To-morrow, first—To-morrow!   240
BAPTISTA   *Petruchio*, hark; she says she'll see thee hang'd first:
   Is this your Speeding?
PETRUCHIO   Oh! be patient, Sir,
   If she and I be pleas'd, what's that to you;
   'Tis bargain'd 'twixt us Twain, being alone,   245
   That she shall still be curs'd in Company.
CATHARINE   A Plague upon his Impudence! I'm vex'd—
   I'll marry my Revenge, but I will tame him.
                              [*Aside.*]
PETRUCHIO   I tell you, 'tis incredible to believe
   How much she loves me; Oh! the kindest *Kate!*   250

She hung about my Neck, and Kiss on Kiss,
She vy'd so fast, protesting Oath on Oath,
That in a Twink she won me to her Love.
Oh! you are Novices; 'tis a World to see
How tame, when Men and Women are alone—   255
Give me thy Hand, *Kate*, I will now away
To buy Apparel for my gentle Bride:
Father, provide the Feast, and bid the Guests.

BAPTISTA   What dost thou say, my *Catharine*? Give thy Hand.

CATHARINE   Never to Man shall *Cath'rine* give her Hand: 260
Here 'tis, and let him take it, an' he dare.

PETRUCHIO   Were it the Fore-foot of an angry Bear,
I'd shake it off; but as it is *Kate*'s, I kiss it.

CATHARINE   You'll kiss it closer, e'er our Moon be wain'd.

BAPTISTA   Heav'n send you Joy, *Petruchio*—'tis a Match.   265

PETRUCHIO   Father, and Wife, adieu. I must away,
Unto my Country-house, and stir my Grooms,
Scower their Country-rust, and make 'em fine,
For the Reception of my *Catharine*.
We will have Rings, and Things, and fine Array,   270
To-morrow, *Kate*, shall be our Wedding-day.

[*Exit.* PETRUCHIO.]

BAPTISTA   Well, Daughter, tho' the Man be somewhat wild,
And thereto frantic, yet his Means are great;
Thou hast done well to seize the first kind Offer,
For by thy Mother's Soul 'twill be the last.   275

CATHARINE   My Duty, Sir, hath followed your Command.

BAPTISTA   Art thou in Earnest? Hast no Trick behind?
I'll take thee at thy Word, and send t'invite
My Son-in-law, *Hortensio*, and thy Sister.
And all our Friends to grace thy Nuptials, *Kate*.   280

[*Exit.* BAPTISTA.]

CATHARINE   Why yes; Sister *Bianca* now shall see
The poor abandon'd *Cath'rine*, as she calls me,
Can hold her Head as high, and be as proud,
And make her Husband stoop unto her Lure,
As she, or e'er a Wife in *Padua*.   285
As double as my Portion be my Scorn;
Look to your Seat, *Petruchio*, or I throw you.
Cath'rine shall tame this Haggard;—or if she fails,
Shall tye her Tongue up, and pare down her Nails.

[*Exit.* CATHARINE.]

Act II

Enter BAPTISTA, HORTENSIO, CATHARINE, BIANCA *and*
ATTENDANTS.

BAPTISTA Signior *Hortensio*, this is the 'pointed Day,
That *Cath'rine* and *Petruchio* should be married;
And yet we hear not of our Son-in-law.
What will be said? what Mockery will it be,
To want the Bridegroom when the Priest attends   5
To speak the ceremonial Rites of Marriage?
What says *Hortensio* to this Shame of ours?
CATHARINE No Shame but mine; I must, forsooth, be forc'd
To give my Hand oppos'd against my Heart,
Unto a mad-brain Rudesby, full of Spleen,   10
Who woo'd in Haste, and means to wed at Leisure.
I told you, I, he was a frantick Fool,
Hiding his bitter Jests in blunt Behavior:
And to be noted for a merry Man,
He'll wooe a Thousand, 'point the Day of Marriage,   15
Make Friends, invite; yea, and proclaim the Banes,
Yet never means to wed where he hath woo'd.
Now must the World point at poor *Catharine*,
And say, lo! there is mad *Petruchio*'s Wife,
If it would please him come and marry her.   20
BIANCA Such hasty Matches seldom end in Good.
HORTENSIO Patience, good *Cath'rine*, and *Bianca* too;
Upon my Life, *Petruchio* means but well,
Whatever Fortune stays him from his Word;
Tho' he be blunt, I know him passing wise;   25
Tho' he be merry, yet withal he's honest.
CATHARINE Wou'd I had never seen his Honesty.—
Oh! I could tear my Flesh for very Madness.

[*Exit* CATHARINE.]

BAPTISTA Follow your Sister, Girl, and comfort her.

[*Exit* BIANCA.]

I cannot blame thee now to weep and rage,   30
For such an Injury would vex a Saint;
Much more a Shrew of thy impatient Humour.
HORTENSIO Was ever Match clapt up so suddenly!
BAPTISTA *Hortensio*; faith I play a Merchant's Part,
And venture madly on a desp'rate Mart.   35
HORTENSIO 'Twas a Commodity lay fretting by you;
'Twill bring you Gain, or perish on the Seas.
BAPTISTA The Gain I seek is Quiet in the Match.
HORTENSIO No doubt *Petruchio*'s got a quiet Catch.

Enter BIONDELLO.

BIONDELLO   Master, Master, News; and such News as you   40
   never heard of.
BAPTISTA   Is *Petruchio* come?
BIONDELLO   Why no, Sir.
BAPTISTA   What then?
BIONDELLO   He is coming; but how? Why in a new Hat, and an   45
   old Jerkin; a Pair of old Breeches, thrice turned; a Pair of Boots
   that have been Candle Cases, one buckled, another lac'd; an
   old rusty Sword, ta'en out of the Town Armory, with a broken
   Hilt, and chapeless, with two broken Points; his Horse hip'd
   with an old mothy Saddle, the Stirrups of no Kindred; besides   50
   possess'd with the Glanders, and like to mose in the Chine,
   troubled with the Lampasse, infected with the Farcy, full of
   Windgalls, sped with Spavins, raied with the Yellows, past Cure
   of the Fives, stark spoiled with the Staggers, be-gnawn with
   the Bots, waid in the Back, and Shoulder shotten, near legg'd   55
   before, and with a half check'd Bit; and a Head-stall of Sheep-
   leather, which being restrained, to keep him from stumbling,
   hath been often burst, and now repaired with Knots, one girt
   six Times piec'd, and a Woman's Crupper of Velure, which
   hath two Letters for her Name, fairly set down in Studs, and   60
   here and there piec'd with Pack-thread.
BAPTISTA   Who comes with him?
BIONDELLO   O Sir, his Laquey, for all the World caparison'd like
   the Horse, with a Linnen Stock on one Leg, and a Kersey
   Boot Hose on the other, gartered with a Red and Blue Lift, an   65
   old Hat, and the Humour of forty Fancies prick'd upon it for a
   Feather; a Monster! a very Monster in Apparel, and not like a
   Christian Foot-Boy, or a Gentleman's Lacquey.
BAPTISTA   I am glad he's come, howsoever he comes.

Enter PETRUCHIO, *and* GRUMIO, *fantastically habited.*

PETRUCHIO   Come, where be these Gallants? Who is at Home?   70
BAPTISTA   You're welcome, Sir.
PETRUCHIO   Well am I come then, Sir.
BAPTISTA   Not so well 'parell'd as I wish you were.
PETRUCHIO   Why were it better, I should rush in thus:
   But where is *Kate*? where is my lovely Bride?   75
   How does my Father? Gentles, methinks you frown:
   And wherefore gaze this goodly Company?
   As if they saw some wond'rous Monument,
   Some Comet, or unusual Prodigy?
BAPTISTA   Why, Sir, you know this is your Wedding-Day,   80
   First, we were sad, fearing you would not come,
   Now sader, that you come so unprovided,

Fye! doff this Habit, Shame to your Estate;
An Eye-sore to our solemn Festival.

HORTENSIO   And tell us what Occasion of Import   85
Hath all so long detained you from your Wife.
And sent you hither so unlike yourself?

PETRUCHIO   Tedious it were to tell, and harsh to hear:
Let it suffice, I'm come to keep my Word;
But where is *Kate*? I stay too long from her;   90
The Morning wears; 'tis Time we were at Church.

HORTENSIO   See not your Bride in these unreverent Robes;
Go to my Chamber, put on Cloaths of mine.

PETRUCHIO   Not I, believe me, thus I'll visit her.

BAPTISTA   But thus I trust you will not marry her.   95

PETRUCHIO   Goodsooth, even thus; therefore ha' done with
Words;
To me she's married, not unto my Cloaths:
Could I repair what she will wear in me,
As I could change these poor Accoutrements,
'Twere well for *Kate*, and better for myself.   100
But what a Fool am I to chat with you,
When I should bid Good-morrow to my Bride,
And seal the Title with a lovely Kiss?
What ho! my *Kate*! my *Kate*!

[*Exit* PET.]

HORTENSIO   He hath some Meaning in this mad Attire: 105
We will persuade him, be it possible,
To put on better e're he go to Church.

BAPTISTA   I'll after him, and see the Event of this.

[*Exeunt all but* GRUMIO.]

GRUMIO   He's gone swearing to Church with her. I wou'd
sooner have led her to the Gallows. If he can but hold it, 'tis   110
well—And if I know any Thing of myself and Master, no two
Men were ever born with such Qualities to tame Women.—
When Madam goes home, we must look for another-guise
Master than we have had. We shall see old Coil between
'em.—If I can spy into Futurity a little, there will be much   115
Clatter among the Moveables, and some Practice for the Sur-
geons. By this the Parson has given 'em his Licence to fall together by the Ears.

Enter PEDRO.

PEDRO   *Grumio*, your Master bid me find you out, and speed
you to his Country House, to prepare for his Reception, and if   120
he finds not Things as he expects 'em, according to the Direc-

tions that he gave you, you know, he says, what follows: This
Message he delivered before his Bride, ev'n in her Way to
Church, and shook his Whip in Token of his Love.

GRUMIO   I understand it, Sir, and will convey the same Token to   125
my Horse immediately, that he may take to his Heels, in order
to save my Bones, and his own Ribs.

                                        [*Exit* GRUMIO.]

PEDRO   So odd a Master, and so fit a Man,
Were never seen in *Padua* before.

        Enter BIONDELLO.

Now, *Biondello*, came you from the Church?   130
BIONDELLO   As willingly as e'er I came from School.
PEDRO   And is the Bride, and Bridegroom coming home?
BIONDELLO   A Bridegroom say you? 'tis a Groom indeed;
A grumbling Groom, and that the Girl shall find.
PEDRO   Curster than she? why, 'tis impossible.   135
BIONDELLO   Why, he's a Devil; a Devil! a very Fiend!
PEDRO   Why she's a Devil; a Devil! the Devil's Dam.
BIONDELLO   Tut! she's a Lamb, a Dove, a Fool to him:
I'll tell you, Brother *Pedro*, when the Priest
Should ask if *Catharine* should be his Wife?   140
Aye, by Gogs-Wounds, quoth he, and swore so loud,
That all amaz'd the Priest let fall his Book;
And as he stoop'd again to take it up,
This mad-brain'd Bridegroom took him such a Cuff,
That down fell Priest and Book, and Book and Priest.   145
Now take them up, quoth he, if any list.
PEDRO   What said the Wench, when he rose up again?
BIONDELLO   Trembled and shook; for why, he stamp'd and swore,
As if the Vicar went to cozen him.
But after many Ceremonies done,   150
He calls for Wine; a Health, quoth he, as if
H'ad been aboard carousing to his Mates
After a Storm; quafft of the Muscadel,
And threw the Sops all in the Sexton's Face;
Having no other Cause, but that his Beard   155
Grew thin and hungerly, and seem'd to ask
His Sops, as he was drinking. This done, he took
The Bride about the Neck, and kiss'd her Lips
With such a clamorous Smack, that at the Parting
All the Church echo'd; and I seeing this,   160
Came thence for very Shame; and after me
I know the Rout is coming:
Such a mad Marriage never was before—

[*Musick.*]

Hark, hark, I hear the Minstrels play.

Enter PETRUCHIO (*singing*) CATHARINE, BIANCA,
HORTENSIO, *and* BAPTISTA.

PETRUCHIO   Gentlemen and Friends, I thank you for your Pains; 165
I know you think to dine with me to-day,
And have prepar'd great Store of Wedding-Cheer;
But so it is, my Haste doth call me hence;
And therefore, here I mean to take my Leave.

BAPTISTA   Is't possible you will away To-night?   170

PETRUCHIO   I must away To-day, before Night come.
Make it no wonder, if you knew my Business,
You would intreat me rather go than stay;
And honest Company, I thank you all,
That have beheld me give away myself   175
To this most patient, sweet and virtuous Wife:
Dine with my Father, drink a Health to me,
For I must hence, and farewell to you all.

HORTENSIO   Let me intreat you, stay till after Dinner.

PETRUCHIO   It may not be.   180

BIONDELLO   Let me intreat you, that my Sister stay;
I come on Purpose to attend the Wedding;
And pass this Day in Mirth and Festival.

PETRUCHIO   It cannot be.

CATHARINE   Let me intreat you.   185

PETRUCHIO   I am content.—

CATHARINE   Are you content to stay?

PETRUCHIO   I am content, you shall intreat my Stay;
But yet not stay, intreat me how you can.

CATHARINE   Now if you love me stay.   190

PETRUCHIO   My Horses, there; what ho, my Horses, there—

CATHARINE   Nay then,
Do what thou can'st, I will not go To-day;
No, nor To-morrow, nor 'till I please myself:
The Door is open, Sir, there lies your Way;   195
You may be jogging, while your Boots are green.
For me, I'll not go, 'till I please myself;
'Tis like you'll prove a Jolly surly Groom,
To take it on you at the first so roundly.

BAPTISTA   O *Kate* content thee; pr'ythee be not angry.   200

CATHARINE   I will be angry; what hast thou to do;
Father be quiet, he shall stay my Leisure.

HORTENSIO   Ay, marry, Sir, Now it begins to work:

CATHARINE   Gentlemen, forward to the bridal Dinner.
I see a Woman may be made a Fool,   205

If she had not a Spirit to resist.
PETRUCHIO   They shall go forward, *Kate*, at thy Command.
   Obey the Bride, you that attend on her:
   Go to the Feast, revel and domineer;
   Carouse full Measure to her Maidenhead;   210
   Be mad and merry, or go hang yourselves;
   But for my bonny *Kate*, she must with me.
   Nay look not big, nor stamp, nor stare, nor fret,
   I will be Master of what is mine own;
   She is my Goods, my Chattles; she is my House,   215
   My Houshold-stuff, my Field, my Barn,
   My Horse, my Ox, my Ass, my any-thing;
   And here she stands, touch her whoever dare;
   I'll bring my Action on the proudest he,
   That stops my Way in *Padua*; *Petruchio*,   220
   Draw forth thy Weapon, thou'art best with Thieves;
   Rescue thy Wife then, if thou be a Man;
   Fear not sweet Wench, they shall not touch thee, *Kate*;
   I'll buckler thee against a Million, *Kate*.

                              [*Exuent* PET. *and* CATH.]

BAPTISTA   Nay, let them go, a Couple of quiet Ones.   225
HORTENSIO   Of all mad Matches never was the like.
   What's your Opinion of your gentle Sister?
BIANCA   That being mad herself, she's madly matched.
BAPTISTA   Neighbours and Friends, tho' Bride and Bridegroom
   want
   For to supply the Places at the Table;   230
   You know there wants no Junkets at the Feast:
   Hortensio, you, supply the Bridegroom's Place,
   And let *Bianca* take her Sister's Room.
BIANCA   My Sister's Room! were I in her's indeed,
   This Swaggerer shou'd repent his Insolence.   235

                                       [*Exeunt Om.*]

      Enter GRUMIO.

GRUMIO   Fie, fie on all Jades, and all mad Masters, and all foul
   Ways! Was ever Man so beaten? Was ever Man so raide! was
   ever Man so weary? I am sent before to make a Fire, and they
   are coming after to warm them: Now were I not a little Pot,
   and soon hot, my very Lips might freeze to my Teeth, my   240
   Tongue to the Roof of my Mouth, my Heart in my Belly, e're I
   should come by a Fire, to thaw me, but I with blowing the
   Fire shall warm myself, for considering the Weather, a taller
   Man than I will take Cold: Holla, hoa, *Curtis*!

Enter CURTIS.

CURTIS   Who is it that calls so coldly?   245

GRUMIO   A piece of Ice. If thou doubt it, thou may'st slide from
my Shoulder to my Heel, with no greater a Run but my Head
and my Neck. A Fire, good *Curtis*.

CURTIS   Is my Master and his Wife coming, *Grumio*?

GRUMIO   Oh, ay, *Curtis*, ay; and therefore, Fire, Fire, cast on no   250
Water.

CURTIS   Is she so hot a Shrew as she's reported?

GRUMIO   She was, good *Curtis*, before the Frost; but thou
know'st Winter tames Man, Woman, and Beast, for it hath
tam'd my old Master, and my new Mistress, and my self,   255
Fellow *Curtis*.

CURTIS   Away, you thick-pated Fool, I am no Beast.

GRUMIO   Where's the Cook? Is Supper ready, the House trim'd,
Rushes strew'd, Cobwebs swept, the Serving-men in their new
Fustian, their white Stockings, and every Officer his Wedding- 260
garments on? Be the *Jacks* fair within, the *Jills* fair without,
Carpets laid, and every Thing in Order?

CURTIS   All ready: and therefore, I pray thee, what News?

GRUMIO   First know my Horse is tired, my Master and Mistress
fall'n out.   265

CURTIS   How?

GRUMIO   Out of their Saddles into the Dirt; and thereby hangs
a Tale.

CURTIS   Let's ha't good *Grumio*.

GRUMIO   Lend thine Ear.   270

CURTIS   Here.

GRUMIO   There.

[*Strikes him.*]

CURTIS   This is to feel a Tale, not to hear a Tale.

GRUMIO   And therefore is call'd a sensible Tale: And this Cuff
was but to knock at your Ear, and beseech listning. Now I   275
begin: *Imprimis*, we came down a foul Hill, my Master riding
behind my Mistress.

CURTIS   Both on one Horse?

GRUMIO   What's that to thee? tell thou the Tale. But had'st
thou not crost me, thou should'st have heard how her Horse   280
fell, and she under her Horse, thou should'st have heard in
how miry a Place, how she was bemoild, how he left her
with the Horse upon her, how he beat me because her Horse
stumbled, how she waded through the Dirt to pluck him off
me; how he swore, how she pray'd, that never pray'd before!   285
how I cry'd, how the Horses ran away, how her Bridle was

burst, how I lost my Crupper; how my Mistress lost her Slippers, tore and bemit'd her Garments, limp'd to the Farm-
house, put on *Rebecca*'s old Shoes and Petticoat; with many
Things worthy of Memory, which now shall die in Oblivion,   290
and thou return unexperienc'd to thy Grave.

CURTIS   By this Reckoning he is more Shrew than she.

GRUMIO   Ay, for the Nonce—and that, thou and the proudest of
you all shall find, when he come home. But what talk I of
this? call forth *Nathaniel, Joseph, Nicholas, Philip, Walter,*   295
Sugarsop, and the rest: let their Heads be sleek-comb'd, their
blue Coats brush'd, and their Garters of an indifferent Knit;
let them curt'sy with their left Legs, and not presume to touch
a Hair of my Master's Horse Tail, till they kiss their Hands.
Are they all ready?   300

CURTIS   They are.

GRUMIO   Call them forth.

CURTIS   Do you hear, ho! *Nathaniel, Joseph, Nicholas,* &c.
Where are you?

> *Enter* NATHANIEL, PHILIP, &c.

NATHANIEL   Welcome home, *Grumio.*   305

PHILIP   How now, *Grumio?*

PETER   What, *Grumio!*

NICHOLAS   Fellow *Grumio!*

NATHANIEL   How now, old Lad!

GRUMIO   Welcome you; how now, you; what you; Fellow you;   310
and thus much for greeting. Now, my spruce Companions, is
all ready, and all things neat?

NATHANIEL   All things are ready, how near is our Master?

GRUMIO   E'en at Hand, alighted by this; and therefore be not—
Cock's Passion! Silence, I hear my Master.   315

> *Enter* PETRUCHIO *and* CATHARINE.

PETRUCHIO   Where are these Knaves? What no Man at
Door, to hold my Stirrup, nor to take my Horse?
Where is *Nathaniel, Gregory, Philip?*

ALL-SERVANTS   Here, here, Sir; here, Sir.

PETRUCHIO   Here, Sir; here, Sir; here, Sir; here Sir?   320
You loggerheaded, and unpolish'd Grooms:
What no Attendance, no Regard, no Duty?
Where is the foolish Knave I sent before?

GRUMIO   Here, Sir, as foolish as I was before.

PETRUCHIO   You peasant Swain, you whoreson Malt-horse   325
Drudge,
Did I not bid thee meet me in the Park,
And bring along these rascal Knaves with thee?

GRUMIO   *Nathaniel's* Coat, Sir, was not fully made:
And *Gabriel's* Pumps were all unpink'd i'th' Heel:
There was no Link to colour *Peter's* Hat,   330
And *Walter's* Dagger was not come from Sheathing:
There were none fine but *Adam, Ralph,* and *Gregory,*
The rest were ragged, old, and beggarly:
Yet as they are, here are they come to meet you.
PETRUCHIO   Go, Rascals, go, and fetch my Supper in.   335

> [*Exeunt* SERVANTS.]

> *Sings.*

"Where is the Life that late I led?
"Where are those"—Sit down, *Kate,*
And welcome. "Soud, soud, soud, soud."

> *Enter Servants with Supper.*

Why, when, I say? Nay, good sweet *Kate,* be merry.
Off with my Boots you Rogue: you Villains, when!—   340

> *Sings.*

"It was a Fryar of Orders grey
"As he forth walked on his Way."
Out, out, you Rogue: you pluck my Foot awry.
Take that, and mind the plucking off the other.

> [*Strikes him.*]

Be merry, *Kate*; some Water here. What hoa!   345
Where's my Spaniel *Troilus*? Sirrah, get you hence,
And bid my Cousin *Ferdinand* come hither:
One, *Kate,* that you must kiss and be acquainted with.
Where are my Slippers?—Shall I have some Water?

> *Enter Servant with Water.*

Come, *Kate,* and wash, and welcome heartily.   350

> [*Servant lets fall the Water.*]

You whoreson Villain, will you let it fall?
CATHARINE   Patience, I pray you, 'twas a Fault unwilling.
PETRUCHIO   A whoreson, beetle-headed, flap-ear'd Knave!
Come, *Kate,* sit down; I know you have a Stomach.
CATHARINE   Indeed I have: 355
And never was Repast so welcome to me:
PETRUCHIO   Will you give Thanks, sweet *Kate,* or else shall I?
What's this, Mutton?
SERVANT   Yes.

PETRUCHIO   Who brought it?   360
SERVANT   I.
PETRUCHIO   'Tis burnt, and so is all the Meat—
  What Dogs are these! Where is the Rascal Cook?
  How durst you, Villain, bring it from the Dresser,
  And serve it thus to me, that love it not?   365
  There; take it to you, Trenchers, Cups and all.

      [*Throws the Meat, &c. about.*]

  You heedless jolt Heads, and unmanner'd Slaves.
  What, do you grumble? I'll be with you straight.

                              [*Exeunt all the* SERVANTS.]

CATHARINE   I pray you, Husband, be not so disquiet,
  The Meat was well, and well I could have eat,   370
  If you were so disposed; I'm sick with fasting.
PETRUCHIO   I tell thee, *Kate*, 'twas burnt and dry'd away,
  And I expresly am forbid to touch it:
  For it engenders Choler, planteth Anger;
  And better it were that both of us did fast,   375
  Since of ourselves, ourselves are choleric,
  Than feed it with such over-roasted Flesh—
  Be patient; to-morrow it shall be mended,
  And for this Night, we'll fast for Company.
  Come, I will bring thee to thy Bridal Chamber.   380

                                        [*Exeunt.*]

      Enter NATHANIEL *and* PETER.

NATHANIEL   *Peter*, didst thou ever see the like?
PETER   He kills her in her own Humour. I did not think so good
  and kind a Master cou'd have put on so resolute a Bearing.
GRUMIO   Where is he?

      Enter CURTIS.

CURTIS   In her Chamber, making a Sermon of Continency to 385
  her, and rails, and swears, and rates; and she, poor Soul,
  knows not which Way to stand, to look, to speak; and sits as
  one new risen from a Dream. Away, away, for he is coming
  hither.

                                        [*Exeunt.*]

      Enter PETRUCHIO.

PETRUCHIO   Thus have I, politickly, begun my Reign,   390
  And 'tis my Hope to end successfully:
  My Falcon now is sharp, and passing empty,

And 'till she stoop, she must not be full gorg'd,
For then she never looks upon her Lure.
Another Way I have to man my Haggard,   395
To make her come, and know her Keeper's Call:
That is, to watch her, as we watch these Kites,
That bit and beat, and will not be obedient.
She eat no Meat to-day, nor none shall eat:
Last Night she slept not, nor To-night shall not;   400
As with the Meat, some undeserved Fault
I'll find about the making of the Bed;
And here I'll fling the Pillow, there the Bolster,
This Way the Coverlet; that Way the Sheets;
Aye, and amid' this hurly, I'll pretend   405
That all is done in reverent Care of her;
And in Conclusion she shall watch all Night:
And if she chance to nod, I'll rail and brawl,
And with the Clamour keep her still awake.
This is a Way to kill a Wife with Kindness,   410
And thus I'll curb her mad and head-strong Humour—
He that knows better how to tame a Shrew,
Now let him speak, 'tis Charity to shew.

                                                      [*Exit.*]

Act III

Enter CATHARINE *and* GRUMIO.

GRUMIO   No, no, forsooth, I dare not for my Life.
CATHARINE   The more my Wrong, the more his Spite appears:
What did he marry me to famish me?
Beggars that come unto my Father's Door,
Upon Intreaty have a present Alms;   5
If not, elsewhere they meet with Charity:
But I, who never knew how to intreat,
Nor ever needed that I should intreat,
Am starv'd for Meat, giddy for lack of Sleep;
With Oaths kept waking, and with brawling fed;   10
And that which spights me more than all these Wants,
He does it under Name of perfect Love:
As who would say, if I should sleep or eat,
'Twere deadly Sickness, or else present Death!—
I pr'ythee go and get me some Repast;   15
I care not what, so it be wholesome Food.
GRUMIO   What say you to a Neat's Foot?
CATHARINE   'Tis passing good; I pr'ythee let me have it.
GRUMIO   I fear, it is too flegmatick a Meat:
How say you to a fat Tripe, finely boil'd?   20

CATHARINE   I like it well; good *Grumio*, fetch it me.
GRUMIO   I cannot tell,—I fear, its cholerick:
  What say you to a Piece of Beef and Mustard?
CATHARINE   A Dish that I do love to feed upon.
GRUMIO   Aye, but the Mustard is too hot a little.   25
CATHARINE   Why then the Beef, and let the Mustard rest.
GRUMIO   Nay, that I will not, you shall have the Mustard,
  Or else you get no Beef of *Grumio*.
CATHARINE   Then both, or one, or any thing thou wilt.
GRUMIO   Why then, the Mustard, Dame, without the Beef.   30
CATHARINE   Go, get thee gone, thou false deluding Slave,

    [*Beats him.*]

  That feed'st me only with the Name of Meat:
  Sorrow on thee, and all the Pack of you,
  That triumph thus upon my Misery.
  Go, get thee gone, I say.   35

    Enter PETRUCHIO.

PETRUCHIO   How fares my *Kate*?
  What, Sweeting, all amort? Mistress, what Cheer?
CATHARINE   Faith as cold as can be.
PETRUCHIO   Pluck up thy Spirits, look chearfully upon me.
  For now my Honey-love we are refresh'd—   40
CATHARINE   Refresh'd, with what?
PETRUCHIO   We will return unto thy Father's House,
  And revel it as bravely as the best,
  With silken Coats, and Caps, and golden Rings,
  With Ruffs, and Cuffs, and Fardingals, and Things: 45
  With Scarffs, and Fans, and double Change of Brav'ry,
  Now thou hast eat, the Taylor stays thy Leisure,
  To deck thy Body with his rustling Treasure.

    Enter TAYLOR.

  Come, Taylor, let us see these Ornaments.

    Enter HABERDASHER.

  Lay forth the Gown—What News with you, Sir?   50
HABERDASHER   Here is the Cap your Worship did bespeak.
PETRUCHIO   Why this was moulded on a Porringer;
  A velvet Dish: Fye, fye, 'tis lewd and filthy:
  Why 'tis a Cockle, or a Walnut-shell,
  A Knack, a Toy, a Trick, a Baby's Cap.   55
  Away with it, come, let me have a bigger.
CATHARINE   I'll have no bigger, this doth fit the Time,
  And Gentlewomen wear such Caps as these.

PETRUCHIO   When you are gentle, you shall have one too,
 And not till then.   60
CATHARINE   Why, Sir; I trust I may have Leave to speak,
 And speak I will; I am no Child, no Babe;
 Your Betters have endur'd me say my Mind;
 And if you cannot, best you stop your Ears;
 My Tongue will tell the Anger of my Heart,   65
 Or else my Heart concealing it, will break:
 And rather than it shall, I will be free,
 Ev'n to the utmost as I please in Words.
PETRUCHIO   Thou say'st true, *Kate*, it is a paultry Cap,
 A Custard Coffin, Bauble, silken Pie,   70
 I love thee well, in that thou lik'st it not.
CATHARINE   Love me, or love me not, I like the Cap,
 And I will have it, or I will have none.
PETRUCHIO   Thy Gown? why aye; come, Taylor, let me see't.
 O Mercy Heav'n! what masking Stuff is here?   75
 What's this, a Sleeve? 'Tis like a Demi-canon;
 What up and down, carv'd like an Apple-tart!
 Here's snip, and nip, and cut, and slish, and slash,
 Like to a Censer in a Barber's Shop.
 Why, what the Devil's Name, Taylor, call'st thou this?   80
GRUMIO   I see she's like to've neither Cap nor Gown.
TAYLOR   You bid me make it orderly and well,
 According to the Fashion of the Time.
PETRUCHIO   Marry and did: but if you be remember'd,
 I did not bid you marr it to the Time.   85
 Go, hop me over every Kennel home;
 For you shall hop without my Custom, Sir:
 I'll none of it; hence, make your best of it.
CATHARINE   I never saw a better fashion'd Gown,
 More quaint, more pleasing, nor more commendable: 90
 Belike you mean to make a Puppet of me.
PETRUCHIO   Why, true; he means to make a Puppet of thee.
TAYLOR   She says your Worship means to make a Puppet of her.
PETRUCHIO   Oh! most monstrous Arrogance!
 Thou lyest, thou Thread, thou Thimble,   95
 Thou Yard, Three-quarters, Half-yard, Quarter, Nail.
 Thou Flea, thou Nit, thou Winter-cricket, thou!
 Brav'd in mine own House, with a Skein of Thread!
 Away thou Rag! thou Quantity, thou Remnant,
 Or I shall so be-mete thee with thy Yard,   100
 As thou shall think on prating whilst thou liv'st:
 I tell thee, I, that thou hast marr'd the Gown.
TAYLOR   Your Worship is deceiv'd, the Gown is made just as my
 Master had Direction; *Grumio* gave Order how it should be
 done.   105

GRUMIO   I gave him no Order, I gave him the Stuff.

TAYLOR   But how did you desire it should be made?

GRUMIO   Marty, Sir, with a Needle and Thread.

TAYLOR   But did you not request to have it cut?

GRUMIO   Tho' thou hast fac'd many Things, face not me: I say 110
unto thee, I bid thy Master cut the Gown, but I did not bid
him cut it to Pieces. *Ergo*, thou liest.

TAYLOR   Why, here is the Note of the Fashion to testify.

PETRUCHIO   Read it.

TAYLOR   *Imprimis*, a loose-bodied Gown.   115

GRUMIO   Master, if ever I said a loose-bodied Gown, sew me up
in the Skirts of it, and beat me to death with a Bottom of
brown Thread: I said a Gown.

PETRUCHIO   Proceed.

TAYLOR   With a small compass Cape.   120

GRUMIO   I confess the Cape.

TAYLOR   With a Trunk Sleeve.

GRUMIO   I confess two Sleeves.

TAYLOR   The Sleeves curiously cut.

PETRUCHIO   Ay, there's the Villany.   125

GRUMIO   Error i'th' Bill, Sir; Error i'th' Bill; I commanded the
Sleeves should be cut out, and sow'd upon again, and that I'll
prove upon thee, tho' thy little Finger be arm'd in a Thimble.

TAYLOR   This is true that I say; an' I had thee in a Place thou
shoud'dst know it.   130

GRUMIO   I am for thee, straight: come on you Parchment
Shred!

[*They fight.*]

PETRUCHIO   What, Chickens sparr in Presence of the Kite!
I'll swoop upon you both; Out, out, ye Vermin—

[*Beats 'em off.*]

CATHARINE   For Heav'n's Sake, Sir, have Patience! how you 135
fright me!

[*Crying.*]

PETRUCHIO   Well, come, my *Kate*; we will unto your Father's,
Even in these honest, mean Habiliments:
Our Purses shall be proud, our Garments poor;
For 'tis the Mind that makes the Body rich;   140
And as the Sun breaks through the darkest Cloud,
So Honour peereth in the meanest Habit.
What, is the Jay more precious than the Lark,
Because his Feathers are more beautiful?
Or is the Adder better than the Eel,   145

Because his painted Skin contents the Eye?
Oh no, good *Kate*; neither art thou the worse
For this poor Furniture, and mean Array.
If thou accounts't it Shame, lay it on me;
And therefore frolick; we will hence, forthwith.   150
To feast and sport us at thy Father's House:
Go call my Men, and bring our Horses out.

CATHARINE   O happy Hearing! Let us strait be gone;
I cannot tarry here another Day.

PETRUCHIO   Cannot, my *Kate*! O fie! indeed you can—   155
Besides, on second Thoughts, 'tis now too late,
For, look, how bright and goodly shines the Moon.

CATHARINE   The Moon! the Sun; it is not Moon-light now.

PETRUCHIO   I say it is the Moon that shines so bright.

CATHARINE   I say it is the Sun that shines so bright.   160

PETRUCHIO   Now, by my Mother's Son, and that's myself;
It shall be Moon, or Star; or what I list,
Or e're I Journey to your Father's House:
Go on, and fetch our Horses back again;
Evermore crost, and crost; nothing but crost!   165

GRUMIO   Say as he says, or we shall never go.

CATHARINE   I see 'tis vain to struggle with my Bonds;
So be it Moon, or Sun, or what you please;
And if you please to call it a Rush Candle,
Henceforth I vow, it shall be so for me.   170

PETRUCHIO   I say it is the Moon.

CATHARINE   I know it is the Moon.

PETRUCHIO   Nay, then you lye; it is the blessed Sun.

CATHARINE   Just as you please, it is the blessed Sun;
But Sun it is not, when you say it is not;   175
And the Moon changes, even as your Mind;
What you will have it nam'd, even that it is,
And so it shall be for your *Catharine*.

PETRUCHIO   Well, forward, forward, thus the Bowl shall run,
And not unluckily, against the Biass: 180
But soft, some Company is coming here,
And stops our Journey.

        Enter BAPTISTA, HORTENSIO *and* BIANCA.

Good-morrow, gentle Mistress, where away?
Tell me, sweet *Kate*, and tell me truly too,
Hast thou beheld a fresher Gentlewoman?   185
Such War of White and Red within her Cheeks!
What Stars do spangle Heav'n with such Beauty,
As those two Eyes become that heav'nly Face?
Fair lovely Maid, once more good Day to thee,
Sweet *Kate*, embrace her for her Beauty's Sake.   190

BAPTISTA What's all this?

CATHARINE Young budding Virgin, fair, and fresh, and sweet,
Whither away, or where is thy abode?
Happy the Parents of so fair a Child;
Happier the Man whom favourable Stars   195
Allot thee, for his lovely Bedfellow.

BIANCA What Mummery is this?

PETRUCHIO Why, how now, *Kate*; I hope thou art not mad!
This is *Baptista*, our old reverent Father;
And not a Maiden, as thou sayst he is.   200

CATHARINE Pardon, dear Father, my mistaken Eyes,
That have been so bedazled with the Sun,
That every thing I look on seemeth Green;
Now I perceive thou art my reverent Father:
Pardon, I pray thee, for my mad mistaking.   205

                    [*Kneels.*]

BAPTISTA Rise, rise, my Child; what strange Vigary's this?
I came to see thee with my Son and Daughter.
How lik'st thou Wedlock? Ar't not alter'd *Kate*?

CATHARINE Indeed I am. I am transform'd to Stone.

PETRUCHIO Chang'd for the better much; ar't not my *Kate*?   210

CATHARINE So good a Master, cannot chuse but mend me.

HORTENSIO Here is a Wonder, if you talk of Wonders.

BAPTISTA And so it is; I wonder what it bodes?

PETRUCHIO Marry, Peace it bodes, and Love, and quiet Life,
And awful Rule, and right Supremacy;   215
And to be short, what not, that's sweet and happy.

BIANCA Was ever Woman's Spirit broke so soon!
What is the Matter, *Kate*? hold up thy Head,
Nor lose our Sex's best Prerogative,
To wish and have our Will.—   220

PETRUCHIO Peace, Brawler, Peace,
Or I will give the meek *Hortensio*,
Your Husband, there, my taming Recipe.

BIANCA Lord, never let me have a Cause to sigh,
'Till I be brought to such a silly Pass.   225

GRUMIO *to* BAPTISTA Did I not promise you, Sir, my Master's
Dicipline wou'd work Miracles?

BAPTISTA I scarce believe my Eyes and Ears.

BIANCA His Eyes and Ears had felt these Fingers e're
He shou'd have moap'd me so.   230

CATHARINE Alas! my Sister—

PETRUCHIO *Catharine*, I charge thee tell this headstrong Woman,
What Duty 'tis she owes her Lord and Husband.

BIANCA Come, come, you're mocking, we will have no telling.

PETRUCHIO Come, on, I say.   235

BIANCA   She shall not.

HORTENSIO   Let us hear for both our Sakes, good Wife.

PETRUCHIO   *Catharine*, begin.

CATHARINE   Fie, fie, unknit that threatening, unkind Brow,
And dart not scornful Glances from those Eyes;   240
To wound thy Lord, thy King, thy Governor,
It blots thy Beauty, as Frosts bite the Meads,
Confounds thy Fame, as Whirlwinds shake fair Buds,
And in no Sense is meet or amiable.

PETRUCHIO   Why, well said *Kate*.   245

CATHARINE   A Woman mov'd is like a Fountain troubled,
Muddy, ill-seeming, thick, bereft of Beauty;
And while it is so, none so dry or thirsty
Will dain to sip, or touch a Drop of it.

BIANCA   Sister, be quiet—   250

PETRUCHIO   Nay, learn you that Lesson—On, on, I say.

CATHARINE   Thy Husband is thy Lord, thy Life, thy Keeper,
Thy Head, thy Sovereign; one that cares for thee,
And for thy Maintainance: Commits his Body
To painful Labour, both by Sea and Land,   255
To watch the Night in Storms, the Day in Cold,
While thou ly'st warm at home, secure and safe;
And craves no other Tribute at thy Hands,
But Love, fair Looks, and true Obedience;
Too little Payment for so great a Debt.   260

BAPTISTA   Now fair befall thee, Son *Petruchio*,
The Battle's won, and thou can'st keep the Field.

PETRUCHIO   Oh! fear me not—

BAPTISTA   Then, my now gentle *Cath'rine*,
Go home with me along, and I will add   265
Another Dowry to another Daughter,
For thou art changed as thou hadst never been.

PETRUCHIO   My Fortune is sufficient. Here's my Wealth:
Kiss me, my *Kate*; and since thou art become
So prudent, kind, and dutiful a Wife,   270
Petruchio here shall doff the lordly Husband;
An honest Mask, which I throw off with Pleasure.
Far hence all Rudeness, Wilfulness, and Noise,
And be our future Lives one gentle Stream
Of mutual Love, Compliance and Regard.   275

CATHARINE   Nay, then I'm all unworthy of thy Love,
And look with Blushes on my former self.

PETRUCHIO   Good *Kate*, no more—this is beyond my Hopes—

[*Goes forward with* CATHARINE *in his Hand.*]

Such Duty as the Subject owes the Prince,
Even such a Woman oweth to her Husband: 280

And when she's froward, peevish, sullen, sower,
And not obedient to his honest Will;
What is she but a foul contending Rebel,
And graceless Traitor to her loving Lord?
How shameful 'tis when Women are so simple   285
To offer War where they should kneel for Peace;
Or seek for Rule, Supremacy and Sway,
Where bound to love, to honour and obey.

Finis.

COLE PORTER

Kiss Me Kate (1948)†

[Cole Porter (1891–1964), born in Peru, Indiana, is one of America's most popular composers and songwriters. A prolific talent, he wrote musical comedies, including *Fifty Million Frenchmen* and *Anything Goes*. His clever lyrics are replete with witty rhymes, and his amusing take on the Shakespearean battle of the sexes has remained popular since its first performance.]

I've Come to Wive It Wealthily in Padua

I've come to wive it wealthily in Padua,
If wealthily then happily in Padua.
If my wife has a bag of gold,
Do I care if the bag be old?
I've come to wive it wealthily in Padua.

I heard you mutter, "Zounds, a loathsome lad you are."
I shall not be disturbed one bit
If she be but a quarter-wit,
If she only can talk of clo'es
While she powders her goddamned nose,
I've come to wive it wealthily in Padua.

I heard you say, "Gadzooks, completely mad you are!"
'Twouldn't give me the slightest shock

---

† from *The Complete Lyrics of Cole Porter*, ed. Robert Kimball (New York: Da Capo, 1992). "I've Come To Wive It Wealthily In Padua" and "I Hate Men" (from *Kiss Me Kate*). Words and Music by Cole Porter, © 1948 by Cole Porter, Copyright Renewed and Assigned to John F. Wharton, Trustee of the Cole Porter Music & Literary Property Trusts Publication and Allied Rights Assigned to Chappell & Co., Inc. All Rights Reserved. Used by Permission of Alfred Publishing Co., Inc.

If her knees now and then should knock,
If her eyes were a wee bit crossed,
Were she wearing the hair she'd lost,
Still the damsel I'll make my dame,
In the dark they are all the same,
I've come to wive it wealthily in Padua.

I've come to wive it wealthily in Padua.
I heard you say, "Good gad, but what a cad you are!"
Do I mind if she fret and fuss,
If she fume like Vesuvius,
If she roar like a winter breeze
On the rough Adriatic seas,
If she scream like a teething brat,
If she scratch like a tiger cat,
If she fight like a raging boar,
I have oft stuck a pig before,
I've come to wive it wealthily in Padua.
With a hunny, nunny, nunny,
And a hey, hey, hey,
Not to mention money, money
For a rainy day,
I've come to wive it wealthily in Padua

I Hate Men

I hate men.
I can't abide 'em even now and then.
Than ever marry one of them, I'd rest a virgin rather,
For husbands are a boring lot and only give you bother.
Of course, I'm awfly glad that Mother had to marry Father,
But I hate men.

I hate men.
I hate 'em all, from modern man 'way back to Father Adam,
He sired Cain and Abel though the Lord above forbade 'em,
I'd hate both Cain and Abel though Betty Grable had 'em,
Oh, I hate men!

I hate men.
Their worth upon this earth I dinna ken.
Avoid the trav'ling salesman though a tempting Tom he may be,
From China he will bring you jade and perfume from Araby,
But don't forget 'tis he who'll have the fun and thee the baby,
Oh, I hate men.
If thou shouldst wed a businessman, be wary, oh, be wary.
He'll tell you he's detained in town on business necessary,

His bus'ness is the bus'ness which he gives his secretary,
Oh, I hate men!

I hate men.
They should be kept like piggies in a pen.
You may be wooed by Jack the Tar, so charming and so chipper,
But if you take him for a mate, be sure that you're the skipper,
For Jack the Tar can go too far. Remember Jack the Ripper?
Oh, I hate men.
Of all the types I've ever met within our democracy,
I hate the most the athlete with his manner bold and brassy,
He may have hair upon his chest but, sister, so has Lassie.
Oh, I hate men!

I hate men.
Though roosters they, I will not play the hen.
If you espouse an older man through girlish optimism,
He'll always stay home at night and make no criticism,
Though you may call it love, the doctors call it rheumatism.
Oh, I hate men.
From all I've read, alone in bed, from A to Zed, about 'em.
Since love is blind, then from the mind, all womankind should
    rout 'em,
But, ladies, you must answer too, what would be do without 'em?
Still, I hate men.

CHARLES MAROWITZ

The Shrew[†]

[Charles Marowitz (b. 1936) is a prolific writer as well as director and
playwright. *The Marowitz Shakespeare* contains seven free adaptations
of Shakespeare's plays. *The Shrew* (1975) presents Kate's transformation in the modern context of brainwashing.]

PETRUCHIO   *(Kindly)* Where is my wife?
KATE   Here, noble lord. What is thy will with her?
PETRUCHIO   *(Kindly)* Are you my wife and will not call me
    husband?
    My men call me `lord'; I am your goodman.
KATE   My husband and my lord, my lord and husband.
    I am your wife in all obedience.

---

† From Charles Marowitz, *The Marowitz Shakespeare* (New York: Drama Book Specialists,
    1978). Reprinted by permission of Marion Boyars, Ltd.

PETRUCHIO   (*Comes forward, takes her in his arms and kisses her tenderly*)
Madam, undress you and come now to bed.
KATE   (*Suddenly fearful*)
Let me entreat of you
To pardon me yet for a night or two,
Or, if not so, until the sun be set.
My physicians have expressly charged
In peril to incur a former malady,
That I should yet absent me from your bed.
I hope this reason stands for my excuse.

> (*There is a pause as* PETRUCHIO's *kindliness slowly evaporates, and everyone else follows suit. Slowly,* KATE *turns from one to the other seeing only grim and cruel faces on all sides.*)

BAPTISTA   (*Suddenly fierce*) O monstrous arrogance!

> KATE *is backed over to the table and then thrown down over it. Her servants and* BAPTISTA *hold her wrists to keep her secure.* PETRUCHIO *looms up behind her and whips up her skirts ready to do buggery. As he inserts, an ear-piercing, electronic whistle rises to a crescendo pitch.* KATE's *mouth is wild and open, and it appears as if the impossible sound is issuing from her lungs.*)

Black out

Selected Bibliography

Editions of *The Taming of the Shrew*

Dolan, Frances, ed. *The Taming of the Shrew: Texts and Contexts*. Boston: Bedford, 1996.
Heilman, Robert, ed. *The Taming of the Shrew*. Signet Classic. New York: Penguin, 1999.
Mowat, Barbara, and Paul Werstine. *The Taming of the Shrew*. New Folger Library Shakespeare. New York: Washington Square P, 2004.
Raffel, Burton, ed. *The Taming of the Shrew*. The Annotated Shakespeare. New Haven: Yale UP, 2005.
Schafer, Elizabeth, ed. *The Taming of the Shrew*. Shakespeare in Production. Cambridge: Cambridge UP, 2002.
Thompson, Ann, ed. *The Taming of the Shrew*. New Cambridge Shakespeare. Cambridge: Cambridge UP, 2003.

Collections of Essays

Aspinall, Dana E., ed. *The Taming of the Shrew: Critical Essays*. New York: Routledge, 2002.
Bloom, Harold, ed. *William Shakespeare's* The Taming of the Shrew. New York: Chelsea, 1988.
Marvel, Laura, ed. *Readings on* The Taming of the Shrew (Literary Companion Series). San Diego: Greenhaven, 2000.

Other Works

• indicates a work included or excerpted in this Norton Critical Edition.

Abate, Corinne S. "Neither a Tamer Nor a Shrew Be: A Defense of Petruchio and Katherine," *Privacy, Domesticity, and Women in Early Modern England*. Ed. Corinne S. Abate and Elizabeth Mazzola. Aldershot: Ashgate, 2003. 31–44.
Alexander, Peter. "The Original Ending of *The Taming of the Shrew*." *Shakespeare Quarterly*] 20.2 (1969): 111–16.
Bamber, Linda. *Comic Women, Tragic Men: A Study of Gender and Genre in Shakespeare*. Stanford: Stanford UP, 1982.

351

Baumlin, Tita French. "Petruchio the Sophist and Language as Creation in *The Taming of the Shrew*. *Studies in English Literature* 29.2 (1989): 237–57.

Bean, John C. "Comic Structure and the Humanizing of Kate in *The Taming of the Shrew*." *The Woman's Part: Feminist Criticism of Shakespeare*. Ed. Carolyn Ruth Swift Lenz, Gayle Green, and Carol Thomas Neely. Urbana U of Illinois P, 1980. 65–78.

Berek, Peter. "Text, Gender, and Genre in *The Taming of the Shrew*." *"Bad" Shakespeare: Revaluations of the Shakespeare Canon*. Ed. Maurice Charney. London: Associated UP, 1988. 91–104.

• Bloom, Harold. "The Taming of the Shrew." *Shakespeare: The Invention of the Human*. New York: Riverhead, 1998. 28–35.

• Boose, Lynda E. "Scolding Brides and Bridling Scolds: Taming the Woman's Unruly Member." *Shakespeare Quarterly* 42.2 (1991): 179–213.

———. "*The Taming of the Shrew*, Good Husbandry, and Enclosure." *Shakespeare Reread: The Texts in New Contexts*. Ed. Russ McDonald. Ithaca: Cornell UP, 1994. 193–225.

Bradbrook, M. C. "Dramatic Role as Social Image: A Study of *The Taming of the Shrew*." *Shakespeare Jahrbuch* 94 (1958): 132–50.

Brooks, Dennis S. " 'To Show Scorn Her Own Image': The Varieties of Education in *The Taming of the Shrew*." *Rocky Mountain Review of Language and Literature* 48.1 (1994): 7–32.

Brown, Carolyn E. "Bianca and Petruchio: 'The Veriest Shrew[s] of All.' " *Re-Visions of Shakespeare: Essays in Honor of Robert Ornstein*. Ed. Evelyn Gajowski. Newark: U of Delaware P, 2004. 35–56.

• Brunvand, Jan Harold. "The Folktale Origin of *The Taming of the Shrew*." *Shakespeare Quarterly* 17.4 (1966): 345–59.

Burns, Margie. "The Ending of *The Shrew*." *Shakespeare Studies* 18 (1986): 41–64.

Burt, Richard A. "Charisma, Coercion, and Comic Form in *The Taming of the Shrew*." *Criticism* 26.4 (1984): 295–311.

Charlton, H. B. "*The Taming of the Shrew*." *Shakespearean Comedy*. London: Methuen, 1938.

Christensen, Ann C. "Of Household Stuff and Homes: The Stage and Social Practice in *The Taming of the Shrew*." *Explorations in Renaissance Culture* 22 (1996): 127–45.

———. "Petruchio's House in Postwar Suburbia: Reinventing the Domestic Woman (Again)." *Post Script* 17.1 (1997): 28–42.

Cioni, Fernando. "Shakespeare's Italian Intertexts: *The Taming of the/a Shrew*." *Shakespeare, Italy, and Intertextuality*. Ed. Michele Marrapodi. Manchester: Manchester UP, 2004. 118–28.

Cohen, Ralph. "Looking for Cousin Ferdinand: The Value of F1 Stage Directions for a Production of *The Taming of a Shrew*." *Textual Formations and Reformations*. Ed. Laurie E. Maguire and Thomas L. Berger. Newark: U of Delaware P, 1998. 264–80.

Conaway, Charles. " 'Thou'rt the Man': David Garrick, William Shakespeare, and the Masculinization of the Eighteenth-Century Stage." *Restoration and 18th Century Theatre Research* 19.1 (2004): 22–42.

Crocker, Holly A. "Affective Resistance: Performing Passivity and Playing A-Part in *The Taming of the Shrew*." *Shakespeare Quarterly* 54.2 (2003): 142–59.

Daniell, David. "The Good Marriage of Katherine and Petruchio." *Shakespeare Survey* 37 (1984): 23–31.

Dash, Irene G. *Wooing, Wedding and Power: Women in Shakespeare's Plays*. New York: Columbia UP, 1981.

Dessen, Alan. "The Tamings of the Shrews: Rescripting the First Folio." *Rescripting Shakespeare: The Text, the Director, and Modern Productions*. Cambridge: Cambridge UP, 2002. 185–208.

Detmer, Emily. "Civilizing Subordination: Domestic Violence and *The Taming of the Shrew*." *Shakespeare Quarterly* 48.3 (1997): 273–94.

- Dolan, Frances. "Household Chastisements: Gender, Authority, and 'Domestic Violence.' " *Renaissance Culture and the Everyday*. Ed. Patricia Fumerton and Simon Hunt. Philadelphia: U of Pennsylvania P, 1999. 204–25.
- Dusinberre, Juliet. "*The Taming of the Shrew*: Women, Acting, and Power." *Studies in the Literary Imagination* 26 (1993): 67–84.

Duthie, G. I. "*The Taming of a Shrew* and *The Taming of the Shrew*." *The Review of English Studies* 19.76 (1943): 337–56.

Eriksen, Roy. "*The Taming of a Shrew*: Composition as Induction to Authorship." *Nordic Journal of English Studies* 4.2 (2005): 41–63.

Fineman, Joel. "The Turn of the Shrew." *Shakespeare and the Question of Theory*. Ed. Patricia Parker and Geoffrey Hartman. New York: Methuen, 1985. 138–59.

Friedman, Michael D. "The Feminist as Shrew in *10 Things I Hate about You*." *Shakespeare Bulletin: A Journal of Performance Criticism and Scholarship* 22.2 (2004): 45–65.

- Garner, Shirley Nelson. "*The Taming of the Shrew*: Inside or Outside of the Joke?" *"Bad" Shakespeare: Revaluations of the Shakespeare Canon*. Ed. Maurice Charney. London: Associated UP, 1988. 105–19.

Goldschmidt, Lucien, Robert F. Fleissner, Thomas A. Pendleton and Barbara Hodgdon. "*The Taming of the Shrew*, by Shakespeare and Others" (in Forum). *PMLA* 108.1 (1993): 151–54.

Gray, Henry David. "*The Taming of the Shrew*." *Philological Quarterly* 20 (1941): 325–33.

Greenfield, Thelma. "The Transformation of Christopher Sly." *Philological Quarterly* 33 (1954): 34–42.

Haring-Smith, Tori. *From Farce to Metadrama: A Stage History of* The Taming of the Shrew. *1594–1983*. Westport: Greenwood P, 1985.

Hazlitt, William. "*The Taming of the Shrew*." *Characters of Shakespeare's Plays*. London: Oxford UP, 1934. 255–60.

Heilman, R. B. "The Taming Untamed, or, the Return of the Shrew." *Modern Language Quarterly* 27 (1966): 147–61.

- Hibbard, George. "*The Taming of the Shrew*: A Social Comedy." *Shakespearean Essays*. Ed. Alwin Thayer and Norman Sanders. *Tennessee Studies in Literature*. Special Number 2. Knoxville: U of Tennessee P, 1964. 15–28.

Hodgdon, Barbara. "Katherina Bound; or, Play(K)ating the Strictures of Everyday Life." *PMLA* 107.3 (1992): 538–53.

Holderness, Graham. "Text and Performance: *The Taming of the Shrew*." *New Casebooks: Shakespeare in Performance*. Ed. Robert Shaughnessy. New York: St. Martin's, 2000. 123–41.

Hosley, Richard. "Sources and Analogues of *The Taming of the Shrew*. *Huntington Library Quarterly* 27 (1964): 189–308.

———. "Was There a 'Dramatic Epilogue' to *The Taming of the Shrew*?" *Studies in English Literature, 1500–1900* 1.2. Elizabethan and Jacobean Drama (1961): 17–34.

Houk, Raymond A. "Shakespeare's Shrew and Greene's Orlando." *PMLA* 62.3 (1947): 657–71.

Jardine, Lisa. *Still Harping on Daughters: Women and Drama in the Age of Shakespeare*. Sussex: Harvester, 1983.

Kahn, Coppelia. *Man's Estate: Masculine Identity in Shakespeare*. Berkeley: U of California P, 1981.

———. "*The Taming of the Shrew*: Shakespeare's Mirror of Marriage." *Modern Language Studies*. 5.1 (1975): 88–102.

- Korda, Natasha. "Household Kates: Domesticating Commodities in *The Taming of the Shrew*. *Shakespeare Quarterly* 47.2 (1996): 109–31.

Leggatt, Alexander. *Shakespeare's Comedy of Love*. London: Methuen, 1974.

MacDonald, Jan. " 'An Unholy Alliance': William Poel, Martin Harvey, and

The Taming of the Shrew." Theatre Notebook 36 (1982): 64–72. Rpt. in
The Taming of the Shrew: Critical Essays. Ed. Dana E. Aspinall. New York:
Routledge, 2002.

Maguire, Laurie E. " 'Household Kates': Chez Petruchio, Percy, and Planta-
genet." *Gloriana's Face: Women, Public and Private in the English Renaissance.* Ed. S. P. Cerasano and Marion Wynne-Davies. Detroit: Wayne
State UP, 1992. 129–65.

• ———. "The Naming of the Shrew." Written for this Norton Critical Edition.

Marcus, Leah. "The Shakespearean Editor as Shrew-Tamer." *English Literary Renaissance* 22.2 (1992): 177–200.

Martin, Randall. "Kates for the Table and Kates of the Mind: A Social
Metaphor in *The Taming of the Shrew." English Studies in Canada.* 17.1
(1991): 1–20.

Mikesell, Margaret Leal. " 'Love Wrought These Miracles': Marriage and
Genre in *The Taming of the Shrew." Renaissance Drama* new series 20
(1989): 141–67.

Miller, Stephen. "*The Taming of a Shrew* and the Theories: Or, 'Though This
Be Badness, yet There Is Method in't.' " Textual Formations and Reforma-
tions. Ed. Laurie E. Maguire and Thomas L. Berger. Newark: U of
Delaware P, 1998. 251–63.

Mincoff, Marco. "The Dating of *The Taming of the Shrew." English Studies*
54 (1973): 554–65.

• Mitchell, Marea. "Performing Sexual Politics in *The Taming of the Shrew."*
Written for this Norton Critical Edition.

Moisan, Thomas. " 'What's That to You?' or, Facing Facts: Anti-Paternalist
Chords and Social Discords in *The Taming of the Shrew." Renaissance
Drama* n.s. 26 (1995): 105–30. Rpt. in *The Taming of the Shrew: Critical
Essays.* Ed. Dana E. Aspinall. New York: Routledge, 2002.

Moore, William H. "An Allusion in 1593 to *The Taming of the Shrew?"
Shakespeare Quarterly* 15.1 (1964): 55–60.

Muir, Kenneth. *The Sources of Shakespeare's Plays.* New Haven: Yale UP,
1978.

Neely, Carol Thomas. *Broken Nuptials in Shakespeare's Plays.* New Haven:
Yale UP, 1985.

• Newman, Karen. "Renaissance Family Politics and Shakespeare's *The Taming of the Shrew."* Spec. issue of *English Literary Renaissance* 16 (1986):
86–101. Rpt. in Karen Newman. *Fashioning Femininity and English Renaissance Drama.* Chicago: U of Chicago P, 1991.

Novy, Marianne L. "Patriarchy and Play in *The Taming of the Shrew." ELR* 9
(1979): 264–80.

Orlin, Lena Cowen. "The Performance of Things in *The Taming of the
Shrew." Yearbook of English Studies* 23 (1993): 167–88.

• Parker, Patricia. "Construing Gender: Mastering Bianca in *The Taming
of the Shrew." The Impact of Feminism in English Renaissance Studies.*
Ed. Dympna Callaghan. Basingstoke: Palgrave Macmillan, 2007.
193–209.

Perret, Marion D. "Petruchio: The Model Wife." *Studies in English Literature* 23.2 (1983): 223–35.

Pittman, L. Monique. "Taming *10 Things I Hate about You*: Shakespeare and
the Teenage Film Audience." *Literature/Film Quarterly* 32.2 (2004):
144–52.

Priest, Dale G. "Induction, Theatrically, and Power in *The Taming of the
Shrew." Shakespeare Bulletin: A Journal of Performance Criticism and
Scholarship* 17.2 (1999): 29–31.

• Quiller-Couch, Sir Arthur. "Introduction." 1928. *The Taming of the Shrew.*
Cambridge: Cambridge UP, 1962.

Ramsey-Kurz, Helga. "Rising above the Bait: Kate's Transformation from

Bear to Falcon." *English Studies: A Journal of English Language and Literature* 88.3 (2007): 262–81.

Ranald, Margaret Loftus. "Shakespeare and His Social Context." *Essays in Osmotic Knowledge and Literary Interpretation.* New York: AMS P, 1987.

Rebhorn, Wayne A. "Petruchio's 'Rope Tricks': *The Taming of the Shrew* and the Renaissance Discourse of Rhetoric." *Modern Philology* 92.3 (1995): 294–327.

Ribner, Irving. "The Morality of Farce; *The Taming of the Shrew.*" *Essays in American and English Literature Presented to Bruce Robert McElderry, Jr.* Ed. Max F. Schulz, with William T. Templeman and Charles R. Metzger. Athens, OH: Ohio University Press 1968. 165–76.

Roberts, Jeanne Addison. "Horses and Hermaphrodites: Metamorphoses in *The Taming of the Shrew. Shakespeare Quarterly* 34.2 (1983): 159–71.

Rose, Mary Beth. *The Expense of Spirit: Love and Sexuality in English Renaissance Drama.* Ithaca: Cornell UP, 1988.

Rutter, Carol. *Clamorous Voices: Shakespeare's Women Today.* London: Women's Press, 1988.

———. "Kate, Bianca, Ruth, and Sarah: Playing the Woman's *Part in The Taming of the Shrew.*" *Shakespeare's Sweet Thunder: Essays on the Early Comedies.* Ed. Michael J. Collins. Newark: U of Delaware P, 1997.

———. "Looking at Shakespeare's Women on Film." *The Cambridge Companion to Shakespeare on Film.* Ed. Russell Jackson. Cambridge: Cambridge UP, 2000. 241–60.

Saccio, Peter. "Shrewd and Kindly Farce." *Shakespeare Survey* 37 (1984): 33–40.

Scragg, Leah. "Scolding." *Shakespeare's Mouldy Tales: Recurrent Plot Motifs in Shakespearean Drama.* London: Longman, 1992. 67–96.

Sears, Jayne. "The Dreaming of the Shrew." *Shakespeare Quarterly* 17.1 (1966): 41–56.

Seronsy, Cecil C. " 'Supposes' as the Unifying Theme in *The Taming of the Shrew.*" *Shakespeare Quarterly* 14 (1963): 15–30.

Shapiro, Michael. "Framing the Taming: Metatheatrical Awareness of Female Impersonation in *The Taming of the Shrew.*" *The Yearbook of English Studies* 23 (1993): 143–66. Rpt. in *The Taming of the Shrew: Critical Essays.* Ed. Dana E. Aspinall. New York: Routledge, 2002.

• Shaw, George Bernard. "The Taming of the Shrew." *Shaw on Shakespeare: An Anthology of Bernard Shaw's Writings on the Plays and Production of Shakespeare.* Ed. Edwin Wilson. New York: Applause, 2002. 178–82.

Shurgot, Michael W. "From Fiction to Reality: Character and Stagecraft in *The Taming of the Shrew.*" *Theatre Journal* 33 (1981): 327–40.

Shroeder, John W. "*The Taming of a Shrew* and *The Taming of the Shrew*: A Case Reopened." *Journal of English and Germanic Philology* 57 (1958): 424–42.

Slights, Camille Wells. "The Raw and the Cooked in *The Taming of the Shrew.*" *Journal of English and Germanic Philology* 88.2 (1989): 168–89.

Smith, Amy L. "Performing Marriage with a Difference: Wooing, Wedding and Bedding in *The Taming of the Shrew.*" *Comparative Drama* 36.3–4 (2002): 289–32.

Smith, Molly Easo. "John Fletcher's Response to the Gender Debate: *The Woman's Prize* and *The Taming of the Shrew.*" *Papers on Language and Literature: A Journal for Scholars and Critics of Language and Literature* 31.1 (1995): 38–60.

Thomas, Sidney. "A Note on *The Taming of the Shrew.*" *Modern Language Notes* 64.2 (1949): 94–96.

Thompson, Ann, and Sasha Roberts, eds. *Women Reading Shakespeare, 1660–1900: An Anthology of Criticism.* Manchester: Manchester UP, 1997.

- Tillyard, E. M. "The Fairy-tale Element in *The Taming of the Shrew*." *Shakespeare, 1564–1964; a Collection of Modern Essays by Various Hands*. Ed. Edward A. Bloom. Providence: Brown UP, 1964. 110–14.
Wayne, Valerie. "Refashioning the Shrew." *Shakespeare Studies* 17 (1985): 159–87.
Wentersdorf, Karl. "The Authenticity of *The Taming of the Shrew*." *Shakespeare Quarterly* 5.1 (1954): 11–32.
Wentersdorf, Karl. "The Original Ending of *The Taming of the Shrew*: A Reconsideration." *Studies in English Literature* 18 (1978): 201–15.
Zajko, Vanda. "Petruchio Is 'Kated': *The Taming of the Shrew* and Ovid." *Shakespeare and the Classics*. Ed. Charles Martindale and A. B. Taylor. Cambridge: Cambridge UP, 2004. 33–48.